THE
Money Trail

RELATED TITLES FROM POTOMAC BOOKS

Bullets, Bombs, and Fast Talk: Twenty-Five Years of FBI War Stories
by James Botting

The Meinertzhagen Mystery: The Life and Legend of a Colossal Fraud
by Brian Garfield

On-Scene Commander: From Street Agent to Deputy Director of the FBI
by Weldon L. Kennedy

THE
Money Trail

How Elmer Irey and His T-Men
Brought Down America's Criminal Elite

ROBERT G. FOLSOM

POTOMAC BOOKS, INC.
WASHINGTON, D.C.

Copyright © 2010 by Potomac Books, Inc.

Library of Congress Cataloging-in-Publication Data
Folsom, Robert, 1930–
  The money trail : how Elmer Irey and his T-men brought down America's criminal elite / Robert Folsom. — 1st ed.
      p. cm.
  Includes bibliographical references and index.
  ISBN 978-1-59797-488-2 (hbk. : alk. paper)
  1. Irey, Elmer L. (Elmer Lincoln), 1888–1948. 2. Tax evasion—Investigation—United States—History. 3. Organized crime—United States—History. I. Title.
  HV6344.U6F65 2010
  363.28—dc22
  [B]
                                        2009051148

Printed in the United States of America on acid-free paper that meets the American National Standards Institute Z39-48 Standard.

Potomac Books, Inc.
22841 Quicksilver Drive
Dulles, Virginia 20166

First Edition

10 9 8 7 6 5 4 3 2 1

Contents

1. LAW ENFORCEMENT PROBLEMS LIKE NONE BEFORE

On a weekday morning in mid-May 1919, Daniel C. Roper, the commissioner of the Bureau of Internal Revenue, boarded a train at Washington's Union Station for New York City, where he was to address the twenty-fourth annual meeting of the National Association of Manufacturers (NAM) at the Waldorf Astoria Hotel.[1] Roper had been dealing with the "tide of resentment" against the six-year-old income tax and had been invited before the influential business group to explain his position.[2] Roper was entering the lion's den, and he knew it. No one in Woodrow Wilson's cabinet wore a bigger bull's-eye on his chest. Roper had become commissioner five months after the United States entered World War I. To meet the critical need for revenue to support the war effort, the federal government instituted the income tax—and those concerned about handing over their money were now looking at Roper. In particular, members of the NAM, many of whom were captains of the nation's industries, had been surrendering whopping sums to Washington. The U.S. Steel Corporation, the nation's biggest company, was paying taxes in excess of $250 million ($5 billion in 1990 dollars).[3] In March 1919 one New York City corporation paid a tax bill of $20 million ($400 million in 1990 dollars), using Treasury certificates of indebtedness.[4]

Until the twentieth century, Americans had steadfastly opposed an income tax. And until Roper took over, the Bureau of Internal Revenue had led an unsettled but fairly tranquil existence. Abraham Lincoln established it on July 1, 1862, to collect income taxes as a means of financing the Civil War; just fourteen months after that bitter conflict ended, Congress reduced the income tax. Two years later, stamp taxes on liquor and tobacco were instituted and became "the backbone of the system of internal taxes."[5] Three decades then passed before advocates of an income tax gained a foothold with the passage of the Wilson Tariff Act of 1894, which taxed incomes derived from real estate and from state and municipal bonds. To monitor income, Internal Revenue established an Income Tax Division, which brought an immediate and successful court challenge. In April 1895 the U.S. Supreme Court ruled in *Pollock v. Farmers' Loan and Trust Co.* that the provisions of the Tariff Act were unconstitutional, and the Income Tax Division was disbanded. Advocates of an income tax, including Robert M. LaFollette of Wisconsin, didn't give up, however, and worked for the next eighteen years to make it come true. As Laurence F. Schmeckebier and Francis X. A. Eble observed, "If Congress did not have the power to tax incomes the next best thing to do was to ask the people of the United States to grant them the power."[6] This was accomplished when the country ratified the Sixteenth Amendment to the Constitution on February 13, 1913. The following October, in President Woodrow Wilson's first term, Congress approved an income tax.

At the outset, the law imposed what most Americans could live with—a tax of 1 percent on the net incomes of individuals, estates, trusts, and corporations. A surtax rate graduated from 1 to 6 percent was placed on net incomes in excess of $20,000 ($484,000 in 1990 dollars). Until then, the government relied on custom duties, not taxes, to meet its debt. The New York Customs House had been the government's financial keystone. Located near the tip of Manhattan, the magnificent seven-story structure with its four Daniel Chester French mounted sculptures representing Asia, Africa, Europe, and North America had been completed in 1907 at an unheard of cost—$5.1 million ($107.4 million in 1990 dollars). From that impressive temple of trade, the collector of customs for the Port of New York annually generated 80 percent of the entire federal revenue.[7] But the outbreak of war in Europe in 1914 lowered revenues from duties, and that ideal financial source was no longer enough to maintain the national debt. In 1916 Congress approved an inheritance tax and raised the income tax rate by 15 percent. With the U.S. entry into the war in April 1917 and the critical need to finance its huge costs, both the Bureau of Internal Revenue and the income tax became institutionalized.

In the nineteen months that doughboys were involved, World War I cost the United States approximately $34 billion, including approximately $11 billion loaned to the Allies, and was the reason why Congress raised corporation and excess profit taxes and steeply graduated income and inheritance rates. Only about a third of the war was defrayed by taxes. As James Blaine Walker notes, "The balance was to be supplied by an extensive resort to borrowing." This was done through the new Federal Reserve banks, which had been established by the Act of 1913.[8] In 1917 income tax rates were raised 67 percent, and in 1918 they were increased to 77 percent. The income tax wasn't a mass levy, but it was steeply progressive. In 1917–1919 those with incomes above $20,000 ($200,000 in 1990 dollars) paid more than 70 percent of the income collected in those two years. When Daniel Roper was appointed Commissioner on September 25, 1917, Americans were paying the highest income tax rates in the nation's history. And the agency Roper had taken over faced an overwhelming task. In 1916, 778,289 income tax returns were filed, bringing in $512 million. In 1917, 3,824,316 income tax returns were filed, bringing in $908 million. And now, because many thought the income tax was unreasonable, the thunder of opposition was no longer distant: tax fraud and evasion were becoming thorny issues. Roper's approach to the new order was bonded in realism. There could be, he knew, "no perfect tax law, none which could be administered to the satisfaction of all the people."[9] He would have sought to eliminate exemptions if it lowered rates, but he felt that exemptions didn't contribute to "the integrity of results."[10]

Yet, the income tax wasn't Roper's only concern even in the face of a paper flood of tax returns and the mounting problem of tax fraud. Since coming to Internal Revenue, he also had been handling unparalleled, complicated, and deeply divisive measures new to the country. No federal agency head had ever faced such daunting law enforcement tasks. Simmering for decades, a whole range of issues, such as drug enforcement and organized crime, exploded on the national conscience on Roper's—and Elmer Irey's—watch, and still perplex law enforcement today.

When the twentieth century began, the market was saturated with opiates. Patent medicines containing opiates were sold at every drug store in the United States. Heroin, a synthetic alkaloid made from morphine that was stronger than ether, had come into use in 1898. A gleeful advertisement in *Ainslee's* general circulation magazine called heroin "the greatest boon to mankind since the discovery of morphine in 1803."[11] Bayer, the German pharmaceutical family, was advertising heroin as a cough sedative. Until 1906 cocaine was an ingredient in Coca-Cola. In 1908 the St. James Society of New York hailed heroin as a "remarkable remedy," which left those addicted to morphine "entirely recovered." But the clock on opiates, always easy for Americans to obtain, had been ticking since the turn of the century. Dr. Harvey A. Wiley, the Agriculture Department official who dealt with jaw-breaking disputes over caffeine and narcotic use and who was behind the indictment of the Coca-Cola Company over unlabeled additives, noted that the use of drugs in the nineteenth century was not considered "un-American" but "peculiarly American."[12] The medical profession, reflecting public consensus, exhibited a favorable attitude toward the medicinal properties in opiates. In sum, physicians had total freedom to prescribe narcotics. As the number of drug addicts soared in the century's first decade, however, public opinion began to turn against the use of opiates.

In 1910, spurred by the reform efforts of Hamilton Wright, an Ohio physician who came to be known as "the father of American narcotics law," Representative David Foster of Vermont introduced legislation in Congress. It was Wright's idea to control drug traffic through the federal powers of taxation. Foster's bill would require every drug dealer to register, pay a small tax, and record transactions. But the measure turned out to be too uncompromising. "In his enthusiasm and political naiveté," wrote Dr. David Musto, "Wright had not taken into consideration the great threat his bill posed to everyday routine and sales in the drug trades."[13] The bill died in early 1913 owing to opposition from the pharmaceutical industry. In June, Representative Frances B. Harrison, a Tammany Democrat from New

York City, introduced its gentler and compromising successor. A year and a half passed before his measure was approved. As Christmas 1914 neared, Congress, in a rush to adjourn for the holidays, passed it in a few minutes. On December 17, President Woodrow Wilson signed the Harrison Act of 1914. Remarkably, the most significant drug control legislation in American history escaped final notice—until two weeks and two days later. The *New York Times*, on January 2, 1915, almost as an afterthought, ran a four-paragraph story, buried on page nine, that said the bill had passed the House. It didn't mention the remarkable achievement of its original sponsor, Hamilton Wright. He would see only the opening chapter of the struggle over narcotics. He died in 1917 at age forty-nine, following injuries he received in an automobile accident in France, where the energetic crusader had gone to help the Allied cause.

Enforcement of the Harrison Act, which became effective on March 1, 1915, went to the Bureau of Internal Revenue along with the duty of collecting taxes on drug sales. When Roper took over, the act's legitimacy was still being tested in the courts, and he found himself in the choppy wake of a struggle with the medical profession. At its heart was the issue of whether physicians should provide addiction maintenance to addicts. The Treasury opposed maintenance, and while Roper was hesitant to go after the medical profession, it was clearly an obstacle. Doctors, at least certain elements, were not ready to relinquish the ironclad authority they had held on the maintenance issue, dating from the mid-nineteenth century. Just before the Civil War, Oliver Wendell Holmes Sr., dean of the Harvard Medical School, blamed the prevalence of opium addiction "on the ignorance of physicians."[14]

Initially, differences over police powers in the Harrison Act slowed enforcement. The U.S. Supreme Court tried to rest the argument, ruling in 1916 that the act's police powers weren't very broad. In their annual reports for 1916, 1917, and 1918, Treasury officials, including Roper, tried to deal with this setback by imploring Congress "to counteract this emasculating decision" by amending the Harrison Act—to no avail.[15] The U.S. Public Health Service—then a part of the Treasury—took the position that the act contained no police powers, a view opposite from Roper's. Rupert Blue, the highly regarded U.S. surgeon general and a renowned plague fighter, believed the act was intended simply to gather information and that physicians could continue to prescribe drugs such as morphine to patients, whether addicted or not. To add to the discord, the Justice Department "was having considerable trouble convincing federal district judges that registered physicians did not have the right to prescribe as they wished to anyone they wished."[16]

In early 1919 the addict maintenance issue boiled over in New York City, then a city of 5.6 million and the center of the nation's addict population. It was where the largest population of addicts existed (estimates ranged as high as 200,000) and where the medical profession was favorably inclined to dispense drugs to addicts. The Associated Physicians' Economic League of New York, a federation formed in 1914, included a Manhattan group called the Physicians' Protective Association (PPA). One of its leaders was Dr. John P. Davin, a "familiar medicopolitical figure in New York State" who opposed "any encroachments by the state on the private practitioner."[17]

Daniel Roper, meanwhile, had been receiving reports from the city indicating a steady increase in the use of cocaine, heroin, morphine, and other narcotic poisons. He also was following the warnings of New York City's commissioner of health, Dr. Royal A. Copeland, a fifty-year-old eye surgeon who assumed the post in early 1918. One of every thirty New Yorkers, Copeland said, was addicted to drugs (approximately 150,000). Pointing out that "drugs were fast becoming a menace to the city," Copeland said that manufacturers were estimated to have sold more cocaine to wholesalers in the city in January 1919 than was sold in all of 1918.[18] And he left not a shred of doubt about his feelings: physicians who prescribe drugs to addicts "should be boiled in oil."[19]

In February 1919, three months before his NAM address, Roper dispatched a seasoned investigator, Daniel L. Porter, to New York City to review the drug scene firsthand. A member of Internal Revenue's Alcohol Division, Porter had acquired the sobriquet "Shadow" for his work in "practically banning illicit stills from the mountains of Tennessee, Virginia and the Carolinas."[20] Visiting each of New York City's five boroughs, Porter discovered that doctors were, indeed, a primary source of supply for addicts. His findings clearly sparked alarm. "Unscrupulous physicians" were writing as many as 200 prescriptions a day to addicts, and over the past year "1,500,000 prescriptions for the illicit procuring of narcotics had been issued and filled." He also found that "thirty physicians are in a sort of drug ring issuing prescriptions for narcotics for fees ranging from 25 cents to four dollars." The principal drug being dispensed was heroin, and it was being "obtained through the regular channels at $12 to $15 an ounce [$240 and $300, respectively, in 1990 dollars] and is retailed through the prescriptions at $60 to $75 [$1,200 to $1,500, respectively, in 1990 dollars] an ounce."[21]

In early March, Porter returned to Washington to report his findings to Roper—at the very time the Supreme Court, to everyone's surprise, reversed itself and came down on the government's side by upholding the police powers in the Hamilton Act and banning addiction maintenance in two separate rulings. In one ruling, the jurists upheld the indictment of a San Antonio physician who had provided morphine to a known addict. In effect, this affirmed the constitutionality of the Harrison Act. The other ruling, involving a Memphis physician and a druggist, concluded the critical question, Does the legitimate practice of medicine include the maintenance of addicts? The jurists ruled it did not: to maintain an addict by medical prescription "would be so clear a perversion of meaning [of the word "prescription"] that no discussion of the subject is required."[22]

That settled any doubts Roper had about launching a crackdown on physicians. In what was an entirely new undertaking for Internal Revenue, Porter worked "for some weeks" to recruit and train a "strong force of special agents."[23] In March, with training completed, Porter and his new force left for New York City, where he "immediately got in touch" with Lt. Henry Scherb, who had been heading the NYPD's sixteen-man drug investigative unit since 1913. In their first full year, 1914, the year Congress passed the Harrison Act, Scherb's squad arrested 950 drug violators and boasted a conviction record never again equaled: only three of the 950 weren't convicted. Joining forces, Porter and Scherb launched a systematic investigation of the city's drug traffic. They carried a rather unusual mandate: to take action against physicians and pharmacists, not underworld drug traffickers.

In what was the first drug sting carried out by a federal agency, agents in the strike force for weeks "loitered at night near drug stores, keeping tab on the customers, and observing from window corners the relations between purchaser and seller." Posing as "cokeys" with "twitching faces" and wearing "unkempt attire," three of the force visited the office of Dr. Leopold Harris on East Thirteenth Street to seek treatment. There, they found that for 50 cents each ($10 in 1990 dollars), they could get prescriptions written for 15 grains of dope; for $1 ($20 in 1990 dollars), 25 grains; and for $2 ($40 in 1990 dollars), 30 grains. They were directed to a pharmacy at First Avenue and Sixteenth Street, where the prescriptions were filled. Other squads carried out similar stings. All were successful: In each case the agents disguised their real intent behind getting a fix. The next time, they would return for real.

On the evening of Tuesday, April 8, "with the suddenness of a shot," the strike force launched its first raid. In one pharmacy, agents found a box containing 50,000 drug prescriptions, all dated within the last ten months. In another pharmacy, records showed 100,000 orders for narcotics had been dispensed in one year. They arrested six physicians and four pharmacists in Manhattan, including Dr. Harris and his nephew, Dr. Henry Harris, who practiced with him, and confiscated $30,000 in narcotics ($600,000 in 1990 dollars). The physicians were charged with illegally prescribing, the druggists with illicit selling. A day later, all ten were released on bonds ranging up to $5,000 ($100,000 in 1990 dollars). As the crackdown continued, it left the city at a critical juncture, an eventuality that Roper and Dr. Copeland had foreseen. On April 9, the morning after the first raid, the Department of Health opened a narcotic supply clinic at 145 Worth Street. The same day Dr. Copeland held a press conference at the Department of Health, noting that between thirty-five and sixty addicts had already telephoned his office seeking drugs. He explained, "The clinic would be conducted to effect cures through gradual reduction of the amount of narcotic furnished."[24] Seven doctors were on hand to help the addicts, who were given drugs "for much less than they had been accustomed to pay." Only twelve people showed up the first day; by the next day, 135 arrived for treatment. Thereafter there was a steady influx.

In Washington, as Roper worked to resolve the addict maintenance furor, he had to confront an even mightier issue: Prohibition. Idling in the back of his mind was the ominous development of January 1919: the last of the required thirty-six states, Nebraska, ratified the Eighteenth Amendment to prohibit the manufacture, distribution, and sale of alcoholic beverages. Prohibition would become effective in January 1920.

On Capitol Hill, Rep. Andrew J. Volstead of Minnesota, chairman of the House Judiciary Committee, filed a bill laying out the enforcement requirements (HR 6810). The measure was moving through Congress, and while Roper wanted no part of it (he opposed Prohibition), he knew his bureau would be chosen to enforce Prohibition.

■

A lean, handsome man with closely cropped hair, soft features, a penetrating gaze, and clean-cut looks that he carried into his late years, Roper was a follower of South Carolina's populist governor, Ben Tillman, whom he admired for his "spine of steel and a deeply rooted purpose."[25] Of Scottish ancestry, Roper was born in Marlboro County, a rich farming region along the northeastern top of South Carolina, where the thrifty farmers found that by making cotton a surplus crop they would never be broke. An only child, he was raised in a rural environment where the three Rs were highly valued. He received a solid upbringing from a strong and loving father; his mother died when he was three, and his father remarried. More than fifty years later, Roper still spoke fondly of him, noting that "in his modest way, he was a scholar" who quoted Shakespeare. There were no daily newspapers. On winter nights by an open fire (the family got their first kerosene lamp when Daniel was ten), the father would read aloud from Benson J. Lossing's *Eminent Americans* and "constantly prepared" Daniel "for the day when I would start to school" by teaching him the ABC's "from a New Testament of large print."[26] In high school, where the entire student body totaled 125, he learned Latin and Greek from the principal, a one-legged man named William G. Quackenbush, who had three assistants, "all men of strong Christian character." They "taught with unrelenting zeal," Roper recalled, "at all times seeking to inspire us with a heartfelt desire for knowledge and its blessings."[27] After high school he attended Trinity

College and then became a teacher for a salary of $40 a month ($1,000 in 1990 dollars) and "my board"—until he decided to run for office.[28]

Roper started his political life as a state legislator in November 1892 at age twenty-five, a time when he described himself as "inexperienced, unsure of myself and unacquainted with the bearded farmers and Confederate heroes Tillmanism had swept into office."[29] When Roper entered the legislature's lower house, Prohibition was a driving issue in South Carolina. On the ballot that November was the simple question: Prohibition, yes or no.

A substantial majority voted yes, but no provision had been made to institute it. Two weeks after the legislature convened, Roper turned out to be the House member picked by the Prohibition forces to introduce the enacting legislation. They had gone to Roper because he "had no prestige to endanger and no ambition to continue in public service." Also, Marlboro County was dry; not one saloon had existed there for seventy-five years.[30] After some wrangling in the state Senate—Governor Tillman, who controlled that body, opposed a bone-dry law and favored a restricted method to control the sale of liquor—a revised measure was approved.

South Carolina was the first state to make such an experiment in the distribution of liquor. It established a dispensary system, an idea from Sweden that was first adopted in the South by the college town of Athens, Georgia. The bill also set up a state control board along with county boards, and the "dispenser had to be a man who could prove he did not drink and had had no past connection with liquor interests." Purchasers had to file applications. Liquor was sold in sealed packages only in daylight hours, no package could be opened on the premises, and none could be sold to an "intoxicated man, minor, or man known to have used liquor to excess." The system quickly created a "stormy wave of protest and rebellion."[31] At one point, Governor Tillman had to appoint constables to enforce the law. There had been 613 bars in the state in 1892. The number of dispensaries was never to exceed 146. Though state ownership brought in close to half a million dollars a year, which largely went to finance schools, the system soon became corrupted and mismanaged and "blind tigers" (illegal saloons) sprang up everywhere.

The Prohibition forces had been right about picking Roper to introduce the bill. He was their sacrificial lamb, and the bitter dispute that ensued ended his brief legislative career. It also changed his life. He didn't expect that his loyalty to Ben Tillman in supporting the Senate measure would be rewarded. Less than a month after returning home, he received a telegram from Urey Brooks, clerk of the state supreme court in Columbia, to come see him at his office. Brooks handed Roper a telegram. It was from Brooks's uncle, Matthew C. Butler, the U.S. senator from South Carolina, and it read, "Ask D. C. Roper to come to Washington to see me as early as convenient for him."[32]

Roper wasn't a member of the landed gentry, though his father owned a 500-acre farm. To pay his way to the nation's capital, he borrowed $50 ($1,350 in 1990 dollars) from a friend, Pressley Mangum, who lived in Mc-Coll. His visit to Senator Butler in May came during the "Panic of 1893," when the collapse of the Reading Railroad, dramatic plunges in the stock market, and a gold drain were rocking the economy. These issues helped end Grover Cleveland's presidency and gave the Republicans a lock on the White House for the next sixteen years. For Roper, this marked the beginning of a long career in Washington. Butler offered him the job of clerk of the House Commerce Committee, and he accepted. It was an important assignment in light of the 1887 passage of the Interstate Commerce Act, whereby the powers in Washington sought to regulate big business. He would later serve as clerk of the House Ways and Means Committee before earning a reputation as an organizational wizard.

In 1913, after Woodrow Wilson entered the White House, the federal government underwent one of its biggest expansions: the inauguration of parcel post delivery, which required reorganizing the post office, and the appointment of 7,000 first-class, 11,000 third-class, and 40,000 fourth-class postmasters. As the newly appointed first assistant postmaster general at the U.S. Postal Service, Roper masterminded the massive task. As a result, the nation's postal system became, because of the number of employees, scope of operations, and volume of business, "the biggest business in the world."[33] He stayed at the post office until 1916, when Wilson made his second run at the presidency. Roper had helped Wilson in his first campaign, and now he was put in charge of the New York organization. Wilson was victorious on November 7, though barely, against the formidable Charles

Evans Hughes of New York. The next September, Wilson named Roper to lead Internal Revenue at a salary of $6,000 a year ($126,000 in 1990 dollars). Roper had just turned fifty. It happened to be the point when Internal Revenue was beginning to deal with issues that no other federal agency had ever handled. He quickly began to understand that the new post demanded more than his respected and polished organizational skills. In short, it required "a spine of steel."

2. THE SPECIAL INTELLIGENCE UNIT

As he sat on the dais at the National Association of Manufacturers convention in New York City, Daniel Roper listened to William P. White, the head of the NAM's Committee on Taxation, denounce the income tax as "unsound public policy" and call for its repeal. White went on to urge the imposition of a "well-devised non-cumulative sales tax." Expecting this hostility, Roper remained undeterred. In his address, he warned against "unethical tax advisers" who were showing people how to avoid taxes and minced no words about the tax evader. "He is a criminal. Tell me where he is and I will point the way to his winter quarters."[1]

Some of his audience was probably aware that three months before, Roper had picked a case in the nation's leading metropolis to make his point. Seymour L. Rau, a New York City life insurance broker, had become the first person in modern times to be tried and convicted for failing to pay his income tax. On February 7, 1919, Rau was sentenced in the U.S. District Court in Manhattan to thirty days in the city prison and fined $300 ($6,000 in 1990 dollars) plus twice the amount of income tax due, which came to $334 ($6,513 in 1990 dollars).[2]

Roper knew where he stood, once noting that the income tax "had not come upon the scene with a halo of popularity." Since war's end, he had been getting reports of serious charges of irregularities that involved "important taxpayers"—whom he never named.[3] But not only were Americans

— 13 —

falsifying their returns, Internal Revenue collectors were conspiring with taxpayers in fraudulent schemes to evade paying what they owed. And evasions were mounting. Since the war, the country's tax rolls had jumped spectacularly. In 1916, the year before Roper took over Internal Revenue, 450,000 Americans sent in an income tax return. In 1917 the figure jumped to 3,824,000, in 1919 it went to 5,652,000, and in 1920 (the year he left) it went to 7,605,000.

In cracking down on tax evaders, Roper knew he needed a strategy different from the one he was using to deal with drug enforcement. He had picked an able investigator in "Shadow" Porter to handle the crackdown in New York City, and there had been measurable success. But that had been makeshift and had brought more problems than it solved. Still, despite his difficulties with Porter's mission, Roper thought he would be able to shift drug enforcement away from Internal Revenue by setting up a separate agency to handle it when Prohibition came in—which he knew was imminent. A separate agency was going to be required. What Porter—and Roper too—had learned was that drug enforcement wasn't ordinary police work, like going to the scene of a crime and trying to solve it (or in Porter's rural experiences, smashing stills and arresting their operators). In drug enforcement, conspiracy was paramount. Breaking up a drug smuggling ring is a painstaking operation, requiring heavy manpower, long bouts of surveillance, and seemingly exhaustive detail. Moreover, then and now, drug enforcement agents often faced failure and had to start their investigations all over again.

While tax fraud was entirely different, it was going to require similar action. Roper couldn't turn to agents at Internal Revenue. He had none. He had taken Porter from the Alcohol Division, a highly valued arm of Internal Revenue, and he knew he couldn't raid it again. The division had been enforcing the liquor stamp tax since 1868, and over that time the nation's liquor traffic had grown into the federal government's largest single source of revenue. The division had no agents to spare. Handling tax evasion was going to be far-reaching and long-term, and Roper understood he had to handle it that way.

A few days after returning from the NAM convention, Roper called in Joseph Callan, his special assistant who had been his chief aide when both were serving at the Post Office Department. They tossed around some ideas, and eventually Roper decided to set up a new branch. It would be a small operation with limited authority. They decided to call it the Special Intelligence Unit, and it was to have two purposes: to investigate "large-scale evasions" of income taxes and to keep Internal Revenue and its personnel free of wrongdoing.[4]

Both men were well acquainted with the outstanding work of the crack Postal Inspection Division. Postal inspectors "can spot a missing penny quicker than anybody in the world," cracked Callan.[5] Authorized by Congress in July 1836, the division, operating with fewer than 100 inspectors until well into the twentieth century, had the assignment of investigating "mail depredations." Over time it had become the most esteemed and efficient investigative unit at the federal level, and its work drew comparisons to Scotland Yard. Roper proceeded to make a personal request to the postmaster general, Albert Burleson, for "six men of my own choosing—but no more." Burleson and Roper were longtime friends. Burleson had been the go-between when President Wilson wanted Roper to serve as vice chairman of the Tariff Commission, before naming him as commissioner of Internal Revenue. The "always cooperative" Burleson was willing to give up six postal inspectors. Roper, however, pushing his friendship a bit more, "got away with seven."[6] The seventh man would be the Special Intelligence Unit's leader, and Callan already had someone in mind for the post: Elmer Irey, a man he had served with in the Postal Inspection Division. Irey's temperament and essential decency had made a lasting impression on Callan, whose wife had attended high school with Irey in Washington. Callan had come to admire Irey's quiet reserve, maturity, and most of all, what he perceived as an intrinsic, steel-rail honesty. An unspoken trust had grown out of their friendship, and Callan wasted no time getting Irey on board.

They met in his office in early June. Elmer Irey came over from Lynchburg, in western Virginia, where he was serving as a postal inspector. Afterward, Callan said, "I had to talk the big ox into leaving the Post Office sinecure." Said Irey, "I wanted the job as soon as it was offered. Callan just took a long time getting around to telling me I'd get $2,500 a year" ($50,000 in 1990 dollars).[7] That was three times the pay in Lynchburg, where he was earning $700 a year ($14,700 in 1990 dollars). Thus Irey, age thirty-one, would be heading the Special Intelligence Unit. The six other handpicked inspectors—Hugh McQuillen, Arthur A. Nichols, Everett Parker, Arthur Smith, Herbert B. Lucas, and Frank Frayser—were all older and had more investigative experience than Irey.

In late June, Irey and his wife, Marguerite, moved to Washington with their two young sons, Hugh and Robert, and rented an apartment on Euclid Street. At the Treasury, a structure with dingy corridors that dated back to Andrew Jackson's presidency, he was given a roomy corner office on the third floor with a prized view of Pennsylvania Avenue. Placing his collection of Abraham Lincoln photographs on a bookshelf behind his desk, he went to work there on July 1, 1919. On that day, federal law enforcement changed forever.

3. ELMER LINCOLN IREY

At the beginning of the twentieth century, Charles Irey moved his family of nine—wife Emma, four sons, and three daughters— from Kansas City, Missouri, to Washington, D.C., where he went to work for the Government Printing Office.[1] Charles may have looked at it as a new destiny. The nation's capital, its population at 250,000, was thriving and growing, its future alluring. The automobile was just around the corner. The city's main thoroughfares were paved, some with cobblestones. Though big, marbled government buildings dominated, people could walk right up to a fenceless White House. On bustling Pennsylvania Avenue, pockmarked by well-dressed street vendors, an underground cable pulled the cable cars, and horses were used to pull a variety of vehicles. A large bus known as the Herdic, drawn by two horses, regularly climbed the hill to the Capitol. When the Herdic reached the foot of the hill, a second team was added, and the four horses, "with the exhortation of two drivers and great effort," were able to pull the bus to the Capitol entrances.[2]

Charles Irey was an admirer of Abraham Lincoln, and he had given Elmer, born in Kansas City on March 10, 1888, the third youngest of the four brothers, "Lincoln" as his middle name. That, however, appeared to be as far as the elder Irey's Lincolnesque characteristics went. Shortly after settling his family in the Lincoln Park area, he deserted them, with no explanation, never to return, his whereabouts uncertain. Within the family, the reason for his leaving remains obscure. Afterward, it "was something the family never talked about," according to Elmer Irey's oldest son, Hugh.

Elmer was twelve at the time. Two brothers, Walter and Edwin, and a sister, Matty, were older. Another sister, Maude, died in the 1918 influenza pandemic. The two oldest boys "were not the type to take over the responsibilities that needed to be taken over in the family circumstances," said Hugh. Elmer's mother turned to him "to keep things going." This trait was "the interesting part of my father's personality," Hugh said. Elmer already had the strong virtues that would help him overcome a broken home and early hardship—and that would carry him throughout his life. He helped his mother raise the two smallest children, Alice and Hugh, the youngest boy, then two years old. Hugh (for whom Elmer named his first son) grew up to worship his older brother.

Irey, a good but not an outstanding student, graduated from Eastern High School at age eighteen in 1906. At Eastern High, he had met slim, brown-haired Marguerite Wagner, who was a year younger, and they became sweethearts. Even before his graduation, they were firm about marriage but decided to put off their wedding until Elmer had a secure future. Marguerite was already secure: She came from an established family in the District. Her father, William, a prominent gunsmith, a skilled marksman, and a skeet-shooting companion of Theodore Roosevelt, owned a sporting goods store on Pennsylvania Avenue, three blocks from the Capitol. Wagner was a frequent visitor to the White House, giving advice to President Theodore Roosevelt, an outdoorsman and skilled marksman himself.

Upon graduation from high school, Irey, working part-time to support his mother and the younger siblings, attended night classes at a business school where he learned to type and acquired shorthand. Stenography had become a popular art in the 1890s (Daniel Roper had taken a course in shorthand at a night school when he first arrived in Washington). In 1907, at age nineteen, Irey got his first full-time job as a clerk in the Postal Inspection Division at the Post Office Department. His knowledge of shorthand opened up his future. He had become so proficient in the art that when William J. Vickery, the Division's chief inspector since 1904, learned of his talent, he brought Elmer into his office as his personal secretary.

At the postal inspector's office, Irey had become a part of the oldest, most capable investigative unit in the federal government. Even before the turn of the century, it was such a well-organized force that post office inspectors were frequently "borrowed by other branches of the Government to travel extensively in this country and abroad engaged in sleuthing not connected with the mails."[3] In the beginning, their work concerned mail fraud, but eventually evolved into a more cunning game—solving mail car robberies. The author Joe Jackson called train robbery an American invention that sprang "from the chaos following the Civil War."[4] After the first recorded train stickup—by John Reno and his three brothers in Seymour, Indiana, on October 6, 1866, netting $12,000 in loot ($312,000 in 1990 dollars)—Washington made outlaws pay a high price for robbing the mail. Congress passed the Mail Fraud Act in 1872, making mail robbery a federal offense punishable by life imprisonment. The act marked the first time that Washington extended its law enforcement reach into the states' jurisdiction.

Jesse James found that sticking up a train was more lucrative than robbing a bank, but he always left the mail alone. In their time, the Jesse James–Cole Younger gang robbed a total of twelve banks and seven trains, turning their deeds into class warfare. During the stickup of the Iron Mountain Railroad in Missouri in 1874, a gang member announced that he would examine each male passenger's hands before taking his money. "Hard-handed men have to work for their money—the soft-handed ones are capitalists, professors, and others that get easy money," the outlaw reportedly said. That instruction "transformed the bandits into folk heroes," wrote Joe Jackson.[5]

As the century changed, train robberies were still a constant, actually becoming a bigger target for more daring outlaws. By 1900 railroads were booming: 1,224 companies were operating trains on 258,784 miles of track that crisscrossed the United States. In 1905 John Gideon, an ex-railroad worker, single-handedly held up a Union Pacific express near Moscow, Idaho, and escaped with $50,000 ($1,250,000 in 1990 dollars) from the mail car. Caught and convicted, Gideon was sent to Leavenworth for life.

Irey was there to see the last of the big train robberies. As Vickery's right hand, he was always in the thick of the drama. Barely into his twenties, he could be counted upon to handle instructions and take down daily reports in shorthand from field investigators by telephone from the scene. He was learning, always learning, listening, and paying attention to details. One day in 1909, the drama heightened like never before for Irey.

He had been on the job two years when the celebrated Mud Cut mail car robbery occurred, an event that became such a controversial and drawn-out issue that it eventually landed in the Oval Office. Mud Cut was a heady learning experience and became a cautionary tale for Irey. Leading the investigation was his old boss, William Vickery, who had left Washington in January 1908 to take over the Kansas City office. On a larger scale, the case represented the clash between the old ways of law enforcement coming to terms with the slowly expanding federal role.

Late on Saturday night of May 22, 1909, the Union Pacific's Overland Limited, one of the crack trains of the West, pulled into the Fremont station, twenty-five miles outside Omaha. Bound from San Francisco to Chicago and carrying eighty passengers, the train included the Omaha and Ogden Railroad Post Office, the official designation for the car holding eight mail clerks and the U.S. mail. At the Fremont stop, a number of robbers slipped aboard the engine tender. Minutes before the train was to arrive in Omaha, two of the robbers jumped onto the engine deck, pointed pistols at the engineer and fireman, and ordered the train to halt. The locomotive stopped near Forty-second Street on the edge of the city. Ignoring the passengers, the robbers went straight to the mail car, where they had to shoot out a window before the clerks would unlatch the metal door. Hopping aboard, they tossed out seven bags of mail, each shaped "like a heavy sausage" that reached from a man's shoulder to the ground, then ordered the clerks and trainmen to carry the bags back down the tracks, near a stone bridge between high clay banks the locals called the Mud Cut.[6]

By the time the Overland Limited pulled into the Omaha station at 12:20 a.m., fifteen minutes late, the robbers had made a clean getaway. Before dawn broke, Omaha and South Omaha police forces, the Douglas County sheriff's office, U.S. marshals, Union Pacific special agents, and the postal inspectors (and soon Pinkerton agents too) were swarming over Mud Cut. William Vickery, now running the Kansas City office, took charge of the investigation. Only $700 ($17,500 in 1990 dollars) had been taken. The outcome was swift: inside three weeks, five men were taken into custody in the robbery.

On June 12 a federal grand jury indicted Jack Golden, Frank Grigware, Dan Downer, and Fred "Fritz" Torgensen for robbing the U.S. mails and endangering the lives of the mail clerks. A fifth indictment for a "John Doe" was also handed down; he turned out to be the presumed ringleader, forty-five-year-old Bill Matthews, a suspect in train robberies similar to Mud Cut. "A heavy-set bear of a man who looked and sounded like an old-time fur trapper," Matthews had used his job as "a stage driver through Colorado and Idaho as a front for scouting out robberies."[7] Downer and Torgensen were small-time criminals who operated out of Spokane and had been involved in horse and cattle rustling. They were a trio with little future. On the other hand, Golden and Grigware didn't appear to be criminals so much as drifters trying to latch onto a good thing. They knew the trio and had been keeping company with them, but that didn't make Golden and Grigware train robbers.

The outcry from an indignant public provoked a speedy rush to judgment. Trial was scheduled for early July, but the case wouldn't come together and didn't start until October 25. Less than three weeks later, the five were convicted and given sentences of life in prison. As far as William Vickery was concerned, however, matters didn't end there. As he sat daily in the courtroom, the more he heard the more questions he began to ask himself. Was there perjured testimony? Were Grigware and Golden a part of the robbery? The case troubled him. Specifically, he doubted their guilt. The robbers were masked, but one witness said he knew Grigware by his "stature and carriage," though he never heard him speak. Charles A. Goss, the U.S. attorney who prosecuted the case, "would admit to the difficulty of tying all of the defendants directly to the robbery," and so the trial didn't go as planned.[8] In addition, U.S. District Judge Frank C. Munger allowed "lots of speculation into evidence."[9]

The investigators were another important aspect of the case. The foremost investigator was the legendary James McParland, head of the Pinkerton National Detective Agency's western office. The Pinkerton name was legendary, but in fact James McParland, not William or Allan Pinkerton, was the nineteenth century's most famous detective. McParland almost single-handedly solved the Molly Maguire case in Pennsylvania, chased Butch Cassidy and the Sundance Kid across the West, sent Tom Horn to work for cattlemen in Wyoming, and may have been behind the lynching of the four train-robbing Reno brothers by a masked posse. Most notably, McParland coaxed a confession from Harry Orchard, the assassin of Governor Frank Steunenberg of Idaho. Dashiell Hammett had memorialized McParland in his novel *The Continental Op*. Before becoming a best-selling writer and a legend of his own, Hammett had been a Pinkerton agent for eight years, serving in seedy Spokane and elsewhere. He fashioned his "Old Man" of the fictional Continental Agency after McParland. Hammett's Old Man was "rather strict and like an implacable god, [he had] no feelings at all on any subject." In *Red Harvest*, the famed writer of hard-boiled detective fiction was thinking of McParland when he wrote, "The agency wits said he could spit icicles in July."

McParland was called into the Mud Cut investigation. Three years had passed since he coaxed a confession from killer Harry Orchard, a feat writer Anthony Lukas termed "the most extraordinary confession in the history of American criminal justice." By then McParland was in his sixties, his short figure was portly, and he wore extra thick lenses, but he was as unrelenting as ever.[10] The Pinkerton style had always been to co-opt the local police, thus giving "any abuses an official veneer."[11] The Pinkerton style also included the famed "sweatbox," a heated cell where confessions were beaten out of suspects. But McParland no longer needed such tactics. He had honed his technique into an art, using his mountainous reputation and his knowledge to establish an easy rapport, as he did with Orchard. But whether McParland used his personality to help decide the course of the Mud Cut investigation, how much of a role he played behind closed doors, and if he was instrumental in deciding the course of events from July to October was never revealed publicly. And if Vickery, in his own way as strong as McParland, was at odds with the renowned crime fighter, it never became public. In the end, the jury believed the prosecution. For Vickery, however, ostensibly in charge of the investigation, and the one responsible for passing on the evidence to ensure conviction, the Mud Cut trial was a botched trial, loaded with holes: there was questionable and perjured testimony; there were uncertainties from the presiding judge, and there was a range of prosecutorial failings. Vickery recommended that the Postal Division launch an investigation. The inquiry took four years and would become a part of post office lore. Working under the keen and careful Vickery and watching Mud Cut come to a final resolve—through all its faults and failures—would serve Irey well: he would handle his future post and career with the same kind of great prudence.

In August 1913 the Postal Inspection Division's report on Mud Cut was sent to the White House. Accepting the report's recommendation, President Woodrow Wilson commuted Jack Golden's sentence and declared him innocent of all charges, and he was released from Leavenworth. The evidence—or lack of evidence—against Golden, Joe Jackson noted, was basically the same as that against his good friend, Frank Grigware, and he could have been released too. But Grigware wasn't around to enjoy that possibility. He had escaped from Leavenworth in April 1910—with a flourish. When the Leavenworth train made its weekly trip into the prison yard to deliver lumber and other materials, he commandeered it and rode to his freedom. Over the next twenty-four years, Grigware was the nation's most elusive fugitive.

During his dozen years at the postal unit, where the custom was to change the reins every four years, Irey served under three chief inspectors. He also married his sweetheart from Eastern High, Marguerite Wagner, in 1912. The next year, his sixth at the unit, saw the great post office expansion in the Wilson presidency, masterminded by Daniel Roper. Out of that expansion Irey was named to one of the most coveted investigative posts in the government—postal inspector, at a yearly salary of $1,800 ($39,600 in 1990 dollars). Six years later, Roper picked him as the first chief of a new investigative branch no bigger than the crack unit he left.

A slightly overweight man nearly six feet tall who wore steel-rimmed spectacles and a trim haircut, Irey would achieve his ends in a quiet way, his public life never at odds with his private life. Clearly reserved, with few contradictions, journalists went away from Irey impressed. "Irey was the most modest human being I ever met," said William J. Slocum, the writer who collaborated on Irey's memoir. "He was a genial, soft-spoken human being who gave no outward sign that most of his life had been spent chasing hoodlums and larcenous politicians and other forms of con men."[12] Alan Hynd called him a "devout family man, deeply affected in an emotional way by violence of any kind."[13] William G. Mann noted that it was "a tribute to the morale" of the SIU that four of the original six agents were still at the branch twenty years later.[14] Of his investigative skills, the noted political columnist Marquis Childs wrote, "Irey pursued evildoers with the fine impartiality of a force of Nature."[15] "Undoubtedly, much of Elmer's success was due to his ability to organize," observed Harry Anslinger, noting that trait was put to the test in the Lindbergh kidnapping.[16]

Irey never wanted nor sought attention. Early on, he displayed a naiveté about the trappings of power. After being named chief of the Special Intelligence Unit, according to his son, Hugh, he was given a special perk—his own automobile license number, 800. Shortly after, he stopped his sedan at a red light in downtown Washington. Two men at the curb glanced at the 800 plate, and Irey overheard one of them say, "Yeah, that's Elmer Irey. That's his car." The next day, Irey turned in the plate and got a regular number.[17]

4. CORRUPTION ON A STAGGERING SCALE

The Special Intelligence Unit's first case dealt with corruption within the Treasury's ranks. It involved an Internal Revenue inspector, Morris Rosenblum, who, with two certified public accountants, had set up a tax fraud scheme at a firm, Sterling Accounts and Audit Company, in New York City. The trio solicited wealthy taxpayers and falsified their income tax returns. Rosenblum would accept the return as filed. For this, they charged a 20 percent fee for the amount of taxes defrauded. But a business executive, Adolph Pricken, the vice president and principal owner of Coastwise Warehouse Inc., whom Rosenblum tried to shake down, blew the whistle on him. Irey devised a sting. He had Pricken hand the fee to fix the tax return, $2,000 ($38,000 in 1990 dollars), in marked bills to Rosenblum. When Rosenblum left the office, SIU agents stopped him, found the marked bills, and arrested him. The SIU found that the trio had prepared tax returns for 115 firms and individuals, and more than $1 million ($19 million in 1990 dollars) that the trio accumulated was recovered.

Tax corruption, of course, was an old story. The Whiskey Ring, a brazen band of conspirators made up of revenue agents and distillers, operated out of St. Louis from 1871 to 1875 and cheated the government out of millions of dollars.[1] "It seems astonishing," the trial judge said, "that a conspiracy so enormous in its proportions and which was depleting the revenue of such vast sums, should so long remain undiscovered by the uncorrupted officers of the government."[2] This was because the entire St. Louis office, including the Internal Revenue supervisor, was bought off—along with every agent that was assigned there or who even visited occasionally. In 1872 an agent named Brashear visited the St. Louis office on a revenue matter, saw what was going on, and was handed $5,000 ($115,000 in 1990 dollars) to keep his mouth shut. In 1873 Brashear returned and this time was given $10,000 ($230,000 in 1990 dollars) to write a false report on the condition of the distilleries in St. Louis. In 1894 an agent named Hogue received $10,000. In the spring of 1875 the distillers raised $10,000 to be used as "a corruption fund in Washington to stop threatened proceedings."[3] The Whiskey Ring, however, resembled two-year-olds training on the potty when compared to the numbing level of corruption among Prohibition agents.

Congress passed the Volstead Act (officially the National Prohibition Enforcement Act) in late 1919. (President Wilson vetoed it, but Congress quickly overrode the veto within hours.) At 12:01 a.m. on January 16, 1920, Prohibition went into effect. To enforce this ignoble experiment, the act established the Prohibition Unit as a subdivision of the Bureau of Internal Revenue. Ironically, Daniel Roper, who had big misgivings about Prohibition and who had fought against giving Treasury any role in enforcement, was given the task of putting the unit together. The trouble, he knew, would be unending. The Prohibition Unit represented the biggest one-time establishment of federal police powers in the nation's history, dwarfing everything before. The initial force of 1,550 agents and investigators would reach 2,800 by the decade's end. The unit was not placed under Civil Service, instantly creating a spoils system. And to even entertain the breadth of enforcement that was needed to do the job was an invitation to wreck the senses.

The unit had to contend with illegal activity on five fronts:

1. Prescription of alcohol by doctors and sale of alcohol by druggists. There were 11 million prescriptions issued nationwide yearly for cases that seemed suspicious. In New York City, by 1925, seventeen agents were available to keep check on 1,200 drugstores and to investigate approximately a million prescriptions issued yearly by the city's 5,100 doctors.

2. Breweries manufacturing illegal beer. Massive cheating was going on in the production of near beer from genuine beer, and there weren't enough agents to determine if it was legally de-alcoholized.
3. Liquor smuggled across the borders. By 1924 the U.S. Coast Guard had been enlisted in the effort to watch the Atlantic Seaboard's 2,069 miles, but even its most dedicated couldn't make it more than a hit-and-miss endeavor. There were thirty-five agents posted along a Mexican frontier 1,744 miles in length, and they also had to watch the states of Texas, New Mexico, and Arizona. Including the Atlantic, Pacific, Gulf of Mexico, and Great Lakes, the total distance vulnerable to smuggling was approximately 18,700 miles.
4. The diversion of industrial alcohol. By 1925 the country's thirty denaturing plants that manufactured industrial alcohol were "nothing more or less than bootlegging organizations."
5. The illicit still. This was potentially the largest source of supply and "the source with which the [Prohibition Unit] was least equipped to deal."[4]

The depth of official corruption surrounding this ignoble episode in American history is staggering. From the start, the Prohibition Unit emitted a stench as foul as the cheap booze that legions of bootleggers produced. From 1920 to 1928, 706 agents were fired for larceny; 257 others, almost two-thirds of the original force, were prosecuted for larceny. This averages an astonishing arrest or dismissal rate of two agents each week of every year for eight years.

Irey's SIU was assigned to police the unit, and for most of the 1920s he had to use his tiny force not to uncover criminal tax fraud but to track down corruption in the Treasury's ranks, specifically at the Prohibition Unit. In June 1921 the SIU consisted of Irey; his second-in-command, William H. "Harry" Woolf; three clerks; a mail messenger; and thirty-nine special agents, the first six of whom had been brought on in 1919. (For half of Irey's twenty-seven-year tenure, the SIU's ranks stayed at approximately 100.) They were backed up by a field force of revenue inspectors and agents that in 1921 numbered 2,394. Revenue agents handled all tax matters except for criminal cases, which were turned over to the SIU. Irey admitted that policing Prohibition agents was an impossible mission, noting, "I am astonished that so many agents did remain honest."[5]

The SIU's first target turned out to be New York City, where Prohibition's onset had loosed an avalanche of applications for permits to withdraw and sell alcoholic liquors. Irey likened the scene to the mad rush of gold seekers in the Klondike of 1897. A legally obtained permit for withdrawal could be compared to a sack of gold dust. The numbers said it all: A permit holder who obtained a boxcar of alcohol, which holds 120 drums with fifty gallons in each drum, paid the warehouse price of 62 cents a gallon, for a total outlay of $3,720. The boxcar of alcohol was then sold to a bootlegger for $8 a gallon, or $48,000. The bootlegger, in turn, promptly cut each gallon three times, bringing its value to $24 a gallon, or $144,000. These were minimum figures too. Explained Irey: "This minimum is important because a price of $12 a gallon was not unusual and only three cuttings was quite unusual. One freight car filled with alcohol could, and often did, mean a quarter of a million dollars for a basic outlay of $3,720, plus bribe, plus transportation."[6]

After a number of Prohibition agents put together a scheme to sell counterfeit liquor permits (at $500 each), Irey launched an inquiry that led to ninety-four arrests, including seventeen agents in New York City's Prohibition office. In 1921 Irey sent a two-man force (including a newly hired agent named Frank J. Wilson) to Philadelphia to gather evidence that led to the indictment of Pennsylvania's Prohibition director, William C. McConnell, for issuing fraudulent liquor permits.[7] One of the SIU's most notable Prohibition cases, known as "The $5 Million Conspiracy," involved the former chief of the Philadelphia Secret Service office, Matthew F. Griffin. Upon retiring after thirty years of service, Griffin opened a detective agency for the ostensible purpose of guarding the legal export of whiskey. While working on another case, SIU agents came across a scheme Griffin had hatched. A company had been organized to handle export shipments of liquor (worth $5 million) to Greece. But SIU agents found that after obtaining legal authorization for the shipments, the company planned to substitute water for the whiskey. In a lengthy and sensational trial, Griffin and other principals in the plot were found guilty.

From these experiences, Irey quickly lost any illusions about the benefits of Prohibition, observing, "There were no Civil Service requirements, and, as a result, the most extraordinary collection of political hacks, hangers-on, and passing highwaymen got appointed as [Prohibition] agents."[8] Stanley Walker, city editor of the *New York Herald Tribune* and a chronicler of the scene, called them "swinish" and said it was common to see a group of Prohibition agents enter a New York speakeasy "at noon, remain until almost midnight, eating and drinking, and then leave without paying the bill."[9]

With faith a fleeing object, the numerous scandals bore on John Kramer, whom Roper had named the first Prohibition director. He was called "Honest John" by his supporters back in his hometown of Mansfield, Ohio, for not participating in the "business of party plunder."[10] Yet, overwhelmed and under fire, Kramer was gone in nineteen months. He was replaced by Roy A. Haynes, the former mayor of Hillsboro, Ohio, and a member of the "Ohio Gang," the political machine that grew out of the Mark Hannah age. Hannah, a wealthy Cleveland banker-industrialist and kingmaker, created "the businessman in politics," according to William Allen White. "In 1880 he learned that politics, properly controlled, prospered every business that he touched. So he set out to make a brand of politics as profitable as his mines, his ships, his railways, and his banks."[11] This infamous band of mercenaries, with Attorney General M. Harry Daugherty in the lead, came to Washington after Warren Harding was elected president and "traded in liquor withdrawal permits, protection to bootleggers, appointments to office, illegal concessions, immunity from prosecution, pardons, paroles, privileges, and general graft."[12] Unlike Kramer, Haynes didn't mind the business of party plunder. Frank Wilson called Haynes "an incompetent weakling."[13] Daniel Roper's successor, Millard West, turned out to be one of those "passing highwaymen" Irey cited. West barely warmed Roper's old chair before a federal grand jury indicted him for turning over 4,000 cases of bonded whiskey to the Kentucky congressman who had sponsored him for the office, Rep. John W. Langley, a seventeen-year member of the

House. In 1921 Irey's agents arrested Langley after he sold the whiskey for $100,000 ($1.9 million in 1990 dollars).

During this time, Daniel Roper was also working to secure legislation to set up an expanded narcotics bureau. Established on January 1, 1920, the new bureau (a forerunner to the Drug Enforcement Administration) had one striking feature—an absence of bureaucracy. Roper named a highly experienced hand to lead it: Levi G. Nutt, an ex-Ohio pharmacist and a nineteen-year Treasury veteran who was the same age as Roper. Nutt started out at the turn of the century with the Division of Chemistry, popularly known as the ATF (Alcohol, Tobacco, and Firearms) Revenue Laboratory. Set up in 1866 after passage of the Oleomargarine Act, the lab had been variously used to examine adulterated butter, alcoholic products, patent medicines, cosmetics, wines, and a host of other preparations for tax classification. After passage of the Harrison Act, it took on the task of analyzing narcotics and dangerous substances.

Nutt commanded a force of 255 agents and inspectors, including agents in charge, all under civil service. As senior officer, he would play a dual role in both Prohibition and drug enforcement. (Prohibition's enforcement side, of course, quickly turned sour, and he had to be called in to assist.) Field offices were established in New York City, Chicago, Philadelphia, Boston, Baltimore, Jacksonville, Nashville, Detroit, Minneapolis, Kansas City, San Antonio, Denver, Seattle, San Francisco, and Honolulu. There were only thirty-eight clerk-typists or stenographers in the fifteen offices. The lone legal adviser was based in Washington. Salaries of the agents in charge ranged from $5,200 ($98,800 in 1990 dollars) in New York City and Chicago, to $4,600 ($87,400 in 1990 dollars) in Denver and Seattle.

■

Roper's thirty months as commissioner had been a historical turning point for federal law enforcement. In taking Internal Revenue into uncharted waters, he had kept it on sure footing, handling many matters with almost flawless skill. He maintained restraint, stayed dedicated, and met each concern with a practical sensibility, not necessarily a solution. He had followed the Wilson policy, a policy that "generally practiced a collegial style of leadership [allowing] others to present initiatives and develop programs."[14] He was not a close friend of Woodrow Wilson (few who served him were), but there had been no better soldier in the president's last four years. In that fateful year of 1919, the challenges of tax, drug, and liquor enforcement had reared up together. No one before Roper had been handed such an array of complicated issues. He had come away from them with great success and without the controversy that plagued the Department of Justice and the Bureau of Investigation (BI). He had met the challenges, and masterfully too, and had kept his own counsel. There is not one complaint from him on the public record, nor a word from him about the missteps of others. In all of this he had showed a spine of steel (like he had found in Tillman). But the pressures had been enormous and had finally started to wear on him. Early in 1920, nearing a nervous breakdown, he decided to resign. Also, politically astute, he knew that a Republican era was about to begin, and he would be out in any case.

Upon deciding to leave, Roper called Irey to his office. There was a "glum silence," Irey recalled, because Roper was disappointed that the Treasury had been handed the role of enforcing Prohibition. Roper spoke: "We frequently underestimate the wisdom of the Justice Department. Justice was just too smart for us. Lord knows, I pulled every string I could to get it shifted to them. But they were too smart. I'm afraid you're stuck."

"Yes, I guess we are stuck, Mr. Roper."

"No, Mr. Irey, we're not stuck. You're stuck. Me . . . I'm resigning."[15]

Roper had taken enough cold plunges that he didn't want to face the Götterdämmerung of Prohibition too. He had as good an understanding of what was about to happen with Prohibition enforcement as anyone in government. That was going to be a mission unlike anything Washington had undertaken before—and it wasn't going to be pretty.

On March 6, 1920, Roper received a 160-word letter from the president, accepting "with regret" his resignation and indicating a recognition of the Herculean tasks Roper had faced. Your "duties," Wilson wrote him, "have been immensely difficult and complex, but you have discharged them with singular efficiency. I want you to know with what satisfaction I have watched your conduct of the affairs of your office."

On March 31, sixty-five days after Prohibition became law, Roper left. Shortly thereafter he entered a Baltimore clinic, where he spent several weeks for "frayed nerves," and he was thankful that the "great tension" of his tenure "had not impaired my health."[16] Though he never complained, much of his concern had come from being saddled with the insurmountable problem of Prohibition. Still, Roper left an indelible mark.

5. SPLENDID CLIMATE
FOR ORGANIZED CRIME

The political-criminal alliances that formed in the big cities in the Prohibition era had little to worry about from the federal constabulary, a shaky, ill-funded apparatus, its effectiveness in severe question. Prohibition had turned the world of commerce upside down, making enforcement close to insurmountable. Lawful businesses such as restaurants and bars, which once sold liquor, had become speakeasies engaged in illegal activity. The number of locations that practiced vice had increased geometrically and fallen prey to the alliances. As Matthew DeMichele and Garry Potter noted, "Where illegality is occurring with regard to liquor, it is a small step to also provide gambling, prostitution and other vice-related goods and services. . . . The underworld [that] operated in a segregated environment which assured the delivery of services to customers, but which also assured that 'respectable' folk would have little or no contact with the vices if they so chose, now was invited into everyday life."[1] Corruption was no longer clandestine.

It wasn't a pretty picture. The enormous bounty from bootlegging, along with the proceeds from a variety of prospering rackets and vice, was the charm that bound the three elements together in the political-criminal alliances—corrupted elected officials, their police cohorts, and the criminal combines—in mutually beneficial fashion.

The racketeers who would rule organized crime for the next quarter century were coming of age. The federal constabulary, as it stood, was never going to cope with this clever criminal element. Aside from a shaky foundation, whatever tradition existed at the federal level rested in the small, specialized units such as Irey's old unit, the postal inspectors, and the Secret Service, originally set up in 1865. The new Prohibition branch, the biggest force in the federal constabulary, was shooting itself in the foot almost daily. And when it came to achieving local cooperation, the door was usually slammed in the face of federal agents, often with a bang. A decade before, with passage of the Mann Act—the first law that overrode local jurisdiction—the locals believed their role had been usurped. It wasn't left unspoken that they didn't look kindly at federal detectives, even in the face of the cooperation given "Shadow" Porter's drug task force in New York City. Drugs, of course, weren't a thriving commerce like liquor. But local enforcement had always been dominant, and it was easy to see why. In April 1926 Police Commissioner George V. McLaughlin asked the Board of Estimate to appropriate money for 3,000 new officers in a New York Police Department that was already more than 10,000 strong—a force bigger than the entire federal constabulary.

At the Treasury, Irey's Special Intelligence Unit, with its limited statutory power, wasn't going to give the political-criminal alliances any trouble. Internal Revenue had always maintained that income from illegal enterprise was taxable, but ambiguities existed. Ironically, when Daniel Roper was commissioner, Internal Revenue on March 10, 1919, issued an interpretation about criminal activity that provided a sizeable pass to those earning illegal incomes. Internal Revenue had received an inquiry from an individual in "a Southern state" who asserted, "I was engaged last year in the business of making whisky, which the revenue says is illegal. I was raided by the revenues and my still was taken and I was fined. I have not quit the business but want to know whether I have to make income return of the money I made off the whisky and whether I can deduct the loss of my still or my fine."[2] Internal Revenue ruled that both the loss of the still and the fine could be deducted in determining net income subject to taxation. At the same time, it decided to allow gamblers and other participants in illegal practices to deduct a part of their losses. The owner of a gambling house whose place was raided and whose furniture and gambling equipment were destroyed could deduct those losses along with any court fines he paid. Internal Revenue also ruled that poker players could deduct losses if they didn't exceed winnings.

Two years later, in the Revenue Act of 1921, Congress made it statutory that taxes be deducted on earnings from an illegal enterprise. The next year, however, the statute became a court test involving Manly S. Sullivan, a dealer of farm equipment and marine engines in Charleston, South Carolina. Convicted in federal district court in 1922 for refusing to file a tax return on his 1921 income of $10,000 ($190,000 in 1990 dollars), Sullivan had made no secret that part of his earnings came from bootlegging. He decided to fight the verdict and chose a set of unusual grounds as his defense. His lawyer, Frederick W. Aley of Charleston, contended Sullivan's proceeds from bootlegging were not subject to income tax under the Revenue Act of 1921. Congress, Aley argued, could not have intended to include gains from crime and thus put legitimate and illegitimate transactions on the same footing.[3] In addition, Aley invoked a constitutional question, arguing that if Sullivan did report the income it would violate his rights against self-incrimination under the Fifth Amendment. By 1924 the case was still winding its way through the federal courts, far from a decision.

Though mandated to bring in tax conspirators, Irey was a reluctant warrior who drew strict lines. Aside from tax criminality, he had no intention of becoming a crime fighter, and when he did, it wasn't exactly by his own initiative. He knew the SIU was never going to be popular, and neither was the income tax. He understood a human trait: people don't like for their hard-earned money to be taken by the government, nor do they want Washington digging into their finances. The watchful legislators who held the SIU's purse strings shared this belief. The guardians on Capitol Hill attended Irey's branch with special care, limiting the means of the SIU to carry out any more responsibilities than was needed—after all, Irey could look at their tax returns too. For his part, Irey felt Internal Revenue's primary objective was to collect money for Uncle Sam, not to catch crooks. After taking over in 1919, he recommended to Roper that the Treasury not prosecute any delinquent taxpayer who admitted the error of his own volition and then made a voluntary disclosure before investigation. Penalties and interest would be levied, but the taxpayer wouldn't be criminally prosecuted. Roper agreed. The custom is still followed today.

■

As the 1920s opened, President Harding made a brilliant selection as his secretary of the Treasury: Andrew W. Mellon, a wealthy banker. Parallel to Prohibition's vast and deep corruption, the country was undergoing great economic growth. No public figure was more responsible for the Roaring Twenties than the gaunt, white-haired Mellon, born in 1855. And no banker was as gimlet-eyed as Mellon, an attitude he brought to Washington. His sure-handed policies not only helped wipe out the huge war debt; he also instituted major tax cuts and initiated programs that turned the country into an economic dynamo that became mobile like nothing before. In 1919 there were 6,677,000 passenger cars. In 1929 there were 23,121,000. Presidents Warren Harding, Calvin Coolidge, and Herbert Hoover, in succession, kept Mellon as the secretary of the Treasury.

At the same time, Harding picked a smooth mercenary, Harry Daugherty (who had managed Harding's presidential campaign), as his attorney general. The Justice Department was already on uncertain footing, besieged by its handling of controversial episodes arising out of World War I: the 1917 dragnet of draft evaders, the 1919 May Day bombing, and a 1919 Senate investigation that found the Bureau of Investigation (yet to become the FBI) was probing the opinions and affiliations of prominent people suspected of being pro-German. All of this was topped off in November 1919, when the Bureau of Investigation began seizing dissidents and aliens in what became known as the Palmer Raids (named after then–attorney general, A. Mitchell Palmer). Furthermore, it took just thirteen months for scandal to descend on the Harding White House from three fronts: Secretary of the Interior Albert B. Fall came under a cloud for his role in the Teapot Dome affair involving the secret leasing of oil reserves without competitive bidding; Charles R. Forbes, a Harding appointee named to head the Veterans Bureau, came under fire; and then Daugherty himself became the target of Senator Burton K. Wheeler, who thought the scandals were a conglomerate Daugherty held in his hand and should have acted on. Talk had spread across the Hill about Daugherty's inclination to go easy on the big trusts that Washington's regulatory agencies monitored. "Tips came to me in bunches that Daugherty was up to his neck in massive graft," said Wheeler.[4] This warfare, which included an attempt to impeach Daugherty, continued in one fashion or another but never gained real momentum. Then, in August 1923 President Harding died of an embolism in San Francisco. The new president, Calvin Coolidge, tolerated Daugherty until the next March, when he fired him for failing to turn over files on Senator Wheeler to congressional investigators.

The new attorney general, Harlan Fiske Stone, a respected New Englander who had been dean of the Columbia Law School, worked to fix the mess left by Daugherty. One of Stone's most notable tasks was to find a new director for the Bureau of Investigation, which he noted had an "exceedingly bad odor" and was "filled with men with bad records, and many of them had been convicted of crime."[5] Stone narrowed his choice between J. Edgar Hoover, age twenty-nine, the bureau's assistant director since August 1921, and Irey, now thirty-six, who had been acquiring a measure of recognition for running down corruption in the Prohibition Unit. Irey had kept his record and that of his unit in pristine fashion, but he wasn't a lawyer, a consideration in a department run by lawyers. In the government, Secretary of Commerce Herbert Hoover, who had watched the events at Daugherty's Justice Department and the BI with disdain, passed a favorable word to Stone on Hoover, based on the recommendation of his confidential assistant, Larry Richey, once a Secret Service agent and a friend of J. Edgar. Outside the government, Roger N. Baldwin, a lawyer who founded the American Civil Liberties Union, supported Hoover. Baldwin had been disturbed by the surveillance activities of the bureau's General Intelligence Division under Hoover. But after visiting with Hoover, he told his colleagues, "We were wrong in our estimate of [Hoover's] attitude."[6] On May 10, 1924, Stone made Hoover the acting director; he then made his choice permanent the following December. The seventh man to lead the bureau in its then sixteen-year history, Hoover began a forty-eight-year reign as director.

Despite Stone's efforts at reform, the scholarly John W. H. Crim, who served as a special assistant attorney general to Stone in 1924–1925, had been a prosecutor in the Southern District of New York, and was Justice's leading trial prosecutor, believed that the department's dominant weakness lay with politics. So disillusioned by the politicization of the department, Crim told a congressional committee that "it would be a very good idea to take the Attorney General out of politics by taking him out of the Cabinet."[7]

Crim's period at Justice had given him the opportunity to observe the work of the U.S. attorneys around the country. He didn't think much of them, noting, "Not more than ten of the Federal District Attorneys were competent to handle their offices. They had been elected not because of their ability but because of their fealty to some politician."[8] In his misgivings about federal prosecutors, Crim had many localities in mind, including Chicago, where he went to handle the prosecution of Charles Forbes and seventy-year-old John W. Thompson, a Chicago and St. Louis contractor, on charges of defrauding the government. Forbes was found guilty and sentenced to two years in Leavenworth. Crim and a team of three others from Justice handled the prosecution, not the U.S. attorney for the Northern District of Illinois, Edwin A. Olson. Olson's office was up to its neck in Prohibition cases. Among them was a series of cases Olson botched arising from the sensational murder (by Al Capone and his henchmen) of a twenty-six-year-old assistant state attorney, William H. "Bill" McSwiggin, and involving seventy-eight indictments that were handed down for violations under the Volstead Act. A year elapsed before the cases were called, owing to court congestion. By then, two key witnesses had been murdered, and all seventy-eight cases were dropped because of lack of evidence.

At the time, Olson's first assistant, William F. Waugh, was handling the case of Johnny Torrio, the slightly built, button-eyed racketeer who gave Al Capone his start in Chicago and whom Elmer Irey called "the father of modern American gangsterdom."[9] In May 1924, in a setup maneuvered by the bootlegger-racketeer Dion O'Banion, Torrio was arrested by police—his first and last time—during a raid of the Sieben Brewery. Since Torrio was involved, the police turned the case over to Olson's office. A Torrio henchman offered $50,000 ($900,000 in 1990 dollars) to William Waugh if he would drop the prosecution. Torrio went to jail, but neither Olson nor Waugh pursued the bribe offer. After Torrio went down, his lawyer, Robert W. Childs, once Olson's first assistant, stopped in for a friendly chat with Waugh. Shortly thereafter Torrio was transferred from the Wheaton jail to the better sanitized Waukegan jail, where during his nine-month stay he was allowed to furnish his cell with a large bed, a thick carpet, a dressing table, and bulletproof screens over the two windows. Waugh, upon leaving for private practice, represented Capone when the master racketeer was trying to cover up his role in the 1929 St. Valentine's Day massacre.

■

Crim was at the Justice Department when Harland Stone arrived, and worked closely with William J. Donovan. One of Stone's prize pupils at Columbia Law School, Donovan earned a degree in the same graduating class as Franklin D. Roosevelt. Stone brought him from Buffalo, where he was serving as the U.S. attorney for the Western District of New York (appointed by President Harding in 1922). Donovan's zealousness had made him few friends in Buffalo, where he was born on January 1, 1883. He padlocked the Country Club of Buffalo and the exclusive Saturn Club, the city's most elaborate speakeasy. The list of those arrested at the two clubs read like a who's who of Buffalo's leading businessmen (for which Donovan was "being cursed in drawing rooms throughout the Delaware District").[10] In a final insult to the city's power elite, Donovan busted the mayor, Francis X. Schwab, for manufacturing and selling beer at his brewery, and he personally prosecuted the case. Schwab was fined $500 ($9,500 in 1990 dollars) on the liquor charges and $10,000 ($190,000 in 1990 dollars) in civil penalties. Donovan, of course, was the intrepid "Wild Bill" Donovan, the World War I hero, and World War II spymaster who was in the thick of conflict all his life. In 1916 he was in a U.S. cavalry unit under Gen. John J. Pershing that tried to run down Pancho Villa for killing Americans on border raids. As a thirty-five-year-old lieutenant colonel in New York's Fighting Sixty-ninth, he won the nation's three highest awards for combat heroism (the Congressional Medal of Honor, Distinguished Service Cross, and Purple

Heart) in France's grimy trenches, and led the celebrated unit up Manhattan's Fifth Avenue upon its return in 1918.

When Stone and Crim left Justice, Donovan stayed, taking over the Antitrust Division in March 1925 and becoming a vigorous enforcer of the antitrust laws. Over the next four years he brought more cases (sixty-five) than anyone before, argued half a dozen cases before the Supreme Court, was effective in getting J. Edgar Hoover's help in carrying out antitrust investigations, and was responsible for a number of landmark rulings. He also tried to use the antitrust laws against Chicago's labor racketeers, sending Assistant Attorneys General Mary G. Connor and William R. Benham to the Windy City to handle a key case involving the Candy Jobbers Association, a racketeering front, in November 1927. Federal indictments were returned against eleven current and past officers of the association, including business agent, Simon J. Gorman, along with thirty-four others, charging violations of the Sherman antitrust law and a series of bombings, stabbings, and beatings of candy dealers who refused to join the association's plans to maintain fixed prices in what was a $7 million ($75.6 million in 1990 dollars) enterprise in Chicago.

One of Donovan's most significance moves was to send a twenty-nine-year-old lawyer, John Harlan Amen, to New York City late in the Coolidge administration to launch a drive on the rackets. Amen carried upper-crust lines. He attended Phillips Exeter Academy, where his father was headmaster; went on to Princeton University and Harvard Law; and wed Grover Cleveland's daughter. He would turn out to be one of the sturdiest rackets prosecutors in the annals of New York City. Donovan's choice of Amen was memorable; yet, his move was akin to sticking a finger in a broken dike.

Donovan only had resources enough to apply a Band-Aid to Washington's effort against racketeering. The 1920s was the Golden Age for racketeers, a time of virtually unimpeded growth, when organized crime figures were building wealth and influence. Burdette G. Lewis, who served as New York City's commissioner of corrections in the early 1900s, was the Justice Department's most outspoken critic. On the day he took over as corrections chief, Lewis said that twenty-eight racketeers were serving terms in New York City's jails. Since 1910, he noted, rackets had been operating "in the handling of perishables of all kinds, in certain trades of the building industry and in the clothing industry particularly." He blamed Justice for not using the 1914 Clayton Antitrust Act against racketeers, instead concentrating its efforts on trust-busting. Because "nothing effective was done to check extortion, intimidation, and even murder-for-hire in many of our northern, Midwestern and Far Western cities," Lewis said, "racketeering has been growing for more than thirty years."[11]

After the irreplaceable Crim left, Justice lost more of its footing. Nine months into the job, Harlan Stone went to the Supreme Court as its youngest member at age fifty-two. His departure brought three months of upheaval over a successor. In January 1925 President Coolidge, even in the face of Republican opposition, nominated Charles B. Warren, a Michigan lawyer serving as ambassador to Mexico. Coolidge withdrew Warren's name after his nomination sparked a tie vote in the Senate. In mid-March sixty-five-year-old John G. Sargent, a former state's attorney and attorney general of Vermont, accepted the post. "A fine old Yankee lawyer from a small country town more or less bewildered by the executive vastness of his job," Sargent "was not a fit man. . . . [He] disliked Washington and stayed away as often as he could."[12] When he took over, Justice's staff numbered 452, of which 151 were lawyers, 52 of those in the Claims Division alone. The Criminal Division consisted of an assistant attorney general, six lawyers, a secretary, and seven stenographers. The Division of Prohibition and Taxation had four assistant attorneys general, ten lawyers, two secretaries, and seven stenographers. Unlike the Treasury and its strong tradition, Justice had been a limited operation well into the twentieth century. In 1891 the department moved into its own building (sixteen of the ninety-eight employees were custodial help).

Beginning with Harlan Stone, the department was occupied with clearing away the corruptive ash the Ohio Gang left on the Harding White House—an effort that carried into the next decade with questionable success. Harry Daugherty went free after his trial in the Southern District of New York ended in a mistrial. The case of Albert Fall, who had resigned under fire in 1923, carried until 1931, when he was convicted of conspiracy to defraud the government and was sent to prison for one year.

■

At the Bureau of Investigation, J. Edgar Hoover had taken command of a matchstick force with a questionable image, no prestige, and serious questions about the way it had operated. The bureau was carrying out broad statutory responsibilities: The investigation of bootleggers, antitrust violations, Army and Navy frauds, bank frauds, automobile theft, and Mann Act violations. Still, it wasn't a major crime-fighting operation because Hoover had little political capital. Bathed in one compelling controversy or another since the war and ridiculed as the Department of Easy Virtue, the bureau's standing remained at a low point during the 1920s. Congress, beginning in 1920 (when the BI was eleven years old), kept its annual appropriations in the $2 million range, and by the end of the decade the BI's personnel force had plunged from a high of 1,127 to 591—339 of them special agents. After taking control, Hoover issued yearly reports "designed to convince the Congress of the Bureau's efficiency."[13] But until the early 1930s, when it began pursuing the celebrity bank robbers, the BI maintained a certain anonymity.

Actually, the entire federal constabulary stayed at low ebb during the 1920s. Aside from the corruption, missteps, and lack of appropriations, an even greater drawback yoked it: the simple and defeating sentiment that law enforcement was local. From the start—in Theodore Roosevelt's presidency—the concept of a federal detective force was strafed with doubts. During the congressional debate at the end of TR's tenure over establishing the Bureau of Investigation, many on Capitol Hill looked unfavorably at the idea of a general police system at the federal level. Opponents were fearful of "a Federal secret police" and "a spy system" and even a "central secret-service bureau such as there is in Russia today."[14] A comment in the Congressional Record summed up the alarm: "There is no desire for a general detective service or national police organization in connection with the Federal Government. On the contrary, there is in Congress an utter abhorrence of such a scheme. . . . It is considered absolutely contradictory to the democratic principles of government."[15] This sentiment carried into the Prohibition era, despite the accompanying rise in violent crime in the big cities.

The provenance of the time was summed up in an editorial in the *New York Times* about gang warfare in Chicago. It came several days after the daylight machine-gunning on busy South State Street on October 11, 1926, of Hymie Weiss, a well-known racketeer (and mortal enemy of Al Capone); Weiss's bodyguard, Patrick Murphy; his chauffeur, Sam Peller; William W. Wilson, a leading criminal lawyer; and Benjamin Jacobs, a private investigator working for Wilson. The five men had spent most of that Monday at a trial at the criminal court building, and had driven to racketeer Dion O'Banion's old headquarters—his flower shop on South State Street. Peller parked in front of Holy Name Cathedral. As they walked across the street, they were cut down by machine-gun fire from the window of a second-story flat adjoining the flower shop. Weiss and Peller were killed; the other three were wounded.

Of this incident, an editorial in the *Times* asserted: "A new outbreak of ferocious crime in Chicago, including this time murder by machine guns, has apparently led some people in that city to despair. They raise loud laments that the municipal police force can no longer be depended upon and that the prosecuting authorities have shown themselves to be powerless. So, according to newspaper reports, the eyes of citizens are lifted to Washington. Whatever the truth, it is not to be believed that Chicago will confess herself so impotent. There is no warrant in the Constitution or the laws for Federal intervention except in cases of crime under Federal statutes, and there is no reason to support that if there were Federal intervention it would be effective. Crime is local in this country and must be dealt with by the local authorities. Otherwise our whole system of government would break down.[16]

In those cities where the criminal-political alliances dominated, there was this harsh handicap: a sizeable and influential body of opinion stood against federal expansion into criminal activity. Against this background, Washington's highest levels were clearly aware of what was happening in Chicago. At a session of Congress on the morning of Saturday, February

24, 1926, Vice President Charles G. Dawes took the House floor to read a petition from a group called the "Better Government Association in Chicago and Cook County." The moment was unannounced, unceremonious, ordinarily a time of little activity with minimum attendance, and came three months after Dawes won the Nobel Prize for his plan on German reparations. The petition spelled out what was happening in Chicago and called for a congressional investigation. It said, in part,

> There has been for a long time in this city of Chicago a colony of unnaturalized persons, hostile to our institutions and laws, who have formed a supergovernment of their own—feudists, black handers, members of the Mafia—who levy tribute upon citizens and enforce collections by terrorizing, kidnapping and assassinations. There are other gangs, such as the O'Donnells, the McErlanes, Ragens Colts, Torrio and others, some of whom are citizens of the United States. Many of these aliens have become fabulously rich as rum-runners and bootleggers, working in collusion with police and other officials, building up a monopoly in this unlawful business and dividing the territory of the county among themselves under penalty of death to all intruding competitors.
>
> Evidence multiplies daily that many public officials are in secret alliance with underworld assassins, gunmen, rum-runners, bootleggers, thugs, ballot box stuffers and repeaters, that a ring of politicians and public officials operating through criminals and with dummy directors are conducting a number of breweries and are selling beer under police protection, police officials, working out of the principal law enforcement office of the city, having been convoying liquor—namely alcohol, whisky and beer—and that one such police officer who is under Federal indictment is still acting as a police officer.[17]

This was a defining moment. Petition in hand, Dawes had put crime in Chicago on the national agenda. He had condemned the conspiratorial alliance of police officials, elected officials, and organized crime elements such as the Mafia. For the first time, the Mafia had been pinpointed in name from the highest levels in Washington. If misunderstandings had existed about the Mafia's presence or influence, it was in the open now. Notably, too, in spelling out how a criminal-political "supergovernment" had come together in Chicago, Dawes marked the way for law enforcement to act against the Mafia and organized crime—forces that were just then becoming a problem for law enforcement.

The petition Dawes read was sent to the Senate Immigration Committee, chaired by Hiram W. Johnson, a sixty-year-old California Republican who had served as governor. And that happened to be where the petition would stay—for good. Not even Dawes, with his prestige and influence, could carry the day. There were no congressional hearings, no outcry to act, and no support at all. The belief on Capitol Hill was against any expansion of the federal role in law enforcement.

No one was more aware of Chicago's criminality than Dawes. Chosen in 1925 as the vice president under Calvin Coolidge, he should have been the president of the United States instead of Coolidge. The two were opposites who barely got along. Coolidge, a lawyer, tired easily, was shy and cautious, and had few friends. Dawes, a lawyer, was a dynamo with an unyielding countenance and made admirers everywhere. He acted when it counted and was out front on issues when Coolidge was not, particularly on the political-criminal alliance that ran Chicago. An Ohioan, Dawes began practicing law in suburban Evanston at age thirty in 1895. The next year he managed William McKinley's presidential campaign in Illinois, served as the comptroller of currency after McKinley won, and then ran unsuccessfully for the U.S. Senate. Leaving politics, he organized the Central Trust of Illinois and became wealthy. When the country entered World War I, he was commissioned a major in the U.S. Army, rose to brigadier general, and was named chief of supply procurement for the American Expeditionary Force. For his achievements, he was awarded the Distinguished Service Medal, but after the war he faced hostility from a congressional committee investigating charges of overpayment for supplies. To an accusing question, he parried, "Sure we paid. We didn't dicker. . . . We would have paid horse prices for sheep if sheep could have pulled artillery to the front. . . .

Hell and Maria, we weren't trying to keep a set of books, we were trying to win the war!"[18] This outspokenness earned him the sobriquet "Hell 'n' Maria" Dawes and the admiration of many, including Warren Harding.

In 1921 newly elected President Harding named Dawes to head a committee to investigate and recommend reorganization of the War Risk Board (later the Veterans Bureau) and develop plans for the care of war veterans. The committee's eleven members included Mabel T. Boardman, the wealthy secretary of the American Red Cross. At its first meeting, members found a note requesting their presence at a social affair at Boardman's home that evening. Dawes, at the head of the table, read it, and picked up another note telling him that a suite of seven rooms was ready for his use in a new building on the site of the old Arlington Hotel. He read it and turned to the director of the War Risk Board.

"How long do you think we are going to be here?" Dawes asked.

"Six or seven months."

"Well, I am not going to be here even six or seven days," Dawes snapped, turning to Boardman. "Now, Miss Boardman, we are not going to your party tonight or to any other social event until we solve this problem. I see the Surgeon General sitting there. We are going to give him just fifteen minutes for his testimony, and that will apply to all other witnesses. If we can't get all we want in that time, perhaps we can extend it slightly, but I don't think we will have to do so."[19] Three days after this initial meeting, the committee's report was in preparation.

A granite-like figure who quickly left his mark on Washington's provincials, Dawes was not a man to dicker, and his political star never stopped shining. Soon, Harding named him the first director of the Budget Bureau, where his reform measures in the bureau's first year saved two billion dollars. In April 1924 as chairman of the Reparations Committee, he devised a plan to reduce Germany's reparations payments, which helped stabilize that country's economy and won him the Nobel Prize. In November he was picked as Coolidge's running mate. Among many complaints "Silent Cal" made about his vice president, one was that he was too forthright: Dawes once sent the president a letter saying that he wasn't going to attend cabinet meetings.

Watching from suburban Evanston before Prohibition came, Dawes knew what was happening to law and order in Chicago—that the city's only voices of protest against crime and corruption, outside a tiny number of honest politicians and police, were watchdog groups and business elements. All had been largely ineffectual. Even before Prohibition's lawlessness, they were trying to fight crime. In 1919, sparked by a business group called the Association of Commerce, the Chicago Crime Commission, the first in the nation, was established.

In April 1923 the commission published its first list of criminals who were constantly in conflict with the law, twenty-eight in all. The commission's dogged director, Henry Barrett Chamberlin, a former reporter-editor, maintained a close vigilance on crime and regularly issued informed accounts of what was happening. "Deprivation and want cause few crimes in Chicago," he said. "[Crime] is an organized business and it must be fought with business methods."[20] He used techniques the Federal Bureau of Investigation adapted forty years later in gathering intelligence on organized crime leaders. Frank J. Loesch, the commission's illustrious president and a tenacious crime fighter, applied the name "Public Enemies."[21] Heading the list was "Alphonse Capone, alias Scarface Capone, alias Al Brown." Second was one of his bodyguards, Tony "Mops" Volpe, and third was Al's older brother, Ralph. Under Chamberlin, who served from 1919 to 1941, the commission had many little victories, but they never added up to the totality needed to thwart Chicago's criminal combines and their political alliances—certainly not against the background of the Great Experiment, Prohibition. The commission's effort was far outweighed by the dishonesty of public officials, the legal technicalities that allowed racketeers to avoid jail and thrive, and the illegal wealth that Capone and others earned and wisely spread around. Fred Pasley observed, not too facetiously, that the U.S. Marines would have been powerless against the forces behind Chicago's criminal life.

In the early 1920s Chamberlin and the reformers, Dawes among them, achieved a modicum of success: the end of Mayor William Hale "Big Bill" Thompson. Born in Boston and raised in Chicago, where his father made a fortune in real estate, Big Bill "developed a natural gift for campaign tent oratory" and "knew instinctively how to tickle the prejudices of ethnic and national groups."[22] He got into politics as a thirty-five-year-old alderman in the Second Ward in 1900, a time when one official said, "The worst you can say about Bill is that he's stupid."[23] After that, opponents and observers sought new heights to describe him: Big Bill was "a buffoon in a tommyrot factory"[24] and a "man with the carcass of a rhinoceros and the brain of a baboon."[25] Still, this wasn't as direct as what was said about Governor Lennington Small, known as Thompson's "puppet": "We have a governor who ought to be in the penitentiary."[26]

In the 1915 mayoralty, Thompson rode in on a campaign to clean up the city, capturing the seat by the biggest plurality ever registered for a Republican in Chicago. With such a margin he decided he could do what he wanted and reform wasn't on his agenda. He kept the city wide open, becoming "the hero of every pimp, whore, gambler, racketeer and bootlegger."[27] His first eight months in office produced twice as many police complaints as the entire preceding year. Johnny Torrio and Al Capone were able to build their political-criminal alliance during Thompson's reign.

In 1923 he was ready to run for a third term when his campaign manager, Fred Lundin, an ex-congressman, was indicted with twenty-three co-conspirators for misappropriating more than $1 million of school funds ($19 million in 1990 dollars). Big Bill withdrew his name, and the mayoralty went to a Democrat, William E. Dever, a former judge and alderman. Dever initiated true reform that included closing 200 downtown handbook parlors operated by "Mont" Tennes. Tennes's life history, if known, would have disclosed "practically all there is to know about syndicated gambling as a phase of organized crime in Chicago in the last quarter century," according to the Illinois Crime Survey.[28]

Mayor Dever achieved a measure of success against the criminal combines. Torrio tried to buy off the new chief of police, Morgan A. Collins, offering $100,000 a month; Collins answered by padlocking Torrio's headquarters, a four-story redbrick building at 2222 South Wabash Avenue that contained his offices, a saloon, gambling rooms, and a brothel. In May 1924 Collins had led the Sieben Brewery raid that brought Torrio's incarceration. Dever's offense also forced Torrio and Capone to consider havens beyond the mayor's reach. With the help of a Republican commit-teeman named Ed Konvalinka, Torrio established operations in Cicero, a flourishing suburb of 70,000 thirty minutes west of the Loop by the ele-vated railway. With Cicero as their centerpiece, Torrio and Capone began expanding the scope of their operations—and influence.

■

What Chicago needed was an honest and zealous prosecutor. What it had was Robert Emmett Crowe, who would serve as the state attorney of Cook County from 1921 until 1929, the period when bootlegging and racketeering flourished virtually unimpeded. The scholarly Columbia Uni-versity law professor, Raymond Moley, ventured that there was no more "extraordinary example of the political exploitation of a prosecutor's of-fice" than under Robert Crowe.[29] A Yale Law School graduate from Peo-ria, Crowe rode into office in 1921 on the Thompson ticket. He brought rounded experience, serving as an assistant state attorney, assistant corpo-ration counsel, and a Cook County circuit court judge for one year be-fore becoming chief justice of the criminal court in 1917 at thirty-eight, the youngest man to sit on that bench. He broke with the Thompson-Small machine following the conviction of Fred Lundin in the school funds scan-dal, which reformers thought had ended Big Bill's political career. During Crowe's tenure, the city turned into a labor-racketeering hell. "Trade as-sociation" was the designated phrase for the hollow fronts that racketeers established and used to maintain control over a trade through terror and murder, while stealing from their dues-paying members. These fake orga-nizations always resulted in the public being forced to pay higher prices. In the 1920s insurance rates skyrocketed. Chicago householders paid $27.20 for each $1,000 of burglary insurance, while Milwaukee citizens paid $12.10. Auto theft premiums for Chicagoans were $25.40, compared to $7.20 paid by Cleveland motorists.

By autumn 1927, according to Gordon L. Hostetter and Thomas Quinn Beesley, some fifty rackets were flourishing "like jungle plants" in Chicago.[30] "There is not a business, not an industry, in Chicago that is not paying a tribute directly or indirectly to racketeers and gangsters," Fred Pasley pointed out.[31] "Racketeer" wasn't even a word in American dictionaries of the 1920s, but in December 1927 the *Chicago Journal of Commerce* presented its own definition:

> A racketeer may be the boss of a supposedly legitimate business association; he may be a labor union organizer . . . or he may be just a journeyman thug. Whether he is a gunman who has imposed himself upon some union as its leader, or whether he is a business association organizer, his methods are the same; by throwing a few bricks into a few windows, an incidental or accidental murder, he succeeds in organizing a group of small businessmen into what he calls a protective association. He then proceeds to collect fees and dues he likes, to impose what fines suit him, regulates prices and hours of work, and in various ways undertakes to boss the outfit to his own profit. Any merchant who doesn't come in or who comes and doesn't stay in and continues to pay tribute, is bombed, slugged or otherwise intimidated.[32]

In November 1927 the *New York Times* sent a special correspondent, Glenn Griswold, to Chicago for a firsthand account. He wrote, "No business is too small for exploitation."[33] Maxie Eisen, called "Maxie the Immune," may have been Chicago's most notorious racketeer. Since 1918 he had been arrested and brought to court twenty-eight times on charges ranging from burglary to assault to kill and never went to jail. The president of the Kosher Meat Peddlers' Association, he operated five other associations—all with high-sounding names—the Master Jewish Butchers Association, the Jewish Chicken Killers, the Poultry Dealers, the Master Bakers of the Northwest Side, and the Wholesale and Retail Fish Dealers Association. Every pushcart peddler on Maxwell Street, where Eisen was known as the Simon Legree of the pushcart peddlers, paid tribute to him.

■

Under Chief Morgan Collins, the Chicago Police Department was doing its job. In 1926 the police were bringing in felony violators in droves, close to fifty a day. The police that year made 20,186 felony arrests. Of that number, 647 went to jail. The prosecutor responsible for determining what happened in those 20,186 arrests was State Attorney Crowe. If 647 felons were sent away, Crowe and his staff decided not to prosecute the other 19,539. None of the convicted felons, incidentally, were racketeers and cut-throats from the various criminal combines.

William Dever was that rarity, an honest mayor. Edward Dean Sullivan called him "one of the best executives Chicago ever had."[34] Dever, along with Collins, had tried hard, but the mix of circumstances overwhelmed them. While Dever was mayor, Cook County Sheriff Peter M. Hoffman, a Republican, allowed two gangsters, Terry Druggan and Frankie Lake, who were confined to the city jail, to come and go as they pleased. Druggan spent most of his evenings with his wife "in their $12,000-a-year [$216,000 in 1990 dollars] duplex apartment on the Gold Coast, whose distinctive appurtenances included a solid silver toilet seat engraved with his name." For this unhealthy impropriety, U.S. Circuit Judge James H. Wilkerson sent Sheriff Hoffman to jail for thirty days, supposedly ending his public career. However, the Democratic head of the county board, Anton J. Cermak, appointed Hoffman as assistant chief forester of the forest preserves at a salary of $10,000 annually ($180,000 in 1990 dollars).

Chief Collins had brought credibility to the department, but murders in the city had increased each year of Dever's mayoralty. In Crowe's eight-year tenure, there were 349 murders, 215 of which were underworld figures. His office obtained 128 convictions for murder, none involving an underworld figure. The Illinois Association for Criminal Justice pronounced Frank McErlane, an alcoholic who had the build of a wrestler, "the most brutal gunman who ever pulled a trigger in Chicago."[35] When McErlane was arrested for killing a driver for the O'Donnell brothers, a lesser known but important criminal element, Crowe put him under house arrest at the Hotel Sherman, then ordered his unconditional release until "the pressure of public opinion" forced him to seek a grand jury indictment.[36] After months of legal maneuvering, Crowe decided not to pursue the case. He obtained another indictment against McErlane for a double slaying. Then later, decided not to pursue that either.

From the start, Dever could not overcome his own party's soiling of city hall. To get the nomination, he had made a deal with George E. Brennan, boss of the Illinois Democratic machine, that with the exception of a few show-window positions, Brennan would be permitted to dispense all the patronage of the office. This effectively renounced "the lever that might have pried Chicago corruption apart."[37] Politically, the city was divided into fifty wards, each headed by an alderman or committeeman. To understand Chicago's ward politics is to understand how racketeers such as Torrio and Capone flourished. Party affiliation meant little. The criminal combines didn't really have to deal with city hall; an alderman who wanted his cut of the vice and bootlegging in his ward was enough. The mayor set the tone because his office controlled the police department (as in New York City). But the alderman and underworld figures brokered alliances at the ward level that permitted, on the one hand, ballot-box stuffing, fraudulent counting, and roving, pistol-packing terrorists on Election Day, and on the other hand, gambling joints, houses of prostitution, illegal breweries, and speakeasies.

Dever had "tried hard to dehydrate Chicago," but the police department, under Collins, began to invade homes and jail people for possession of as much as a single bottle of liquor, "a crusade that turned the public against them."[38] This would turn out to be the final insult for the reform effort. Furthermore, Big Bill Thompson was making noises and, to the chagrin of the reformers, decided to seek the mayoralty again. The reformers had one ace in the hole: Vice President Dawes. He was fully informed on the Chicago scene, visited the city occasionally, and talked regularly with others—in particular, to his brother, Rufus, a respected Chicago financier who lived in Evanston and would later serve as president of the Chicago World's Fair Centennial Celebration.

Chicago's deeply-embedded political corruption, racketeering, and criminality had brought about Dawes's speech on the House floor in early 1926, yet nothing resulted from the grim hand he had played. Though he was a man of grit who did not stand alone amid the provenance of the time, Dawes decided his days as a public spear-thrower for Chicago's reformers were at an end. From then on, he would work quietly behind the scenes.

6. "THE MASTER OF ALL HE SURVEYED"

On April 13, 1927, William "Big Bill" Thompson took over the mayoralty of Chicago after whipping William Dever, 515,716 votes to 432,678. This wasn't a substantial margin, but the point was, Big Bill was back and that's what a majority of Chicagoans wanted—though some observers were appalled. Said newspaperman Fred Pasley, "On the record of its electorate, [Chicago] was the sap town of America."[1]

But it was Al Capone, not Thompson, who was the "Mayor of Crook County."[2] By then, Capone, who started his climb in Big Bill's first term as mayor, was sitting at the top of Chicago's gangland and had rewarded Big Bill for past favors: he put up $260,000 ($4,680,000 in 1990 dollars) to return him to city hall. By then, too, Capone's mentor, Johnny Torrio, was gone. Ten weeks after three assassins rubbed out Dion O'Banion in his flower shop, it was Torrio's turn. As he carried groceries into his apartment building, he took four slugs in the jaw, chest, right arm, and groin from "Bugs" Moran and three other assailants. O'Banion had been their leader, and Moran believed Torrio was behind his slaying. Moran would become Capone's No. 1 enemy. As for Torrio, he made a miraculous recovery, spending only three weeks in the hospital. It would take him even less time to decide to turn the keys of the kingdom over to his burly, scar-faced lieutenant, just twenty-six years old. After paying a $5,000 fine ($90,000 in 1990 dollars) in federal court and serving a nine-month sentence for the Sieben Brewery arrest, Torrio, with wife Ann at his side, left Chicago for good.

Within a month, Capone enlarged his quarters at the Hotel Metropole (which was convenient to both city hall and the Chicago Police Department) to fifty rooms. Law and order soon became the equivalent of a massive car wreck. Not even the cold-blooded murder of William McSwiggin, age twenty-six, and the ensuing outcry had stopped Thompson's reelection or the continued rise of Capone—at whose hands McSwiggin had died. McSwiggin's slaying raised a hue and cry like few others in Chicago's criminal history.

On the evening of Tuesday, April 27, 1926, McSwiggin, a highly regarded assistant state's attorney in Robert Crowe's office, had gone to Cicero, which joined Chicago to the west, to carouse and drink with five friends from his school days—Tom "Red" Duffy, Jim Doherty, Edward Hanley and the brothers, Myles and William "Klondike" O'Donnell. Duffy, a barber and the son of a policeman, had been involved in bootlegging. Hanley was a former policeman. Doherty and the O'Donnells were as disreputable a trio of bootleggers as anyone would want to chauffeur around. They were in Doherty's green Lincoln sedan and decided to stop at the Pony Inn at 5613 West Roosevelt Road, a mile from Al Capone's Hawthorne Inn, in the town Capone had chosen for his stronghold. ("If you smell gunpowder, you're in Cicero.") Capone used the Hawthorne, with bulletproof shutters on every window, as his headquarters.[3]

As McSwiggin and the other five alighted from the Lincoln, an armada of cars suddenly drove up. Its occupants poured more than a hundred machine-gun bullets at them and fled. McSwiggin, directly in the line of fire, took seven bullets in the back and neck and died almost instantly. Duffy and Doherty also died at the scene. The O'Donnells and Hanley survived. McSwiggin, whose father was a sergeant in the Chicago Police Department, had grown up with the five in the Irish colony on the West Side, and despite once unsuccessfully prosecuting Doherty and Myles O'Donnell for a bar murder, they had remained fast friends. Duffy, Doherty, and the O'Donnells had spent that day wearing the badges of ballot watchers for the Crowe machine during a recount of the Republican primaries at the county building in downtown Chicago.

The scenario behind this killing field wasn't difficult to determine. Capone's lookouts had spotted Doherty's Lincoln, loaded with six men whom they believed were hostile, and alerted Capone. Still trying to prove himself to his henchmen (Torrio hadn't been gone long), Capone couldn't put up with such an intrusion: Cicero was his stronghold, and he was ready to protect it with a special ruthlessness. An armada of armed cars drove off after the Lincoln, with a tactical plan that resembled a military pincer attack. The lead car would ram any vehicle that tried to interfere; two flanking cars behind the lead car would hug each curb ready to block side-street traffic; the fourth car, carrying Capone, holding a Thompson submachine gun, would stay behind this interference and do the killing; the fifth and last car would cover their getaway. Unlike military victors, however, Capone and his killers didn't stay around.

McSwiggin's cold-blooded murder became a contentious and complicated issue and left many questions for the public to ponder, the most riveting of which echoed daily across the city all that spring of 1926: Who killed McSwiggin and why? For two weeks, the *Chicago Examiner* put that question in eight columns of black type across the top of its editorial page. Chicagoans also asked, Even if they were his friends in a loyal Irish clan, why was McSwiggin driving around Cicero with them? Crowe, who called it the most brazen murder ever committed in Chicago, put up $5,000 ($90,000 in 1990 dollars) of his own money as a reward, immediately launched a massive crackdown, and led the raiding party in Cicero. They hit both the Hawthorne Inn and the adjoining Hawthorne Smoke Shop; they tore into gambling dens, brothels, and liquor joints, smashing hundreds of beer barrels and cases of booze; and they scooped up loads of denizens and boxes of records. Capone took a beating, in a way. He controlled twenty-five of the thirty-three resorts the raiders overran, inflicting "costly damage upon Capone's suburban empire."[4]

Robert Crowe knew Capone killed McSwiggin and two of his friends, but unearthing the evidence to convict them was another matter. A week after the slayings, Crowe said, "It has been established to the satisfaction of the state's attorney's office and the detective bureau that Capone in person led the slayers of McSwiggin. . . . It has also been found that Capone handled the machine gun."[5] McSwiggin's father, Anthony, a Chicago police sergeant, reached the same conclusion. He had conducted his own investigation and named Capone, Frank Rio, Frank Diamond, and Bob McCullough as his son's slayers. Rio was a crack Capone triggerman, Diamond was the captain of Capone's bodyguards, and McCullough was a former Torrio gunsel. About the incident, John H. Lyle, a municipal court judge, noted, "All of the investigators agreed with Sgt. McSwiggin that Capone was responsible for the slaying, but it's my opinion that Capone was solely after the O'Donnell crew and had not known McSwiggin was in the party. Capone would have foreseen the heat that was raised by killing the prosecutor."[6]

On May 7, U.S. Attorney Edwin A. Olson called a grand jury. Twenty-two days later, it handed down an indictment against Al Capone, brother Ralph, Charlie Fischetti, and Peter Payette, Harry Madigan, owner of the Pony Inn, and the three O'Donnell brothers (a murderous bootlegging trio from the South Side and no kin to the West Side O'Donnells), but not for the McSwiggin incident. Olson had no evidence linking Capone to that. Instead, the eight were charged with conspiracy to violate the Volstead Act, with Olson using evidence gathered by federal agents that Cicero policemen tried to cover up the town's wide-open bootlegging.

When the federal indictment came down, Capone, fearful the police would gun him down amid the outcry over McSwiggin, hid out in Indiana. When he returned to Chicago, Crowe filed charges alleging he was responsible for the Cicero killings. On the day of the court proceedings, Crowe sent his chief assistant, George E. Gorman, to handle the case. To everyone's surprise, Gorman withdrew the murder charge, explaining to the judge, "This complaint was made by Chief of Detectives [William] Schoemaker on cursory information. Subsequent investigation could not legally substantiate the information."[7]

After Capone walked free, Crowe called a special grand jury to seek an indictment in the case, which was now becoming a political comedy. Over the next six months, five more special grand juries were called (a state law limited special grand juries to one-month terms). Crowe asked Illinois Attorney General Oscar Carlstrom to direct the first special grand jury after Harry E. Kelly, the president of the Union League Club, questioned his motives. "Crowe is the directing head of a faction organized for politics and politics only," Kelly said. "Citizens cannot expect Mr. Crowe to prosecute the kind of investigation this city requires."[8] Kelly could have questioned Carlstrom's motives too. The attorney general proceeded to concentrate not on McSwiggin's slaying but on the causes of crimes in Chicago, and he blamed the crime on "the parole abuses at Joliet from which convicts had been buying their way out"—an accusation actually aimed at the administration of Governor Small.[9] Neither Carlstrom nor Crowe, as it turned out, were subtle about using this venue to get back at Governor Small's open door policy on felons: from January 10, 1921, to January 13, 1929, it was later calculated, Small had "sold" 8,000 pardons. None of the evidence Carlstrom presented to the first panel led to an indictment. In addition, the Cook County coroner, Oscar Wolff, "an official as notorious for his ineptitude as he was for his association with gangsters," called a coroner's jury.[10]

The five grand juries produced stark revelations. Charles A. McDonald, a former judge who directed the second jury, declared, "I know who killed McSwiggin, but I want to know it legally and be able to present it conclusively." To support his claim, he offered that "two new clues and two new witnesses had been found."[11] His assertions eventually brought the empanelling of the fifth jury. However, McDonald's new clues and new witnesses never materialized. The fourth grand jury, ignoring the killing of McSwiggin, did return indictments against forty elections officials in the Forty-second Ward—which the state supreme court later quashed. After pending for two years, the Volstead Act violations brought by U.S. Attorney Olson against the Capone brothers and the five others were dismissed. Capone, besides having a laugh at justice in Chicago, did learn an important lesson: it would be the last time he pulled the trigger himself in a killing.

■

With Big Bill Thompson back, Chicago had "opened up like a dropped watermelon."[12] Sitting in city hall as the war for dominance of Chicago's illicit liquor trade raged around him, Thompson bragged that he "was wetter than the middle of the Atlantic Ocean."[13] The number of speakeasies ranged from the *Chicago Tribune*'s estimate of 10,000 to the *Chicago Daily News*'s estimate of 6,000. Fred Pasley speculated the city had 20,000 speakeasies, noting, "The disparity lies in the fact that the newspapers have not listed the drug stores and cigar stores peddling gin and Bourbon, and the beer flats." No city, Elmer Irey observed, held the Volstead Act in more contempt than Chicago. As murders and bombings increased, the deaths of public figures went unsolved. John A. Swanson, a circuit judge and major reformer who escaped injury when a bomb was tossed at his car as he turned into the driveway of his home, said, "The pineapple industry grew up under [Thompson's] administration."[14]

Under Big Bill, the matrix of order was under assault. The chief judge of the traffic court, Harry Olson, showed up at a meeting of the city council's committee on traffic one morning in November 1927 to tell the panel that "so many police tickets are being fixed every day through political pull" that the court's judges were "dismayed by their helplessness." Olson continued, "One day last week the clerk of the court showed me $205 worth of slips [$3,690 in 1990 dollars] withdrawn that day. At this rate the city is losing $600,000 a year [$24.8 million in 1990 dollars] and the traffic violations go merrily on." A chuckle ran around the table, then hearty laughs. A committee member, holding back another laugh, suggested that an inquiry be made to see how many aldermen had fixed slips for their friends, but nobody pressed the proposal. "After several moments of embarrassing silence, the chairman asked if anybody wished to ask any questions but receiving no response, thanked the judge, and the committee hurriedly resumed other business."[15] From his days as a municipal judge, John Lyle said, "Some court attaches were on the payrolls of top gangsters. Others had political sponsors who were linked with the mobs. The employee had to obey instructions or sacrifice his job."[16]

Johnny Torrio had always been the prudent diplomat. He theorized that since "there's enough here for everybody," the Chicago underworld's "wolfpacks" should operate within their own territories.[17] Capone quickly breached his mentor's theory. Inside of two years, he had wiped out all the rival gangs except "Bugs" Moran's, taken their territory, and set up a boot-legging operation that was annually netting $20 million ($354 million in 1990 dollars). In 1928, three years after he took command, the income of the Capone operation—America's first empire of crime—would approach a staggering $100 million ($1.7 billion in 1990 dollars). The criminal goliath was the master of all he surveyed.[18] Capone tooled around in a mobile fort, a seven-ton, $20,000 sedan ($340,000 in 1990 dollars) with a steel body, bulletproof windows, and nondentable fenders. To help him rule the city in ex-officio style, Capone had set up a "highly efficient information network," which writer Frederic Sondern said could have been a model for a government espionage agency and Judge Lyle noted was "as effective for their purposes as the Kremlin."[19] Sprinkling cash rewards like cheap rice, Capone's cohorts enlisted everybody from shoeshine boys and manicurists to hotel clerks and doormen to call in tips on the authorities. To keep the network operating, Capone's combine paid out more than $15 million ($255 million in 1990 dollars) annually, including payments to the police and every other official they could enlist.

Breaking down Capone's $100 million criminal empire, Elmer Irey's agents would eventually produce enough evidence to estimate that $25 million came from gambling, $10 million from organized prostitution, $10 million from narcotics, and $50 million from bootlegging.

Judge Lyle, who had followed Capone's rise, called him "a reptile [who] deserves to die."[20] Yet, he achieved worldly status. A poll of students at Chicago's Medill School of Journalism ranked the racketeer among the "ten outstanding personages of the world . . . the characters that actually made history."[21] Capone was ranked with Benito Mussolini, Charles A. Lindbergh, Adm. Richard F. Byrd, George Bernard Shaw, Bobby Jones, President Herbert Hoover, Mahatma Gandhi, Albert Einstein, and Henry Ford. As for those twenty-eight figures named on the Chicago Crime Commission's "Public Enemies" list, which Capone had been on, back in 1923, not one had been brought to justice. The Europeans joined in too. An editorial in a Viennese newspaper, quoted by the Chicago press, called Capone "the real mayor of Chicago" and "wondered why the voters did not make him so by law as well as in fact."[22] He and his principality had moved from the Metropole and were now making their home at the once lofty, ten-story Hotel Lexington, where they occupied the entire fourth floor, most of the third, and various other rooms where they put up their women. Capone maintained a six-room suite at a yearly cost of $18,000 ($304,000 in 1990 dollars). In the lobby and at other strategic points lounged his shooters. One was a twenty-two-year-old named Tony Accardo, sometimes seen with a tommy gun across his knees.

The violence in Chicago had become deafening by 1928, when there were 367 murders. In New York, there were 200 murders; in London, there were 18. The slaying of Bill McSwiggin was pretty much forgotten—and unsolved. Watching from his teaching post at the University of Chicago, Charles Merriam observed, "Chicago is unique. It is the only completely corrupt city in America."[23] Edward Dean Sullivan portrayed the magnitude of the failure in Chicago: "Pirates on the high seas and American Indians far from civilization in the pioneer days have duplicated, but not greatly surpassed, the bloodthirstiness of the new caste of American apache that is winning control of our cities by murder."[24]

7. GETTING CAPONE

Elmer Irey maintained a small, crack SIU contingent in Chicago made up of Arthur P. Madden, the special agent in charge, and five special agents—Clarence Converse, William Hodgins, Archie Martin, Patrick Roche, and Nels E. Tessem. Gutsy, incorruptible, loyal, and dependable as the ocean tide, they carried special capabilities. The graying, nondescript Madden, who would later lend great assistance to Irey in the Lindbergh kidnapping case, resembled a less jolly Oliver Hardy. Usually clad in a vest with coat, his round, unsympathetic face and small mustache made him look more like a banker ready to turn down the next mortgage application, not a savvy supervisor of men about to make history. Archie Martin, according to Irey, had "encyclopedic knowledge" of Capone's enterprises. Irey called Nels Tessem "a human comptometer,"[1] and Frank Wilson tagged him a "fearless investigator."[2] Pat Roche carried the most battle stars. A twenty-five-year-old policeman when Prohibition started, he was not impressed that size counted in enforcing the law, noting, "A one-legged Prohibition agent on a bicycle could stop the beer in the Loop in one day if he were honest."[3] Roche, along with Clarence A. Converse, handled the Chicago SIU's first case of merit—involving another Treasury adjunct, the Narcotics Bureau. Hearing reports that federal narcotics agents were protecting drug dealers and that Will Gray Beach, the special agent in charge, could be "fixed," their digging produced evidence that the agents were exchanging morphine and cocaine for stolen jewelry and that two of Chicago's largest drug dealers had Beach on their payroll.[4] The Chicago office had been tainted almost from its beginning. On January 31, 1920, William H. Sage, chief of the office, was indicted for violation of the Harrison Act. He was accused of "accepting money" from A. L. Blunt, who was already serving a five-year term in Leavenworth for violation of the act.[5]

For most of the 1920s, the Chicago unit was occupied with policing Prohibition agents, though occasionally it went after bigger game. Roche and Converse once mounted a raid on a Capone brewery, which, Roche noted, "was immune so far as the police was concerned. There were always police flivvers around it and the trucks would go out with a guard of motorcycle cops." Capone biographer Robert J. Schoenberg described with relish what happened after Roche and Converse struck: "One of the employees knew what to do. He eased up to the feds. 'Al Brown owns the place,' he whispered, 'everything will be squared.' He gaped, dumbstruck, when the magic name and usual gracious offer failed to dispel the problem. Nobody turned down the Big Fellow!"[6]

Roche left the SIU in 1928 (just before Irey got the order to move against Capone, and after John A. Swanson won the state attorney's office from Robert Crowe) to become Swanson's chief investigator and did yeoman's work in uncovering payoffs between the brothel operator, Jack Zuta, and various state, city, and police officials. A member of the Chicago Crime Commission's original twenty-eight public enemies, Zuta (number 9) worked for the Moran combine and had the "best business brains in the underworld."[7] After Zuta tried to muscle into an area of the Loop, the Capone combine rubbed him out on August 1, 1930. In the aftermath, Roche unearthed evidence from three of the bank vaults retained by Zuta under various aliases, which partly indicated the extent of police corruption. One set of Zuta's papers showed $3,500 ($54,500 in 1990 dollars) was paid weekly to one police station—the East Chicago Avenue Precinct. Among a lot of material, a letter was found, written on the official stationary of the City of Evanston, which read,

Dear Jack:

I am temporarily in need of four 'C's' for a couple of months. Can you let me have it? The bearer does not know what it is, so put it in an envelope and seal it and address it to me.

Your old pal,

Bill Freeman

Four "C's" of course was $400 ($6,800 in 1990 dollars). "Bill Freeman" was William O. Freeman, the chief of police of Evanston, then known as "the world's wealthiest suburb." Freeman kept his job, incidentally. Explained the mayor of Evanston, a man named Bartlett, "The loan was censurable but his need of the money was legitimate."[8]

■

The Manly Sullivan case would change everything for the Chicago SIU contingent.[9] Sullivan, a Charleston, South Carolina, machinery dealer, had maintained his income from bootlegging wasn't taxable, and in addition, he argued that to report the income would violate his rights against self-incrimination under the Fifth Amendment. After his conviction in federal court in Charleston in 1922 for refusing to file a tax return on his 1921 income, his case slowly began to wind its way to the U.S. Supreme Court.

Along the way, the appeals court sided with him on his Fifth Amendment argument, holding that the Revenue Act of 1921 "requires one who has violated the National Prohibition Law to file a return under oath, giving the details of his legal transactions; and thereby, in our opinion, compels him to be a witness against himself in a criminal case, within the meaning of the [Fifth] amendment." Congress, the ruling went on, "had manifested an intention to tax gains derived from criminal operations, it had failed to give immunity from prosecutions under such disclosures."[10]

Rebuffed, the Justice Department took the case to the Supreme Court. On April 27, 1927, the justices heard the case. Assistant Attorney General Mabel Walker Willebrandt argued the government's side before the august body, which included William Howard Taft, the only man to serve both as president and chief justice; Harlan Stone, now an associate justice; Louis D. Brandeis; and Oliver Wendell Holmes Jr. The court's ruling came on

May 16, twenty days later, in a ruling written by Holmes (he was eighty-six years old). The lofty Holmes, who was a student at Harvard before the Civil War and had been named to the bench in 1902 by Theodore Roosevelt, used wit and logic in rejecting Sullivan's argument that crime income was not taxable. "It is urged that if a return were made the defendant would be entitled to deduct illegal expenses such as bribery," Holmes wrote. "This by no means follows, but it will be time enough to consider the question when a taxpayer has the temerity to raise it." He brushed off the Fifth Amendment argument, declaring its protection "was pressed too far."

Holmes's ruling was a turning point for federal law enforcement: it put into place an imperative that would shape Elmer Irey's future, catapulting the SIU into the wider picture of financial criminal inquiry, a task Irey turned out to be superbly fitted for. He would pioneer the strategy of using the money trail to uncover criminal activity—and would find no upside. Investigating financial criminal conspiracies was a grinding roller-coaster ride with an uncertain ending. It has never changed. It is a formidable and complex undertaking, requiring skilled investigators practiced in finance and accounting. Almost as importantly, Irey would find that such inquiries required staying power because investigators are submerged in detail that can lead anywhere. Even today, financial conspiracy investigations are still the most financially burdensome, politically touchy, and probably the least rewarding task in law enforcement.

■

At first, reluctant to investigate criminal activity in Chicago, Irey stepped gingerly. At least half of the SIU had been occupied with policing their own within Treasury, in particular, corrupt Prohibition agents. Regular cases were left to revenue agents. Fred Pasley wrote that "an official close" to Chicago's collector of internal revenue confided to him that Capone's "sources of income are known to us." The official went on: "We know, for instance, that he owns a lot of Chicago realty, but we can find little property in his name. His sources of income are known to us. We believe he could cash in for $20,000. But where has he hidden it? Our men get so far, then they find themselves in blind alleys."[11] In short, the office wasn't sitting on its hands, but the task of finding the sources was beyond their capability.

Actually, since 1926, Chicago's revenue office had been handling the tax case of Ralph Capone, Al's older brother by five years, who was called "Bottles" for his persuasiveness with saloonkeepers who were reluctant to stock Capone merchandise. Irey knew about the case, and he left it to the revenue agent who was handling it, a "pleasant young agent" named Eddie Waters. As a revenue agent, Waters handled civil cases only and had no enforcement powers (like SIU special agents), but according to Irey, he made "a place for himself by persuading gangsters that it was only right and decent that they pay their taxes."

In 1925 Congress had approved a major tax cut—pushed by Secretary of the Treasury Mellon—which reduced taxes on an income of $100,000 ($1.8 million in 1990 dollars) from $17,020 ($306,360 in 1990 dollars) to $12,360 ($222,480 in 1990 dollars), thus giving a substantial break even to racketeers and bootleggers. Eddie Waters saw he could use the new reduction as leverage, and in early 1926 one of the gangsters he called on was "Bottles" Capone. He warned Bottles that he'd get in trouble "some time" if he didn't pay his taxes. When Bottles told him that "filling out them things" was too much work, Waters offered to make out the forms and told him, "Then all you gotta do is sign." Bottles said he'd made $15,000 ($285,000 in 1990 dollars) in 1922 and 1923, and $20,000 ($360,000 in 1990 dollars) in 1924 and 1925, explaining that he was a "gambler" and made "the dough bettin."[12]

Waters went to his office, filled out four delinquent returns and took them back to Bottles, who signed them. They showed he owed a total of $4,065 ($73,170 in 1990 dollars). But Bottles didn't pay. Months and months passed, with Waters regularly pestering Bottles to pay. Finally, tired of waiting, Chicago's Internal Revenue collector, C. W. Herrick, issued warrants of distraint in January 1927, meaning the government could seize Bottles's property.

At that point, Bottles decided to work an angle. He and his lawyer visited Herrick's office to explain that he was broke and would borrow a thousand dollars and make part payment, if that would be acceptable.

Herrick agreed, had Bottles put it in writing, and sent the papers off to Washington—where Internal Revenue Commissioner David H. Blair's office decided the case needed further investigation before it could accept the offer. All during this time, Irey continued to leave Waters on his own, allowing the case to remain a civil, not a criminal action. When Blair's office referred Bottles's case to Irey, he bounced it back to Arthur Madden, the Chicago SIU chief.

Madden was still dealing with Bottles's case when Irey, in early 1928, decided, in his first major tax initiative in Chicago, to move on a well-known pair of racketeers—Terry Druggan and Frankie Lake. They had made the Chicago Crime Commission's "Public Enemies" list back in 1923, and since then, their escapades regularly kept them in the headlines. After Capone purchased his bay-front mansion in Miami at a cost of $375,000 ($6,750,000 in 1990 dollars), the two bought a place nearby and "maintained open house during the tourist season."[13]

Druggan and Lake ran the Standard Beverage Corporation of Chicago, one of a number of companies involved in a dispute with the Bureau of Internal Revenue over the taxing of illegal income. For the years 1922 to 1924, Standard Beverage had been assessed $616,917 ($11,721,423 in 1990 dollars) in unpaid taxes. The company disregarded Internal Revenue demands for payment until the Supreme Court's May 1927 ruling in the Sullivan case on illegal income, then made a compromise offer of $50,000 ($900,000 in 1990 dollars), submitting with it a statement of its assets. The Internal Revenue commissioner in Washington rejected the offer and in early 1928 handed the case to Irey. But he didn't hand it back to Madden; instead, he dispatched Frank J. Wilson to Chicago. Wilson was his best agent, and Irey wanted it boxed and tied into a ribbon and quickly.

While Wilson was conducting his investigation of Druggan and Lane, both Internal Revenue and the SIU were still bending over backward to work out a compromise with Ralph Capone. Irey speaks of Waters bracing Bottles "for the twentieth time" to pay up, making it apparent Irey didn't place urgency on the case.[14] In July 1928 Bottles "begged" the SIU to give him more time because the racing season was on and he held or shared ownership in four horses that he wanted to race. The SIU relented. Not until November 1928 did Bottles finally offer to pay the entire $4,065 that Eddie Waters, back in 1926, told him he owed. But Bottles "haughtily refused to pay about $1,000 in penalties and interest" that had been tacked on since 1926.[15]

In late fall 1928, after he still refused to fork over the $1,000, Madden stopped negotiations, decided to target Bottles for criminal tax fraud and assigned Archie Martin to investigate him. It soon became grinding work, for Bottles had hidden his bootleg money trail in a very clever fashion. An entire year would pass before it bore fruit. At one point, the outspoken Martin tired of tracing Ralph's income. "Chief," he told Madden, "to hell with all this looking for needles. You know Bottles has ten grand in his pocket. I know the so-and-so has ten grand in his pocket. Everybody in Chicago knows it. Please, Chief, can I go down and stick this gun in his belly and take the dough away from him? I'll do it right in the middle of the street. We'll have a thousand witnesses. Please, Chief." Madden sent him back to look for the needles.[16]

■

The SIU contingent had been working with U.S. Attorney George E. Q. Johnson on both the Ralph Capone and Druggan-Lake cases, and Johnson had come away impressed. Frank Wilson, chomping on the five-cent cigars he liked to smoke, had wasted no time on Druggan and Lake. In March 1928, two months after getting the assignment, he uncovered evidence that the pair concealed their assets. E. Q. Johnson called a federal grand jury that indicted Druggan and Lake for failing to file their income taxes, and later for falsifying their statement of assets. The two eventually pleaded guilty and were sent to Leavenworth—Druggan for two and a half years, Lake for eighteen months. Impressed with Wilson's work, Irey made him the special agent in charge of the Baltimore office.

E. Q. Johnson, rail honest, able, and experienced, had succeeded Edwin Olson in February 1927 as the U.S. attorney for the Northern District of Illinois. Then age fifty-four and on the backside of a long and unblemished career, he had been practicing law in Chicago since 1900, the year he got his law degree from Lake Forest University. Bespectacled, tall, and lean-jawed with a big mound of wavy, silver gray hair, and slightly rumpled in his tweedy suits, Johnson's individualistic style was no hindrance. He added the initials, E.Q., to distinguish himself from countless other George Johnsons. He might have been mistaken for a poet or a drama critic—that is "until he opened his mouth, when it became apparent that he combined a scholarly demeanor with an unlimited capacity for indignation in the face of injustice."[17] No U.S. attorney sat on a bigger hot seat, and Johnson knew this before taking the post. Few better choices had ever been made, and the individual who played a big hand in his selection was Vice President Dawes.

Two years had passed since Dawes had climbed out on a limb to mobilize support against Chicago's underworld and then watched silently as it was sawed off beneath him. The reelection of Big Bill was a slap in the face of every reformer. The city stayed awash in racketeering. Capone's power and wealth was yet to peak. Dawes, however, began to move behind the scenes, his handiwork so well hidden that most of what he accomplished has been lost to history. Not even his biographer offers an insight into his role to rein in Chicago's crime and corruption. Dawes kept a diary but rarely divulged any details of his role. He did make a revealing entry in August 1928, noting that Frank Loesch asked him "to undertake the coordination of the work of some seven hundred local associations now existing and devoted to constructed civic progress." Dawes turned him down, writing, "Loesch and his Crime Commission are in the midst of a crusade against the lawlessness and corruption existing in our city and its government which promises results. The public is at last aroused and the movement, refused support by the City Council, has been financed by popular subscription. It is impossible for me to undertake the work while occupying my present office, but I have a sincere feeling of regret that I cannot help in the fight upon the lawless element there."[18]

In noting that "the public is at last aroused," Dawes had taken heart in the events of four months before: On April 6, 1928, a day known as the "Pineapple Primary," former Judge John Swanson toppled Robert Crowe from his eight-year reign as the state's attorney, whipping him by more than 200,000 votes. The Pineapple Primary (in Chicago's underworld, a bomb was a "pineapple") was a day unlike any in Chicago's electoral annals.

On March 26 a bomb wrecked the front of the three-story frame residence of U.S. Senator Charles S. Deneen, Republican of Illinois. Another bomb was tossed in the driveway of Swanson's home, exploding three seconds before he turned his automobile into it. The U.S. marshal in Chicago, Palmer Anderson, pleaded to Attorney General John Sargent for 500 deputy marshals to guard the polls. Senator George W. Norris, Republican of Nebraska, went Anderson one better, urging President Coolidge to withdraw the U.S. Marine contingent from Nicaragua and send it to Chicago. Coolidge did neither.

In the Twentieth Ward, Octavius Granady, a black attorney who had challenged the ward's boss, Judge Morris B. Eller, was mowed down on Pineapple Primary day. Granady was standing outside a polling place when a bullet from a passing car barely missed him. He hopped in his car to flee and was followed by assassins who pursued him and put a dozen slugs in him. At various polling places, thousands of anti-Crowe votes were destroyed, and Capone's shooters "menacingly paced the rooms where the counting took place."[19] None of the violence could have taken place, wrote John Kobler, "without the connivance of the police." Police captains in the various precincts, obeying orders from ward bosses, assigned patrols to duties that were remote from the polls. Judge Eller, Big Bill Thompson's choice for Republican committeeman in the Twentieth Ward, put it tersely: "The police are with us."[20]

Along with the bombings, the mix of culpability and conspiracy had finally awakened Chicago's citizenry, bringing the classic backlash that resulted in Crowe's ouster—and in time, in the retirement of Big Bill Thompson. In Crowe's eight-year reign, there had been 369 bombings without a single conviction. Now, maybe, it wasn't "to be believed" as the *New York Times* editorialized back in 1926, that "Chicago will confess herself so impotent." In March 1926 the *Chicago Daily News* had been more to the point when it editorialized that "what is needed in Chicago is an irresistible movement on the part of the citizens, through a strong and fearless judge, a special State's attorney, and a special grand jury to bring out the facts."[21] The first need wasn't met until U.S. District Judge James H. Wilkerson was picked to preside at Al Capone's trial, still years away. But after the Pineapple Primary, the other two needs were quickly filled. Swanson, the new state's attorney, was "special," and he wasted no time in naming Frank Loesch, the dedicated crime-fighter and lawyer who had served as president of the Chicago Crime Commission, as a special state's attorney. Loesch began working with a series of special grand juries.

On June 15, a special grand jury indicted ten office holders and their fellow travelers, chiefly from the Twentieth Ward. One of those indicted, Johnny Armondo, a political worker for the Eller forces, was identified as having shot Octavius Granady. The special grand jury had retained a private investigative agency, headed by Sheridan A. Bruseaux, to gather evidence, and it was Bruseaux's agency, not the Chicago Police Department, that developed the evidence leading to Armondo's arrest. Another Loesch special grand jury answered Eller's comment about the police by declaring in its report that the Chicago Police Department was rotten to the core.

In the face of this, E. Q. Johnson had been moving aggressively, under pressure from Dawes and others to do something. The federal presence up to then had been nonexistent. Washington had done little about racketeering. And since the beginning of Prohibition, a turf war had developed between the Chicago Police Department and the federal forces. In July 1920 the Chicago Prohibition office reported it was "greatly concerned over the failure of state and city law officers to cooperate with Prohibition agents." In November 1928 the Prohibition commissioner in Washington reported that it was still getting practically no cooperation from the police department in Chicago.

Soon after taking over, Johnson caught a train to Washington to plead to his superiors at the Justice Department for a larger federal presence. They agreed, and a special force of Prohibition agents, led by a veteran agent named George E. Golding, was put together to work with Johnson. The Treasury, meanwhile, had relinquished control of the Prohibition Bureau to Justice, and Prohibition agents finally received civil service status. But no sooner had the special Prohibition squad begun work than one of its agents, Myron C. Gaffey, shot Municipal Court Bailiff William Beatty in the back during a raid on a South Side speakeasy. The incident created a furor, topped by sophistry from Mayor Big Bill Thompson, who publicly declared, "Deneen is filling this town with Dry agents from Washington, who run around like a lot of cowboys with revolvers and shotguns. Our opponents would have us believe we don't know how to run our town. Vote for the flag, the Constitution, your freedom, your property, as Abraham Lincoln and William Hale Thompson would like to have you do."[22] Chief of Police Michael Hughes and a phalanx of officers marched into the federal building with a warrant for Gaffey's arrest, faced off with George Golding, and left empty-handed. Gaffey maintained that Beatty drew a gun, and a federal grand jury indicted him for resisting a federal officer.

Irey, in his memoir, handled the episode with tongue in cheek: "The agent had to go into hiding in the Federal Building, sleeping and eating in an Assistant U.S. Attorney's office until his victim disappointed the critical Chicago press and recovered from his wound. But George E. Q. Johnson had had enough of Prohibition agents and begged that the special crew be withdrawn before somebody got lynched."[23]

■

Only three weeks after E. Q. Johnson took over as U.S. attorney, a thirty-year-old, prematurely gray lawyer, Dwight H. Green, was sent from the Bureau of Internal Revenue in Washington to Chicago and given the official title of special assistant to the general counsel at the Internal Revenue office. In practice, Green would act as the adviser and attorney for Chicago's revenue collector, revenue agents, and SIU agents. Upon arriving there, one of his first moves was to confer with E. Q. Johnson, who would confer a special status on him, special assistant U.S. attorney, and find him an office in the federal building. The move had Charles Dawes's fingerprints on it.

Green, a native of Indiana, had already made a "name for himself as one of the smartest tax experts in the Bureau."[24] In fall 1925 he had gone to work for Internal Revenue in Washington, trying cases before the Board of Tax Appeals. Before that, he had put a big dose of Chicago history under his belt. He had served as a U.S. Army pilot in World War I, flying Jenny aircraft, but he saw no combat. Mustered out, he went to work as a part-time reporter and legman for William Randolph Hearst's *Chicago Examiner* in Prohibition's early days while getting his law degree at the University of Chicago. Then he took a post with Internal Revenue in Washington.

According to Green biographers Robert J. Casey and W. A. S. Douglas, he was sent to Chicago with a plan to use the tax laws against the criminal combines. Green's plan of action to strike "at the gangsters through the revenue law was less nebulous when he came back to Chicago than it had been during his early days in Washington," his biographers wrote. It was going to take time, of course, to develop a legal strategy that would permit the use of revenue laws against underworld figures. Green "worked over it for nearly a year before he felt safe in trying it out in a court," Casey and Douglas wrote. "It is one thing to argue a technical point of law with lawyers—quite another to bring the same point home to a jury of laymen—and the use of the revenue act for the purpose of stopping a murder epidemic was nothing if not technical."[25]

While there was no real design in what was happening, the stage was slowly being set for Washington to move against Chicago's underworld in a new and different way. Aside from the work of Chicago's reformers, particularly among the business elements associated with Vice President Dawes, bits and pieces were happening, seemingly of little significance, like Ralph Capone's tax case, E. Q. Johnson's appointment, and Dwight Green's arrival. All of this—along with the Manly Sullivan tax case, which was winding its way to the U.S. Supreme Court—would soon become part of a bigger, history-making picture.

8. "WE'LL GET RIGHT ON IT"

It was October 18, 1928, a Thursday. In nineteen days, the nation would elect Herbert Hoover to the presidency. Vice President Charles Dawes would soon be gone, but because of his quiet, able hand, tectonic changes were occurring in Chicago's criminal life.

On that Thursday, Secretary of the Treasury Andrew Mellon called Elmer Irey to his office and told him through "grim lips" that he was being given the assignment to get Al Capone. "Your men seem to be having great success with one Capone," Mellon told him. "George E. Q. Johnson says the unit has done a grand job gathering evidence on Al's brother, Ralph. He thinks maybe you can do it on Al."

"Yes, Mr. Mellon," replied Irey. "We'll get right on it."[1]

■

That is how Irey, in his 288-page memoir, described the assignment to go after the figure who had become the nation's most notorious, most untouchable, and wealthiest criminal. Though SIU agents were already on the money trail of Al Capone's lieutenants, Irey didn't want the assignment to go after him, and he wasn't pleased about it. The best part didn't come until he had left Mellon's office. Walking back to his corner office, he wondered why the Treasury, "charged with fighting tax, customs, and narcotics fraud," had been assigned "to nab a murderer, a gambler, a whoremonger, and a bootlegger." In the same breath, he took a sarcastic swipe at the one party he invariably clashed with, for one reason or another, over much of his career: the Department of Justice. "Justice," he said in his memoir, "was willing to prosecute (by law nobody else could), but in case of failure Treasury would have to take the blame, although Justice had its own investigative agents, the famous F.B.I."[2]

For a man of Irey's probity, it was an extraordinary comment. It represented his years of frustration in dealing with the Justice Department, the Bureau of Investigation, and J. Edgar Hoover. It also was one of the rare comments he put on the record about his feelings. Public figures usually pick their fights carefully. During his first decade on the job, Irey preferred not to pick any fights. Abetted by a remarkable temperament, he took Washington's ways in stride, even a silken attempt at securing his loyalty (Clarence True Wilson of the Anti-Saloon League invited him to lunch one day and offered him the job of assistant secretary of the Treasury). Irey, of course, did not think his role was to chase down criminals. Internal Revenue, he believed, was a tax collection agency first, an enforcement agency second. He didn't consider himself, nor did he pretend to be, the crime fighter who rides into Dodge, guns blazing, and calls news conferences to set criminals straight. Irey wouldn't have been caught dead posing with a Thompson submachine gun at the ready—like J. Edgar Hoover did to burnish his image and send a message to bank robbers such as John Dillinger and Pretty Boy Floyd. Irey's duties didn't involve marching into unknown criminal territory. He knew the tax fraud laws were an airy set of statutes that could rebound on the enforcer and that required precisely drawn evidence. This made him even more prudent. The chaotic conditions Prohibition placed on his small band of investigators didn't make him a reluctant warrior, but a careful one. Irey never sought to seize the day in Chicago. He wanted nothing to do with Capone, and it was clear he was not going to initiate the effort.

In all of this is a riddle: Who suggested deploying Irey to Chicago? Neither the power brokers who sought to bring about Capone's downfall, nor the circumstances leading up to it have been completely spelled out. Herbert Hoover has been given the credit for initiating the Capone investigation, but that was already under way when Hoover entered the White

House on March 4, 1929. He did move it along, but he didn't originate it. "Silent Cal" Coolidge was sitting in the White House when Secretary of the Treasury Mellon called Irey to his office and told him to get Capone. John Sargent was attorney general. It is important to pinpoint this because the takedown of Capone remains the landmark achievement in the history of American law enforcement. And while Mellon gave the order to Irey, it is still unclear whether Mellon actually initiated it.

In his conversation with Irey that October day, Mellon implied that E. Q. Johnson was behind it. In Washington protocol, of course, U.S. attorneys don't call up a cabinet member like the secretary of the Treasury, then put the arm on them to launch a major criminal investigation. What they really do is call up their superior at the Justice Department, and then the attorney general calls up the secretary of the Treasury. A combination of voices likely contributed to the decision. One was Charles Dawes, the first high official to bring Chicago's criminal plight before the nation in his February 1926 House speech. A multipronged strategy involving Dawes and Chicago business elements he knew, such as the Chicago Crime Commission, was already under way. Though Dawes, content to work behind the scenes, remained silent about his role, he played a part in the appointment of E. Q. Johnson. Dawes also may have had a hand in the assignment of Dwight Green, along with the dispatch of that special squad of Prohibition agents to Chicago, led by the veteran George Golding.

Irey sought to clear up this confusing mix of history. There's reason to believe his version is authentic; still, it's not the whole story. While always generous in giving credit, Irey was secretive in his dealings, never revealing more than he had to. He chose not to go beyond his account of Mellon's order to him that day, nor mention E. Q. Johnson. Irey was bothered by press reports that Hoover had Capone investigated because Hoover resented the attention given Capone one day as they both entered the lobby of a Miami hotel. For Irey, such reports meant Hoover's motive was merely spiteful, and he called the reports an "apocryphal libel."[3] Irey's assertion in his memoir that "I recently got the information on what really set Mr. Hoover after Capone" makes it clear that Hoover provided impetus but didn't initiate the investigation.[4] By the time Hoover took office, Frank

Wilson and his team had been on the job for approximately a month. Hoover pushed things along only after a visiting delegation, led by William F. "Frank" Knox, publisher of the Hearst-owned *Chicago Daily News* and later FDR's secretary of the Navy in World War II, urged him to act. The *Daily News* had long been outspoken about the political scene, once editorializing that Big Bill Thompson was "a calamity to the people of Chicago."[5]

In his memoir, Frank Wilson isn't clear on what date the Capone investigation started or how it got off the ground. Irey, in his memoir, did not cite exactly when Mellon called him in and gave him the order to get Capone. Actually, Irey revealed that during his testimony at Capone's trial three years later. As he sat in the witness chair on Friday, October 9, 1931, three days into the trial, Assistant U.S. Attorney Samuel G. Clawson asked Irey, "When were you authorized to begin an investigation into the income tax affairs of the defendant, Alphonse Capone?" Irey answered, "October 18, 1928."[6] This date calls into question E. Q. Johnson's assertion, which Secretary Mellon used, that Irey's unit "has done a grand job gathering evidence on Al's brother, Ralph." At that time, Ralph was still stonewalling the SIU on the taxes he owed, prompting a frustrated Archie Martin to want to stick a gun "in his belly" and take it.

Irey and Wilson also gave differing accounts about the events following Mellon's order. Irey said, in "about as long as it takes for a crack train to get from Chicago to Washington I had a conference under way . . . with Art Madden, and agents Frank Wilson and Pat O'Rourke."[7] Wilson gave two different accounts of how the investigation started. In a 1947 article, he describes getting an urgent phone call at his Baltimore home, ordering him to come to Washington, where he met with Irey and Robert Lucas, the commissioner of Internal Revenue. Wilson didn't pinpoint the time, noting only that "this was in 1928."[8] In his 1965 autobiography, Wilson said he was given the assignment after the St. Valentine's Day massacre in 1929, when Capone's henchmen, in a carefully plotted move, lined seven members of the "Bugs" Moran combine up against a wall and machine-gunned them to death. In the outcry, Wilson said, the "Chicago Chamber of Commerce decided to appeal directly to our new President, Herbert Hoover."[9] Wilson went on to explain, "The day after the Chicago Committee called on President Hoover, he issued special instructions to Andrew Mellon, Secretary of the Treasury, who in turn relayed them to Commissioner Lucas of the Internal Revenue Bureau. The next day I was called to Washington." Wilson's memory doesn't serve him well. He didn't mention the Mellon-Irey meeting that took place a month before Hoover was elected president. Wilson was already in Chicago before Hoover entered the White House, according to Wilson's biographer, Frank Spiering, who cites a memorandum that Wilson sent to Irey asking for permission to drive his car to Chicago by way of Washington, Baltimore, and Buffalo on December 22, 1928.

Given these varying accounts, a number of scenarios arise. The investigation of Capone did not result from a presidential order, though Vice President Dawes could have spoken to President Coolidge about it. No record exists of this, nor does documentation show that Dawes was working behind the scenes. Business elements in Chicago certainly demanded action, tried to do something, and were vocal about it. Dawes was at the top of this mix, had few inhibitions when he felt the need to act, and was aware the Treasury was investigating members of the Capone combine. He had close ties to Charles S. Deneen, Illinois's Republican senator, who submitted E. Q. Johnson's name to the White House for nomination as the U.S. attorney. The Chicago newspaperman George Murray, in his book on Capone, gives Dawes credit for Johnson's appointment to succeed Edwin Olson but offers no details about the move. There was one certainty leading up to Irey's assignment to get Capone: It was an answer to a dismal situation.

■

After leaving Secretary Mellon's office on that Thursday in October, Irey "worried the thing out in the privacy of my office" before setting the investigation into motion.[10] He assigned Art Madden, who "had made a professional and amateur hobby of Al Capone for almost a decade," to coordinate matters and help run the case.[11] He sent Pat O'Rourke to Chicago to go undercover to penetrate Capone's combine. A talented disguise artist, O'Rourke knew "more thugs, gangsters, cutthroats and highwaymen than any other honest man in the world."[12] And he called Frank Wilson to Washington to make him the lead investigator in the case. Among a slew of capable, experienced special agents, Wilson was at the top. Like Irey, Wilson "wasn't too happy" about the assignment.[13] Irey sought to pacify him, telling him he could choose his own team, and furthermore, he could bring his new wife with him.

■

Frank Wilson (age forty in 1928, the same age as Irey) was an unimposing five feet eight and 180 pounds but carried a personality that would have tested the 101st Airborne. He had steely eyes, a razor thin mouth, and a strong, straight nose in a face like a granite block, more rectangular than square, and topped off by thinning hair. His rimless glasses, for nearsightedness that kept him out of military service in World War I, didn't soften his demeanor. The son of a Buffalo, New York, policeman, he had been an investigator for the Food Administration when Herbert Hoover headed it. Irey, who hired Wilson after the agency closed down following the war, came to admire Wilson's "genius for detail" and relentless style: "He will sit quietly looking at books eighteen hours a day, seven days a week, forever, if he wants to find something in those books."[14] A colleague saw another side of him: "Harry" Woolf, Irey's second in command. A lawyer three years older than Irey, Woolf "felt intimidated" around Wilson, considering him "utterly ruthless when he went after something" and ready to "investigate his own grandmother."[15] When Wilson did sit a suspect down, Irey said, he'd fasten "two of the coldest eyes this side of the Fulton Fish Market on his prey."[16]

Wilson had handled one of Prohibition's dirtiest cases, years-long in resolving, and one that reflected John Crim's skeptical view of U.S. attorneys: The mean tale of William McConnell, the federal Prohibition director for Pennsylvania, who was indicted in 1921 along with three of his staff and forty-five others in a scheme to issue fraudulent liquor permits. Wilson and two other SIU agents spent six months gathering evidence, working with the assistant U.S. attorney, T. Henry Walnut, in Philadelphia. When the case was ready to be presented to a federal grand jury in Philadelphia, two aides of Attorney General Harry Daugherty showed up to take over the case. The next day Walnut was fired. More than two decades later, Wilson, still upset, would characterize the U.S. attorney in Philadelphia, George

Cole, as "a sour old gentleman impressed with his own importance."[17] Two years passed before McConnell went to trial; Frank Wilson gives credit for the case going to trial to an unsung assistant U.S. attorney in Philadelphia named Francis Biddle, who would become the wartime attorney general under Franklin D. Roosevelt.

At the time of Mellon's order, Wilson was the special agent in charge in Baltimore. He had just married a slim, twenty-two-year-old lass named Judith Barbaux, whom he met in Washington, where her father worked for the State Department. They bought a "little yellow house with white shutters" in Baltimore, where Wilson, who rarely relaxed, "set out beds of roses and azaleas." He didn't get to tend them long.

Just before Christmas 1928, Wilson and his wife set out in their DeSoto for Chicago, where they lived out of the Sheridan Plaza Hotel. He didn't tell her the real reason they were there; he only said that he was going to look into the affairs of "a fellow named Curly Brown." If he had told Judith the truth, Wilson later said, "She'd have turned the car right around and made me take up some respectable trade like piano tuning."

For his team, Wilson chose Converse, Hodgins, and Tessem. James N. Sullivan was brought in from New Haven—he and Wilson had worked together in Philadelphia on the McConnell case. Dwight Green also started working with them.

For an office, the five were given "an overgrown closet" on the eighth floor of the federal building, where the U.S. attorney's offices were also located. The glass on the office's door was cracked, there were no windows, no ventilation, the green walls were peeling "as if they'd been sunburned," and all five agents had to use the same flat-topped double desk. Wilson complained to Irey, "I could hardy scratch my head without sticking my elbow in somebody's eye."[18] At another point, Wilson tried to borrow a cabinet. They are "to let me know about it," he told Irey, adding, "That is the usual stall around here."[19] Irey, still operating on a shoestring, couldn't help. Congress, exasperated with the scandal-scarred Prohibition Bureau, was in no mood to build up another Treasury operation, particularly a small, unheralded operation like the Special Intelligence Unit, a virtually obscure entity with no achievements other than bringing down crooked

Prohibition officials. And why would anyone consider that an achievement when bunches of Prohibition agents were released every month for one wrong or another?

■

Irey and his agents devised a simple strategy to bring down Capone: He could be held accountable for not paying his income taxes over a six-year period covering 1924 through 1929. Since the authorities couldn't pin any criminality on him, Wilson and his colleagues centered the investigation on unearthing criminal evidence by tracking Capone's money trail, which included examining his spending habits to determine if he had spent more income than he declared. The aim: find evidence that he had a gross income of $5,000 or more, and determine whether he had stated all items of his gross income on his income tax return, along with allowable deductions and credits, including any amounts derived illegally.

The agents worked the winter of 1929, without getting a step closer to Capone. Wilson himself prowled Cicero's "crummy streets" and came away with nothing, except the firm knowledge of how well entrenched Capone was.[20] There was no money trail. Capone had no bank account, endorsed no checks, signed no receipts, had no property in his name, had never filed a tax return nor made a declaration of assets or income. He paid cash for everything and easily obtained funds whenever and wherever.

Winter turned to spring, and on the morning of Friday, May 17, 1929, Chicago was abuzz with the news that Capone had been arrested the night before in Philadelphia. It was rigged, of course. The killings (like the St. Valentine's Day massacre) had been piling up, so at his sit-down with Johnny Torrio at the Atlantic City crime summit in May 1929, Capone agreed to let things cool down (see page 117). He left for Philadelphia, where he and his bodyguard, Frank Rio, were arrested after they came out of the Stanley Theater. The two spent the night sleeping on a bench in the detective bureau. On Saturday morning, they were charged with being suspicious characters and carrying concealed deadly weapons, indicted, and after a trial that started around 11:30 a.m., Judge John E. Walsh, at 12:15 p.m., sentenced Capone to a year in prison. No speedier justice had ever been handed down on a leading racketeer.

On the eighth floor of the federal building, there was surprise but no celebration. After learning the details, Wilson and his team felt the jailing of Capone hadn't changed a thing. He'd been put on the shelf, but he would be back.

That spring, too, Wilson's relentless style had put Judith in harm's way. On a sunny Saturday he took her with him in the DeSoto to a suburban golf club where he wanted to serve a subpoena on an elusive Capone associate named O'Dwyer. He and Judith sat and waited the entire day; O'Dwyer never showed. They returned the next morning. Around 11:00 a.m., according to Wilson, "Four of the toughest looking characters I ever saw showed up."[21]

Wilson followed them into the clubhouse and checked their identities on the register. O'Dwyer's name was there. He climbed back in the DeSoto, and he and Judith waited. A few hours later, the four men came out. Wilson got out, walked over to O'Dwyer, and held out the subpoena. O'Dwyer snatched it and cursed him. Two of his gunsels drew their revolvers. Judith, sitting behind the wheel, slammed her hand on the car's horn and held it down. The blast brought people running from the golf club. O'Dwyer motioned his gunsels to the car and drove off. There were no more weekend forays with Judith.

For the rest of 1929, Wilson inched along. He and his team laboriously dug up Capone's records, compiling a long, but partial, list of goods and services he had purchased. Over the full length of the investigation, they may have examined more than 1.7 million separate items. The list included $26,000 ($442,000 in 1990 dollars) worth of chairs, sofas, tables, beds, and rugs for his homes in Miami and Chicago and his Hotel Lexington headquarters, where his bill came to $1,500 a week. Telephone bills totaled $3,000 a year ($51,000 in 1990 dollars). Clothing purchases included custom-made suits with extra-strong pistol pockets, silk monogrammed shirts, and diamond belt buckles. Tracing every available source, they concluded Capone had $165,000 of taxable income ($2,795,000 in 1990 dollars). But that sum was covered in uncertainty; it had little meaning overall because of the tricky ramifications the tax laws presented. It was no secret that Capone flaunted his wealth. But, under the law, the mere possession of wealth wasn't a crime. Nor was his lavish spending, in itself, an evidence of income, though it became quickly clear to Irey and Wilson—Dwight Green was in the mix too—that Capone's calculated income of $165,000 was trivial compared to the millions he was earning illegally from bootlegging, gambling, and whoremongering. At an early point they agreed that evidence would have to be uncovered to link Capone directly to the enormously profitable rackets he operated—evidence that could stand up in court.

Meanwhile, in late fall 1929, Archie Martin hit pay dirt on Bottles Capone. With Tessem's help, he had spent most of a year digging up evidence that Bottles, who was still balking on the matter of paying $1,000 ($17,000 in 1990 dollars) in penalties and interest on his income tax debt, had used at least five aliases to hide $1,751,840.60 ($29,781,290.20 in 1990 dollars) in bank accounts from 1924 to 1929.

With Dwight Green presenting the case, a federal grand jury indicted Bottles; on the evening of October 8, Clarence Converse and a deputy U.S. marshal picked up him up at a boxing match at Chicago Stadium and whisked him to the federal courthouse, where Green was waiting to question him. Bottles admitted the phony names on the bank accounts were his aliases, explaining that he did it because the money was from gambling proceeds and it was against state law to operate a handbook. Green questioned him late into the night, but Bottles admitted little else. He did identify dozens of checks as those belonging to him but "shuddered piously" when Green told him that they were payments he had made to speakeasy owners for booze. Bottles maintained the speakeasy owners were "heavy gamblers." When Green dropped the heavyweight question on him about his brother's illegal activities, he professed ignorance. Though Al had designated him as the combine's acting head (in his Pennsylvania prison cell, Al had handed his $50,000, eleven-and-a-half-carat diamond ring to his lawyer to give to Ralph as the symbol of transference of power), Bottles said "he hadn't the slightest idea how Al made [his] money."[22]

The next day Ralph was taken before U.S. Circuit Judge Wilkerson, who set his bail at $35,000 ($595,000 in 1990 dollars) and his trial for May 1930. The indictment of Bottles was the first big crack in the Capone combine. He was part of the combine's upper echelon, a tiny, exclusive group that included Jake Guzik, the business manager, and Frank "the Enforcer" Nitti, who had risen from triggerman to treasurer and who was the combine's link to the Mafia. Yet the SIU was no closer in getting the goods on the top guy.

In helping to finance the investigation, Irey turned to the "Secret Six," a group of crusaders and public-spirited businessmen who maintained a $75,000 ($1,275,000 in 1990 dollars) fund to fight the underworld.[23] The six, whose names were guarded, though some were highly public figures, were Julius Rosenwald, head of Sears, Roebuck, and Co.; Samuel Insull, the oil and gas magnate; Frank Loesch; Robert Isham Randolph, president of the Chicago Chamber of Commerce; Edward E. Gore, a public accountant; and George A. Paddock, a stockbroker. According to Irey, the group made the fund "available to us with no questions asked or answered." Still, Irey was tight in his own ways about spending. He mentions using the fund only twice. Malone received funds "to buy some of the gaudy clothes the gangsters affected." Late in the investigation, Irey used some of the money to hide a valuable informant, Fred Ries. Some also may have gone for Wilson's travel expenses; he put a lot of miles on his DeSoto, hunting down leads as far away as Florida.

Toward the end of 1929, the little operations room at the federal building was "crammed with the reports of thousands of interviews, and a bewildering mass of calculations."[24] What had been twelve-hour days in the beginning now lengthened to sixteen and eighteen hours with no time off for holidays or vacations. The task, to Dwight Green, "seemed to get more hopeless day by day."[25] Irey was commuting on weekends from Washington to Chicago. Amid the dark clouds, Arthur Madden arranged a meeting with Police Commissioner William P. Russell and found out how well Capone was entrenched with the "rotten-to-the-core" Chicago Police Department. Madden recounted,

> I reminded him of the fact that if an accident occurred in the street
> and a crowd gathered in such a way as to obstruct traffic, the police
> officers would disperse the crowd peacefully if they could, but forcibly
> if they must. I asked him if the police, in the ordinary exercise of their

authority, could disperse a crowd on the street, why they could not and did not break up a criminal organization that maintained flamboyant headquarters in a well-known city hotel. I suggested driving the organization from the Lexington Hotel, and from any other point within the limits of the city where it might congregate. The Commission listened with attention [and] stated that he would like to discuss the matter with me at some later date when more time was available. He did not say so, but I distinctly gained the impression that, so far as the Capone organization was concerned, he would not be permitted to take the direct action which he himself probably was disposed to take.[26]

9. A THREE-YEAR STRUGGLE

When Frank Wilson arrived in Chicago shortly after Christmas 1928, Arthur Madden told him, "Hanging an income-tax rap on Alphonse Capone would be as easy as hanging a foreclosure sign on the moon."[1] Now it was January 1930. Wilson had spent an entire year in Chicago, living out of the Sheridan Plaza Hotel with Judith, and he was no closer to finding enough evidence on Capone, who was still languishing in a prison cell in Pennsylvania.

Wilson, nevertheless, continued his merciless style. He did not need to be egged on by Irey, who was always calm and steadfast. There was little or no recognition that federal law enforcement was carrying out the most important criminal investigation of its existence. Nothing like this had ever been done before, and it was being held together by only a bond of hard work, will, and Irey's steady hand. In a world of treachery and puzzle, with few constants, there may not have been a better pairing of two criminal investigators. The thread between the two men kept the investigation together. They may have also chuckled at the ludicrous scene: Alphonse Gabriel Capone, just thirty years of age, was running the nation's biggest empire of crime and was not even at the peak of his influence and notoriety.

Wilson and his team had gathered a volume of material on Capone's spending (which even included the number of towels his minions took to the laundry), an outpouring so huge that the team hadn't gotten to all of it. Yet, in what they had examined, they still couldn't tie criminality to Capone. Not a single break had come from their laborious task. Wilson told Irey they couldn't even find a witness who was reliable.

Capone's money trail had yielded clear indications of his great wealth. Whenever he stayed at his mansion in Miami, cash was wired to him through a Western Union office at the Hotel Lexington. On eighteen occasions in a period from January 14 to April 3, 1928, Wilson and his team learned, Capone received a total of $31,000 ($527,000 in 1990 dollars) in amounts ranging from $300 to $5,000. Jake Guzik sent some in money orders to "Albert Costa" in Miami. They were picked up and cashed by Parker Henderson, the son of a former Miami mayor who was the owner-manager of the Ponce de Leon Hotel in Miami, where Capone and his entourage stayed in the winter of 1927. Henderson had helped sell Capone the estate on Palm Island. Henderson was given $50,000 in cash ($900,000 in 1990 dollars) as down payment, and he put the property in his name. The title was later transferred to Capone's wife, Mary. Capone had been offered an estate in the Bahamas for $500,000 ($8.5 million in 1990 dollars) but turned it down.

Then, a few clouds parted. Pat O'Rourke's penetration of Capone's circle paid off. At a party for Capone at the New Florence Restaurant across the street from the Lexington Hotel, O'Rourke overheard someone comment that Frank Nitti had dealings with the Schiff Trust and Savings Bank. The next day Tessem, with a federal subpoena in his pocket, showed up at the bank. Schiff officers temporarily stonewalled him before Tessem turned stern and demanded to see the bank's general ledger. Pouring over it, he found a list of checks credited to Nitti and coaxed bank president Bruno Schiff to admit that he had entered into a secret agreement with Nitti to clear checks and deliver cash without showing his name on the records.

When Irey showed up in Chicago on the first weekend in January, Wilson told him, "I think we've got Nitti and Guzik. I know where Al gets his money, but it'll take a little proving. I can prove where Nitti gets his, and how much. The same goes for Guzik. I think we should get them first and then go for Al. Nobody wants to talk much about Al, so maybe if we put a couple of his big shots away people'll be more cooperative."

Nitti, a Sicilian born in Augori who was ten years older than Capone, ranked near the top of the syndicate. He arrived with his family at Ellis Island at age two and a half. They settled in Brooklyn, where he became a barber who fenced on the side before hooking up with Capone. He was a crack triggerman before he took over as treasurer. Irey said Nitti "had what it takes."[2] A man with a small mustache and wary eyes, his demeanor didn't reflect the image of the stone killer. Capone biographer Robert J. Schoenberg described Nitti as looking "like a bank teller worried about what the head cashier meant by that remark a week ago last Tuesday," yet he "somehow instilled more terror precisely because of his flaccid smallness."[3] And he had slipped up.

On March 14, 1930, three days before Capone was released from prison in Pennsylvania, a federal grand jury secretly indicted Nitti, charging him with accumulating $744,887 ($12,663,079 in 1990 dollars) for the years 1925, 1926, and 1927 without filing a tax form. But no Chicago grand jury, federal or otherwise, could keep a secret and the usual occurred: a courthouse informer told Nitti of the indictment, and he went into hiding. While he was being hunted, the Capone operation suffered its first big setback. On April 25, after a fifteen-day trial, a federal jury found Ralph Capone guilty, and the judge sentenced him to three years in prison and fined him $10,000. His appeals took eighteen months before he went to Leavenworth on November 6, 1931.

■

Capone returned to Chicago in mid-March to face a concern like nothing before. He'd lost nothing in prison, only chewable time. Sent to Holmesburg, one of the nation's worst prisons, he was soon transferred to the nicer surroundings of Eastern Penitentiary, where he pulled duty as a library clerk and got the warden to furnish his cell with rugs, a desk, a bookshelf, and other conveniences. While he was behind bars, an archenemy, Joseph Aiello, had taken over as the head of the Unione Siciliane chapter. Not now, nor ever, was Capone going to tolerate any threat to his power.

On October 23, 1929, Aiello was slain on a neighborhood street, caught in the crossfire of two machine-gun nests set up in second-story flats.

Of the triumvirate that had ruled in his absence, two had gone down: Ralph Capone and Frank Nitti. The third, Jake Guzik, was in trouble. In tracking Guzik's money trail, Wilson found a name that counted: Fred Reis. Reis was the operator of a Capone gambling parlor and an ex-teller at the Pinkert State Bank in Cicero, who handled Guzik's money. The bank was across the street from Capone's Hawthorne Hotel headquarters. Reis's modus operandi was that he would keep $10,000 for the parlor's expenses, take the profits to Pinkert, buy cashier's checks, and give them to Guzik. But Reis had disappeared. Wilson, however, found a small-time hood and traded him his freedom for Reis's whereabouts—a hotel in St. Louis. Recounted Wilson, "We found out from the Post Office inspectors that a special-delivery letter was about to be delivered to him, so we simply tailed the messenger boy and I crossed Ries' palm with a Federal subpoena." The special-delivery letter was from Capone's headquarters; it ordered Ries to flee to Mexico because government agents were on his trail.

After the arrest, Wilson recalled that Reis, "cocky, beady-eyed [and] cop-hating," immediately clammed up. 'Nuts to you!' was all we could get out of him." But Reis was a "hard boy who feared nothing in this world—except maybe little insects like cockroaches and bedbugs." Wilson had learned this from a Pinkert teller and decided to turn Reis's affliction to horror.

He stuffed Reis in a downstate Illinois jail where "cockroaches and other wild life were virtually holding a convention upon the premises." Eyeing the cell, Wilson recounted, Ries barked, "This ain't fit for a dog!" Before leaving, Wilson told the jailer Reis "would probably be calling for us in less than a week." He had already asked a judge in East St. Louis, where he had obtained Reis's commitment papers, to put them in his safe, "so there wouldn't be any docket record and the shysters and their bondsmen would never find out where Ries was."[4]

Forty-eight hours later, Wilson learned that Capone's headquarters had put out a reward for information on Reis's whereabouts. Five days passed before Reis started begging to be let out of his vermin-infested cell.

Federal marshals brought him back to Chicago, and on September 15, he began talking to Wilson.

On October 3, a federal grand jury indicted Guzik for failing to pay his income tax for 1927, 1928, and 1929, years in which he had earned up to $1 million ($17 million in 1990 dollars) and had paid only $60,240 ($1,024,080 in 1990 dollars) out of the $250,000 ($4,250,000 in 1990 dollars) he actually owed. E. Q. Johnson put Guzik on trial in near-record time, and Ries testified that Guzik was his immediate boss and that he had others, namely, Al Capone, Ralph Capone, and Frank Nitti. It was the first time anyone implicated Capone in direct testimony. Guzik was convicted on November 19 and sentenced to five years in prison, the longest term ever handed up for such an offense. As for Ries, the government's star witness, he was still going to be needed to testify against Capone. With funds provided by Chicago's Secret Six, he was spirited away to Brazil, guarded by a marshal, until he was needed again.

The year before the SIU began investigating Capone, the Justice Department at the behest of E. Q. Johnson, undertook its own effort to bring down Capone by attacking his bootlegging operation—but botched it. Shortly after taking over in 1927, Johnson had gone to Washington "to beg" for "a force of fresh, unspoiled prohibition agents and got it." That was the year Congress enacted a law placing the Prohibition Unit under civil service and making it a bureau. The special force was headed by an experienced agent named George Golding, who had acquired the sobriquet "Hard-Boiled" (the *New York Times*, however, called him "high-handed"). Golding "led his men through miles of popping photographers' flash guns as he rounded up dozens of illicit backroom gin mills and bathroom alcohol stills. He even knocked off a few breweries." These "melodramatics began to pall" when one of Golding's agents shot an innocent bystander during a raid. The agent, according to Irey, "had to go into hiding in the Federal Building, sleeping and eating in an Assistant United States Attorney's office until his victim disappointed the critical Chicago press and recovered from his wound." As a result, E. Q. Johnson "begged that the special crew be withdrawn before somebody got lynched."[5]

Taking over from Golding was an agent named Alex Jamie, who had worked in Army intelligence during World War I. As his assistant, Jamie picked twenty-eight-year-old Eliot Ness, a University of Chicago graduate on his first government mission. Upon transfer of the Prohibition Bureau to Justice from Treasury, W. E. Bennett became chief of the Chicago branch, and Ness became his assistant. A few months later, Ness was put in charge of a six-man squad assigned to go after Capone's liquor establishment. They were dedicated and incorruptible. Driving a ten-ton truck with a reinforced steel bumper and a flat bed to support scaling ladders, Ness's crew battered down the doors of nineteen distilleries and six breweries that Capone ran and seized or destroyed more than $1 million ($17 million in 1990 dollars) worth of trucks, equipment, beer, and whiskey.

Ness, like Golding, loved personal publicity and had a penchant for calling out the press and newsreel cameras before hitting a bootlegging operation. Though little known outside Chicago, Ness and his crew by 1931 were being referred to as the "untouchables."[6] Not until much later did Ness achieve mythical status and become the centerpiece of what turned into one of the most overblown law enforcement stories of the twentieth century. As Frank Wilson said of Ness, "A handsome, dashing figure, but his love of notoriety severely limited his effectiveness. He undoubtedly did cause Capone considerable loss. However, he did not, as he later claimed, dry up Chicago, with its 20,000-odd places where one could buy a drink, nor did he destroy Al Capone."[7]

A natty dresser who parted his dark hair down the middle, the handsome Ness bore a resemblance to Robert Stack, the actor who made him famous forty years later in the television series, *The Untouchables*. Even today, Ness is still characterized regularly as a "legendary cop" and "the man who brought down Al Capone." As writer Anthony Scaduto noted, "The deifiers of Eliot Ness have made him a household god invested with superhuman qualities."[8]

Robert Bridges, an unsung Prohibition agent who happened to be as much of a hero as Ness, failed to achieve the same mythical status. Bridges served in Detroit and Cleveland, where he took on an underworld power named Frank Milano. After Milano declared a heavily populated Italian district of the city off-limits to federal agents, Bridges called him to a meeting. At the meeting, "the agents placed submachine guns on the conference table and told Milano they would go into the area whenever they desired and would shoot anyone who tried to stop them."[9] Bridges, incidentally, said of Ness, "[he] never made an arrest in his life."[10] Though Ness and his raiders played longer on television than they did in Chicago, it became popular legend, too, that his operation was run in tandem with Irey's investigation of Capone's money trail, thereby giving it greater legitimacy. It spawned the distortion, too, that Ness played a bigger role than Irey in bringing down Capone. Nothing is further from the truth. Neither was there a two-way punch designed in tandem by Justice and Treasury to bring down Capone. During the 1920s the Justice Department, always an underfunded entity, never acted against racketeering in Chicago, except in the Candy Jobbers case initiated by William Donovan.

Ness's operation did gather enough evidence to prompt a federal grand jury to indict Capone for conspiracy to violate the Volstead Act. That dutiful act has been used to foster the claim that his operation was so effective it dried up Chicago. Capone was running a $100 million ($1.7 billion in 1990 dollars) empire. To conclude, as observers have, that destroying some of Capone's bootlegging outlets, as Ness and his crew did, would bring the country's most powerful racketeer to his knees and dry up the country's second-largest city borders on the ludicrous.

Throughout the SIU's long investigation of Capone, the Justice Department undertook various attempts, such as the one by Ness, to get Capone, inexplicably trying to strike any kind of deal. At one point, Capone, pleading illness, ignored a subpoena to appear before a federal grand jury in Chicago. He was brought before U.S. District Court Judge James H. Wilkerson for contempt of court, and the judge proceeded to lecture him that this time he was not in a municipal courtroom where he could bribe and intimidate everyone from the judge down to bailiffs. Judge Wilkerson sentenced him to a period of six months in jail. Capone posted a $5,000 bond and never served a day.

On June 8, 1931, it was announced that a federal grand jury had indicted Capone on income tax evasion. It was based on solid evidence the SIU had accumulated over more than two years of rugged inquiry, evidence on which E. Q. Johnson was confident he could use to obtain a guilty verdict. Yet, the Justice Department decided that "the government would be satisfied with a two-and-a-half-year jail sentence on a plea of guilty by Capone, rather than run the hazards of hostile witnesses and frightened jurors." On June 16, 1931, Capone came into court and pleaded guilty before Judge Wilkerson to everything, including "5,000 indictments for bootlegging." His lawyers then requested and received a two-week delay in sentencing so that Capone "could arrange his affairs." Later that same day, Judge Wilkerson learned the Justice Department was willing to give him a two-and-a-half-year sentence—and hit the ceiling. Fourteen days later, Capone, back in court, withdrew his guilty pleas, and Wilkerson tossed out every one of the 5,000 indictments, declaring, "[It is] an unheard-of thing . . . that anybody, even the court itself, could bind the court as to the judgment which is to be made by the court. The court will listen to recommendations of the district attorney, but the defendant cannot think that the court is bound to enter judgment according to those recommendations."[11]

Then, Judge Wilkerson ruled that Capone would have to face trial beginning October 6 on charges of income-tax evasion. Wilkerson recognized that this took precedent over the bootlegging indictment. If Capone had been prosecuted for Volstead Act violations instead, there is every likelihood he would have been back on the street in the time it took to down a glass of beer.

■

It had taken two hard years of tedious detail and disappointment for Frank Wilson and his tiny band of investigators to arrive at this point. Wilson had lived out of a suitcase, trudged down narrow roads in the cold and heat from Chicago to Miami, and once drove all night from Chicago to St. Louis. There had been hard-won successes (Ralph Capone, Frank Nitti, and Jake Guzik had gone down), but hard failure in finding substantial criminal evidence on Capone. As a result, Wilson had found himself in "a real sweat."[12] He had come up with a lot of circumstantial evidence on Capone's spending but nothing else. Then he made a lucky discovery.

One evening in late fall 1930, working in his cramped office in the federal building, he got up to look for a place to store papers (he had sent another memo to Irey in Washington pleading for better facilities). Seeing nothing at hand, he walked into the hallway. Sitting there were four dusty file cabinets filled with material the state attorney had sent over. He opened the top drawer of one. In it was a large package tied up in brown paper. He broke the string. Out tumbled three black ledgers with red corners. He opened one. Entries totaling hundreds of thousands of dollars had been made in pen in differing sums. Beside each figure was an initial, apparently indicating to whom the money went. The initials looked familiar, particularly those with a capital "C." He knew instantly that these were the financial records of a big gambling operation.

"Who could have run a joint that size?" Wilson asked himself.[13] The answer: Al Capone. He went back to his cubbyhole and began comparing entries from other ledgers. Before long he hit pay dirt. The "C" of course was for Capone; the other initials were those of his various cohorts. The figures tallied how gambling profits were split up.

The ledgers, Wilson learned the next day, had been seized in a raid on the Hawthorne Smoke Shop, the first gambling house Capone opened in suburban Cicero, where the Chicago crowd came to lay down $3 million a year in wagers. Ironically, the raiders had been part of the group mounted after the murder of Bill McSwiggin by Capone and his henchman in Cicero four years before. The Hawthorne Smoke Shop was next door to the Hawthorne Inn—site of a vivid incident still being dramatized in the movies fifty years later—where Capone wined and dined a roomful of cohorts, then grabbed a baseball bat and used it to club three of them to death as betrayers.

The ledgers showed $587,721.95 ($10,578,996.20 in 1990 dollars) in entries from gambling profits Capone had made there over an eighteen-month period from 1924 to 1926, none of which he reported as income. "If I could hang that income around the neck of Capone, we'd have a case," Wilson recalled.[14] And he did.

His discovery served up ironclad evidence of the wealth Capone's empire was generating. More than half a million dollars had come from just one gambling spot in Cicero, the Hawthorne Smoke Shop, and Wilson found the bookkeeper, Leslie Shumway, in Miami. "In great secrecy," Wilson brought him back to Chicago, where Shumway talked to secret grand-jury proceedings.[15] On March 13, 1931, the jury charged Capone with evading income taxes. When the other rackets were added up, the $100 million ($1.7 billion in 1990 dollars) cited as Capone's annual racketeering income proved reasonable.

Capone had already tried to escape that fateful day. Internal Revenue Commissioner David Burnet tells of a telephone conversation he had with Harry Curtis (whom he did not identify), who suggested "that it was time to stop all prosecutions in the Chicago gang group [and if so] he would guarantee that at least $3.5 million [$374.5 million in 1990 dollars] would be paid to the Collector of Internal Revenue at Chicago voluntarily by various racketeers, gangsters, etc."[16] At another point, Capone dangled a $1.5 million ($160.5 million in 1990 dollars) bribe. A "suave young man" visited Irey's longtime friend, Joseph Callan, in New York, where he was now an executive of the Crucible Steel Company, to offer the bribe.[17] Callan kicked him out of his office, literally. Then, two weeks after Wilson personally questioned Capone at the federal building, Wilson was tipped that four mafiosi had been brought in from New York City to assassinate him, E. Q. Johnson, Madden, and Roche. This did not happen, but Capone still didn't stop. Two weeks before the trial was to open, Wilson learned from Edward J. O'Hare that Capone obtained a list of the jurors—a list that not even the trial judge, Wilkerson, or U.S. Attorney Johnson had been given. Early in his investigation, Wilson met O'Hare in St. Louis through a mutual friend, John Rogers, a Pulitzer Prize–winning reporter for the *Post-Dispatch*. Rogers told Wilson that O'Hare had decided to inform on Capone. A wealthy lawyer and dog-track operator, O'Hare first met Capone when he installed a mechanical rabbit at the Hawthorne Kennel Club outside Cicero.

"Don't be silly," Wilson cracked to O'Hare when he told him in a telephone call about the scheme to bribe the jurors. O'Hare replied, "Capone's boys have a complete list of the prospective jurors. They're fixing them one by one. They're passing out $1,000 bills [$17,000 in 1990 dollars]." The two met an hour later on a street corner on Chicago's far north side. Wilson "felt his heart stop" when O'Hare handed him a list of ten names and addresses. "There you are," he pointed. "They're right off the jury list—names 30 to 39."[18]

Wilson hurried the list to E. Q. Johnson, and Judge Wilkerson thwarted the scheme. On Tuesday, October 6, 1931, the day Capone went on trial for tax evasion, Wilkerson, in black robe, entered the courtroom, sat down, and immediately motioned the bailiff to the bench. "Judge Woodward has another trial commencing today," he said in a crisp, stern tone. "Go to his courtroom and bring me his entire panel of jurors. Take my entire panel to Judge Woodward."

Frank Wilson looked over at Capone, whose "features clouded with fury," but he didn't make a move.[19] And that was that. After hearing the case over an eleven-day span, the jury retired at 2:40 p.m. on Saturday, October 17. That evening, shortly before 11:00 p.m., the jurors returned with a guilty verdict on twenty-two counts of tax evasion. The following Saturday, October 24, Judge Wilkerson sentenced Capone to eleven years in prison and ordered that he pay fines of $50,000 and court costs totaling $30,000. It was six days short of three years from the day Secretary Mellon gave Irey the order to bring down Capone. Wilkerson was going to send Capone immediately to Leavenworth, where his brother Ralph was, but relented to pleas from Capone's lawyers.

Two years later, in the dead of a hot August night, Capone was in a group of inmates at the Atlanta penitentiary hurried to a special chartered train and taken cross-country to an eight-by-four-foot cell in their newly refurbished but still bleak quarters at what would become the nation's most celebrated prison. Attorney General Homer Cummings had been seeking an inaccessible, secure location for celebrity inmates like Capone and got the War Department to give up a military prison he believed was the closest thing to fitting the bill. Twenty-five military prisoners were still in their cells when Capone arrived. The prison compound consisted of a stark cluster of masonry structures, guard towers, and a water tower, all stacked together on a twelve-acre island resting abrasively in the middle of one of the nation's most beautiful and natural settings—San Francisco Bay. The prison was Alcatraz, which became known as the "Rock." Capone would remain there until he was at death's door, riddled with syphilis. In an extraordinarily brief period by historical standards—he lived in Chicago just over a decade and led a criminal domain for only half of that period—Capone had become a racketeer who virtually worked his will over the nation's second-largest city, amassed a fortune greater than the budget of many countries, and left a name that will live in infamy.

10. GRIM JOURNEY TO MANHATTAN

On Thursday, April 2, 1931, five months before Al Capone went to trial, David Burnet, the commissioner of Internal Revenue, and Elmer Irey met in Manhattan with George Z. Medalie, the U.S. attorney for the Southern District of New York, and his chief deputy, twenty-nine-year-old Thomas E. Dewey. Sitting in was Hugh McQuillen, chief of the SIU's New York office and one of the original seven Daniel Roper had brought on when he established the SIU in 1919. The closed, daylong session was to acquaint Medalie and Dewey with the Capone case and how the strategies the SIU learned could be used to bring down his racketeering counterparts in New York City.

Irey's mission to New York City grew out of a memorandum Herbert Hoover sent to Attorney General William DeWitt Mitchell on March 16, 1931, which read,

> My dear Mr. Attorney General:
>
> The special organization set up for prosecution of gangsters in Chicago has worked out most successfully and has been a contribution to the whole of that community.
>
> I am wondering if you would consider setting up such a special organization in New York with view to prosecution of evident grafters on federal counts which are available. I believe that such an activity

might be salutary to the country and a contribution to the enforcement of other laws.

Yours faithfully,

Herbert Hoover[1]

The president's memorandum was passed on to the Treasury and then the Special Intelligence Unit. Irey wasted no time, showing up in New York City sixteen days after the memorandum's date. His mission was heralded by the *New York Times* in its lead story in Friday's morning front page this way: "An intensive drive against New York gangsters, smugglers, bootleggers and other racketeers through the medium of income tax law enforcement was begun yesterday." Though this was going to be a Treasury show, the *Times* noted, "The Department of Justice was anxious to deliver a smashing blow at the flourishing industry of racketeering, which, as in other large cities, is said to have obtained a firm hold here, especially in connection with bootlegging, operation of speakeasies, lottery and poll ventures and smuggling."[2] This was Justice's way of asserting its place, for up to now, it had achieved little success in its drive on racketeers. It was also a way of recognizing Irey's value because fate had sided with the SIU chief. He had the great fortune to work with a trailblazer like E. Q. Johnson in Chicago. Now, he was joining up with two other highly capable prosecutors, Medalie and Dewey. Indeed, despite John Crim's dour feelings about U.S. attorneys, New York City had been served by superior talent in the Southern District through the 1920s into the 1930s.

Medalie, a forty-seven-year old moon-faced man of average height and the first Jew named to the office, was considered the finest trial lawyer at the New York Bar. The White House had named him to the post in January. Writer Nat Ferber called him "the ablest United States Attorney in the history of the Southern District."[3] Born on the Lower East Side, the son of a rabbi, Medalie got his law degree at Columbia. He spent five years on the staff of famed New York County District Attorney Charles Whitman, where he "gained a deep respect for the tedious essence of any investigation, which is detail," and became an authority on the grand jury as "a community's chief investigative tool."[4] His pet phrase for the single telling detail that might, in one electric moment, excite a jury's outrage was, "How do we put a ruby rose on it?"[5] Tom Dewey was working at a Wall Street law firm for $35 ($602 in 1990 dollars) a week when he found himself in a bank claim case with Medalie. He so impressed Medalie that after taking over as U.S. attorney, Medalie named him his chief deputy. A Protestant from a small town in Michigan who earned a law degree from Columbia, Dewey was a classmate of William O. Douglas. Brisk and brainy, he stopped going to law professor Rexford G. Tugwell's seminars after one semester because they were "too undemanding."[6]

Facing the press after the closed-door session, Irey declined to go into detail on the new initiative, but he did disclose he was bringing in "a special squad of about fifty Federal operatives."[7] This was revealing. The force that took down Capone was nowhere near that number; fifty operatives made up half of the SIU in the 1920s. While the number of operatives indicated the seriousness of the New York task, the special force would be largely peopled by Revenue agents and accountants, those handling the details of evidence and records. Investigating financial conspiracies was a battle over every inch of paper. They were backed up by the New York SIU office, including McQuillen; his assistant, Walter Murphy; and a force of seven special agents, the criminal investigators. Irey was also sensitive to Frank Wilson's complaints about the cramped quarters in Chicago. The Treasury rented the nineteenth floor of the twenty-nine-story Park Row Building, once the world's tallest skyscraper, to house the force.

While Irey would return to Chicago to testify at Al Capone's trial, the SIU's investigative role for all intent was at an end there. E. Q. Johnson had solid evidence for conviction and had begun preparing for the trial. Not known publicly was that a federal grand jury, in a secret session on March 13, had indicted Capone for attempting to evade an income tax of $32,488.91 ($559,321.47 in 1990 dollars) on a net income of $123,102.89 ($2,235,852.02 in 1990 dollars) for the year 1924. The indictment took effect two days prior to the expiration of the six-year statute of limitations for tax offenses committed in 1924. According to Frank Wilson, "Johnson requested that the grand jury not make its verdict public until the investigation for the years 1925 to 1929 was completed."[8] That investigation was wrapped up in late May. On June 5 the jury convened again, and an indictment was announced on Friday, June 8. Capone was charged on twenty-one counts of willful evasion of income taxes amounting to $215,080.48 ($3,655,568.16 in 1990 dollars) covering the years 1925–1929. "There was no contention that the $215,080.48 represented all Capone might owe the government if he paid an honest income tax. Rather, the government alleged that this amount is due on net income of $1,038,654 [$18,156,818 in 1990 dollars] for those years. Neither was it contended that this was all the Capone income of those five years, but it represented what the prosecutors expected to be able to prove actually reached his pockets."[9]

From Irey's first day in Manhattan, press speculation centered on the new force's targets. Medalie was "believed to be concentrating his attention against more than 1,000 tax evaders." McQuillen and his agents "are expected to find plentiful material for their work in the inquiry into magistrates' courts, which has already revealed that several members of the Police Department have received large sums for which no accounting is said to have been made to the income tax authorities."

The key question was, Which racketeers would be investigated? At that point, Irey wasn't going to say, and Medalie "declined to name the outstanding subjects of the Federal inquiry."[10] To an extent Irey knew his targets but almost nothing about what was really ahead. New York City, not Chicago, was the country's real capital of crime. The hard truth was that neither Irey nor his force was aware that they faced a situation unlike any before in federal law enforcement. Irey showed up at the exact moment when New York City's political and criminal life had taken on a new dimension. Chicago, a second home to the SIU chief over the last two and a half years, had the country's best-known racketeer, the vaunted Thompson machine, more street-side gang shootings, and maybe more speakeasies, but nowhere had Prohibition served as a more luxuriant seeding ground for organized crime and racketeering than in the town where Mayor James J. "Beau James" Walker reigned and where Tammany Hall, the longest-running, most reptilian political machine in U.S. history, lorded over the town's five boroughs.

Long before Al Capone, and even before Beau James, New York City had called on the Justice Department in Washington for help in exposing corruption in the building trades. In October 1920 Samuel Untermeyer, the counsel for a state legislative committee investigating racketeering in the building trades, noted, "It would take almost an army of judges, lawyers and experts to exterminate and punish any considerable number of them . . . the true way to deal with the situation is by rigid governmental regulation."[11]

After Beau James Walker, the epitome of the flamboyant, amoral politician, won city hall at age forty-four in 1925, Tammany corruption entered a new era. It was no joke that the popular mayor may have transacted more of the city's business at his favorite haunt, the Central Park Casino, than at city hall. The Casino, one of the swankiest restaurants in the city with an entrance that cost $22,000 alone ($374,000 in 1990 dollars), was where Beau James would regularly wine and dine with his young, blond mistress, Betty "Monk" Compton, an actress who had appeared with Fred Astaire in a Broadway musical. In an upstairs room at the Casino, Beau James would hold court, handing out favors and contracts until the cup ran over. No one was more eager to accept the opportunities and rewards of the new constellation of organized crime coming into being: the celestial sphere of Mafia and Jewish racketeers willing to buy Tammany protection. His timing was exquisite.

Two politically well-connected factions ran the city's underworld: the Mafia, primarily Sicilian-born racketeers who had immigrated to the United States after the century turned, and a loose grouping of homegrown Jewish racketeers. In Prohibition, racketeers from both elements became major players in the liquor rackets, vice, gambling, and drug trafficking on the Eastern Seaboard, enterprises that provided undreamed of levels of wealth. Don Joseph Bonnano, the head of one of New York City's Five Mafia Families, called Prohibition "the golden goose."[12]

There was a key difference between the two sides. Under their code of *omerta* (noble silence), the Mafia brethren hewed to silence and anonymity. Wrote Gay Talese, "These people would no more squeal on a countryman to the New York police in the Twenties than they would to the Saracen conquerors in the ninth century, the Byzantine Greeks in the tenth century, or the cruel French in the thirteenth century. Suspicious of all alien authority, they had learned to accept the art of silence—learned it through centuries of biting their lips."[13] The high-living Jewish racketeers, on the other hand, couldn't keep out of the headlines. One was Dutch Schultz. Born Arthur Flegenheimer in the Bronx in 1902, he "grew up to be such a savage character that he was named Dutch Schultz after a well-known bully of that time."[14] In their misplaced loyalty and savageness, only a handful of Jewish racketeers, unlike many mafiosi, won an extended life. One of the wisest of the wise, Meyer Lansky, befriended more mafiosi than Jewish racketeers. Of the Jewish racketeers, a number went on to achieve criminal infamy: Irving (Waxey Gordon) Wexler; Louis (Lepke) Buchalter, who had "a directional genius for lawlessness";[15] Jacob (Gurrah) Shapiro; and John Thomas "Legs" Diamond. Schultz's lawyer, J. Richard "Dixie" Davis, called "Kid Mouthpiece," said Diamond organized "the first really modern mob in New York. As distinguished from the old loosely knit gangs, the mob was a compact business organization with a pay roll of gunmen who worked for a boss."[16] But he never really drew loyalty. He "was as likely to steal from his employer as from a stranger," observed Leo Katcher. [17]

Of the racketeers in both factions, Arnold Rothstein was the slickest. Cunning and private, influential and wealthy, he was New York City's Al Capone without the murderous attitude, rank excess, and organization. Always acting with lone-wolf stealth and vaccinated against arrest, he built a criminal empire that didn't match Capone's income but was far more devious and diversified. He was a one-man corporation of crime, unrivaled before or since, with a hand in virtually every important racket and a gaming operation that flourished in the city's five boroughs.

Writer Edward Dean Sullivan called Rothstein "a true master mind [with] perhaps the keenest anti-social brain in criminal history."[18] Nat Ferber, a reporter for the first four decades of the twentieth century, watched Rothstein's dealings and observed, "As a fixer and a go-between, he stood alone."[19] He "openly violated our legal code every day of his adult life in New York City," said Donald Henderson Clarke, a *New York World* reporter.[20] "He wanted an advantage in every transaction he participated in and was completely blind to any moral or ethical standard which denied him that advantage," said Russel Crouse.[21] "He never gave a thing in his life without a quid pro quo," said writers Craig Thompson and Allen Raymond.[22] Edward M. Fuller, a brokerage firm owner caught up in the bucket-shop scandals involving Rothstein and Tammany Hall chieftains, said, "That fellow liked money."[23] Lloyd Morris, the social historian, described Rothstein as "the J. P. Morgan of the underworld; its banker and master of strategy." Charlie Luciano: "He could spend it so fast just livin' that it even made my head spin, and I was a pretty good spender."[24] Rothstein set no boundaries on Wall Street or in organized labor. He worked both sides of the union street, offering protection as a middleman for the unions or running strike-breakers. "He didn't know or care about the politics of a strike," said union activist Morris Malkin. "[It was whoever] got to him first or if they paid him more."[25] F. Scott Fitzgerald bowed to Rothstein, making him the character Wolfsheim in *The Great Gatsby*. One of Rothstein's favorite expressions was "I am 100 per cent right."[26] George Medalie had even represented Rothstein once.

Before Prohibition landed, Rothstein had ties to virtually everyone involved in the city's burgeoning rackets. In his stock and trade, he held a special place in the heart of every New York racketeer: he represented what they wanted to become. One of the first gangs he put together, circa 1919, included Legs Diamond, who started out as Rothstein's bodyguard, along with Lepke, Gurrah, Gordon, and Luciano. Dutch Schultz served an apprenticeship as a truck driver. "With the coming of Prohibition, a new type of gang came into being," wrote Leo Katcher. "It had discipline and order. It possessed a chain of command. And, most important, it was financially independent."[27] Rothstein paid his crew $7.50 ($142.50 in 1990 dollars) a day; the average wage was $6.27 ($119.13 in 1990 dollars) a day. Frank Costello was associated with Rothstein as early as 1921. Meyer Lansky met Rothstein at a bar mitzvah of a mutual friend's son in Brooklyn. "Rothstein taught me some valuable business lessons that day we met," he said. "He invited me to dinner at the Park Central Hotel and we sat talking for six hours. It was a big surprise to me. Rothstein told me quite frankly that he had picked me because I was ambitious and 'hungry.'"[28]

By the mid-1920s Rothstein had become the foundation on which the edifice of organized crime was formed in New York City. He cornered the market on narcotics because he dealt in lots too big for anyone else to compete against, just as he had done in financing bucket shops, running gambling houses, bootlegging, and loan sharking. Writer Leo Katcher credits Luciano with alerting Rothstein to both the potential of drugs and the international market. Before Rothstein, foreign interests demanded and received their money before the drugs were shipped. Under Rothstein's scheme, drugs were sent from abroad on a short-term credit basis. Until 1925 Rothstein limited his drug purchases to European sources, but late that year he turned to the Asian market, sending one of his mechanics, Sid Stajer, to China, Formosa, and Hong Kong to arrange purchases. Rothstein also was the underworld's ace in the hole. With his impeccable financial standing, he could arrange credit with banks for felonious sorts who couldn't borrow a dime. He advanced $9,000 ($153,000 in 1990 dollars) to rumrunner Eddie Costello, Frank's brother, on "a note payable to the 42nd Street branch of the National City Bank."[29] When Frank needed $40,000 ($680,000 in 1990 dollars) to purchase a brewery, he borrowed it from Rothstein, giving him a note.

■

On November 4, 1928, Rothstein was found shot once in the abdomen, lying at the service entrance to the Park Central Hotel on Seventh Avenue and West Fifty-sixth Street. He died on November 6, the day Herbert Hoover was elected president of the United States over Alfred E. Smith of New York. George "Big George" McManus, a thirty-six-year-old gambler known as one of the city's biggest bookmakers and a longtime acquaintance of Rothstein's, was sought for his murder. On the evening he was slain, Rothstein was at his hangout, Lindy's, the Broadway restaurant made famous by Damon Runyon. Around 9:45, Rothstein, at his table with gambler Jimmy Meehan, received a phone call from McManus. Rothstein left the table to take it; when he returned, he and Meehan walked outside, where he handed Meehan a long-barreled .38-caliber revolver and said, "Hold this for me. George McManus wants to see me, and I'm going up to his room. I'll be back in an hour." He left for the Park Central Hotel, six blocks away, where McManus's floating poker game was going on.

McManus had registered at the Park Central several days before under the name "George Richards" and was given Room 349. At 10:53 p.m., the desk sergeant at the old West Forty-seventh Street station house received a call from a police box informing him that a man had been shot at the Park Central Hotel. That same hour, from a phone booth at the corner of Fifty-seventh Street and Eighth Avenue, McManus called James J. "Jimmy" Hines, the Upper East Side district leader who was four years away from taking command of Tammany Hall. McManus then walked to the corner of Fifty-ninth Street, where approximately fifteen minutes later, a Buick driven by Abraham "Bo" Weinberg, a very tough gunsel (and Dutch Schultz's chief lieutenant), stopped. McManus climbed in. Over the next twenty-four days, while the NYPD was conducting a coast-to-coast manhunt for McManus, he hid in an apartment Schultz provided him on Mosholu Parkway in the Bronx.

The first of many cover-ups in the case, it was masterminded by Jimmy Hines, who had close ties to Rothstein. Hines allowed his wife, Geneva, to entertain her friends at a hotel Rothstein owned, the Fairfield, at Rothstein's expense. For his generosity, Rothstein received "warm notes of thanks" from Geneva.[30] Her husband and Dutch Schultz, meanwhile, were like crossed fingers. "More than once," recalled "Dixie" Davis, Schultz's lawyer, "I sat late with Hines and Dutch Schultz in a mob night club as we plotted ways by which, with the Dutchman's mob and money, Hines might extend his power over still other districts and seize absolute control of Tammany and the whole city government."[31]

To the unknowing, Tammany Hall was a mathematical formula consisting of four-dimensional spheres of corruption—in short, a tangled web. But there was a commonality to what was happening. "Rothstein alive had been an unsavory article, Rothstein dead was a calamity," wrote Ernest Cuneo, Fiorello La Guardia's law clerk.[32] Rothstein was well connected, and in Tammany's collective desperation, Hines's cover-up, like the rest, would stall embarrassing disclosures at the least, criminality at the worst.

Once the shock wave of Rothstein's murder hit Tammany Hall, the rush was on to keep the enormity of his dealings from the spotlight. No one was more clandestine than Rothstein, but everyone leaves a money trail. His lay in the records he kept on his myriad enterprises, including art galleries and antique shops. In the records that were uncovered, he had kept his accounts down to the penny. From the start, the press smelled a cover-up. On the morning of November 9, three days after Rothstein died, the *New York Daily News* editorialized, "There has been a strange lassitude hampering the activities of detectives seeking to solve this crime." That afternoon, William H. Hyman, the lawyer retained by Rothstein's family, handed over books, records ledgers, and any papers on his business and financial affairs to sixty-year-old New York County District Attorney Joab H. Banton, declaring, "If these papers are ever made public, there are going to be a lot of suicides in high places."[33]

The day after Rothstein was shot, Charlie Luciano and two Rothstein henchmen, George Uffner and George "Fats" Walsh, had showed up at his office. Luciano and Uffner were deeply involved in Rothstein's drug ring. The NYPD was there, however, and charged them with being "suspicious characters." But that was all the police had on them, and they were released. Said Leo Katcher, "The police did not know that their visit had been to check the whereabouts of the different caches of narcotics in this country, the supplies awaiting shipment from foreign countries, and any unfilled orders that ought to be met without delay."[34] Rothstein also had letters, documents, and other data in steel filing cabinet drawers at his home at 912 Fifth Avenue that had been removed. The NYPD was aware that he was involved in drug trafficking but never pinned down his role. In 1921 drug squad agents began shadowing Rothstein, according to Sara Graham Mulhall, deputy commissioner of the New York State Department of Narcotic Control. "Much evidence [was] gathered against him but it [was] difficult to find anything conclusive," Mulhall said.[35] She didn't disclose this until after Rothstein's slaying.

The U.S. attorney for the Southern District, Charles H. Tuttle, wanted a look at the records Banton was given but wasn't quick enough. Tuttle had succeeded the highly respected Emory R. Buckner in April 1927 and had been on Rothstein's drug trail since late 1927, when agents in the Manhattan office of the federal Narcotic Division heard that an unusually large amount of drugs had been smuggled into the United States by traffickers with headquarters in France, Holland, and Belgium. Three agents in the office, Louis J. Kelly, James R. Kerrigan, and Thomas McGuire, began working the case. In tracing the shipment, the trio came to believe that one group controlled drug smuggling in the city and that Rothstein was one of its principals. Days after his murder, they learned that another shipment of drugs had reached the city and even knew the identities of some of the principals. They got one of their sources to cough up a name: Rothmere, which turned out to be the Rothmere Mortgage Corporation, one of many corporate identities Rothstein operated under in a building at 45 West Fifty-seventh Street.

On Thursday, December 6, exactly one month after Rothstein died, Assistant U.S. Attorney John M. Blake obtained a warrant to search Rothmere's offices. Blake, Kelly, Kerrigan, McGuire, and a fourth agent, Ray Connally, went there and couldn't believe their good fortune. In the files they found ten folders containing the names of people involved in Rothstein's drug ring, along with a wealth of information about their activities. They had struck the mother lode: Rothmere was the front for Rothstein's drug trafficking. Indeed, what they found in the files was so explosive that it required them to move immediately.

The name Joseph Unger, age forty-six, had popped up in the files. The agents found he was staying at a midtown hotel. Quickly putting a tail on him, they learned he'd been in touch with a thirty-year-old beautician in Chicago named June Boyd. On Friday afternoon, December 7, they watched as two large steamer trunks were taken from the hotel to Grand Central Terminal. Two of the agents stationed themselves in the baggage room and stood within ten feet of Unger when he walked up and ordered the trunks placed in the baggage car of the Chicago-bound Twentieth Century Limited. Moments before the train pulled out, they ran to the baggage car, flashed badges, and pulled the two trunks onto the platform. Inside was an estimated $2 million ($34 million in 1990 dollars) in narcotics.

Several hours later, the agents ordered the Limited to stop just before it reached Buffalo and arrested Unger. At the same time, agents in the Chicago bureau went to the Hotel North Sheridan, arrested June Boyd, and confiscated a trunk containing an estimated $1 million ($17 million in 1990 dollars) in narcotics. She was charged with being the representative of Rothstein's drug ring in Chicago. Two other people also were arrested: Mrs. Esther Meyers, a lingerie manufacturer, and Samuel "Crying Sammy" Lowe, who had a long sheet of drug violations.

Tuttle wasted little time in breaking this bombshell. On Saturday, December 8, he called a press conference to announce the seizures, declaring, "It was the biggest single raid on a narcotic ring in the history of this country."[36] He set off a stick of political dynamite, too, by using his press conference to bare the machinations among Tammany pols; Banton, the district attorney since 1921; and the NYPD on the Rothstein files. Tuttle had been trying for a month to get the files, sitting and stewing as he watched Banton stall and maneuver. On November 14 Banton said, "his search of the papers had yielded a goldmine of pertinent information" but gave no details.[37] On November 21 Banton said, "the press of other duties was forcing him to assign the search of the papers to two of his assistants, and a police lieutenant, Richard Oliver."[38] On November 22 Banton changed his mind, declaring that a search "promised little" and would be a "dreary and onerous task" that would take "many, many weeks" and that he couldn't spare his two assistants from their regular tasks. As for the papers, Banton "was releasing them to attorneys who represented the different claimants to the Rothstein estate," one of whom was Nathan Burkan, a Tammany district leader.[39] This was like handing the keys to the neighborhood bank to a ring of safecrackers.

At that, Tuttle obtained a court order to go through the papers. John Blake and another assistant U.S. attorney, Alvin McK. Sylvester, went to Burkan's office. Leo Katcher described what happened next: "Burkan informed the court that they had, somehow, disappeared. They were, he swore, either lost or stolen. Filing case, ledgers, books—all gone!"[40] That finished Tuttle's trust in Joab Banton. Blake and Sylvester began building a case for a search warrant. On December 6 Blake obtained an order to descend on the Rothmere Mortgage Company, where he and the drug agents found the mother lode.

Now, at his Saturday press conference, it was payback time. "The local police and District Attorney Banton," Tuttle said, "had no part in uncovering the information about the drug conspiracy from the Rothstein secret files or aided in bringing about the arrests." He also revealed he was getting another court order on Monday allowing him to see other Rothstein papers a federal grand jury had impounded.

George McManus had turned himself in on November 27, twenty-four days after Rothstein died. In that span, controversy had been building over the NYPD's handling of the case. On December 4, the *New York Times* reported that Police Commissioner Joseph A. Warren would "tender his resignation" to Mayor Walker because of "the seemingly unsatisfactory work of the police in the case" and would do so after McManus was indicted in Rothstein's murder. The next day, December 5, a grand jury indicted McManus, Hyman "Gillie" Biller, his payoff man, and two unnamed individuals called "John Doe" and "Richard Roe" on first-degree murder charges.

A few hours later, with the press gathered in his office, District Attorney Banton was luminous: "We have an airtight case in this Rothstein murder. . . . The only thing that now remains is the work of preparation for the trial, which is not far off. . . . There is no doubt in my mind that Rothstein was lured to the Park Central Hotel and then killed in cold blood, and that the four men now under indictment were participants in that murder. . . . I think the shooting took place in McManus's room in the hotel but that doesn't preclude our obtaining more definite information later for use at the trial."

A reporter asked him if he had evidence on who fired the fatal shot. "I prefer not to answer until the trial," he replied. "The police have done hard work in this case and they have been conscientious in what they have done."[41] Banton was right about that. It was Jimmy Hines, not the NYPD, who had McManus spirited from the murder scene. But in Tammany's arena, the NYPD had to operate within the machinery of consequences. In Mayor Beau James's first term, Police Commissioner George V. McLaughlin set up a squad to crack down on gambling in Tammany clubhouses, headed by a cop who would become a legend: Lewis J. Valentine. Angered by McLaughlin's action, Beau James replaced him with his former law partner, Joseph Warren, "who could be trusted not to interfere."[42] Now, Warren was taking the fall.

A few days after a leading Republican, W. Kingsland Macy, sent a letter to every GOP state legislator calling for an investigation of the NYPD and recommending Emory Buckner, the former U.S. attorney for the Southern District who prosecuted Harry Daugherty, as the inquiry's counsel. Beau James named Grover Aloysius Whalen, the general manager of Wanamaker's and New York City's official greeter, as the police commissioner. Eighteen months before, in a memorable moment for the nation, Charles Lindbergh, back from Paris after his historic transatlantic flight, rode down Broadway to a blizzard of ticker tape, confetti, and the cheers of onlookers. Sitting in the open roadster with Lindbergh were Beau James and Grover Whalen.

Tall in stature, Whalen had "the perfect teeth of an aluminum comb," wore a magnificent waxed mustache, a homburg tilted at a rakish angle, and a gardenia in his lapel. His flashy personality and expensive wardrobe had detractors. One wag said he's "as handsome a figure as ever nodded from the waist."[43] He was, however, an old hand at Tammany's ways. In taking over the nation's biggest police department he didn't have a thimble of police experience (neither did Warren). One of his first statements was, "I want to have every underworld crook have it impressed on him that New York is an unhealthy place in which to remain."[44] But Whalen did know his way around Tammany and its history of interfering with the NYPD. Much of the mayor's power rested with his control of that force. Whalen laid down six impressive conditions under which he'd take the job. They included no interference by Beau James in "appointments, transfers or promotion"; no encumbrance of crackdowns on gambling (Whalen specifically mentioned Tammany clubhouses); and allowance of demotions of any police officer who got his job through political pull.[45] To his surprise, Beau James accepted all the conditions.

On Monday, November 18, 1929, two weeks short of a year since Rothstein's slaying, George McManus went on trial. Both sides knew the case was weak. McManus still wouldn't talk. "Gillie" Biller, his "pay-off man," had skipped town after his indictment and was believed to be in Havana, Cuba. Biller knew more than anybody, except McManus, about that night at the Park Central Hotel. The NYPD sent Detective Sgt. James Garvey to Cuba to find him—without success.

McManus had hired one of the city's top barristers, James D. C. Murray, a New York Law School alumnus who began his practice in 1929 at age twenty-nine. Leo Katcher called him "brilliant and sardonic."[46] Banton countered with his senior criminal prosecutor, bespectacled George N. Brothers, an urbane, quietly mannered, nineteen-year veteran who started out as an assistant district attorney in 1910 under the famed Charles Whitman. Over his career, Brothers had handled close to 1,500 homicide cases and in recent years had been assigned a large share of the high-profile cases.

At trial, one of the most interesting revelations came in the testimony of Al Scher, the cashier at Lindy's the night Rothstein got a phone call between 9:00 and 10:00 from McManus to come to the Park Central Hotel, where he was fatally shot. Asked by Brothers to describe what happened, Scher, "youthful, pale and nervous" testified: "The party wanted to speak to Arnold Rothstein. I said the 'party's' not in. I said would the party care to leave a message, I'd take it, if so. The party said it was George McManus."

After Brothers finished, Murray got up and asked Scher, "This voice over the phone, did you recognize it as the voice of this defendant, George A. McManus?"

"No, I did not," replied Scher.

"If it had been the voice of George McManus, you would have recognized it, wouldn't you?"

"Yes."

"It was the voice of McManus, was it?"

"No, it was not."[47]

Nor did the NYPD help the prosecution's case. After a departmental trial, Patrolman Patrick Flood and Joseph Daly, a first-grade detective and twenty-six-year veteran, were demoted by Police Commissioner Whalen for their work on the case. Flood testified at trial that no superior officer appeared at the scene until four hours after Rothstein was shot. In addition, John F. Cordes, a detective with three honor medals for courage, was demoted because he failed to fingerprint McManus upon his arrest. The end came when Bridget Farry swore—under questioning from Murray and looking directly at McManus from the stand—that McManus wasn't the man she had seen in Room 349 on the night Rothstein was shot. Farry, the maid on duty on the third floor who had identified McManus as being in Room 349, had also said that between 10:20 and 10:30 McManus left the room and didn't return. McManus's hand-tailored Chesterfield overcoat with his name embroidered in the lining was found in 349.

On Thursday morning, December 5, Murray asked Judge Charles C. Nott Jr. for a directed verdict of acquittal "on the ground that the People failed to make out a case." George Brothers stood up, looked back at the clock on the wall and sidelong at the jury, and spoke: "When we started this prosecution it was based upon evidence which has not been forthcoming. From the beginning of this trial until we rested the People's case, with very few exceptions, witnesses were hostile. . . . It was apparent that they did not tell the truth. We have done our best. We fought against odds which we would not overcome."

Answering Brothers, Judge Nott agreed, declaring, "In my opinion, many of the witnesses, in fact most of the witnesses on the material matters, were hostile, and many of them, in my opinion, have demonstrated on the stand there that they have no appreciation whatever of an oath . . . the law governing all cases of circumstantial evidence is reasonable and simple, and can be stated in terms that anybody can understand, but under that law it is not sufficient to prove that a man might have done an act or that he could have done an act. It is necessary to prove that he must have done the act; that under no reasonable hypothesis could anybody else have done it."[48]

Upon finishing, Nott directed a verdict of acquittal. Said Commissioner Whalen, "The failure to present incontrovertible evidence sufficient for a conviction was due entirely to the laxity of the police who had been assigned to the case originally and to the commanding officers of the detective and uniformed forces at the time of the murder."[49] Rothstein's slayer was never found. The case is still marked "open" in the NYPD files.

■

When Rothstein went down, so did his racketeering empire, a point recognized and seized upon by two of his former colleagues, Charlie Luciano and Frank Costello. While Tammany pols scattered for cover, Luciano and Costello used the occasion to host a national gathering of their underworld associates from around the country at Atlantic City. It was held at the Hotel President from Monday, May 13 to Thursday, May 16, 1929, six months and one week after Rothstein's death. Costello shelled out $25,000 ($425,000 in 1990 dollars) of his own money for the accommodations.

It was not the first crime conference. The previous December, a contingent of twenty-seven mafiosi gathered at the Hotel Statler in Cleveland, including New Yorkers Joseph Profaci, thirty-two; Vincent "Ace" Mangano, forty; and Buffalo's Joseph Magliocco, thirty, all future family dons, along with representatives from Newark; Gary, Indiana; St. Louis; and Tampa. As a non-Sicilian, Al Capone wanted to participate but couldn't. An ally, Pasquale "Patsy" Lolordo, the head of Chicago's Unione Siciliane, came. The meeting backfired when the hotel's desk clerk, who didn't like the attendees' dark, somber looks, called the police. They were arrested, booked, and questioned but remained mum, and the police had to let them go.

There would be no interruptions in Atlantic City. The seaside town with its famous boardwalk was run by Enoch L. "Nucky" Johnson, a partner with Luciano in rum-running who "provided each delegate's wife or girlfriend with a fur cape, his personal gift." The crime summit was about carving up Rothstein's empire. In *The Big Bankroll* in 1958, Katcher described how it divided up Rothstein's "hidden assets." Luciano and Louis Lepke took over drug trafficking. At his death, Rothstein had at least $2 million ($34 million in 1990 dollars) tied up in drug deals. On the day he was shot, Luciano showed up at Rothstein's office to check on the whereabouts of the different caches of narcotics. Police questioned him and let him go; he told them he was a waiter. Always up to his nodding eyelids in drug trafficking, Luciano was first arrested for a drug violation in April 1916, a few months before his nineteenth birthday. Frank Erickson, "a beefy, red-faced Scandinavian" who had handled Rothstein's high-level bookmaking business (dealing with big-stakes bettors such as movie mogul Harry Cohn), took over the biggest prize—gambling.[50] He would work hand in hand with Costello, who had a knack for picking the right man; "Dandy Phil" Kastel partnered with him in the 1930s in Huey Long's Louisiana. The last slice of Rothstein's empire, the labor rackets, "what Rothstein still had of it," went to Lepke, who had carried out thuggery for Rothstein in the garment strikes of 1919–1920.[51] New York City, able to draw on cheap labor from the immigration wave at the turn of the century, was the world's garment center, a racketeer's paradise encompassing an area three blocks wide by ten blocks long in the middle of Manhattan and grossing a billion dollars a year in the 1920s. This pie-slicing occurred with little discomfort, along with another issue—bootlegging.

According to Leo Katcher, Luciano was running a bootlegging alliance called Group Seven, which controlled key areas of the Northeast. As Katcher notes, by 1924 "the business of breaking the prohibition law had shaken down," eliminating individual operators and small-timers as the underworld became more organized.[52] By 1928 Group Seven "had struck cooperative alliances—for buying, selling, distilling, shipping and protecting [whiskey]—with twenty-two different mobs from Maine to Florida and west to the Mississippi River."[53] It was made up of Meyer Lansky and Bugsy Siegel in New York; Joe Adonis in Brooklyn; Abner "Longy" Zwillman (later known as the "Al Capone of New Jersey"), and Willie Moretti in Nassau County (in western Long Island), and northern New Jersey (including Newark, Jersey City, and Fort Lee); Waxey Gordon, Nig Rosen, and Bitsy Bitz in Philadelphia; Charles "King" Solomon in Boston (he ruled much of New England); and Nucky Johnson in Atlantic City (southern New Jersey). Luciano and Costello, along with Johnny Torrio, who had partnered up with them, represented the seventh grouping. Torrio, Al Capone's mentor, had laid low after his near-death encounter in Chicago, taking a long sojourn to Italy with his wife. Racketeering, however, was in his DNA. After settling in New York City, where he got his start in the rackets, Torrio linked up with Dutch Schultz in a bail bond enterprise, the Greater City Surety and Indemnity Company, of which they owned two-thirds. With racketeering at its zenith and no strong watch on shady bail bondsmen, it was highly profitable. The two were in a "dandy position to corner the market," writer

Paul Sann observed, "since they happened to be so well acquainted among the people in town who needed bail the most." The market was huge. In January 1930 a federal grand jury under Charles Tuttle handed up a presentment noting that $50 million ($850 million in 1990 dollars) in bail bonds were written yearly in New York City, from which "policemen and attaches of the magistrates' courts reap a rich harvest of 'tribute.'"[54]

According to Tony Sciacca, Torrio, still into bootlegging, wanted to expand his riches. He felt the safest way to do this was through a confederation. This had worked grandly in Chicago, and he wanted to import the idea to the East Coast. Torrio took his idea to Luciano at the posh Barbizon Plaza suite where he lived under the name "Charles Reid." "He looked like a businessman, and behaved as sedately as the most cultured executive," wrote Sciacca.[55] It was a propitious time.

In late 1928 the sinking of a liquor-laden freighter off Cape Hatteras, along with a series of hijackings, conspired to wipe out the Group Seven's inventory of scotch. And none other than Luciano had fallen prey to a hijacking, which arose from a deal he'd made with a Chicagoan named Samuel Bloom, a friend of Rothstein, to import King's Ransom scotch from a distillery in Scotland. King's Ransom was highly valued—its heavy, smoky quality made it easy for bootleggers to dilute without losing its flavor. The deal between Bloom and Luciano involved a shipment of 15,000 cases of King's Ransom that landed in Boston and was loaded on trucks headed to New York. The scotch never arrived. Luciano found out Bloom lost $100,000 ($1.7 million in 1990 dollars) in a Rothstein poker game; had given the gambler his IOU, payable in a week; and then had paid up— the day after the hijacking. For his betrayal, Bloom disappeared, no doubt given a cement funeral and dumped in a river.

Now, Luciano not only bought Torrio's idea that a confederation was a way to overcome these problems, he also put it into play. Torrio's plan was accepted by the crime summit. Group Seven set up a "national headquarters" at the Hotel Belvedere on West Forty-eighth Street in Manhattan, managed by Frank Zagarino, "an old-timer" who was close to Torrio, according to Craig Thompson and Allen Raymond.[56] Among other things, it set the prices to be charged along with volume to be imported. The quota for the New York group was fixed at 50,000 cases a month.

Members of Group Seven showed up in Atlantic City, along with other Luciano associates, including Albert Anastasia, Frank Scalise, and Vincent "Ace" Mangano, all of whom operated in Brooklyn. The Jewish faction included Lepke and Dutch Schultz from New York; Morris "Moe" Dalitz and Louis Rothkopf of Cleveland's Mayfield Road gang; Max "Boo Boo" Hoff of Philadelphia; Abe Bernstein and his delegation of Detroit's Purple Gang; Kansas City's top racketeer, John Lazia, a confederate of Thomas J. "Boss" Pendergast; and Cleveland's Chuck Polizzi. Al Capone came with his twenty-three-year-old bodyguard Tony Accardo, and financial mastermind Jake Guzik. Taking credit for the summit, he defined its theme in one of the great sound bites of the day: "I told them there was business enough to make us all rich and it was time to stop all the killings and look on our business as other men look on theirs, as something to work at and forget when you go home at night. It wasn't an easy matter for men who had been fighting for years to agree on a peaceful business program. But we finally decided to forget the past and began all over again and we drew up a written agreement and each man signed on the dotted line."[57]

The Rothstein and Torrio problems were flourishes compared to two other and more commanding issues swirling at the summit. One involved pudgy Joseph "The Boss" Masseria, fifty-one, and regal Salvatore Maranzano, sixty-three, who had a "Julius Caesar complex," as Joe Valachi called it. The two were unyielding, old-style elders and rivals who had been running the New York brethren for years, and who now were heavy with discontent. Maranzano and Masseria weren't invited to the Atlantic City summit and were deeply offended. The younger elements—the Young Turks, of whom Luciano was the leader—looked upon them derisively as "Mustache Petes" who had outlived their usefulness and stood in the way of their ambitions. "Masseria's a fat old bastard and we don't need him," observed Bugsy Siegel.[58] The Italian and Sicilian racketeers at the crime summit, with few exceptions, were younger men who would populate the underworld for decades to come. The problem, likely decided privately by a nod from those mafiosi Luciano sounded out, was, What to do with the "Mustache Petes?" It would come down to a matter of picking the right time.

The other commanding issue involved Capone. Uneasiness existed among many at the summit about him. There had always been an edgy peace between the New York brethren and Capone, who wanted to be a part of the Sicilian tradition, then represented by the Unione Siciliane. The Unione began as a legitimate fraternal association to aid Sicilian immigrants in the new country; by the mid-1920s it had turned into a front for criminal activity, none more so than the Chicago chapter, the country's biggest with 6,000 members. Casting an eye at those numbers, Capone did all he could to control the chapter, making Frank Nitti his chief link to the Unione. Disapproving of Capone's involvement in prostitution, Masseria blocked his entry into New York's circle. Maranzano, who considered himself the titular head of New York's Mafia, had no such qualms and was out to build an accord with Capone.

To the Young Turks, Capone was bad news. Racketeering was growing and so was violence—personified by Capone. The killings had been piling up, most notable, aside from Rothstein's in November 1928, the St. Valentine's Day massacre in February 1929, and the slaying of racketeer Frank "Yale" Uale on a Manhattan street in July 1928, five months before Rothstein was slain. Capone of course was responsible for the latter two. The St. Valentine's massacre grabbed national headlines, but it was Yale's slaying that really got the New Yorkers' attention. Yale had mentored Capone after hiring him as a bouncer/bartender in his Coney Island saloon. At the time of his murder, Yale headed the Unione Siciliane and wanted Joseph Aiello as the president of Chicago's Unione Siciliane's chapter. This was enough to make Capone choke on his pasta. He had no enemy bigger than Aiello, not even Bugs Moran, whom he had tried to wipe out on St. Valentine's Day, ninety days before the Atlantic City summit.

Laurence Bergreen wrote that Capone's "jealous rivals, especially from New York, had conspired to transfer control of the Chicago organization from his trigger-happy hands to Johnny Torrio's steadier grip."[59] It was evident to the New York brethren at the summit that Capone had ordered Yale's slaying. If he could rub out Yale, nobody was safe. He had come into their territory and taken down one of the city's ranking underworld figures. In contrast, they couldn't step foot in Chicago without Capone's approval.

Chicago was a burial ground for out-of-town button men. Capone was just bad news. Just six days before the summit, he had taken a baseball bat to three Sicilians—Albert Anselmi, John Scalise, and Joseph Giunta, a close associate of Aiello's—whom he thought had double-crossed him. Dr. Frances McNamara, the Cook County jail physician for thirty years, said the punishment inflicted on the trio was unparalleled in his experience. Anselmi and Scalise were cop killers freed by an appeals court; Giunta headed the Unione Siciliane's Chicago chapter.

The summit's burning question over what to do about Capone was handed to Torrio. In their sit-down, according to Tony Sciacca, Torrio told Capone he should leave Chicago "for a time and turn his gang over to cooler heads who would be able to negotiate in good faith." This "first step toward peace" would require Capone "to spend a little time in prison to eliminate the abrasion—Capone himself."[60] All Torrio had to do was outline the facts, murderous and otherwise. Inside of a year, at least fifteen persons connected to Capone had died violently. Irey's SIU was after him. The Thompson machine was facing defeat, and a new city hall was bent on reform. In New York City, where Capone had important connections, Beau James was up for reelection, and the murder of Arnold Rothstein had resulted in shining the heat of a thousand suns on Tammany, including the launching of an investigation of the magistrates court, headed by one of the city's most distinguished lawyers, Samuel Seabury. Torrio was persuasive enough that Capone drove to Philadelphia on Friday, May 17, where he had arranged through a contact to be taken into custody. Two Philadelphia detectives met him as he and his bodyguard left a motion picture theater. Capone handed over his .38 revolver and was placed under arrest on a charge of concealing a deadly weapon. The next morning he was indicted, taken to court less than two hours later, sentenced to a year's incarceration, and sent off to Holmesburg. The next morning, a Sunday, the *Chicago Tribune* streamed in bold type on its front page: "Quaker Justice in Jig Time." Tony Sciacca noted that New York's "wise guys whispered that Luciano, Costello, and their organization were so powerful that they could do what no cop had ever done before—send Capone to jail for the first time in his life."

In particular, Luciano and the New York brethren departed Atlantic City in friendly spirits, their confidence buoyed in knowing a bright future lay ahead for them, even as the Great Depression was building steam. Six weeks before, on March 26, the New York Stock Exchange had seen the biggest stampede of selling in its history. In a national economy headed for the rocks, however, Mafiosi and Jewish racketeers weren't going to be the suffering class. Amid the fellowship and clinking of glass at Atlantic City, it required a few careful words and a knowing nod to reach an understanding. With a minimum of gestures, they had struck mutuality. The outlook was business as usual. And why not? For racketeers, this was the Golden Age. They weren't looking at a downturn; they were looking ahead. Furthermore, they knew Prohibition would end. And when it did, they would turn to depression-proof schemes—such as gambling—that would become their principal sources of income.

Al Capone had left them an inescapable lesson: The limelight could prove your undoing, or stealth is wealth. While most of the racketeers at Atlantic City were walking land mines, they weren't about to conduct open season on their enemies, as Capone did regularly. The New York element, in particular, took to heart Capone's remarks that there was "business enough to make us all rich" and began in earnest to conduct open season on the consuming public in the nation's biggest and wealthiest metropolis. Racketeering underlay their existence. The imperative was to maintain peace and anonymity within the territorial divide. With such an aim, the future looked rosy—and certainly was—for the changing underworld order.

11. WHERE ORGANIZED CRIME REALLY REIGNED

This was the criminal setting Elmer Irey found himself in on that April 1931 day he sat down with George Medalie and Tom Dewey to plan a drive against New York's racketeers. Neither he, nor Medalie, nor Dewey, nor the federal constabulary, nor the NYPD had but the scantiest knowledge of the underworld's key figures, and in particular, the struggle to the death between the Young Turks and the Mustache Petes that had come out of Atlantic City's 1929 crime summit, the gathering that would bring a new Mafia order into being.

The rolling thunder from Arnold Rothstein's slaying twenty-nine months before was still resounding in New York City's political life. Along with the sensational revelations and cover-ups, it had sparked an Albany-launched investigation—the Seabury hearings, which not only revealed that under Tammany Hall's embrace, no city's governance was more corrupt, but also would end Mayor "Beau James" Walker's political career. In addition, U.S. Attorney Tuttle's long inquiry into Rothstein's involvement in drug trafficking enmeshed the Manhattan bureau of the Treasury's Narcotics Division in scandal, resulting in the reorganization of the ten-year-old division into the Federal Bureau of Narcotics and the appointment of Harry J. Anslinger as its commissioner.

For Irey, it was going to be markedly different from Chicago, which had occupied him for the last two and a half years. Though marked by Capone's destructive image, Chicago's reputation as the pinnacle of crime and corruption was misleading. The Windy City didn't have the modifying climate of an unmatched political machine like Tammany Hall. Across the entire constellation of crime, whether in racketeering, drug trafficking, political corruption, or providing a surfeit of clever criminal combatants, no city offered the abundance of political squalor and organized crime that New York's five boroughs did. Edward Dean Sullivan was critical of the way the city treated its criminals, particularly Rothstein. In his view, "the New York method" was to cover up its dirty linen as opposed to the Chicago system of publicizing its own bad reputation. "In Chicago," he wrote, "the crime reporters, urged on by an unquestioned public interest in the feuds, exploits and murders of the gangs, would have known and set forth for months the associations, enmities and activities of Rothstein."[1] New York, of course, did not have a group like the Chicago Crime Commission, which regularly issued a list of that city's public enemies.

As Irey was shaping his drive against racketeers, the Mafia order was undergoing a marked change, an outgrowth of Atlantic City's crime summit. On Wednesday, April 15, thirteen days after Irey arrived, Joe the Boss Masseria and Charlie Luciano drove to Coney Island in Masseria's steel-armored sedan, with plate-glass windows an inch thick, for lunch at the Nuovo Villa Tammaro restaurant, owned by a friend of Masseria's. After lunch was over, and those at the table had left, Luciano and Masseria began playing cards. Luciano excused himself to go to the men's room; gunmen appeared and rubbed out Masseria. The NYPD found five bullets in him.

In early May, a few weeks after Masseria was slain, Salvatore Maranzano called a meeting of the family factions at a resort near Wappingers Falls, south of Poughkeepsie. Maranzano lived on Avenue J in Brooklyn and had a farm in the small town. With Masseria gone, he had become the *Capo di Tutti Capi* (Boss of Bosses), and once and for all sought to settle the feuding between Mafia elements. With Masseria out of the way, Maranzano used the Wappingers Falls gathering to realign the Mafia order. Next, he arranged a meeting with Al Capone at the Congress Hotel in Chicago as his territorial peace offering to the country's most well-known criminal name.

According to Joseph Bonnano, the gathering was the Mafia's first national conference, and it was attended by a "few hundred people." An up-and-coming mafioso who had entered the United States illegally from Cuba in 1924, twenty-six-year-old Bonnano had been asked by Maranzano to accompany him to Chicago, along with his cousin, Stefano Magaddino, and John Montana, a Magaddino confederate. Bonnano called himself "the chief aide of the victorious general" and noted that a pleased Capone sent Maranzano "a gold watch studded with diamonds." One of Maranzano's loyal soldiers, incidentally, was a twenty-two-year-old named Joseph Valachi.

Now, exactly two years after Atlantic City, the first accord between New York's Five Families and the Capone syndicate was put in place at the Congress Hotel—and by a Mustache Pete, Maranzano. Charlie Luciano was there, accompanied by Meyer Lansky. Because Lansky was Jewish, Luciano had to obtain Maranzano's permission to bring him. Maranzano despised Jews, but Luciano did get permission, except that Lansky would not be allowed into the meetings even though Capone would. For Capone, Maranzano had, with his Julius Caesar complex, set aside the requirements of Sicilian heritage—since this was a gathering, as Bonnano explained, "to allow everyone to identify himself within the new political constellation in our world."[2]

Bonnano put the accord this way: "Maranzano would affirm Capone's place in Chicago and Capone would affirm Maranzano's supremacy in the national scene." The pact was the culmination of three years of effort by Capone and Mafia factions to come together—five months before Capone would go to prison. For his part, Maranzano used the gathering as homage to Capone and a way of solidifying the new family structure he had established. Actually, this merely set the stage, and smoothed the way, for the Young Turks, led by Luciano, to take over the New York Mafia.

At approximately 3:45 p.m., on Thursday, September 10, four men, posing as federal agents, walked into Maranzano's suite of offices on the ninth floor of the Grand Central Building on Park Avenue. They lined the six men in the outer office, along with Maranzano's secretary, Grace Samuels, against a wall. Maranzano had come out of his office to greet them. Two of the hit men ordered him back to his office, where they drew knives and began slashing him. Maranzano fought back, crying out, and striking back with his arms. His killers pulled out their pistols and began firing. The NYPD found the Mafia's Boss of Bosses laying across his desk, stabbed six times, his throat cut, and four bullet wounds in his head and body.

Luciano had ordered the killing; Lansky carried it out. Recounted in *The Last Testament*, the lengthy preparations that led up to Maranzano's demise and that took four months from the date of Masseria's rubout on Coney Island, revealed in clear fashion the ruthless and immensely devious enemy that the realm of law and order now faced.

Lansky had brought in three gunsels from out of town, picked Red Levine (Luciano's longtime aide) to head the murder squad; rented a house in the Bronx for the four; gave them "a crash course in the characteristic behavior of federal tax agents";[3] persuaded Thomas Lucchese, Luciano's "closest friend," to be the finger man in Maranzano's office;[4] and ensured the plan by arranging with Maranzano to meet Luciano in his office on September 10 to discuss "pressing matters." Maranzano already was "under investigation for bootlegging, alien-smuggling, tax evasion and a variety of other matters," and his lawyers had told him that government agents "might make a surprise visit, and if they did, he should be cooperative." Maranzano "readily identified himself" to the four confident-looking, well-dressed government "agents" when they walked in and asked to see him. After one of the killers "noticed a quick, almost imperceptible nod" from Lucchese, the four moved quickly, drawing their guns. The five other men, Maranzano's bodyguards, caught completely off-guard, were easily disarmed. Two of the killers marched Maranzano into his office and carried out the plan. It was over in minutes. Lucchese "remained behind momentarily, looking into the inner office to make certain Maranzano was dead." The five bodyguards had rushed out, "not to give chase but in fear of being found in the office with Maranzano's corpse."[5]

■

With that, Luciano had the extraordinary benefit of stepping into a perfect organizational setting, composed of the Five Families, which Maranzano had put together in deft fashion starting with the Wappingers Falls gathering, during the last six months of his life. Under Luciano, the

Five Families again realigned. The consolidation of power among New York City's Sicilians had begun in the late 1920s, resulting in the formation of the Five Mafia Families. The number of families "was formed spontaneously," Bonnano noted, as Sicilian immigrants settled in the city.[6] As Bonnano explained, "The number five was not preordained; it just worked out that way." The Five Families and the dons, under Maranzano's original decree at the Wappingers Falls gathering, along with Luciano's changes, were as follows:

1. Luciano family—Charles Luciano, under Maranzano's original decree, born in Lercara Friddi, Sicily, on November 24, 1897, took over the Masseria family with Frank Costello and Vito Genovese as underbosses and Manhattan as their base. Now the *Capo di Tutti Capi*, he was the preeminent figure in New York City's underworld.

2. Gagliano family—Gaetano Gagliano, born in Sicily about 1888, who had been the underboss to slain gang chief Thomas Reina, assumed control of Reina's family, which operated in the Bronx. Masseria's henchmen had killed Reina, and this in part led to Masseria's downfall. Gagliano's underboss was Thomas "Three Fingers" Lucchese.

3. Mangano family—The brothers Vincent "Ace," born in Sicily on March 28, 1888, and Philip Mangano took over the Mineo family, headed by Frank Scalise. Scalise was deemed "too close" to Maranzano and had to step down. The brothers, with Vincent having the final say, controlled the rackets in the Brownsville section of Brooklyn, including parts of the waterfront. The underboss was Alfred Anastasia.

4. Profaci family—Joseph Profaci, born in Villabate, Sicily, on October 2, 1897, was an ally of Maranzano. His family was split between Profaci and Joseph Bonnano. The Profaci family operated in the Bay Ridge section of Brooklyn and Staten Island.

5. Bonnano family—Born in Castellammare del Golfo, Sicily, Joseph Bonnano carved out the Williamsburg section of Brooklyn and the Bronx at age twenty-six. He would shape himself in the mold of Maranzano with his Caesar complex. Over the years, Bonnano would barely contain his disdain for Luciano. His cousin, Stefano Magaddino, would head the family in Buffalo.

Theirs was a leadership of relatively young, disciplined men who came of age during a tumultuous and failed national experiment. Bonnano was the youngest; Costello, at forty, the oldest. The Five Families would develop coast-to-coast links with other mafiosi and connive endlessly to extort, build rackets, and secretly entwine legitimate business enterprises. At every opportunity, the Five Families sought to take control of a share of the commercial life of New York and New Jersey. They dominated the equally rewarding underworld of narcotics trafficking and organized vice such as prostitution and pornography, extortion, loan-sharking, and thievery in a range of wholesale markets. They corrupted labor unions. They established business associations as fronts to force businessmen to pay tribute for protection. They bribed servants of the legislative, judicial, and executive branches at the local, state, and federal levels.

They were also tolerant of other power bases, the most important being Joe Adonis's operation in Brooklyn. A Neapolitan who smartly kept out of the limelight, Adonis became the most influential racketeer outside of the Mafia—more powerful even than the Jewish racketeers, Waxey Gordon, Dutch Schultz, and Louis Lepke.

Hollywood couldn't have scripted it better. The Five Families became the base of the American Mafia. Each served on a Luciano-created national commission to oversee the rackets, ratify decisions, and resolve problems arising from their criminal activity. The original commission included Al Capone and Frank Milano of Cleveland, a power in the Silent Syndicate, which ruled that city's underworld. The term "Silent Syndicate" was coined by crime historian Hank Messick and was first known as the Mayfield Road Gang. Milano ran a saloon and social headquarters at 12601 Mayfield Road. Ace Mangano chaired the national commission. By no means was this a commission that conspired to centrally control all decision-making on a nationwide basis. The dons had regal powers within a certain territory inside New York City, and they exchanged favors with groupings in various cities. They were never a national crime syndicate, nor a national governing body. They couldn't begin to extend their power nationally. No criminal conspiracy has ever exercised that kind of power. This was a belief driven by ignorance largely because the Mafia structure wasn't yet understood, much less known. The dons knew there were inherent restrictions to power. They placed limitations on their plunder, not because of a lack of greed, but out of an understanding of the dangers they faced if they encroached on another don's authority or territory. To avoid this, they agreed to give cities such as Miami and Las Vegas autonomy so that any don could operate a racket in them.

The phantom-like dons were clever emperors who kept a discreet silence; they gave new meaning to the word "circumspect." They knew if they didn't secretly work for their common greed, they'd destroy what they had built. The commission's members were committed to resolving family disputes, making territorial decisions about rackets, and sharing the cut. They networked ways to hide their extortions and share their plunder. Inside the commission, with Capone gone, Luciano's personal prowess made him the most influential partner. He had the devotion of Meyer Lansky and Frank Costello—partners since youth. Lansky's trustworthiness and merciless judgment gave life to the Mafia. Costello's considerable wealth and coolly persuasive, diplomatic style enhanced the criminal elite.

■

With the coming of the Five Mafia Families, a new and powerful element now ruled New York City's underworld. Their names and allegiances would remain a mystery for decades to law enforcement.

In addition, Edward Dean Sullivan's assertion about the "New York method" can be understood in the glare of the Masseria and Maranzano assassinations. The NYPD appeared informed on their standing. The day after Luciano's gunsels pumped five bullets into Masseria, the *New York Times* reported: "To hear some of the detectives at Police Headquarters tell it, the killing of Joe the Boss is likely to cause an outbreak of gang warfare that will exceed anything this city ever has known. Some police officers who kept tabs on the racketeer's long career insist that he was 'the biggest of 'em all—bigger than Al Capone.'"[7] Two days after Maranzano was slain, an account said, "Maranzano was known to the police . . . and [Police] Commissioner [Edward] Mulrooney said that information gathered by detectives showed that he may have been one of the 'big shot' racketeers of the country."[8] To place both on a scale with the country's best-known racketeer was a revelation warranting a look by the NYPD, but this didn't happen.

Furthermore, lawmen were not snooping around Atlantic City in May 1929 when virtually every influential racketeer in the country was huddling there. Capone's presence drew tiny interest from New York City's ten dailies. There was a six-inch item in the *New York Times* on May 16, written by a stringer in Atlantic City, reporting that W. S. Cuthbert, the city's public safety director, had ordered the police to pick up Capone if they saw him. (They didn't.) In a gesture to celebrity, the *Evening Journal* of New York carried a picture of Al and Nucky Johnson strolling down the boardwalk together, looking like Mutt and Jeff.

A month after the crime summit, law enforcement was handed valuable intelligence, at no cost. On June 15, 1929, the *Literary Digest* published a lengthy article on Al Capone that was built around the theme that "a new day seems about to dawn in Chicago's gangland" and that included a detailed accounting of the Atlantic City gathering. One of the attendees, apparently pleased by what had been accomplished, had turned over a copy of the remarkable treaty—the "written agreement" that Al Capone and the attendees signed "on the dotted line"—to Robert T. Loughran, a United Press reporter in Chicago. Exactly what was in the document only Loughran knew, and he did not disclose his source. Loughran's article cast Torrio in a favorable light, sparking the belief that he was the source. The *Literary Digest* carried a summation of his dispatch.

According to the article, the fourteen-point agreement included the following: the attendees would suspend all killings and settle all controversies by "an executive committee"; Johnny Torrio would become "the king and chief arbiter of the new syndicate"; Capone would disband "his gang" and relinquish his hold on a range of rackets; Capone would agree on a national head for Unione Siciliane and Torrio would make the appointment; and "everyone" would forget all past grievances, "such as the St. Valentine's Day massacre, and hundreds of other gang violences of the past." Loughran also wrote that Torrio, as the head of the new amalgamation, would single-handedly control between $15 million and $16 million

($225 million to $270 million, in 1990 dollars) annually. The *Literary Digest* helped to perpetuate the theme of Capone as folk hero, unwittingly giving legitimacy to the criminal underworld's actions by drawing celebrity comparisons. As a result of the summit, the article said, "Gunmen will have an executive council and a 'czar,' whose duties will presumably be analogous to those of Judge Landis and Will Hays in the domains of baseball and the movies."[9] Torrio and Luciano, always looking for public acceptance, must have grinned from ear to ear at the analogy.

The *Literary Digest* article did not mention the role of New Yorkers in Atlantic City. The real story was that Capone's star was falling, and Luciano's star was on the rise. New York's dailies, despite their crusading, usually fell short of achieving any fix on the criminal underworld other than what was presented to them. The story the *New York Times* splashed atop its front page on April 3, 1931, about Irey and his special force coming to Manhattan, contained this timely assertion about "the flourishing industry of racketeering." That sentence did spark the sharpening of pencils.

On Sunday, May 17, forty-four days later, the *New York Herald Tribune* launched an eight-part series on racketeering in New York City, where of course it had been growing for years. The series ran daily on the front page through the following Sunday. While a valid effort to expose racketeering, the *Herald Tribune*'s series broke no new ground and was published at the time Capone and Maranzano were meeting at the Congress Hotel in Chicago, an event no New York daily covered. It was written by a star reporter, forty-three-year-old Alva Johnston, a Pulitzer Prize winner in 1923. His articles dealt with racketeering in the flour, building, ice, and grape trades, along with the laundry and milk trades on the city piers, at the Fulton Fish Market in Manhattan and at the Wallabout Market in Brooklyn. In the police courts, he wrote, cases made against racketeers were often "nearly always" dismissed because of the "refusal of the fear-stricken witnesses to testify." Johnston never dropped the names of Dutch Schultz and Waxey Gordon, two racketeering kingpins of the era. When Johnston did drop a name, neither the names nor revelations were exactly new—the foremost being Owen "Owney the Killer" Madden and Joseph "Socks" Lanza, marginal underworld figures who were well known on police blotters. Before he gained a reputation as a bootlegger, the British-born Madden, convicted of a gangster's murder in 1914 and paroled in 1923, had been arrested forty-four times. Socks Lanza was already pretty notorious, by then the longest-lasting racketeer at the Fulton Fish Market. Over a twenty-five-year career, he excelled at escaping prosecution. Johnston did ridicule the "governmental policy" toward racketeers, noting that it "is based on the hope that some day the racketeers will wipe themselves off the face of the earth, as the dinosaurs became extinct by eating one another."[10]

In the 1920s and 30s, the NYPD may have had a bead on Mafia activity in the city, but little if nothing came from it. Lewis J. Valentine held the post of NYPD police commissioner longer than anyone in the twentieth century. Born in March 1882 in Brooklyn's Williamsburg section (known as Irishtown), he became a probationary patrolman in the NYPD in November 1903 at a yearly salary of $800 ($20,800 in 1990 dollars). In October 1904 he married the girl next door, Elizabeth, and with her faithfully supporting him over the next thirty years, he climbed every rung of the police ladder to the very top. He went from probationary patrolman to policeman, sergeant, lieutenant, captain, deputy inspector, inspector, deputy chief inspector, chief inspector, and on September 25, 1934, police commissioner, named to the post by newly elected Mayor Fiorello La Guardia.

In short, Valentine, whom Stanley Walker called "almost painfully honest,"[11] was a law enforcement figure who had pretty much seen it all during his thirty-one-year rise through the ranks, and he knew that the NYPD was "the prize of political contention."[12] He retired on September 14, 1945, having served forty-two years in the NYPD. In Lowell Limpus's 1939 biography of Valentine, the only racketeer mentioned is Charlie Luciano, who was called "the overlord of organized vice" in the city.[13] The word "Mafia" does not appear in Limpus's book. Valentine lived through the early days of New York's Mafia, its deadly struggles, the establishment of the Five Families, and their takeover of the city's underworld. The NYPD was aware of the racketeering that was going on. In spring 1930 the department's annual report, summarized superbly by the *New York Times* on May 18, cited the racketeering that was going on in the laundry, milk, and construction industries, but the NYPD's counterintelligence only went so far.

In Washington, when officialdom did show the will to move toward the changes law enforcement required, the imperfect substructure it put into place did not rise to the challenge. This was illustrated by the Wickersham Commission, headed by seventy-one-year-old George W. Wickersham, the attorney general when the Bureau of Investigation was established in 1909. On May 20, 1929, the Hoover White House announced the formation of the Wickersham Commission (formally known as the National Committee on Law Observation and Enforcement), and eight days later, experts were in place and their tasks assigned. For months, little was disclosed about the commission's work.

Toward the end of 1929, criticism started, centering on "secrecy concerning [the commission's] activities." Members of Congress demanded "it reveal to Congress and the public just what has been happening behind closed doors." George Wickersham, the ultimate professional, wasn't hiding anything of course. He had undertaken a vast, complicated task; characteristically, he was being painstakingly thorough. One of the things going on behind closed doors, besides hard work, was a degree of panic by the commission staff. They couldn't cut the Gordian knot. It had taken from May to Christmas 1929 to get a firm grasp on the enormity of their goal.

On January 10, 1930, a Friday, the White House made public a preliminary report on what had been happening. In a statement accompanying the report, Wickersham proclaimed that the country's law enforcement machinery was "entirely inadequate." Then, instead of laying out some of the reasons why, the preliminary report proceeded to list the names of the various experts involved in the study along with a carefully worded explanation on what each had accomplished in their areas. This shined a light on the myriad troubles the commission's staff encountered—which actually may have been Wickersham's intention.

August Vollmer, a professor at the University of Chicago who once served as chief of police of Berkeley, California, headed the study on police conduct, but he could be "secured" only for the month of September. Vollmer handed in "a preliminary report" in early October "but has been prevented by his duties at the University of Chicago from following it up with the large work of application which the commission has desired him to complete. A further staff is being recruited." To study the federal court system, U.S. district court judges were drafted, including Francis Caffey, the very able U.S. attorney for the Southern District who had worked with Daniel Roper on New York City's narcotics problem. But the commission concluded from the judges' "preliminary studies" that "a far more thorough study of the whole matter should be undertaken." That was shorthand for, "This is bigger than anyone thought." Dr. Hastings H. Hart of the Russell Sage Foundation was enlisted to look at penal institutions, probation, and parole. What happened then? Based on what Hart found, a twenty-member board was put together to make "an exhaustive study." On the subject of crime statistics, the commission staff found statistics "so inadequate as to require study and recommendation of administration or legislative action" that it handed the task to a Harvard professor, Sam Bass Warner.

For the commission's members, there may have been a bigger sore point: no compensation. Toward the end of the preliminary report, there was this comment: "Inasmuch as the members of the Commission are serving without compensation, and as eleven out of the fourteen experts in charge of different investigations are also serving without compensation and are assisted by many others, some of whom are likewise giving their services in the national interest, the expenditure of the commission up to the present time has amounted only to about $70,000" ($1,190,000 in 1990 dollars).[14]

The following Monday, January 13, 1930, the White House sent a lengthy message to Congress. It included two extensive reports of the commission's findings on Prohibition enforcement, along with recommendations from Justice and Treasury on moves to reform aspects of federal law enforcement. They dealt with reorganizing the highly congested federal courts, providing additional forces, and raising the salaries of the U.S. attorneys and judges in the districts, transferring the Prohibition Bureau from Treasury to Justice, and establishing a unified border patrol operation. The next day the White House's weighty effort was splashed on front pages across the nation. This was enough to ease the criticism.

The findings the commission sent to the Hill included surveys of criminal activity in Chicago and New York City, both of which were pertinent to Irey's mission. Guy L. Nichols of the Prohibition Bureau wrote the survey on Illinois and made a point of central importance. "Crime is organized in Chicago to an amazing extent," he wrote. "Today it consists of a series of lawless operations practically syndicated by rival gangsters and draws into its elusive web of crime many public officials and politicians who avail themselves of their way to make easy money."[15] One striking aspect of Nichols's survey was the listing of every known racketeer in Chicago, in which the inestimable Frank Loesch had undoubtedly played a hand. The survey named 330 "alleged gangsters," giving their criminal occupations, the neighborhoods where they operated, and their gang association. Al Capone topped a list of twenty-seven names, including Ralph Capone, Johnny Torrio, and Louis "Little New York" Campagna, who started out as Capone's bodyguard and would go on to become a leading figure in the combine that succeeded Capone. In sum, there was a clear awareness and examination of organized crime in Chicago.

The study made on New York could have taken the same approach, but it didn't. Palmer Canfield of the Prohibition Bureau put together a pedestrian report containing nothing out of the ordinary. It piled together statements such as: "It is unnecessary to state that New York City is the chief port of the United States"; and "As everyone knows, it is first in population"; and "The division of State police known as the State troopers was organized in 1917. It has grown each year numerically and in varied law-enforcement activities."[16] Canfield's survey cried out for a measure of what was really happening in the city's criminal underworld, which the Chicago report tried to do.

All of this came five years after Vice President Dawes stood in the well of the House of Representatives and spelled out what was happening in Chicago, specifically citing the Mafia. His warning had cried out for further examination. There was no indication that the Wickersham Commission heeded it. The commission was organized at the exact time—May 1929—that major organized crime figures from around the country had gathered at the crime summit in Atlantic City to plan their future. By the time the commission handed up its final report, in January 1931, the American Mafia was in the throes of organizing into the Five Families, and organized crime was here to stay. Whatever the commission had to say about the state of "law observation and enforcement" was in many regards not wholly relevant.

12. WAXEY, INSTEAD

Against an unparalleled criminal scene and major upheaval in the city's government, Irey's trip to New York City was a journey of uncertainty and questionable success. His special force had moved quickly. By mid-June it provided the evidence for a Medalie grand jury to hand down indictments on Mannie Kessler, whom the writer Stephen Fox called New York's "most celebrated Jewish bootlegger of the early 1920s"; Jose Enrique Miro, a Harlem policy racketeer who banked $1.2 million ($9.6 million in 1990 dollars) from 1928 to 1930 and paid no taxes; James J. Quinlivan, an eighteen-year NYPD vice squad veteran who had acquired a bank account of $57,744.67 ($615,120.39 in 1990 dollars) on which he had paid no taxes; and Albert H. Carlisle, a Wall Street stockbroker.[1]

The four had already been under investigation, and none were major criminal figures. Irey tried to level expectations. On June 18, the *New York Times* reported, "In trying to land the larger fish—the men who have control over various illicit monopolies—the agents will have to work slowly, it was explained. Preparing the case against Capone was a matter of years of weary searching through all kinds of bank records and other documentary evidence, and the same thing is expected here." The story went on to name five "larger fish": "An unofficial report has it that there are approximately 1,500 tax evaders on the government list in this city who have withheld altogether about $3,500,000 ($59.5 million in 1990 dollars) in taxes, but this could not be verified through Mr. Medalie. Among these names, it was said, are those of Jack (Legs) Diamond, Dutch Schultz, Owney Madden, Larry Fay [and] Vannie Higgins."[2] That let the cat out of the bag.

Dutch Schultz was a very large fish to hook, perhaps the biggest—outside Mafia powers like Charlie Luciano. Also, there was another Jewish racketeer not listed among those five names leaked to a curious press: Waxey Gordon. Actually, the SIU had placed Gordon on a level with Schultz (Irey: "There was a good deal of debate as to who was bigger"), and it turned out that Waxey would be the first racketeer the SIU went after.[3] The lucrative and illicit beer breweries he was running in New Jersey made him the leading bootlegger in metropolitan New York City and upper New Jersey. Arnold Rothstein, incidentally, had helped both Schultz and Gordon to make their mark.

First convicted as a pickpocket at nineteen in 1905, Waxey went on to petty and grand larceny, assault and battery, and selling illegal drugs. When Prohibition came in, he and Detroit bootlegger Max "Big Maxey" Greenberg began smuggling liquor from Canada. Leo Katcher credits Waxey with bringing Arnold Rothstein into bootlegging. In fall 1920 Waxey and Maxey needed $175,000 ($3,679,200 in 1990 dollars) to expand their operation and went to Rothstein for help. Gordon had worked for him in the garment center, protecting strikers or strikebreakers, depending on which side Rothstein profited from aiding.

Rothstein, as usual, went everyone one better: he financed the first shipload of Scotch whiskey from England. Scornful of Mafia chieftains such as Joe Masseria, who he believed distributed cheap booze, he decided to import only the best Scotch from Britain and to organize the shipments on a proper business basis and on a cargo-ship scale. He gave Waxey a piece of the deal, from which Waxey built his bootleg empire. Toward the end of the 1920s, using cunning and a "gruesome collection of triggermen," Waxey, like Rothstein, went everybody one better.[4] He took over three beer breweries in three New Jersey cities (Paterson, Union City, and Elizabeth) from the four owners—two were murdered, a third moved away, and the fourth went in with Waxey to save his life, thus giving him a virtual monopoly of the beer business in metropolitan New York and New Jersey. Breweries are large operations, often taking up two city blocks, and building one in Prohibition "was just a little too raw," as Irey noted. Explaining the impact of a beer brewery, it was easy to see why Irey targeted Gordon:

> It took very little room and less talent to make vast quantities of Prohibition gin, rye, or scotch. A closet sink, bottles, labels, alcohol, and flavoring, and the conscience of an Arab slave-trader was all a man needed to turn out $12-per-bottle liquor by the case. But beer was something else again. Barrels, malt, hops and bottles were needed in vast amounts. A brewery was essential, of course, because none of the Prohibition-day alchemists could ever make home brew taste like anything but home brew . . . Waxey's lager factories ran day and night but only a truck or two of beer left the brewery in a week. And that was near beer. The hundreds of thousands of gallons of real beer left via the sewers to bottling and barreling plants in garages a half-mile from the brewery. Waxey pumped it through pressure hoses than ran in the sewers. It would appear that there was a certain amount of connivance—cooperation at the least—on the part of some elected or appointed office holders.[5]

Investigating and prosecuting the Gordon and Schultz cases would take longer than the Capone case did. Gordon's case resembled Capone's in a number of ways. Though separating himself almost entirely from the actual operation of his illicit enterprises, he received the lion's share of profits. When an SIU agent came calling in early 1931 (Irey noted, "just to see what would happen"), Waxey didn't mind telling him where he stood: "I'm a man who keeps no records, no books, and I've never signed a check in my life."[6]

By then, of course, every racketeer of any standing, including mafiosi, recognized the jeopardy of leaving a money trail. Immediately after Ralph Capone's conviction, Irey said, a line began forming at the revenue collector's office in Chicago of people who wanted to pay their taxes. The total they coughed up came to $1 million ($17 million in 1990 dollars).

Until 1931 Waxey Gordon paid an average of $33 ($561 in 1990 dollars) in taxes in each of the three previous years, totaling about half the cost of the pearly fedora he wore. In 1931, with Irey on his money trail, he paid $35,000 ($595,000 in 1990 dollars). But the SIU calculated he had actually taken in more than $4.5 million ($76.5 million in 1990 dollars) he didn't declare as income, secluding it in more than 200 bank accounts under aliases.

Irey handed the investigation to Walter Murphy, assistant chief of the SIU's New York office, and brought in three crack special agents, Ellison Palmer from Atlanta, Paul Anderson from the Washington headquarters, and Cliff Mack from Boston to reinforce the office ("There is always plenty of need for strange faces in big investigations").[7] They began working with Tom Dewey and "his magnificent collection of assistants."[8]

Before climbing into Waxey's spider web, the SIU had gathered the evidence to help the Southern District to successfully prosecute James Quinlivan and Jose Miro for tax evasion. Quinlivan bought a speakeasy from money he made shaking down vice operators and kept it "well supplied by raiding rival establishments and transferring their confiscated stock to his own saloon." Miro's was the first big case Dewey tried, according to Irey. He had banked $1,023,154 ($17,393,618 in 1990 dollars) from 1928 to 1930. "He made these deposits," Irey noted, "despite the undue strain put on his assets by the dozens and dozens of $14 [$238 in 1990 dollars] shirts he kept sending to a Tammany chieftain named Jimmy Hines."[9]

At the time, in a little publicized but significant case, the SIU also went after Wilfred A. "Willy" Brunder, a black Harlem policy banker who had deposited a total of $1,753,342.33 ($29,806,810.61 in 1990 dollars) in the Dunbar National and Chelsea Bank between January 1, 1925, and December 31, 1930. Indicted for evading taxes, Brunder fled to Bermuda in mid-1931, returned in December, and turned himself in at Medalie's office. He pled guilty, was fined, and was sent to prison.

Turning to Waxey, Murphy and his crew began checking banks in Hoboken, the New Jersey town in the glare of New York City's skyline that was "the distributing center of the metropolitan beer industry." The SIU soon ran into "a real headache," Irey related, because most of the banks in that area of New Jersey were "completely dependent upon the huge deposits of the beer-peddling hoodlums." To accommodate Waxey, "bankers were destroying records, perjuring themselves, and doing all sorts of unusual things with deposits to make them difficult to trace."[10] For refusing to hand over Waxey's records, Frederick S. Lang, assistant secretary and treasurer of the Jefferson Trust Company, was sentenced to three months in the Federal House of Detention in New York City. Gordon's henchmen, according to Dewey biographer Richard Norton Smith, bribed New Jersey police and politicians so that when a Treasury agent set foot in Hoboken, he was arrested and held on the pretext of carrying false credentials. For the rest of 1931, 1932, and into 1933, Murphy's team assisted Dewey's prosecutors in talking to 1,000 witnesses, sifting through 200,000 deposits slips, and tracing toll slips of more than 100,000 telephone calls to secure an indictment of Waxey.

The big break came following the murder of William Brady, a truckman in New Jersey for bootleggers. Brady's records furnished the SIU with the first real leads on Waxey. They found a number of checkbook stubs showing sizeable bank accounts: In the name of George Nollman, deposits of $2,095,778.58 were made over a year's time. In the name of Harry Renner deposits of $1,039,012.12 had been made over the same time. In three months, L. J. Sampson had $599,794.12 credited to his account. James Henderson had deposited $1,332,629.05 over six months. Harry Weber had banked $1,192,942.10 in one year. (In 1990 dollars, the five amounts totaled $92,539,250.89.) Four other accounts had been less active.

Slowly, meticulously, SIU agents plowed through a mountain of records, examining every debit sheet in each of the bank accounts for the period covered by the check stubs. The stubs represented payments for a wide range of charges connected to Waxey beer business: machinery for a warehouse for beer barrels located at 818–826 Madison Street, Hoboken; for delivery trucks; for malt used by the Eureka Cereal Beverage Company; and for blacksmith and repair work on brewing machinery and equipment. In the L. J. Sampson account, agents traced a check for $1,400 ($23,800 in 1990 dollars) made as part payment on a Pierce-Arrow sedan Waxey owned. They found a henchman, Samuel H. Gurock, who ran the account.

They also found the head of a cooperage company who swore he had been paid $3,200 ($54,400 in 1990 dollars) in cash for beer barrels by Waxey himself.

Walter Murphy and his team reconstructed Gordon's private financial life in the same exacting fashion Frank Wilson and his team did with Al Capone: they charted the day-to-day expenditures representing his scale of living; this depicted a total income as accurate as the most careful spender could produce for his own outgoes. Waxey leased an apartment at 590 West End Avenue with ten rooms and four baths at $6,000 ($102,000 in 1990 dollars) a year. A bookcase, built to his order by an interior decorator, cost $2,200 ($37,400 in 1990 dollars). He drove two Pierce-Arrows and two Lincolns. His wife drove a Cadillac. He spent winters at Hot Springs, Arkansas. His children went to expensive summer camps. His suits, made by Al Capone's tailor, cost $225 ($3,825 in 1990 dollars); his custom-made shirts cost $13.50 ($229.50 in 1990 dollars); neckties cost $5.00 ($85.00 in 1990 dollars). Waxey claimed he was making $6,000 a year ($102,000 in 1990 dollars). His day-to-day expenditures, as the SIU calculated them, showed that his outlay came to considerably more than $25,000 a year ($425,000 in 1990 dollars).

Then, Irey recalled, the agents "started auditing Waxey's books the hard way." They checked bank accounts of real-estate companies, brewery suppliers, and trucking concerns and "found a stone wall of deceit erected by the theoretically honest businessmen who feared Waxey's guns almost as much as they dreaded the loss of his patronage." One company, "a top-notch trucking concern," rewrote its books at Waxey's demands.[11]

■

Over the three years he was in and out of New York, Irey came to know Tom Dewey and thought "it was a most successful relationship insofar as the taxpayer is concerned."[12] He was never more praiseworthy— and frank—about a public figure than he was of the famed prosecutor who would ride his record to the governor's chair in Albany. Calling Dewey "the perfectionist to end all perfectionists," Irey said he presented him with "a minor morale problem because some of my men found his glacial perfection good for their official records but a bit trying on their disciplined tempers." Dewey pushed the T-Men to thoroughness "beyond description," Irey went on. "Although some of my boys made some handsome efforts to describe it in exquisite flights of profanity."[13]

If Dewey was overbearing—the word Irey used to describe him—it was a helpful trait in dealing with the circumstances of the time. In his first year, the Southern District received 2,500 racketeering complaints, enough to keep its entire complement of fifty-two prosecutors on nothing but racket cases, which were the most difficult to prosecute. Dewey estimated that to try one racket case would require a dozen investigators and prosecutors working full-time for up to a year. Most of that time was taken up by one key factor: finding witnesses who would talk. Threats and intimidations usually rendered mute even the most honest or courageous businessman or unionist.

Medalie's office was overrun with Prohibition cases. If all the Volstead Act violators arrested in New York City during a single month (up to 500) had demanded a jury trial, every federal judge available for Prohibition cases would be occupied for a year. In Washington, by end of the Twenties, Mabel Walker Willebrandt and her Prohibition enforcement division at Justice were handling 40,000 cases a year, 50 percent of which involved bootlegging. After living with Prohibition for almost a decade, she had concluded, "No political, economic or moral issue has so engrossed and divided all the people of America as the Prohibition problem, except the issue of slavery."[14]

To complicate matters, the Southern District's top post had become a politically popular springboard. Medalie's predecessor, Charles Tuttle, captured wide attention for his success in breaking up Arnold Rothstein's drug rings. He also made a dent in bucket-shop operations, a particular specialty of Rothstein's. Tuttle also jumped on bail bond abuses in the federal courts and tried to curb them. One of the companies furnishing bonds was called the Greater City Surety and Indemnity Company, of which the two-thirds owners happened to be Dutch Schultz and Johnny Torrio. In January 1930 Tuttle called a conference of district attorneys from counties in the district to discuss the growth of crime. He did not extend an invitation to District Attorneys Thomas Crain of New York County and Charles

B. McLaughlin of Bronx County. Though he lacked political experience, Tuttle had developed what the *New York Times* called a "consummate skill in feeling the public pulse."[15] In the summer of 1930 speculation started on his seeking the chair in Albany. On September 26 he won the gubernatorial nomination at the Republican State Convention in the state capital and immediately threw down the gauntlet, declaring that the "chief issues of the campaign was whether or not the state was to have a governor that was bigger than Tammany Hall."

The next day the front page of the *New York Times* carried a formal two-column picture of Tuttle, taken by its own photo studio. It showed a thin, pleasant-faced man with short-cropped hair who had aged well. Sporting a stiff high collar and tie with jeweled stickpin, he wore a direct, confident look and bore a striking resemblance to Daniel Roper's firm countenance. In November 1930 Tuttle lost to the incumbent, a man with similarly consummate skills—Franklin Delano Roosevelt.

In January 1932, while the SIU was still deep into the Gordon investigation, Governor Roosevelt, age fifty-one, announced his candidacy for president of the United States and made repeal one of his campaign promises. (Prohibition was a year away from ending.) In September the state's Republican Party picked Medalie to run against the popular incumbent, Democrat Robert F. Wagner, for the U.S. Senate seat. That left Tom Dewey, age twenty-nine, to run the Southern District.

Medalie had little chance in the Democratic landslide of November 1932 that put FDR in the White House. Medalie and Dewey were ready to clear out their desks, a standard practice in a change of administrations in Washington. The new president, however, was in no hurry to disrupt the district's battle against racketeers and let them stay. Dewey had been working with a federal grand jury for almost two years, grilling witnesses such as banker Frederick Lang and gathering evidence in the difficult effort to indict Waxey Gordon.

There was the Seabury investigation too. Irey and the Southern District had been made privy to evidence accumulated by the Seabury hearings, which grew out of Rothstein's slaying and his involvement with Magistrate Albert Vitale of the Bronx. On Sunday evening, December 8, 1929, the

Tepecano Democratic Club held a testimonial dinner for the popular Vitale at the Roman Gardens restaurant in the Bronx. Suddenly, seven masked men with guns burst in, and one hopped atop a table to cover the guests as they were stripped of their valuables, amounting to $5,000 ($85,000 in 1990 dollars). Vitale slipped off his diamond ring and dropped it in his pants. Standing mute was an NYPD detective, Arthur C. Johnson, who handed over his service revolver. Also quiet was forty-year-old Ciro Terranova, one of the city's leading racketeers. Known as the Artichoke King for his control of the commodity, he was there as a representative of the food industry and happened to be the underboss of the Joseph Masseria family, whose territory included the Bronx. He had a police record going back to 1916 that included three charges of homicide. Immediately after the robbery, events took a fascinating turn: By the next morning, Vitale had arranged for the gunmen to return the loot, including Johnson's gun and bullets. One of the robbers had taken the revolver, broke open the barrel, ejected the cartridges and let them fall to the floor before picking them up.

Vitale had already been in the headlines over the past year—during the turbulent period following the slaying of Rothstein and while Beau James Walker was running for reelection. That fall, Fiorello La Guardia, the congressman from East Harlem and archfoe of Tammany, ran against Beau James and built his candidacy on the dispute over Rothstein's missing records. At one point he tied Tammany directly to Rothstein by releasing documents showing that Vitale had borrowed $19,940 ($282,900 in 1990 dollars) from Rothstein and urged Governor Roosevelt to investigate corruption in the city. Roosevelt, however, deemed Vitale's borrowing habits too weak to act upon and demanded specific charges, which La Guardia couldn't provide.

Several weeks after the Roman Gardens incident, Vitale's name was discovered in the files of a drug trafficker named Louis Saccarona by John Blake, the assistant district attorney in Tuttle's office, and his team, which was then investigating Rothstein's drug ties. In early January the Association of the Bar of New York City launched an investigation of the Bronx magistrate and named George Medalie to head it. On January 21 Thomas C. T. Crain, the new Manhattan district attorney, launched a grand jury inquiry into "allegations of unsavory conditions" in the magistrates courts, explaining his move was a "direct result" of Vitale's conduct in the Roman Gardens robbery and said he would present the evidence to grand jurors himself.

In the fall 1929 campaign, Tammany had nominated Crain in place of Joab Banton, now persona non grata for his handling of the Rothstein case. It was a tale in itself on why John Curry, Tammany's chief sachem, even picked Crain for the arduous job. He was approaching seventy-two. Columnist Heywood Braun commented, "The crane is mightier than the Crain and much more stalwart. The crane stands on at least one leg."[16] Crain happened to be the general sessions judge who tossed out the testimony at Ciro Terranova's murder trial in 1918, ruling that it had come from co-conspirators and accomplices and that outside corroboration was required.

On February 15 the New York Bar sent Medalie's report to the Appellate Division of the Supreme Court and called for the removal of Vitale on the ground of official misconduct. At a hearing on March 12, Vitale testified he had amassed $165,000 ($2,805,000 in 1990 dollars). Appointed in 1924 at a salary of $8,000 ($144,000 in 1990 dollars), his salary in 1930 was $12,000 ($204,000 in 1990 dollars). Vitale told the hearing that "much of his real estate had not been listed in his name," explaining he had borrowed money from Rothstein because he "needed it right then and there" for stock investments.[17] Two days later, the appellate justices unanimously removed Vitale as a city magistrate.

On March 14 the special grand jury that District Attorney Crain had impaneled to look into the magistrates courts delivered its report. Crain called the presentment "an exceptionally able document."[18] Actually, it was a scrap of rags Crain made into a tuxedo. It named no names, found no evidence for indictments, warned the magistracy to open its courts on time, and declared that magistrates shouldn't grant interviews in chambers and that all "business" should be heard in open court. It also recommended that no magistrate more than seventy years old be seated as the chief magistrate, an action aimed at seventy-seven-year-old Chief Magistrate William McAdoo, who ignored it and continued to serve.

On June 20, 1930, Governor Roosevelt rejected a plea from the Socialist Party in New York City to investigate scandal in the city. The plea had its beginnings on March 13, when the party's leader, forty-six-year-old Norman Thomas, testified before the Crain grand jury's magistracy inquiry. A sharp-tongued orator who had run for mayor against Beau James and La Guardia and a persistent critic of conditions in the magistrate system, Thomas had assailed Beau James for reappointing a magistrate who had freed a policeman in a shooting incident. Before entering the jury room, he handed out a statement naming eleven magistrates "who should be investigated on specific charges."[19] In addition, he cited curious entries on the court calendar of Magistrate George W. Simpson. On his calendar of July 14, 1925, Simpson had jotted down names of prominent Tammany leaders alongside cases scheduled for hearing. The names "Hamill" and "Hirschfield" appeared opposite a case involving Nicoasia Brothers, Inc. Thomas said the name "Hamill" was for leniency or fixing the case, while the name "Hirschfield" was for prosecution. In effect, Simpson was using a Tammany scorecard to decide a verdict.

Criminal indictments, not political or private appeals, changed Governor Roosevelt's mind. On June 26 William E. Walsh, chairman of the Board of Standards and Appeals, was indicted by a New York County grand jury for accepting a gratuity while holding a public office and by a federal grand jury for failure to file an income tax return for the year 1929. The appeals board ruled over zoning in the five boroughs. Walsh, a personal friend of Mayor Walker's, was regarded as one of the city's upstanding citizens. On July 9, a federal grand jury indicted Magistrate George Ewald for using the mails to defraud.

Governor Roosevelt and his circle were considered Hyde Park aristocrats and were unpopular among Tammany's rank and file, but Roosevelt and the Curry regime agreed on state patronage in the city, and Roosevelt went along with Tammany policy. This peaceful coexistence ended on August 2, 1930, when the governor ordered the Appellate Division to begin an investigation into the magistrate system and approved the appointment of Samuel Seabury, a former judge and an arch Tammany opponent, to head it. Commented the newspaper columnist Walter Lippmann, "A break between Governor Roosevelt and Tammany has been avoided by a kind of tolerant understanding on the part of the Tammany leaders that what Governor Roosevelt had to do under pressure of public opinion to let New York be investigated he had to do, and that what he did not have to do he would not do."[20]

Seabury launched his hearings on September 29, 1930, and they ran until May 14, 1931, a month after Irey came to Manhattan. Seabury and his staff went about the inquiry with unrelenting thoroughness, examining 1,059 witnesses in private hearings. Afterward, his staff waded through 15,000 pages of initial testimony to match testimony with evidence. Those with discrepancies were recalled, this time in public session. Two hundred and ninety-nine witnesses were grilled publicly. The names Dutch Schultz, Waxey Gordon, Louis Lepke, and Jacob Gurrah popped up in the testimony. Bribery was a "way of life for at least some of the nine Deputy Assistant District Attorneys assigned to various Magistrates' Courts in Manhattan."[21] Many small fries also testified about corruption. John C. Weston, a process server in the district attorney's office from 1921 to 1929, told how he played the part of an assistant district attorney to fix cases. Over those eight years, Weston received $20,000 ($360,000 in 1990 dollars) in bribes from lawyers, bondsmen, and policemen "for aiding in the discharge of 600 vice and immorality cases involving 900 defendants."[22]

Seabury's chief counsel was the diminutive Isidor J. Kresel ("he could run under a table wearing a high hat"), a buzz saw who had been counsel to the New York State Assembly during the 1913 impeachment of Governor William Sulzer.[23] He had served with the Justice Department the year before going with Seabury, Kresel knew "where the facts were buried" and that "neither juries nor Tammany judges could dispute records."[24] The staff included young and bright attorneys whose average age was twenty-eight. One was William G. Mulligan, one of Felix Frankfurter's best students at Harvard Law School. At his first full staff meeting, Seabury uttered the memorable slogan, "Old heads for counsel—young heads for war."[25]

Taking a page from Elmer Irey, Seabury's staff checked thousands of bank and brokerage house records, learning the names of policemen, bondsmen, clerks, court attendants, and assistant district attorneys who had stashed hundreds of thousands of dollars from trafficking in payoffs in magistrates courts. This could not have occurred without the knowledge of the magistrates, Seabury concluded. Combing through voluminous evidence, including grand jury transcripts, his inquiry found that scarcely an enterprise in the city failed to pay tribute to protection or labor peace.

The inquiry didn't stop with the magistrates courts. Seabury, whom Fiorello La Guardia would later call "the greatest exterminator of crooks in the history of this country," exposed the workings of Crain's office.[26] An analysis of Crain's indictments by Raymond Moley, then a Columbia University professor, showed that most defendants with serious offenses often pleaded guilty to misdemeanors. Of 1,279 indictments for grand larceny in 1930, 623 resulted in conviction but only 73 for the crime charged; all the rest for lesser crimes.

Seabury exposed Dr. William F. "Horse Doctor" Doyle, one of "the biggest grafters in municipal history."[27] A veterinarian, Doyle practiced before the Board of Standards and Appeals, pleading cases for builders, contractors, and landlords. The inquiry found he won 244 permits for garages where they were forbidden, 52 applications for gasoline stations where applications had previously been turned down by the Bureau of Fire Prevention, and 187 modifications of departmental orders issued under the state labor and tenement-house laws—besides getting the board to reverse itself in many other cases. In one year, the fees he split with Tammany officials amounted to $243,692 ($4,386,456 in 1990 dollars). The SIU produced evidence of tax fraud.

By the time Seabury got to his biggest target, Beau James, the inquiry had been taken over by a special legislative panel headed by State Senator Samuel H. Hofstadter, of which Seabury was named counsel. Seabury laid out fifteen specific accusations of Walker's "gross improprieties."[28] One involved the Equitable Coach Company, which became the basis of one of the most damaging charges against the mayor. Equitable was awarded a bus franchise after Walker induced the Board of Estimate to award a monopolistic franchise to Equitable. It made no difference the company didn't own a single bus. A backer of the company, J. Allen Smith, had "brought Walker a $10,000 ($170,000 in 1990 dollars) letter of credit for use on his European trip" in the summer of 1927. The "beneficences" from such enterprises doing business with the city led Russell T. Sherwood, Walker's agent, to deposit "nearly $1,000,000, of which $700,000 [$11.9 million in 1990 dollars] was cash, in a secret safe-deposit box." Walker "failed to explain the source of this money."[29]

When Beau James took the witness stand in the New York County courthouse off Foley Square on a Wednesday morning in May 1932, the scene was electric. Five thousand persons stood outside and a thousand inside when Beau James arrived, outfitted in a double-breasted blue suit, blue shirt, blue tie, and matching blue handkerchief. "Little boy blue is about to blow his horn—or his top," he cracked.[30] Seabury, prematurely white haired (he had been since he was forty) and wearing a gray suit, looked much older. Actually, only four years separated their ages.

During questioning over the next two days, Beau James bested Seabury, at one point whispering under his breath, "You and Frank Roosevelt are not going to hoist yourself to the Presidency over my dead body."[31] But despite manipulating the cheering crowds (women on each side of the main doorway threw roses as he emerged from the building) and getting a good press ("Mayor James J. Walker fought with rapier-like wit against the ponderous legal attack leveled at him by Samuel Seabury"), the evidence held up.[32]

When the committee's report was presented to Governor Roosevelt for action (with the Democratic National Convention in Chicago only weeks away), he sat on it. No governor, of course, ever faced what Roosevelt faced: he was trying to wrap up his party's nomination for the presidency at the Democratic National Convention while pondering the removal of the idolized chief executive of the nation's largest city. Observers remained unenthused. Wrote columnist Walter Lippmann, "[Roosevelt] has displayed a singular petulance towards everybody who has had any part in putting him in a position where he might have to make a decisive choice between breaking with Tammany and surrendering to it."[33] Roosevelt sat on the report until he won the nomination. On August 11, a month after the Democratic convention, in the executive chamber in the Hall of Governors in Albany, Mayor James J. "Beau James" Walker faced his accusers. When it looked like Governor Roosevelt would replace him, he resigned on September 1, 1932, and sailed to Europe in December to join "Monk." His wife stayed behind.

■

The SIU and Dewey had been working together for more than a year to obtain the indictment of Dutch Schultz, now only weeks away. Schultz's money trail, they found, could not compare to Gordon's, nor was he as extravagant. But he possessed an element almost as important as wealth: political clout. Of all of New York's racketeers, he was the closest to Jimmy Hines, the Eleventh District leader, perhaps the most powerful single man in Tammany Hall, and an ally of FDR.

Schultz helped perfect the modern model in organizing a racket (Dewey conceded he had a "brilliantly inventive mind").[34] As Judge Morris Ploscowe said, "The big money—and success to the criminal is measured in terms of money—is to be made in activities which have a legitimate place in our competitive system but which can be perverted to criminal ends."[35] In its rawest form, the model involved the use of intimidation to take over a trade for the purpose of regularly extorting money. This required the top racketeer, like Schultz, to set up a front to disguise the paying of tribute. He would pick a henchman to run the front, thus shielding Schultz. In turn, the henchmen picked underlings to do the dirty work. As the lone connection to the racket's boss, the henchman had to be clever enough as both front man and shield to avoid the limelight, and not become tainted if the public found out that dirty work was afoot.

Schultz's model included infiltrating and capturing a union local that served the trade. Once racketeers put their people in all the right posts, the local almost always assumed a momentum of its own, making reform and prosecution of the local's racketeer-leader infinitely more difficult. Not to be outdone, the Mafia dons perfected an arsenal of variations on Schultz's model, particularly on the waterfront and in the construction trades.

Schultz introduced his model in New York City's restaurant business early in 1932. He picked a smooth operator named Jules Martin to establish the Metropolitan Restaurant and Cafeteria Association as his front man. The association charged a $50 ($850 in 1990 dollars) initiation fee to join, $30 ($510 in 1990 dollars) per year in dues, and $1,500 ($25,500 in 1990 dollars) "association dues" to avert threatened strikes by the union. One restaurateur who didn't join had a stink bomb thrown down his chimney. A stink bomb "consisted of valerian or butyric acid and gave off an extremely offensive odor which got into the carpets, draperies, the wood of the tables, even into concrete floors and plumbing fixtures. It ruined almost everything in a restaurant, and places had to be closed for months."[36]

Martin opened "a cheap little restaurant as a front and entering wedge" into the trade.[37] Then he hatched a scheme to have two of his waiters and another racketeer take over Local 16 of the Restaurant Employees International Alliance, the waiters' union that served a part of Manhattan. In the next election, Martin had the ballot box stuffed: thirty-eight votes more than the local's total membership were counted. Schultz then had his henchmen take over another waiters' local. All of this happened with "incredible speed,"[38] Dewey said. Schultz was requiring small restaurant owners to pay an initiation fee of $250 ($3,250 in 1990 dollars) and an additional $30 ($510 in 1990 dollars) per year in dues; he learned this through the owner of a small cafeteria, Abraham Finkel. Dewey had him appear before a grand jury, but Finkel denied any knowledge of a racket or shakedown. Only after Dewey took Finkel through a court ordeal lasting almost a year did results occur. "Then he came to our office in secret and told us the truth about a shakedown," said Dewey.[39] During this period Schultz also took over the window cleaners union. After they refused to pay dues to his union, according to Craig Thompson and Allen Raymond, window cleaners began dropping from skyscraper windows to the sidewalks below. Someone had tampered with their safety belts.

■

On January 23, 1933, just as FDR was settling into the White House, a federal grand jury indicted Schultz for failure to pay income taxes of $22,336 ($357,376 in 1990 dollars) on his traceable 1929 income from beer sales of $130,324 ($2,085,184 in 1990 dollars). Schultz immediately took it on the lam. With the master racketeer in hiding, Dewey used the rest of the year to put together the Waxey Gordon case, during which Dewey gave new meaning to the word "dedication." He became so immersed in getting indictments that he showed up at home for dinner only three times in four months, a period when his wife, Frances, gave birth to their first son.

On April 1, 1933, beer became legal, and twenty-seven days later Gordon and two of his henchmen, Sam Gurock and Louis Cohen, were indicted for tax fraud. Along with Maxey Greenberg, they were charged with conspiring to conceal Gordon's income of $1,616,690.90 ($27,473,945.30 in 1990 dollars) in 1930–1931 and to defraud the government of taxes of $347,565.84 in 1930 and $35,408.62 in 1931. But Maxey was no longer around. On April 12 Schultz's henchmen murdered Maxey and Max Hassel, another longtime Gordon mechanic, in an Elizabeth, New Jersey, hotel room. Gordon, in an adjoining room, barely escaped by jumping out of a window. Schultz's motive? Waxey had started flooding the Bronx and Yorkville districts in direct competition to Schultz right after beer was legalized, and a war quickly developed.

Gordon didn't wait to be served the indictment—he fled the city. Sam Gurock had already disappeared; he was arrested in New Jersey in July 1932 as a material witness in the case. Dewey planned to sit him before the grand jury. But he was released on a bond of $1,500 at 1:00 a.m. the day after his arrest—contrary to George Medalie's request to keep him in jail. At the time of his arrest, Gurock gave his address as the hotel where Greenberg and Hassel were killed.

Irey sent his ace undercover man, Pat O'Rourke, and Special Agent Joseph Harvey to find Gordon. Explained Irey, "A little bird—of the genus pigeon—told Pat that Waxey was holed up somewhere in the Catskill Mountains." O'Rourke and Harvey spent a week in Ellenville, Catskill, Calicoon, Liberty, and Loch Sheldrake, with no luck. In Bethel, they found an old associate of Waxey's who ran a boarding house and learned that a number of men had rented a nearby cottage and were annoying neighbors by driving a high-powered speedboat on White Lake late at night. On May 20, a Saturday night marked by thunderstorms, O'Rourke and Harvey sneaked up to the cottage. Caution didn't prevail. O'Rourke stepped in a puddle and fell with a splash on the seat of his pants in three inches of mud and water. In a second, every light in the house went out—it was all O'Rourke needed to know: "Honest people don't douse the lights when they hear noises. They usually put more on."

The next morning O'Rourke and Harvey showed up at the cottage with five New York state troopers, led by Sgt. Thomas Mangan. Guns drawn, they opened the door to confront a sullen-looking, dark-faced man who raised his hands. In an upstairs bedroom, a man was getting out of bed as they walked in. They ordered him to one side. One of the troopers slipped a hand under the pillow and pulled out a loaded .38-caliber revolver. In an adjoining bedroom, they found Waxey sleeping peacefully. O'Rourke walked up to the bed, pocketed the "horse pistol" resting on the bedside table and ordered, "Get up, Waxey. You're under arrest." Waxey blinked and his face "went kind of white and pasty." Sitting up, he blurted—"Well." After that "he didn't say another word," O'Rourke recounted.

Once downstairs, Waxey started protesting. "This is nonsense. I ain't Waxey Gordon. I'm William Palinski. I'm in the tobacco business." Continuing to insist he was Palinski, he told O'Rourke, "I got friends in Albany, I have." O'Rourke retorted, "Look, Waxey, you're talking too much. You oughtn't to keep saying you're William Palinski and walk around in silk drawers that have I. W. embroidered on 'em. I. W. means Irving Wexler, Waxey."[40] Returned to Manhattan, Waxey quickly produced the bail of $100,000 ($1.7 million in 1990 dollars).

■

Dutch Schultz was still in hiding when Waxey's trial on charges of tax evasion opened on Foley Square on Wednesday, November 20, 1933. To find a jury, Dewey, his aides, and SIU agents interviewed 1,000 people, of which 150 were chosen, and "by no means, were they willing," recalled Irey.[41] It was also the same month Medalie, age fifty, retired, and two months before Dewey would leave.

That November, too, in one great and final sweep, Dewey nailed the cream of New York City's racketeers. A federal grand jury indicted 158 persons for violating the Clayton Anti-Trust Act through interference with interstate commerce, including Louis Lepke and Jacob "Gurrah" Shapiro, known as the "Gorilla Boys." In 1931 they had taken over a group of flour trucking and baking industries through their business front, the Flour

Truckmen's Association. The Perfection Coat Front Company was a legitimate garment industry company before Lepke and Gurrah took that over too. Loaded up with rackets cases, it took the district until 1935 before the Gorilla Boys were tried and convicted (Dewey was New York City's special prosecutor by then). Lepke and Gurrah were given two years in prison and fined $10,000 ($160,000 in 1990 dollars), the maximum penalty for a misdemeanor violation under the Clayton Act.

U.S. District Judge John C. Knox, who delivered the sentence, knew this was just a slap on the wrist and turned down bail pending appeal, which the two racketeers immediately sought. This sparked the memorable incident between Dewey, the city's special prosecutor, and Judge Martin T. Manton, the senior member of the Second Circuit U.S. Court of Appeals. Dewey wanted to indict the pair on stronger charges in order to "send them to jail for the rest of their lives."[42] He went to see Manton, who was "cordial and gracious"; explained his plan; and asked him to deny bail "until our indictment could be completed, or at least to fix bail at a high enough level to hold them." Manton "assured" him that "he certainly would not like to see Lepke and Gurrah escape, and that he would bear in mind all that I had said."[43] The next day Manton turned the Gorilla Boys loose on $10,000 bail ($160,000 in 1990 dollars). A week later, Dewey got the indictment, but Lepke and Gurrah had fled. Later, with Manton presiding, the appeals court reversed Lepke's conviction. Six years before, when William "Big Bill" Dwyer appealed his conviction for operating one of New York's biggest bootlegging rings, Judge Manton supported a new trial.

On November 22, two days after Waxey Gordon's trial opened, Tom Dewey was sworn in as interim U.S. attorney; at thirty-one he was the youngest in the Southern District's history. He had benefited from Medalie's mentorship. ("How do we put a ruby nose on it?" Medalie would say as a way of counseling his younger colleagues to find the single, electric detail that would excite a jury's outrage.)[44]

Dewey did that by showing Waxey's hidden income. The deliberations set a world record for a leading racketeer. At 3:34 p.m., on December 1, the jury retired. It returned fifty-one minutes later to announce a guilty verdict. Gordon was fined $80,000 ($1,360,000 in 1990 dollars) and given a ten-year prison sentence. It was just short of thirty-two months since Irey came to Manhattan. It was Dewey's most successful case and his first big leap into public attention. Gordon's conviction so delighted the press, Irey observed, "That for days it failed to refer to us as 'G-Men' or FBI agents."[45] It was also five days before Utah became the thirty-third state to ratify the Twenty-first Amendment, which would end Prohibition.

On January 2, 1934, Dewey left for private practice. He had missed out on prosecuting Dutch Schultz, who was still in hiding and was now the best-known racketeer of his day. The Gordon and Schultz cases had taken Dewey's entire stay in the Southern District. The momentum from the combination of revelations from Arnold Rothstein's slaying, the Seabury hearings, and the work of the SIU and the Southern District continued to drive the reform effort. The massive indictment of 158 racketeers marked the first time the Clayton Act had been invoked against racketeers in New York City. Aware of the light penalty for violating the act, the FDR White House was in the process of preparing new legislation to deal with racketeering. Meanwhile, Irey was already engaged in a contest with a political figure who has never been matched for his audacity and criminality.

13. ANONYMOUS COMPLAINTS ABOUT HUEY LONG

After he won prominence in the Capone case, Elmer Irey began receiving anonymous letters from Louisiana, as early as 1930, complaining that "Long and his crowd" were stealing "a hundred million dollars" from the state—"What was the Treasury Department going to do about it?" A former Louisiana governor, John M. Parker, was a regular visitor to Irey's office in Washington, and "his conversation was always the same: 'When are you going to do something about Long?'"[1]

"Long" was Huey Pierce Long Jr., Louisiana's former governor and now a U.S. senator. Known as "The Kingfish" and called the "most indefatigable campaigner and best catch-as-catch-can stumper the demagogically fertile South has yet produced," Long hailed from rural Winnfield in Louisiana's hill country southeast of Shreveport.[2] He also provoked opposition like perhaps no one else in twentieth century politics. John P. Sullivan of New Orleans, a fierce Long opponent, declared, "Jesse James was a gentleman compared with Long, because Jesse James at least wore a mask."[3] Governor Parker, whom the Kingfish once "campaigned furiously" for, would become one of his harshest critics, calling him a "creature devoid of every element of honor and decency."[4] The British writer Rebecca West, on a visit to the United States, saw a cold intelligence in Long, calling him "the most formidable kind of brer fox."[5] Long practiced a "genial totalitarianism," said historian John Morton Blum.[6] Long's methods were not kingly. A

Louisiana state legislator said, "He knew everything about you and how to get to you."[7] Historian T. Harry Williams spelled out the uniquely awesome measure of his blitzkrieg-like power. Williams said Long

> set out not to contain the opposition or to impose certain conditions on it, but to force it out of existence. Deliberately, he grasped the control of all existing boards and other agencies, and then just as deliberately, by creating new agencies to perform new functions, he continually enlarged the patronage at his disposal. His control of patronage gave him control of the legislature and his control of the legislature enabled him to have law enacted that invested him with imperial authority over every level of local government. He became so powerful finally that he could deny the opposition almost all political sustenance, and if he wished, destroy it. What he was working on before his death, and in effect had brought it off, was creating an arrangement in which the only remaining opposition faction would have to come into his organization to survive.[8]

After serving a tumultuous period on the state's Public Service Commission—where Governor Parker tried to kick him off amid talk of impeachment—Long ran for governor in 1924 and lost. He ran again in 1928 at age thirty-eight and won, though not handily. But from then on, he was going to make certain he would never lose another election. After discharging every state jobholder under executive control who had not actively supported him, the Kingfish, over the next few years, put together, atom by atom, the nuclear political machine that Williams described.

His dictatorial manner was on display from the start. Heeding the cry of reformers to crack down on gambling in New Orleans (where voters never cared for him, giving his gubernatorial opponent 60,568 votes to his 17,815 votes in 1928), the Kingfish employed a technique new to law enforcement in Louisiana. Instead of asking a judge for a search warrant or using the police, he sent in his own raiders. They just kicked open the door of gambling joints, confiscated or destroyed the equipment, seized all money found, and deposited it with the state treasurer. The Kingfish's raider was Raymond H. Fleming, adjutant general of the state national guard. A *New Orleans Item* reporter who punched him in the mouth in retaliation for being called "a sonofabitch" was pinned by bodyguards while the Kingfish returned the deed. (He gave him a black eye.) Another reporter who got on an elevator in which a Long opponent was being rushed away from Huey's tirade had a gun thrust into his ribs. He quickly exited the elevator. Soon, the State House impeached Huey on nineteen counts, including calling out the militia to override the courts and civil authorities—along with fixing the state courts, bribing legislators, misappropriating state funds, gross personal misconduct, habitually carrying concealed weapons, blackmail, releasing convicted prisoners, and trying to bribe his own bodyguard to kill a legislator.

In a special election in January 1930, while still governor, Huey was elected to the U.S. Senate, so he installed an old friend, Alvin King, the president of the state Senate, to act as governor. He supported FDR in his 1932 run for the presidency, along with Arkansas's Hattie Caraway, the first woman to be elected to Congress. Hattie wanted to run for the U.S. Senate, but the state's Democratic machine opposed her candidacy, believing she was a mousey creature who would lose. With Huey's support—he went to Arkansas to campaign for her—she whipped her nearest competitor by two to one, an early indicator of the Kingfish's appeal.

Elmer Irey chose a brassy time to go after the Kingfish. In July 1932, with Herbert Hoover still in the White House, he assigned a trio of agents headed by Archibald "Archie" Burford, the agent in charge of the Dallas office, to look into the allegations. The presidential campaign between Hoover and FDR was heating up, and an investigation of Long could rebound either way. Irey was always prudent in his handling of political subjects; while he may have had political leanings, he never left a scent during his entire career on what he thought of the two major political parties. The newspaper columnist Marquis Childs said that Irey was known as "the country's No. 1 button lip" and elaborated that his "distrust of publicity may have come as a result of the oppressive burden of secrecy that inevitably he carries about with him."[9]

After a preliminary look into Long's activities, which took less than a month, Archie Burford caught a train to Washington. The morning after he arrived, sitting in Irey's office, he reported, "Long and his gang are stealing everything in the state." Irey put together a task force of thirty-two agents, headed by Burford, to investigate the Kingfish. In no time at all, word rocketed back to Long, who marched personally to the office of Revenue Commissioner David Burnet. "Dave was frightened speechless before big-shot politicians," Irey recalled, "so he sat unhappily and listened as Long lectured him on the dangers of investigating United States Senators."[10] The Kingfish wasn't through. He sent a message to Irey through a mutual acquaintance: "You're in his 'Sonuvabitch Book.'" Explained Irey, "That 'Book' was infamous in Louisiana and was getting quite a reputation among civil servants in Washington. It was a book Huey actually kept . . . if he put your name in it you were politically dead in Louisiana and in severe danger in Washington."[11]

Days after FDR was elected in November 1932, Secretary of the Treasury Ogden L. Mills called Irey to his office to ask if he had enough evidence on Long for an indictment before Inauguration Day, March 4. Irey said he needed more time. Mills told him to suspend the investigation, write up a report, and give it to his successor. "After all," Mills told Irey, "the Senator is one of their [the Democrats'] babies; let them decide what to do with him."[12]

Actually, this wasn't entirely the case. Long had "few intimate friends among his Senate colleagues."[13] He "most admired and trusted" Senator Burton Wheeler of Montana.[14] When Long learned that Wheeler was in Shreveport on his way to meet President-elect Roosevelt at his retreat in Warm Springs, Georgia, he had two state policemen intercept him and drive him "in a drenching rain" to the Roosevelt Hotel in New Orleans, where they arrived at 1:00 a.m. The next morning Wheeler had breakfast at Long's house (Huey greeted him wearing green pajamas). The point of the visit was that Long wanted Wheeler to intercede with FDR. "I'd wish you'd talk to him about stopping some of those investigators from Washington they've got down here in Louisiana." Wheeler turned him down, telling him he didn't think it "would be appropriate."[15] Long proceeded to move in another way, through maneuvers that revealed his adeptness as a practitioner of power politics. Shortly, the assistant secretary of the Navy, E. L. Jahncke, who was from New Orleans, learned that a bank in the city had called in his loan of $250,000 ($4,950,000 in 1990 dollars). Harvey Couch, a friend of Long's and a director of the Reconstruction Finance Corporation, telephoned the Kingfish to protest the move, noting that since it was done at the instruction of the state bank examiner, Long must have ordered it.

Long replied, "I don't have anything more to do with that bank examiner than the Assistant Secretary of the Navy has to do with the Treasury Department."

Couch frowned, "Oh, is that it?"

"That's exactly it," Long replied.[16]

Irey knew nothing of these raw power plays. But he followed instructions. When FDR named William H. Woodin, one of his campaign's major financial angels, as the secretary of treasury in March 1933, Irey sent him the SIU's damning report on the Kingfish. Months passed. Then, in poor health, Woodin resigned.

■

The SIU's investigation forged on in the months leading up to the November 1932 presidential election. The Kingfish showed up at the Democratic National Convention in Chicago the previous June, where he probably became the highest-ranking politician yet to be handed wine and favors from Mafia chieftains. After the Five Families realigned in 1931 with Charles Luciano as the Boss of Bosses, the Mafia brain trust wasted no time in building ties to Tammany Hall and their followers. Through Dutch Schultz, they established ties with Jimmy Hines and made their first big splash at no less a political gathering than the convention. Hines led the faction committed to FDR. Albert Marinelli led the other faction, which was committed to Al Smith, in what became a bitter fight for the nomination. Marinelli, the leader of the Second Assembly District (which included the racketeer-run Fulton Fish Market) was a rising star in Tammany who would ride in on the Fiorello La Guardia landslide to become New York County clerk in 1933. Of Marinelli, Tom Dewey said, "He was a politician, a political ally of thieves, pickpockets, thugs, dope peddlers, and big-shot racketeers. I thought the Marinelli story told much about the alliance between crime and politics in New York. In fact, he was one of the most powerful men in town."[17] Marinelli had entered politics in his teens and became an election district captain. His wealth came from a trucking business he established; among his customers were the Borough of Manhattan, the City of New York, and Frankie Yale. His friend, Arnold Rothstein, insured his business and even had a $40,000 ($720,000 in 1990 dollars) policy on Marinelli's life. He lived on a Long Island estate, drove to work in a Lincoln, and employed a Japanese butler named Togo.

Hines shared his suite at the Drake Hotel with Frank Costello. Luciano shared his suite at the Drake with Marinelli; they became "constant companions" and went to Arlington Race Track between convention sessions.[18] Either way, the Mafia brethren would be on the victorious side. Al Smith had lost the presidency to Herbert Hoover in 1928 and decided to challenge FDR for the nomination in 1932. This was Smith's last stand and a losing one too.

During the convention, Huey Long went to Luciano's six-room suite, where he met with Luciano, Costello, Meyer Lansky, and Moe Dalitz. Long, said Luciano, "was sober enough to explore ways to bring new enterprises to his state, and to draw cash to his own pockets." Their meeting in the suite laid the "outlines of a deal" to bring gambling to Louisiana. "We didn't know too much about [Long]," recalled Luciano, "except that he was a loudmouth who liked to drink and he seemed to control his state with an iron fist. . . . That was good enough for me."[19]

By the early Thirties, Costello and his partner, Philip "Dandy Phil" Kastel (Arnold Rothstein introduced Kastel to Costello) had 15,000 slot machines (of an estimated 25,000) operating in mom-and-pop stores throughout New York City's five boroughs, according to Thomas Kessner. In 1932, Kessner said, Costello and Dandy Phil took in $37 million ($429 million in 1990 dollars) from the one-armed bandits.

"A nickel slot at a good location in one of the boroughs could turn as much as $35 a day" ($570 in 1990 dollars), according to Craig Thompson and Allen Raymond.[20] A nickel slot at a poor spot could be counted on for $15 ($240 in 1990 dollars), with the average slot reaching $20 ($320 in 1990 dollars). After taking office on January 1, 1934, Mayor La Guardia made the machines the main target of his anti-gambling crusade. A photograph printed in an October 14, 1934, edition of the *New York Daily News* showed the stubby mayor wielding a sledgehammer to bust up a four-foot-high pile of confiscated slot machines. The police were cracking down too. In one two-week stretch, "police arrested 714 slot machine racketeers together with hundreds of craps shooters, policy and numbers runners, and bookmakers."[21] To put off the authorities, Costello converted his slots into "candy machines" and won a court injunction against further police action. But the heat was too much, and Costello turned to Huey Long, still a ready ally three years after their get-together at the Democratic National Convention in Chicago. At a meeting at the New York Hotel in Manhattan in early 1935, Long and Costello struck a deal to bring the one-armed bandits to New Orleans, where Huey would receive a yearly fee of $30 ($450 in 1990 dollars) per slot. In July 1935 (just two months before the Kingfish was assassinated) 986 slot machines were shipped down. They were operated under a front called the Bayou Novelty Company, which included a number of subsidiary companies. Long, using the legislature like a rubber stamp, had Bayou and the other companies chartered as charitable enterprises. The major portion of the profits was supposedly to be disbursed among worthy organizations in need of funds as a variation on the theme of Long's Share the Wealth crusade. According to Hank Messick, "the slots were closed for two weeks when Huey Long was shot, but Costello made a 'new deal' with New Orleans Mayor Robert S. Maestri and Governor Richard W. Leche. Bayou reopened as the Pelican Novelty Company, which featured pinball machines equipped with an automatic payoff device. Meanwhile, Costello got the state courts to rule that slots machines that paid off in mints with each play were legal. The Louisiana Mint Company was organized in 1942 and continued in operation until 1946."[22]

In its first year of operation, beginning about mid-1934, the Pelican Novelty Company took in a net profit, after operating expenses, of $800,000

($12.8 million in 1990 dollars). Of this amount, some $600 ($9,600 in 1990 dollars), or just enough to validate the charter, was disbursed to charitable enterprises.

■

Though the Kingfish had played an important role in getting the party's nomination for FDR, he gave him fits during his first year in the White House. Shortly after assuming office in March 1933, FDR closed the nation's banks in order to avert a complete financial collapse. His aides worked feverishly with Congress on a bill that authorized the Treasury to reopen the banks that met certain safeguards. Long tried to waylay the bill and broaden it. In April, Long opposed the new Agricultural Adjustment Act, which had cleared the House. He held it up for twelve days over the issue of raising farm prices by inflating the currency. When FDR agreed to accept an amendment authorizing him to inflate with silver, paper, or a devalued dollar, the Kingfish claimed the president had "swallowed our demand, hook, line, and sinker."[23] In June, the last month of the session, the White House brought the National Recovery Act to Capitol Hill—a "bold and imaginative effort to cope with the related problems of falling prices and wages and cutthroat competition in industry"[24]—which Huey fought.

From the floor of the U.S. Senate, the sharp-tongued Huey ridiculed FDR as "Prince Frankling, Knight of the Nourmahal,"[25] and lampooned high administration officials Henry Wallace ("the ignoramus of Iowa"), Harold Ickes ("the Chicago Chinch Bug"), and Hugh Johnson ("the lord high chamberlain").[26] By state legislative fiat, the Kingfish had made certain that no federal relief money could be obtained by any municipality or parish except with the approval and supervision of an agency of his own. By early 1934 Huey had broken with FDR and was vigorously building support among the nation's impoverished with his Share the Wealth plan, launched in February and highlighted by its catchy song, "Every Man a King." He certainly entertained presidential ambitions. But he had also picked just about every conceivable way to become FDR's enemy, both opposing his programs and personally embarrassing the president.

Until then, FDR had not responded to the Kingfish's attacks. Late in June he acted: He took away all of his federal patronage. And he had Postmaster General James Farley ask Huey to come to the White House for a conference, at which he gave him the bad news. Huey showed up in a summer suit and wearing a straw hat, which he did not remove "except to occasionally tap Roosevelt's knee with it."[27] Long "did not seem concerned at his loss of patronage," but after returning to his office, he instructed his secretary to go to Farley's office and get the Louisiana patronage list and tear it up in front of the postmaster general."[28] On January 1, 1934, FDR named Treasury Undersecretary Henry J. Morgenthau Jr. to succeed William Woodin, who, incidentally, had left without so much as a whisper to Irey about the report on Long. Not hearing anything back, Irey left matters alone. But it wasn't going to be that way with Morgenthau. There was another weapon that could be used against Long: Irey's investigative report. FDR left that in the hands of Morgenthau. It had lain dormant for a year in the files of Secretary of the Treasury Woodin. Not any more. Long was more than FDR's political foe. He had become the enemy. And that is why Morgenthau—right after taking over for Woodin—jump-started Irey's investigation.

In his memoir, Irey recalls the moment. Three days after becoming the secretary of treasury, Morgenthau sent for Irey and brusquely came to the point: "Why have you stopped investigating Huey Long, Mr. Irey?"

Irey explained that former Secretary Mills had told him to stop, and turn in the report and that he "had received no instructions to reopen the investigation."

Snapped Morgenthau, "What's the matter, Mr. Irey, are you afraid of Huey Long?"

Irey proceeded to repeat his explanation and finished with, "I'm awaiting instructions."

Morgenthau said, "You did put Capone in jail, didn't you?" Now he was smiling.

After that, Morgenthau told him he wanted to see him once a week, on Friday. And that he could "come in through my secretary's office, not through the main reception room." Irey started doing that.

Once, after he had reported every week for almost a year, he was "particularly short of information, so I decided to skip a meeting. The next morning I got a phone call. 'This is the Secretary. You haven't been to see me in eight days.'"[29]

At age forty-three, three years younger than Irey, the strong-willed Morgenthau easily took the dealer's hand in the Treasury's criminal inquiries, and he was going to actively use it. With both Irey and Harry Anslinger under his wing, he would make a formidable mark on federal law enforcement. In addition, Eleanor Roosevelt once said to Morgenthau that he was one of only two men who "stood up to Franklin" (Louis Howe was the other).[30]

Irey immediately went about organizing a task force. He put Archie Burford back in charge of the case, and he set up their headquarters in the Masonic Building in New Orleans, where they took up a whole floor for offices. Again, Irey was going to see to it that no one would have to endure the cubbyhole existence Frank Wilson had once put up with in Chicago. The investigation of Long started just a year after Al Capone's front-page exodus and the larcenous lifestyles of the two remain unparalleled to this day. No racketeer before or since dominated a major American city the way Capone dominated Chicago. No politician before or since dominated a state the way Long dominated Louisiana.

Working out of the Masonic Building, the SIU task force—it numbered approximately fifty investigators (the Kingfish claimed there were 250)— spent most of 1934 gathering evidence on Long and his gang. Irey had his agents follow the pattern taken in the Capone case—investigate the aides before taking on the "big man himself." The T-Men laboriously tracked the money trail of 232 individuals, 42 partnerships, and 122 corporations; examined bank statements, forged, and unforged checks; and questioned contractors about who had paid bribes.

In gathering a mountain of incriminating material, they were able to chart out the Long hierarchy. After the Kingfish came Seymour Weiss, the glad-handing owner of the Roosevelt Hotel in New Orleans and a long-time Long confidant who handled his financial affairs; Monte Hart, a New Orleans businessman; and Abraham L. "Abe" Shushan, president of the New Orleans Levee Board. Long had, on occasion, entrusted Weiss and Shushan with the key task of raising campaign money.

In each case, agents invited them in to explain their failure to report income. For months, however, they and others under investigation stalled for one reason or another—which helped push the investigative effort further back.

In October 1934 Abe Shushan was indicted; in December, indictments were handed down on Seymour Weiss and State Rep. Joseph Fisher, the first elected official to be caught in the web of conspiracy of Louisiana's politics. When the SIU agents gave him the opportunity to explain, Fisher swore he had no unreported income. But the T-Men had uncovered evidence he'd been taking "commissions" in connection with state highway projects and not reporting the income. Fisher's uncle, Jules, was indicted with him, charged with paying a total of $41.18 ($574.56 in 1990 dollars) on an income of $348,000 ($4,872,000 in 1990 dollars). Fisher's trial was scheduled first but was still months away.

A member of an influential family in Jefferson, the coastal parish next to New Orleans, Fisher first gained notoriety in 1930 as one of the key players in the disappearance of Sam Irby, a former employee of the state highway commission. Why Irby left the commission is uncertain, but he started saying publicly that he had proof of widespread graft at the commission. Irby happened to be a heavy drinker. After a few belts he would turn into a fountain of information for anyone who cared to listen. The Kingfish knew about Irby and his drinking habits—he had become an entry in the "Sonuvabitch Book." But Huey wasn't as bothered by Irby's knowledge of highway graft as by what Irby knew about Huey and his mistress, Alice Lee Grosjean. In those days, that was damaging. The Kingfish had Joe Fisher spirit Irby away from the prying press and take him by boat to a fishing camp on isolated Grand Isle until he could devise a way to control the situation.

The Fisher family, headed by Isidore, the patriarch, and assisted by son Joe, ran a variety of enterprises involving furs, canning, and seafood. Isidore's brother, Jules, was a state senator and president of the Fisher Shrimp Company, whose sales reached to Latin America. The Fisher family commanded the allegiance of people in Jefferson and the surrounding coastal region and represented the kind of important and tightly knit political base Long could call on all over Louisiana.

Meanwhile, Irey was doing something he never had done: finding a prosecutor to his liking—and not from the Justice Department. This was a tactical move that had nothing to do with the qualifications of Justice's prosecutors (and it would come back to haunt him). He believed he had good reason. Pat O'Rourke, working undercover in Louisiana, cautioned him that Long and his gang weren't "worrying much" about the investigation. "They have confidence in local juries," he explained. Wary of Huey's iron grip, Irey decided against bringing a "dam Yankee" prosecutor from Washington.[31]

At one of their Friday conferences, Morgenthau and Irey tossed around names, finally agreeing on Daniel J. Moody. The youngest governor in Texas history, Dan Moody had been elected governor of Texas in 1927 at thirty-four and, before that, had been attorney general since 1925. He started law school at the University of Texas at sixteen. He was a man of modern ideas, one of the first governors to institute civil service requirements to curb patronage in the state bureaucracy. He also was a rawhide-tough trial lawyer with the strength of character and experience to ride down a cattle stampede. In Texas a dozen years later he would lead a losing fight to overturn Lyndon Johnson's "victory" over Coke Stevenson in the U.S. Senate campaign—amid substantive charges of voter fraud.

When Morgenthau approached him, Moody expressed strong reluctance; at that, Morgenthau decided on an end run. On a Sunday morning early in 1935, he took Moody and Elmer Irey to the Oval Office. President Roosevelt was waiting and gave the Texan a particularly warm greeting. Then, Irey recalled, FDR started "pouring on the charm." By the time the meeting ended, Irey said, "Moody would have indicted Sam Houston if FDR wanted him to."[32]

On April 25, 1935, in a New Orleans courtroom where Moody was sitting as prosecutor, State Rep. Joe Fisher of Jefferson parish was found guilty of failing to pay taxes on an income of $122,000 ($1,932,000 in 1990 dollars) that he had received over four years. He was sentenced to eighteen months in the Atlanta penitentiary. He was the first of Huey's lieutenants to go to jail, and no one had been a more loyal and helpful friend to the Kingfish. Fisher had followed Huey's orders in the Irby episode. He was also in a secret club of around 1,000 loyal contributors who would put up from $1,000 ($16,000 in 1990 dollars) to $5,000 ($80,000 in 1990 dollars) each whenever Huey asked them to.

Encouraged by the Fisher verdict, Irey decided to lay the groundwork for the Kingfish's prosecution. Long lived lavishly. He owned more homes and used more hotel quarters than Al Capone. He made frequent train trips to New Orleans. He was carted around Washington in "an expensive car driven by a chauffeur." He "was rumored to own one hundred expensive suits and dozens of costly shirts." He always carried the bulk of his unreported cash in a chest known in his inner circle as the "deduct box." Like a dog on a leash, it went with Long to wherever he spent the night. Most of the contributions to the box came from "salary deductions."

Huey, master political thief that he was, had his own version of kickback heaven. Every state employee was required to return from 2 to 5 percent of their salary to the state's Democratic machine, which meant to the Kingfish. By 1935 the contents of the deduct box had "risen to a million dollars or more," according to historian T. Harry Williams.[33] One little-known tale of how such a sum came to rest in the deduct box was told by James Henry "Blackie" Audett, the career criminal in the employ of Boss Tom Pendergast in Kansas City. "I delivered $260,000 [$3.8 million in 1990 dollars] in cash to Huey Long . . . right down to Louisiana in my billfold like it was cigar coupons. Twenty-six $10,000 bills. It was in the early 1930s sometime, just before the election. I also gave him a message from Mr. Pendergast. He said to tell Huey Long there was no doubt of what the outcome of the election would be—he could rest assured he would be elected."[34]

The Kingfish was also earning fees for being employed as counsel for the Public Service Commission while serving as U.S. senator. This unusual arrangement came out of a Long-sponsored act passed by the legislature in October 1934, giving the commission authority to assess public utilities investigated by the commission with the costs of the investigation, including attorneys' fee. By December 1934 utilities had paid $65,000 ($1,040,000 in 1990 dollars) in such assessments. And Long had a demand in the courts in May 1935 for an additional $20,000 from the Southern Bell Telephone and Telegraph Company, which was fighting a commission order to reduce its rates in Louisiana. In addition, in 1935 he had a bill approved to permit the governor and the attorney general to employ attorneys to represent Louisiana in disputes relating to tax recoveries of the title to land claimed by Louisiana. Under the act, Long received one-third "of the amounts which he can recover for the State and its taxing subdivisions" on account of omissions in assessments and erroneous assessments.[35]

In July 1935 Irey dispatched his top agent, Frank Wilson, to look into the case. Wilson quickly found that "getting people to agree to testify against the all-powerful Kingfish was about as difficult as getting them to give evidence against Scarface and his gang."[36] Running down evidence on Long took him all the way to "the petrified jungle of lower Broadway."[37] At that point, Wilson decided the tax case against the Kingfish "was browned to a turn." Now, as he had done with Al Capone, it "was customary to invite the taxpayer to explain income which we found had not been reported" and he went to New Orleans. He expected "a run-around" before getting in to see him but that didn't happen. When he phoned Long's secretary for an appointment, Long himself called back within five minutes and told them to "come right on over." Wilson, along with several agents in the task force, took the elevator to Long's suite on the ninth floor of the Roosevelt Hotel. As they walked in, Long was standing in his bare feet, hair mussed, wearing a "heavy growth of stubbly beard" and robin's egg blue silk pajamas embroidered with the monogram H. P. L.

"I've heard aboutcha, Wilson." Long peered at him. "Been down here a helluva long time, haven'tcha? Makin' any headway?"

"Oh, yes, we're making a lot of headway," replied Wilson.

Wilson's strategy was to lay down a barrage of questions on completely unsuspicious items. All during the session Huey lay stomach down in his silk pajamas, feet at the head of the bed, answering questions in his high-pitched voice, telling "countless yarns, parables, racy jokes" and laughing. They found he had a prodigious memory, rattling off countless details in his answers. But when they began asking more important questions—such as who had paid off the mortgage on his house—he suddenly lost his memory.

Wilson told the Kingfish that they had evidence that Seymour Weiss had paid off his $25,000 ($400,000 in 1990 dollars) mortgage in cash—laying down twenty-five one-thousand-dollar bills.

Still lying on his stomach, he dropped his forehead into his hands and said, "I don't remember anything about that. Man, that's none of my business. That's my wife's house."

Wilson mentioned expenses such as $1,320 ($16,120 in 1990 dollars) in a two-month period for expensive Wagner & Wagner suits, which Weiss paid for. "I've been getting suits there for years," Long replied. "They're better'n anything in New York or Washington."

The questioning went on until 6:00 p.m., when Huey abruptly cut them off, explaining he had an engagement. He invited them to come back "again sometime."

Wilson made a date for the next afternoon, telling Long that he wanted to bring along a stenographer—a young lady. The Kingfish got the point. "Man, I won't only be dressed! I'll get that gal of yours a swell box of candy!"

The next day Wilson brought a "demure little blonde" who blushed when the Kingfish presented her with a box of candy. He was wearing a double-breasted white serge suit, a silk shirt, a violet tie, a violet pocket-handkerchief, and black-and-white sport shoes. He was "clean-shaven, combed, shining."

It was a long session, Wilson said, with the stenographer taking it all down. At the end, Wilson knew "we had a clear case of tax evasion."

Wilson took everything back to Washington. During his meeting with Commissioner Guy T. Helvering and Irey, Robert H. Jackson, the Bureau of Internal Revenue's forty-three-year old general counsel (who would later serve on the Supreme Court), was brought in. After Wilson laid it all out for them, "they beamed."[38]

■

On Saturday, September 7, 1935, after a long train ride from Washington, Irey met in a hotel room in Dallas with Dan Moody and Archie Burford, who had been on the case from the start—four years had passed. Now, Burford and Irey were going to review the evidence with Moody and decide what to do about Huey Long.

After examining the pile of documents, Moody literally tossed a lighted match into it. He said he didn't think a jury would convict the Kingfish for cheating on his taxes.

Irey said nothing—though he may have been envisioning a spiral of smoke and wondering about the tireless efforts of his investigators.

Moody went on. "Nor are we likely to do it because the Yankee contractors saw fit to pay his gang a few million in graft. We might embarrass him, but he embarrasses hard and anyhow we aren't trying to do that. We want a conviction."

Irey spoke up. "I know all this too well," he said. Nodding at Burford, he said, "He's dug up something that might do the job."[39]

Long, Burford explained, was involved with the Win-or-Lose Corporation, an oil and gas company that bought, sold, or exchanged lands and leases for the drilling and prospecting of oil, gas, and other minerals. He had devised the structure of the company, which was chartered by the state in 1934. The company's president was James A. "Jimmie" Noe of Monroe, president pro tempore of the state senate. Seymour Weiss was vice president. Long owned thirty-one shares in the Win-or-Lose Corporation, Noe owned a like number, Weiss owned twenty-four, and Governor O. K. Allen, Long's handpicked successor, owned twelve shares.

Noe, Burford went on, had acquired twenty sites in proven gas fields near Monroe from Governor Allen for "absolutely nothing" and transferred the leases to the corporation. Win-or-Lose offered the leases to two gas companies at $25,000 per location. The companies said no. Shortly thereafter, the two gas companies changed their mind. They bought the twenty leases from Win-or-Lose for $16,000 each ($256,000 in 1990 dollars). Win-or-Lose realized $320,000 ($5,120,000 in 1990 dollars) on the deal, of which the Kingfish made $62,000 ($998,200 in 1990 dollars).

Irey told Moody he considered these manipulations to be grand larceny. It was a classic scheme of larcenous hearts. In this case, raw political manipulation had shot up the value of the leases. Long benefited from this increase, Irey said, and this was grand larceny. The Kingfish's fingerprints were all over the deal, Burford chimed in.

Then Irey dealt Moody another card he could use on jurors. State Senator Noe had manipulated the sale, Irey said. Noe had announced he planned to introduce a measure to allow the state to increase taxes on natural gas produced in Louisiana from one-fiftieth of a cent per thousand feet to two cents flat per thousand. If passed, oil and gas companies operating in Louisiana would "pay through the nose," Irey said. Yet, after the two companies purchased the leases from Win-or-Lose, the bill quickly dropped from sight.

Then Irey dealt Moody the final card.

These dealings, he said, will reveal Long as "the con man" he really was. Long had always depicted himself as the "archfoe of the soulless corporation," but it was a corporation that had made $320,000 ($5,120,000 in 1990 dollars) for himself and his pals. Tying the Kingfish to the deal will rob him "of his stature as the poor man's friend," he said.

Moody was convinced. "I will go before the grand jury when it meets next month and ask for an indictment against Long."[40] The grand jury hearing was scheduled for October 3.

The next day, Sunday, September 8, Huey Long was at the state capitol, where the legislature was in special session. At about 9:20 p.m., he was standing in the corridor talking to a small group near the main door of the governor's office when Dr. Carl Austin Weiss (no relation to Seymour Weiss), wearing a white suit, "flashed among" the group, pointed a "small pistol" at Huey, and fired a shot. In the sudden aftermath, Long's bodyguards and capitol police mowed him down. In the fusillade, they fired sixty-eight rounds. As Weiss lay on the floor, a number of the bodyguards emptied their guns into him. Up to twenty-four entry wounds were found in Weiss.

A single .45-caliber bullet had entered under Long's ribs on the right side and exited in the back near his spine. Dr. Arthur Vidrine, the superintendent of Charity Hospital in New Orleans, was visiting the legislative session and "with the tacit consent of those present he became the doctor in charge."[41] In the hour-long operation, Dr. Vidrine opened Long's abdomen and found the liver, gall bladder, and stomach free of injury. He saw two perforations in the colon, as the bullet had cut through one fold and then another. He found a small amount of blood in the abdominal cavity and a small blood clot in the small intestine. He sutured the wounds of entrance and exit in the colon and the abdomen was closed.

The next morning, however, Huey was getting worse. Surgeons called in "were shocked" to learn that Dr. Vidrine had not catheterized the bladder to see if it contained blood. At their urging, a catheter was inserted, and the urine was found to be holding a "great deal of blood."[42] The bullet had hit a renal duct in the kidney, but Dr. Vidrine had not discovered it the day before. Long was experiencing internal hemorrhaging from the kidney. The physicians agreed that in his weakened condition another operation to tie off the kidney would be fatal. Though he had been given five blood transfusions, Long continued to weaken.

Approximately thirty hours after being shot, Huey Long, age forty-two, died at 4:06 a.m., Tuesday, September 10, 1935, in a bed at Our Lady of the Lake Hospital in Baton Rouge. His family was at his bedside. No autopsy was performed on Long—or on Dr. Weiss.

"I hated to see that," Irey later told his son, Hugh. "We had him dead to rights. We would have nailed him to the wall."[43]

■

Long's assassination didn't stop the Louisiana investigation. Irey's task force had spent more than a year and a half on it, and in the mountain of evidence, a huge pile centered on the late Kingfish's inner circle. Irey wasted no time in having prosecutors turn to them. Seymour Weiss occupied first place in the pecking order of prosecution, followed by Monte Hart, then Abe Shushan. But after a review of evidence, it was agreed that Shushan would make the strongest case for prosecution.

On October 8, exactly one month after Long's assassination, Shushan went on trial in federal court in New Orleans, charged with accepting $525,732 ($8,311,712 in 1990 dollars) in bribes on which he paid no taxes. His lawyers argued that the money Shushan received came from political contributions he was holding as agent. The jury's verdict was a shocker: "Not guilty."

Irey described his feelings and the courthouse scene immediately after the ruling: "We Intelligence Unit men were a sick lot as we watched the

Huey Long mobsters cheer wildly and then methodically manhandle the newspaper cameramen and smash their equipment."[44] Then, it got worse.

The next trial, that of Seymour Weiss, was set for May 1936. Days before it was to start, and without warning anyone at the Treasury in advance, the Justice Department dismissed all of the remaining cases, eleven in all. Attorney General Homer Cummings had handed the hot potato to the U.S. attorney in New Orleans, Rene A. Viosca. In later accounts, the cases were called "weak."[45] In his memoir, Irey noted that Viosca announced that the "changed atmosphere" in Louisiana since Senator Long's death had made convictions "very improbable."[46] In his motion in court before U.S. Judge Wayne G. Borah on May 29, Viosca said, "I have given the most careful consideration to these cases and am firmly of the opinion that the government has no reasonable hope to secure convictions in any of them."[47] More than two years of hard work had suddenly ended. All the Treasury had to show for it was Joe Fisher's conviction.

A donnybrook ensued. For the first time in his career, Irey publicly attacked the Justice Department, declaring the move came in "an election year." Frank Wilson pointed out that it occurred on the eve of the Democratic National Convention, set for June in Philadelphia (at which FDR gave his "rendezvous with destiny" address.) The press, generally anti-Long, called it "the Second Louisiana Purchase."

The nine members of the federal grand jury in New Orleans (who had taken nine months to bring the indictments) assailed the move in a letter to Viosca. In part, it said, "As to whether the cases are 'weak,' this same United States Attorney . . . presented these 'weak' cases to us for investigation." The letter sarcastically concluded, "We suggest that Representative Joe Fisher, possibly one of the least of the offenders, should be released from prison as he is now the victim of gross and unwarranted official discrimination."[48]

Political or not, the Justice Department had never really been made a part of the ongoing effort to bring down Huey Long. The department had resented that Irey went to an outside source—Dan Moody—to handle Long's prosecution.

For any prosecutor worth his salt, the Long case was the Super Bowl, with the victor getting his name in the history books. But all the Justice Department got to handle were the cases of the lieutenants, not the captain of the ship. Now, it .was payback time. Moreover, the Justice Department had been forced to go along with the case, not because Long was the centerpiece of this high drama, but because it was obligated to provide prosecutorial help. With the Kingfish gone, the ship was in dry dock.

In the middle of this, Elmer Irey, now forty-eight, suffered a heart attack. The Long case had been wearing. Irey was juggling two other major cases at the time—Boss Tom Pendergast in Kansas City and Moses L. Annenberg, the Chicago racing wire tycoon. Irey suffered from diabetes; he didn't know it, and he never had it treated. "Genetically, he came from a family that was riddled with diabetes," explained his son, Hugh, a physician who practiced in Baltimore. Hugh believed the diabetes eventually led to serious heart trouble for his father. The disease had been with him a long time. When the United States entered the war in 1917, Irey, then twenty-nine, had gone to an Army recruiting station to enlist. Doctors gave him his physical, found he had a high blood sugar count, and rejected him. Irey continued to ignore this diabetic symptom.

All his life he had been a teetotaler. "Therapy for a heart condition was very limited in those days," said Hugh. "So the doctor suggested he ought to have a drink or two in the evening. Dad would have a bourbon and water and it helped to relax him. That was the first time he had alcohol in the house."[49]

At the Treasury, meanwhile, Morgenthau didn't allow the Justice Department's dismissal of the Louisiana criminal prosecutions to deter him. He had the cases taken to the U.S. Court of Tax Appeals, It was a civil proceeding in which Justice had no authority to seek dismissal.

In 1937 a special section of the Board of Tax Appeals heard the suits and ruled against the defendants. More than $2 million ($38 million in 1990 dollars) in taxes and penalties were collected from Huey Long's estate, Weiss, Shushan, New Orleans Mayor Robert Maestri, and other prominent figures in Louisiana.

■

Early in 1937 Rufus W. Fontenot, the collector of internal revenue in New Orleans who happened to be born in Crowley and attended Louisiana State University, paid a visit to Elmer Irey at the Treasury. The SIU's chief had recuperated and was in the midst of a tax-evasion case involving Frank Costello (who eventually beat it). Fontenot's duties often brought him to Washington, and since he had helped in the Long investigation, Irey asked him how things were going in Louisiana.

"Elmer, they are absolutely contemptuous not only of us, but of the entire government. They're stealing more than ever."

"You watching their returns?" Irey asked.

"Sure," said Fontenot. The members of Long's old gang were being "very careful" with their income tax statements, he said, but they hadn't gotten any smarter. They were reporting a lot more money on their tax returns, he explained, and calling it "gambling winnings." Fontenot didn't believe it was coming from gambling. "Dick Leche, he's governor now, had a return that said simply, 'Other Earnings $90,000 [$1,380,000 in 1990 dollars].'"

"Somebody's foot'll slip," Irey said.

To Fontenot, Irey seemed interested but reticent. Looking grim, he asked if Irey would go back into Louisiana.

"My ears are still red," Irey cracked. Fontenot left it at that.

A few months later Irey received a phone call from Fontenot. "One of 'em has slipped," he told Irey. "Slipped right up to his neck. I'm catching a train to Washington tonight."[50]

Before his assassination, Huey Long was prophetic about the greed of those around him. "They'll be stealing the emblems off the capitol pretty soon," he told his secretary. He had tried to maintain a semblance of order to the graft. "Huey assumed a certain amount of corruption," one intimate related, "relatively little stuff, enough to make a good living." But what he had left was a legacy of unsurpassed corruption.

Two days later, in Irey's office, Fontenot laid out his case. The man who had slipped up was J. Monroe Smith, the president of Louisiana State University, an academic who got his PhD in educational administration from

Columbia University and was handpicked by Long to run the institution (it was referred to as "Long-Smith University"). The Kingfish had always taken a keen interest in the university, leading the band, giving pep talks to the football team. After Tulane trounced LSU 34-7, he had the football coach fired. He took LSU as his own, Irey observed, to spite Tulane, his old alma mater—after the New Orleans institution refused to give him an honorary degree.

"He's never had a nickel in his life," Fontenot said of J. Monroe Smith, "yet he's speculating heavily in whiskey warehouse receipts and last year he sold more than $130,000 [$1,950,000 in 1990 dollars] worth of stock under a fictitious name. He makes $18,000 [$270,000 in 1990 dollars] a year and his wife spends four times that in parties."

"What's he say in his tax returns?" asked Irey.

"He's never filed any."[51]

After conferring with Commissioner Helvering and Archie Burford (who had been promoted to another post) Irey decided to try again. He sent another team, headed by Frank W. Lohn, to Louisiana.

This time, it took the SIU investigators until early 1940 to pin down the remaining members of the Long gang, all of whom went to jail. This remarkable effort by Irey's Intelligence Unit remains today the most successful investigation ever conducted by any federal agency into state corruption. Seymour Weiss, Monte Hart, Abe Shushan, and J. Monroe Smith were sentenced to two and a half years in prison. (The forty-five-year-old Shushan never went to prison; in 1947 President Harry Truman pardoned him.) H. W. Waguespeck, a member of the Levee Board; Henry Miller, a city accountant in New Orleans; and members of the New Orleans brokerage firm Newman and Harris were given the same sentences. Louis C. Lesage, a Standard Oil Company lobbyist, and J. Emory Adams, a nephew of Monroe Smith, got a year and a day. All were convicted of mail fraud, based on evidence Irey turned over to postal inspectors.

The severest penalty went to Governor Richard Leche, a former judge on the state appeals court who was elected in 1936, shortly after Long's assassination. Leche admitted making $1 million ($15 million in 1990 dollars) in his three years as governor. At his trial, he admitted from the stand that he and Seymour Weiss took $67,000 ($1,005,000 in 1990 dollars) as a bribe in an oil deal. Convicted, Leche was thrown in jail for ten years.

Irey also broke up a flourishing racket in state tax reductions. In all, the Treasury made $6,372,360 ($95,585,400 in 1990 dollars) in additional taxes and penalties from the Louisiana investigation. "I doubt seriously if the investigation cost the American people a quarter-million dollars," Irey said.[52]

Elmer Irey in 1946, shortly before he retired. (Courtesy of Hugh Irey)

To Mrs. Mrs. Irey — my very kindest wishes

Elmer Irey; his wife, Marguerite (far left); and friends; with actress Ginger Rogers on a Hollywood movie set in 1946. At far right is Hugh Irey, his younger brother. Irey went to the movie colony in 1946 for the making of *The T-Men* at RKO, in which he gave the introduction, the only time he ever appeared on film. (Courtesy of Hugh Irey)

The *Washington Evening Star* ran this editorial cartoon by Clifford K. Berryman on its front page on August 31, 1946, the day before Elmer Irey retired.

Dec. 30, 1932

Dear Mr Irey:

I want you to know how much we appreciate all that you have done for us during the past year. It is not possible for me to thank you sufficiently for your own assistance and for that of your department. I know of nothing which could have been done that was not, and I fully realize the time and effort that your organization has spent. It has meant a great deal to us to be able to go to you for advice and I want to thank you again for the many ways you have helped. Time and time again during the past months I have realized the value of federal organization.

Sincerely

Charles A. Lindbergh

Handwritten letter from Charles Lindbergh to Elmer Irey.
(Courtesy of Hugh Irey)

August 13, 1946

Dear Elmer:

The information has reached me that you are retiring from the Government Service at the end of this month and were it not for the fact that I finally retired last December, I would doubt it. The possibility that the time would eventually come when you and I would no longer be in the Government Service never entered my thoughts. I guess that I just took it for granted that we would - just go on. I telephoned Joe Callan's office to get his reaction but found that he is in Bermuda.

You are about the last of a long line of men who were prominent in the Postal Inspection Service and the Treasury Department which included Joe P. Johnston, Joe Callan, Arthur Nichols, Herbert Lucas, Frank Fraser, Everitt Partridge, Commissioners Blair and Helvering, and many others.

In organizing the Intelligence Unit and being its head for twenty-seven years, (through the administrations of five presidents, during which time you had to contend with many unreasonable officials) and bringing the Unit to the high standard that it now has, you have clearly demonstrated that you are not only an excellent executive but are also a top diplomat and President Truman should send you to the Paris Peace Conference to assist Secretary of State Byrnes to handle Molotov and Vishinsky.

You are too young and active to go into complete retirement and my advice to you is to accept one of the many part time positions that are offered to you and to spend the summers at Shady Side and the winters in Florida and I hope to have the opportunity to visit you at both places during the coming years.

With all good wishes for many years of health and contentment for Mrs. Irey and yourself, I wish always to remain,

Your sincere friend,

Hugh McQuillan

Mr. Elmer L. Irey

Congratulatory letters on Elmer Irey's retirement came from Frank Wilson, chief of the U.S. Secret Service who had been the lead agent in the Capone investigation, and Hugh McQuillan, who headed the SIU branch in New York City. (Courtesy of Hugh Irey)

TREASURY DEPARTMENT

WASHINGTON 25, D. C.

August 20, 1946

My dear Chief:

    Your contemplated retirement from active service brings to mind many pleasant memories of the happy years during which I have had the satisfaction of being associated with you. It's a big satisfaction to be associated with a man who does big things in a big way, and that was your continuous program as Chief of the Intelligence Unit and later as Chief Coordinator of the Treasury Enforcement Agencies. Therefore, I had plenty of the best kind of satisfaction during the twenty-six years of our association.

    I wish to express my gratitude for your friendly interest in my official and personal welfare, and for the inspiration you have been to me during that period. I sincerely trust that you and Mrs. Irey have many happy years ahead of you, and that you will be able to continue to enjoy the close association with Hugh and Robert and their families. Also that you and they will be blessed with continued good health and that all of you will have loads of enjoyment at Shady Side and Sarasota.

    With continued high regards and esteem, I am

Cordially yours,

Frank J. Wilson

Mr. Elmer L. Irey
Chief Coordinator
Treasury Enforcement Agencies
Washington, D. C.

Leon Gleckman, right, known as the "Al Capone" of St. Paul, with his attorney, William Anderson, outside the federal building in Minneapolis. (Courtesy of *St. Paul Pioneer Press*)

March 9, 1942

Personal

Dear Mr. Irey:

On March fifteenth neither you nor I
are particularly popular. On this coming March
fifteenth we will be unpopular with more millions
of tax payers than ever before. Since we are to be
companions in misery, I feel I should take a
moment to tell you of my pride in the work of the
Intelligence Unit.

It has just come to my attention that
twenty-three years ago this coming Friday, March
thirteenth, you organized the Intelligence Unit
under my old friend, Dan Roper, who at that time
was Commissioner of Internal Revenue. As the
years have gone by, the Intelligence Unit has
become a shining mark not only of incorruptibility
but what is just as important, of A-1 efficiency.

I know how much quiet pride you have in
the reputation of the Unit. I am taking this
opportunity to let you know I share in that pride.
I hope you will let your staff know of my feeling.

Very sincerely yours,

Franklin D. Roosevelt

Honorable Elmer L. Irey
Chief
Intelligence Unit
Bureau of Internal Revenue
Washington, D. C.

Letters from President Franklin D. Roosevelt and Secretary of the Treasury
Henry Morgenthau on anniversaries of Elmer Irey's career. (Courtesy of
Hugh Irey.)

March 9, 1944

Dear Elmer:

Two very important anniversaries occur in the next two or three days. One is your birthday, and I extend hearty congratulations upon it. The other is the date of your completing twenty-five years of service in the Treasury, and while you are to be congratulated upon this, I think that the warmest congratulations should go to the Treasury Department rather than to you.

As you round out this period of service, I want to tell you again, as I have told you in the past, what a great contribution you have made to the Department and through it to the entire country. We are proud of you and of the record you have made here. As you complete another year of your life and the twenty-fifth year of your service here, I send you my very best wishes for many happy and successful years to come.

Sincerely,

Henry Morgenthau Jr

Mr. Elmer L. Irey
Chief Coordinator, Treasury
  Enforcement Agencies
Treasury Department
Washington, D. C.

14. BOSS PENDERGAST

Just after 9:00 a.m., on the morning of Monday, May 22, 1939, portly, bald, sixty-seven-year-old Thomas J. Pendergast, known as Boss Tom Pendergast and Kansas City's best-known political figure, stood in a dark business suit before fifty-five-year-old U.S. District Judge Merrill E. Otis for sentencing after his conviction for tax evasion. The setting was unusual. The sentencing did not take place in the disciplined atmosphere of a courtroom. The scene was messy, a metaphor for the way Boss Pendergast had run Kansas City. A new federal courthouse was under construction, so court was held in a building normally used for storage and as a printing plant, located directly behind the construction site. The crowd watching the proceedings was so large it spilled into the corridor. Since this day was special—indeed, historic—the media was there in force: radio commentators spoke in muffled tones amid the clatter of teletype machines, and stirring this noisy mix were sounds of construction. In the statement he read before sentencing, Judge Otis, regally ignoring the distraction, noted the significance of the occasion and mercifully distinguished among Pendergast's wrongdoings.

Said Otis, "If the crime charged is, as here, attempted tax evasion, the punishment should be for attempted tax evasion. Not a job or title should be added to the punishment because it is judicially noted that the defendant has been a political 'boss,' nor because it is judicially noticed that the city and county which he has dominated have been governed with inde-scribable corruption and dishonesty. There are those, I know, who think such matters should affect the sentence imposed for attempted tax eva-sion. They who think so err."[1]

The prosecutor who helped fell one of the greatest political dynas-ties ever created in America was Maurice M. Milligan, the U.S. attorney for the Western District of Missouri. A Missouri native, Milligan had been after Pendergast for five years, but he had known about him since 1911, when he was twenty-seven and Pendergast was thirty-eight. This is how he described him the day he saw him in that year: "He wore a black derby hat slightly cocked on one side of a massive head of bulldog proportions. His face was ruddy, and what impressed me most was his thick, bull-like neck that gave him the appearance of a wrestler . . . his voice was deep and throaty. I thought then, and I think now, that he was made to order for the pen of the cartoonist—a burly Irishman with a truculent look, an exagger-ated paunch, and a big head crowned with a small derby. Nast's cartoon of Boss Tweed came to mind. Tweed weighed 300 pounds; Pendergast around 250 pounds."[2]

Since the turn of the century, Boss Tom Pendergast's political machine had run Kansas City. It was a snake pit of crime and corruption, exceeded only by New York's Tammany Hall, and of course, Chicago, because those two cities operated on a much larger scale. Biographer-historian Michael Wallis described Kansas City as "the crown jewel on a gaudy necklace of lawless havens—a corridor of crime—ranging from St. Paul and Detroit in the North to Joplin, Missouri, and Hot Springs, Arkansas, in the South."[3] Irey called the city where he was born "the nation's greatest dope outlet."[4] Lear B. Reed, former chief of police of Kansas City, said: "The Bowery, the Barbary Coast, Chinatown, the Orient, Singapore and other notorious spots on the globe that have been in the spotlight of fact or fancy—none of them had anything on Kansas City."[5] Burton Turkus, the Brooklyn assistant district attorney who successfully prosecuted Louis Lepke, called Kansas City the "hideout haven for lammisters," referring to the hit men of New York–based Murder, Inc.[6] Mendy Weiss, the hulking racketeer and hired killer (of Dutch Schultz, among others) and Lepke's trusted operations chief, hid out in Kansas City for six months in 1941. Though wanted posters with his face on them were everywhere and he even was registered for the draft in the city's Seventh Ward, Weiss was "picked up fifteen times by Kansas City police for traffic violations," an incredulous Turkus exclaimed, "and was let go every time!"[7]

For years, normal law and order did not apply to Boss Pendergast and the criminal-political alliance he ran, a system that existed in other cities around the country—only the names changed. Irey, as he already had in Chicago, New Orleans, and New York City, would send a force of agents to Kansas City.

■

The SIU had already been drawn to John Lazia, the city's most influential racketeer, one of Boss Tom's key lieutenants, and an attendee of the May 1929 crime summit in Atlantic City. In 1932 Special Agent Harry D. Beach called Lazia to the SIU's office at the Federal Reserve Bank Building in Kansas City to discuss the $100,000 ($1.7 million in 1990 dollars) that had passed through his hands in 1928 and 1929, on which he had not filed a tax return. Lazia was defiant, so Beach said, "We shall take the proper steps."[8]

Four days later, two men entered Beach's apartment at the Berkshire Arms Hotel and beat him senseless. He died from injuries and his assailants were never apprehended—whereupon, Irey entered the case in earnest.

Lazia, a slender, dapper man "frequently wearing spats" and carrying a swagger stick, was born in Kansas City's Little Italy district (the Ninth Ward) in 1897. He had made his political mark before he was out of his twenties, seizing control of the ward in 1926 and becoming the "King of Little Italy." He owned the Cuban Gardens, a popular nightclub adjacent to Pendergast's Riverside racetrack, which "took in as much as $8,000 [$120,000 in 1990 dollars] from gambling on a good night." Digging into his background, the SIU found his holdings also included a greyhound racetrack in neighboring Clay County. He had covered his money trail. Neither the track nor the nightclub was listed in his name. The rent went to an employee of the Merchants Bank in Kansas City. At one point, an SIU agent called police headquarters to inquire about Lazia, and Lazia himself answered the phone.

The police deferred to him. For his support of Pendergast, wrote David McCullough, Lazia had "control over liquor and gambling, along with broad powers in hiring policies at police headquarters."[9] This turned out to be a deadly concession. In 1932, when the state legislature gave Kansas City home rule over its police department, Lazia used his powers to hire seventy recently released convicts from Leavenworth for second careers in law enforcement. Canadian-born James Blackie Audett, a bootlegger, thief, and kidnapper who served time in Leavenworth, was a Lazia henchman.

At one time, an estimated 10 percent of Kansas City's policemen possessed criminal records. This was one reason why Lear B. Reed, who had served in the FBI's field office in Kansas City and whom reformers named the chief of police the July after Pendergast's tax conviction, called the city's "gang-ruled police department" the "worst" in the United States.[10] When the daughter of City Manager Henry F. McElroy, Mary, was kidnapped in broad daylight on Saturday, May 27, 1933, authorities called on John Lazia to handle the ransom negotiations. As the lord of Kansas City's underworld, he had the best antenna in that underworld. The kidnappers wanted $30,000 ($480,000 in 1990 dollars). It took him one day to raise it. On a Sunday eight days later, her abductors released her.

The SIU's inquiry of Lazia had been going on for almost a year when in May 1933 Pendergast wrote James Farley, the new postmaster general and FDR insider, to ask the new administration "to go easy on one of my chief lieutenants [Lazia]. . . . I know it was simply a case of being jobbed because of his Democratic activities."[11]

In February 1934, federal prosecutors for the Western District of Missouri took Lazia to trial for evasion of income taxes. A jury convicted him, but the judge released him on bond pending his appeal for a new trial. Carl Sifakis wrote that Lazia was making signs of informing against the machine in exchange for gentle treatment.[12] If that was the case, final retribution took a little more than a year. On July 10, 1934, at 3 o'clock in the morning, Charles Carrollo, Lazia's chief lieutenant, pulled his boss's car up to the front of the Park Central Hotel, where Lazia and his wife had a penthouse apartment. As Lazia got out to open the door for his wife, two trig-germen stepped from the shadows and cut loose, one blasting away with a Thompson submachine gun, the other with a shotgun. Shot eight times, Lazia died twelve hours later. The bullets that killed the Kansas City Godfa-ther were matched with the bullets from the Thompson submachine gun used at the infamous Union Station massacre in Kansas City on the morn-ing of June 17, 1933, when gunmen ambushed a group of lawmen bringing in a fugitive, Frank (Jelly) Nash. Four were killed, including Nash and an FBI agent, and two of the lawmen were wounded. The gunmen escaped.

■

In January 1934 Homer Cummings called Maurice Milligan to Wash-ington to make him the U.S. attorney for the Western District of Missouri in Kansas City, telling him Kansas City was "one of the three 'hot spots' in the United States." Cummings didn't call it a "hot spot" because of the Pendergast machine or the 1933 Union Station massacre. He called it that because Kansas City and two other "hot spots," Chicago and St. Paul, made up the Bermuda Triangle of kidnappings. They were associated "in some manner with every kidnapping that has occurred to date, either as the situs of the crime, the hideout or the place of ransom payment."[13]

New to the job, Milligan, age fifty, was no stranger to what was happen-ing. A Missourian born and raised on his family's farm outside Richmond in Bay County, forty miles northeast of Kansas City, he knew the region's heritage. Jesse James, who in 1866 became the country's first bank rob-ber, maintained a secret hangout in Bay County, on the farm adjoining the Milligan farm. His mother, according to Milligan, "saw the James boys rob the Richmond bank."[14] When Milligan returned from his meeting with Attorney General Cummings, he didn't preoccupy himself with kidnap-pers and bank robbers. He had his hands full with the invincible Boss Tom Pendergast.

In the municipal elections in March 1934, the Pendergast machine faced its first serious challenge. A reform movement, the Fusionists, had put up its own slate of candidates, including Dr. A. Ross Hill, former presi-dent of the University of Missouri, as mayor. Election Day that cold March became known as the "Bloody Election." Cruising bands of thugs intimidated voters and beat others, wielding a gun butt to the head and face of a *Kansas City Star* reporter. Seven shots were fired into the plate glass window of the Fusionist headquarters. At the end of the day, there had been four murders, and "dozens" were injured, "eleven seriously." The Fusionists lost, of course, and nothing was done to bring the violators to justice.

Blackie Audett told of his role in the election: "My first job in Kansas City was to look up vacant lots. I looked them up, precinct by precinct and turned them lists in to Mr. Pendergast—that's Tom Pendergast, the man who used to run Kansas City . . . when we got a precinct all surveyed out, we would give addresses to them vacant lots. Then we would take the addresses and assign them to people we could depend on—prostitutes, thieves, floaters, anybody we could get on the voting registration books. On election days we just hauled these people to the right places and they went in and voted—in the right places."[15]

After the reelection of FDR in November 1936, a citizens' committee in Kansas City turned over evidence about election fraud to Milligan. In the election, upward of 60,000 "ghost" voters had stalked through various polling places. Many were "repeaters," some voted up to thirty times.[16] To get a flavor of the rigged voting that year, the Lawrence McDaniel campaign stands out. McDaniel, a prominent St. Louis lawyer, ran for the state supreme court in the August 1936 primary against Judge Ernest S. Gantt, a Pendergast machine candidate. McDaniel carried a substantial majority of the 114 counties in Missouri and the City of St. Louis. But in Kansas City's First Ward (Boss Pendergast's stomping grounds), Gantt received 18,919 votes whereas McDaniel had 18. In the Second Ward, Gantt got 19,201 votes and McDaniel received only 13. In the November 1936 election, 20,687 votes were cast in the First Ward. The ward had a total population of 19,923, including children.

Milligan took the evidence presented by the citizens' committee and had a grand jury impaneled. J. Edgar Hoover sent a team of special agents to Kansas City to investigate voter fraud. On the team was Charles Appel Jr., an expert examiner who set up a laboratory to study the voting data, including photographing and enlarging ballots and records, studying fingerprints and conducting other tests. It was the bureau's first major field effort to meld its scientific and investigative capabilities (and still stands as one of the most successful of its kind that the FBI undertook).

Beginning in January 1937 and carrying into 1938, Milligan ran a series of grand juries that returned thirty-nine indictments involving 278 election judges, precinct captains, and clerks, many of whom were women, for voting irregularities. Some were criminal enforcers, "but most were essentially honest men and women who were following orders." Pendergast got up a $100,000 defense fund for them—explaining that his nephew James and William Boyle, a contractor, raised the money. The trials, lasting into 1939, used Appel's expert testimony, along with his damning charts and photographs. Juries convicted 63, 36 pleaded guilty, 162 pleaded nolo contendere, and 17 were nolle prossed—for a total of 278. In addition, $60,000 ($900,000 in 1990 dollars) in fines was collected.

It was a remarkable, yet bittersweet, accomplishment for Milligan. The strongman behind all the years of voter fraud—Boss Pendergast—remained untouched, as it had been since before the turn of the century. Thomas was a native Missourian, born in St. Joseph in 1872. Seventeen years later, his older brother, James A. "Big Jim" Pendergast, a gregarious saloon owner and budding politician who resembled the great prizefighter John L. Sullivan, brought his three younger brothers, Thomas, Michael, and John to Kansas City—and thus began a long and corrupt dynasty. When Big Jim died in 1911, he had been boss of the notorious First Ward and a member of the city council for eighteen years. Tom, then age thirty-nine, took over the ward and branched out, eventually controlling the rest of the city and Jackson County, with a voting population then of more than 400,000. At city hall, City Manager Henry "The Judge" McElroy was his front man. By 1931 Boss Tom's machine controlled such a large segment of the state's voting strength that it was next to impossible for a candidate running at large to be elected without the support of his machine. He was not only the undisputed boss of Kansas City but also a major political power statewide. The capitol in Jefferson City was called "Uncle Tom's Cabin."[17]

Pendergast resided in splendor. His $100,000 ($1.8 million in 1990 dollars) home at 5650 Ward Parkway, built in 1927, was one of the city's most palatial structures and fronted one of the most splendid avenues in the Midwest. But he maintained a nondescript second-floor office above a barber supply shop at 1908 Main Street, where decisions were made and favors flowed. His business interests touched just about everyone in Kansas City.[18] With a group of partners, he ran the T. J. Pendergast Wholesale Liquor Company. His chief source of income was his Ready-Mixed Concrete Company, established in 1928 with Michael Ross who controlled Ross Construction, and held the monopoly on concrete. To avoid trouble with city inspectors, all "prudent" independent builders used Pendergast's companies. Such an enterprise was handy when the "lavish Federal aid dispensed by the New Deal gave Kansas City a public building program of enormous proportions," said Maurice Milligan. "These public improvements cost around $50,000,000."[19]

With his iron grip on both the city and state governments, the route through democratic means was never going to bring him down. As Irey observed, "He was second only to Hitler's associates in the practice of stuffing ballot boxes." The political spoils system was another matter, however. Pendergast's millions had come from the graft and unfair advantages in a complicated network of official dealings, like building contracts, public works, relief jobs, and recovery projects from the federal financing that flowed into the state. In the spoils system, where the currency is cash, not ideals, the grip is less firm. What finally brought down Pendergast was that he never passed up the chance for more spoils, particularly since he was staring down enormous gambling debts.

The conspiracy that took him down involved Missouri's insurance industry and a whopping cash prize of $9,020,279.01 ($135,304,185 in 1990 dollars) the industry sorely wanted. In October 1922 the Missouri state superintendent of insurance ordered a 10 percent reduction in fire insurance claims, a move the industry fought all the way to the U.S. Supreme Court and lost. Meanwhile, the industry had raised rates 16 2/3 percent, bringing more litigation from Missouri and a court order that money from the rate increase be impounded until it was decided who would get it. By 1935 the escrow had reached that $9,020,279.01 sum, and the legislature passed a compromise bill (Irey: It "could very easily have been written by the insurance companies") giving 50 percent to the insurance companies,

30 percent for the insurance company's legal fees and 20 percent to policy-holders. Before signing the bill, Governor Guy B. Park took it to Attorney General Roy McKittrick, who said he could "see flaws" in the document and opposed its signing. McKittrick "was astonished" to learn that Park had signed the bill later that day—May 18, 1935. Over the next year and a half, so much controversy ensued over the back and forth at the meeting between Park and McKittrick, that the legislature appointed a committee to investigate the circumstances. After the investigation—Irey called it a "whitewash"—the insurance agreement stood.

At that point—early 1937—Missouri's new governor, Lloyd C. Stark, and Milligan took off to Washington for a meeting at the Treasury with Secretary Morgenthau, who brought in Elmer Irey. Milligan told them, "Pendergast got paid off for that insurance deal and everybody in Missouri says he got a half-million dollars."

Irey asked Milligan, "Do you think Street paid Pendergast off?"

Both Milligan and Stark "were sure."[20]

"Street" was Charles R. Street of Chicago, who ran the fire insurance industry in the West. His formal title was vice president of the Great American Insurance Company and the chairman of the Subscribers Actuarial Committee of the 137 associated insurance companies that would get slices of the $9 million. Charles Street, the classic wheeler-dealer, was already known to Irey, who was also familiar with the insurance settlement (he called it "the 1935 Missouri Compromise"). He didn't like what he found out about Street, which immediately raised his suspicions. (He "gave a much better description of his position in the fire insurance than I could," Irey revealed. Speaking before a "meeting of top fire-insurance executives," according to Irey, Street said, "In all the speeches that I have heard today, cooperation has been stressed. But in my opinion the only man who cooperates is the man who does my bidding, or does as I want him to.")[21]

Street had a "dominating personality," according to Larsen and Hulston, and possessed "the power to make decisions for the companies."[22] Irey had been alerted to the situation back in 1935, when the law partner of R. J. Folonie, the Chicago attorney for the insurance companies involved in the settlement, died. Revenue agents had run a routine check on his estate and discovered that on May 9, 1935 (nine days before Governor Park signed the settlement bill), Folonie's law firm had received $100,500 ($1,608,000 in 1990 dollars) in checks from various insurance firms and had immediately disbursed them. This was a sum of money too attractive not to raise eyebrows.

Visited by SIU special agents, Folonie explained that the money didn't belong to his law firm and had been sent to Street. SIU agents next visited Street, who verified that he got the $100,500 but wouldn't say "to whom he had passed it." Irey, explaining that "we had long heard rumors of a Street-Pendergast tie-up," started getting brief "notes" from Street on his whereabouts and what he was doing. Irey never explained why Street started doing this; it can be surmised that, apprehensive, the SIU had him on their radar; he was more than ready to put on a contrived act. One note Irey received from Street said, "Leaving for South Dakota. On my return next week will take a run to Missouri and see what they have to say. Don't think can do anything at least before Queen Mary comes in." The note intrigued Irey deeply. Actually, it was a dead giveaway. The famed ocean liner was making its maiden voyage from Southampton to the United States and among the names on the passenger list were "Mr. and Mrs. Thomas J. Pendergast."[23]

On March 7, 1937, Internal Revenue issued a summons to Street. He showed up the next day and refused to answer any questions on the grounds that his answers might incriminate him. Thus began, in effect, the gritty two-year, seventy-one-day period of setbacks, compromises, complications, and successes that would end on the day of Boss Pendergast's sentencing. Though Street wouldn't answer agents' questions, he was quick to say that he had filed an amended return that day for the year 1935, showing as income $100,500 ($1,608,000 in 1990 dollars), and that he had paid $47,093 ($706,398 in 1990 dollars) in additional taxes plus interest of $2,825.60 ($42,284 in 1990 dollars). Irey considered having him indicted for tax fraud since he filed his amended return after the SIU inquiry started.

"We had word of a half-million-dollar bribe," Irey said, "so we thought we'd wait until Street filed his 1936 tax. It was considered highly unlikely that he would pay taxes on the balance of about $400,000."[24] Irey was right. When Street filed his 1936 report in 1937 it made no mention of $400,000. The SIU was preparing to look at his books and question him under oath when he suddenly died. That was a short-lived setback.

Charles Street knew Pendergast. They had met on January 22, 1935, at Chicago's Palmer House in the room of insurance executive A. L. McCormack, at which time, it was agreed to pay Pendergast to use his influence to settle the rate agreement so the $9 million in escrow could be freed. Less than ten days before, Street, McCormack, and Robert E. O'Malley, the superintendent of insurance in Missouri and a Kansas City cigar manufacturer, met on two occasions at the Coronado Hotel in St. Louis, where McCormack explained that an agreement could be reached on the $9 million with Pendergast's help. Now, at the Palmer House, Pendergast, after matters were spread out, told Street to make an offer. Street offered $200,000 ($3 million in 1990 dollars). Pendergast replied, "Don't be silly."[25] Street raised the bribe to $500,000 ($7.5 million in 1990 dollars). Pendergast said he would put pressure on O'Malley as soon as he returned to Kansas City. The outcome of that, of course, was never in doubt. A "political hack" associated for years with the machine, O'Malley had been named to the post by Governor Park "at Pendergast's insistence."

Then Pendergast asked to use the phone. He called his secretary in Kansas City and said,

"Bet $10,000 on 'Flying Dere.' To win. Goodbye."

Two months later, according to Irey, nothing had been done to put through the legislation to settle the agreement. "Street knew his Pendergast," explained Irey. The insurance executive told McCormack to tell Pendergast, "We'll give him $750,000 [$11,250,000 in 1990 dollars]." That really settled matters, and the cash transactions, with McCormack acting as bag man, started. On May 1, 1935, McCormack made the first delivery, $50,000 ($750,000 in 1990 dollars) in cash, taking it by plane from Midway Airport to Kansas City, where he handed it to Pendergast and watched him place the cash in his office safe. On May 14, at "stage-managed negotiations" at the Muehlebach Hotel in Kansas City, the agreement was signed.

Governor Park "arrived to give his blessing prior to a signing ceremony" on May 18, attended by McCormack, Street, O'Malley, and their assistants and lawyers.

The rest of the $750,000 was paid on various occasions to Pendergast, who shared $125,000 ($1,875,000 in 1990 dollars) of it with McCormack and O'Malley. "Six months later, Pendergast was broke and needed $10,000 ($160,000 in 1990 dollars) to pay his hospital bills at Menorah Hospital," Irey said. McCormick took "this hint" to Street in Chicago. Street, short of cash "at the moment," telegraphed it a few days later to McCormick. And that was what broke the whole scheme apart. "It was this telegram which eventually led us to McCormack," Irey said.[26]

The SIU began examining Pendergast's financial records for the years 1927 to 1937 and found he had been concealing income he had received from his business enterprises over that period. The evidence convinced Irey that Pendergast "had a genius for political larceny unsurpassed in our time."[27] That said a lot, considering Irey's involvement with Huey Long.

Pendergast's excesses of extravagance and greed were truly staggering. Irey said he "may very easily have been the most abject slave the Sport of Kings ever owned." He bet up to $20,000 a day on the horses. In one year during the 1920s, he lost $600,000 ($24.8 million in 1990 dollars) at the racetrack. Because he had to have that money, Irey said disgustingly, "A Treasury agent had his brains kicked out; you could buy all the morphine or heroin you could lift in Kansas City; and the man who wanted to keep his job as a police captain in Kansas City had better keep his prostitute file correct and up to the minute so Tom's machine would be certain no girl practiced her ancient art without paying full tribute."[28]

The building of an airtight case for tax evasion came amid combustible contrasts. In the last stages of the SIU's investigation of Pendergast's money trail, a turf war broke out between the Treasury and Justice. While the SIU was still gathering evidence for the tax case, U.S. Attorney Maurice Milligan decided to indict Pendergast for tax evasion in the insurance agreement case. In July 1938 the SIU had traced the telegram for $100,000 that Charles Street had sent to McCormick to give to Pendergast. On March 17, 1939, McCormick finally broke down and admitted he was the payoff man.

Milligan felt he had invested too much in his insurance investigation to sit around and wait for Irey's tax inquiry to conclude. He'd never been able to lay a finger on Pendergast, not even in his mighty victory in the vote fraud case. Pendergast had been kicking dirt in his face for a long time. He had the goods on him now, and he wasn't going to wait. He decided to bring an indictment and got the backing of the newly appointed attorney general, forty-nine-year-old Frank Murphy. The former governor of Michigan, Murphy had succeeded Homer Cummings after being upset in his reelection bid in 1938. (One of FDR's key aides, Harry Hopkins, predicted Murphy would win by half a million votes in the off-year election.) When Irey learned of Milligan's plan, he and Revenue Commissioner Helvering went to see Murphy to tell him they had a stronger case and needed a few more weeks to wrap it up.

"If you indict Pendergast only for the insurance-bribe, he'll be getting away with murder," said Irey. He explained that for nine years, from 1935 to 1946, Pendergast had defrauded the government out of $1,181,283 ($17,719,245 in 1990 dollars).

"I will not be party to the obstruction of justice. We will indict Pendergast now," replied Murphy. He wasn't about to compromise in what was the first major skirmish of his term with the Treasury.

Irey persisted. "I don't think you understand. You see, he defrauded the government out of much more than we are charging him with in the present indictment."[29]

Murphy refused to listen.

On Tuesday, April 4, 1939, three days before Pendergast was indicted, J. Edgar Hoover showed up in Kansas City as a way of dotting the "i" on the indictment, sharing in the Justice Department's glory and willing to drink from half a cup.

Just before Pendergast was scheduled to go to trial for bribery in the insurance rate case, Milligan accepted his plea bargain. Pendergast pleaded guilty to a variety of tax charges and threw himself on the court's mercy. Explained Milligan, "Too many prominent persons in Kansas City would have been embarrassed had the whole sordid story of the Pendergast machine been drawn from the witness stand."[30]

Now, on the morning of Monday, May 22, 1939, in the improvised setting, U.S. District Judge Otis was merciful, sentencing Pendergast to one year and three months in Leavenworth, fining him $10,000, and decreeing that he was to pay back taxes, penalties, and interest in the amount of $430,000 ($6,450,000 in 1990 dollars). This was considerably less than the $1,181,283 that Irey maintained Pendergast owed.

Boss Tom's son, Thomas Jr., drove him the thirty-five miles from Kansas City to Leavenworth, where Milligan noted, "There were enough Pendergast henchmen [there] to form a club." A "great many" of the "vote fraud crowd" were doing time in the prison.[31] Robert O'Malley, the insurance commissioner, got one year for tax fraud. Otto Higgins, the chief of police at the time of the Union Station massacre and known by FBI agents to be "dirty," was sentenced to two years for tax fraud. City Manager Henry F. McElroy, who resigned shortly after Pendergast was indicted, died while facing federal indictment for failure to report more than $250,000 ($3,750,000 in 1990 dollars) in income. Later, it was discovered that McElroy had misplaced at least $20 million ($120 million in 1990 dollars), a figure nearly twice the city's annual budget.

For all his despotic deeds, Pendergast didn't fare badly. Incidentally, neither the Oval Office nor Morgenthau made their feelings known in the turf clash between Treasury and Justice. Irey expected a better outcome. The nonpolitical lawman who always thought right made might, Irey wrote in his memoir that the way the Pendergast case was prosecuted left him with "cold feelings."[32] Pendergast not only didn't get the book thrown at him for tax fraud on a huge scale, he escaped an additional two-year prison term on criminal contempt charges in the Missouri fire insurance settlement case. He had fought that accusation all the way to the U.S. Supreme Court, and on January 4, 1943, the jurists found 6-1 that the three-year statute of limitations prevented his conviction. After accruing great wealth through bribery, extortion, intimidation and racketeering, in addition to committing crimes such as rampant vote fraud through more than two decades, Boss Tom served a total of fifteen months in Leavenworth before going free.

15. FINALE IN NEW YORK CITY

The Dutch Schultz case broke wide open during the turbulent Huey Long investigation. On November 1, 1934, Secretary of the Treasury Henry Morgenthau talked by telephone with Mayor La Guardia in an attempt to nudge matters along about "the best-known racketeer in New York."[1]

"The point is," Morgenthau told the mayor, "the Treasury wants this fellow. . . . He's the last of the big gangsters that are out. And if there's anything we can do to work with you I want to let you know that."

A cooperative La Guardia replied, "I think it's a defiance not only to the city but to the whole government that this fellow is at large."

In the conversation, Morgenthau had also brought up Irey. La Guardia said, "I wish that either Hoover or Irey would tell me frankly if there's been any lack of cooperation in any way . . . because at the top it's all right. If there's any feeling then it's down below and then I would suspect that it isn't one of irritation or jealousy but one of rather protecting this particular person."

Morgenthau replied, "I see."

La Guardia said, "I want to get right to it."[2]

On November 28, twenty-seven days after that phone conversation, Dutch Schultz, after hiding out for twenty-two months from his federal indictment for income tax evasion, turned himself in to the authorities in Albany. At his arraignment, he pleaded not guilty.

During the almost two-year-long period that Schultz was hiding out, Tammany power Jimmy Hines had protected him. This reality eventually hit home to Washington, resulting in the phone conversation between Morgenthau and La Guardia. However it was done or who did it, word of that conversation filtered back to Hines, and he acted. As Schultz's longtime political patron, Hines could easily pick up the phone and call Schultz's lawyer, Dixie Davis. Davis made no secret that he was Schultz's "main contact." Davis knew Hines "preferred being seen with me rather with members of the mob."[3]

In addition, the situation regarding Schultz was made even more clear on November 7, six days after the Morgenthau–La Guardia conversation, when Elmer Irey issued "a nationwide directive" calling for Schultz's arrest.[4] According to Paul Sann, Schultz's legal battery offered "the government $100,000 to buy off the case"—just as Al Capone had tried to do before he went to trial for tax evasion in 1931.[5] Morgenthau rejected the offer, and there "was nothing left for Dutch Schultz to do except to come in and get it over with."

After months of legal maneuvering, Schultz's trial was moved from New York City to Syracuse and Schultz moved with it. He hobnobbed around town, looking solicitous, and had his picture taken for the local press as he contributed to the underprivileged. It wasn't exactly on the scale of a soup kitchen for the poor, like Capone arranged in Chicago, but turning angelic can pay off, even for master racketeers. The trial began on September 15, 1935, and ended twelve days later with a hung jury. Retrial was set for May 14, 1936. After reports of jury tampering came out, the trial was reset for July 23 and moved to the hamlet of Malone on the New York–Canada border. Schultz moved to Malone, where he contributed flowers and candy to the sick children at the town's lone hospital.

On August 1, after deliberating for twenty-four hours, a jury acquitted Schultz—to loud applause. Silencing the outburst, U.S. District Judge Frederick H. Bryant (a Malone native), "anger evident in his face," told the "twelve farmer jurors" that "your verdict shakes the confidence of law-abiding people in integrity and truth."[6] Schultz and his lawyers had outsmarted the Justice Department, and the case that Morgenthau thought might slip away did. After the verdict, Mayor La Guardia and Police Commissioner Valentine warned Schultz publicly that if he returned to the city he would be arrested. Schultz moved his operation to New Jersey, where on a clear day from a Manhattan skyscraper, he could be seen smirking. Sitting in his Alcatraz cell, Al Capone must have been kicking himself for not getting his trial moved downstate to "Little Egypt," where the inhabitants would have enjoyed his largess.

On October 10 Schultz was indicted on eleven counts of failing to file income tax returns for 1929–1931, a misdemeanor. He couldn't claim double jeopardy because the original charges involving willful evasion of income tax laws were for a felony. Schultz was prepared. When he turned himself in to authorities in Perth Amboy, at his side was State Senator John E. Tooland of Middlesex County. Shortly thereafter, former New Jersey Governor George S. Silzer was brought into the ranks of his defense team.

By then, Irey and his task force had folded their tent and left New York City. The SIU's work had led to the indictment of one other prominent racketeer, forty-five-year-old Lawrence "Larry" Fay. But a lot of work went for naught. Just before his trial, a doorman at the nightclub Fay operated on West Fifty-sixth Street, disgruntled at the cutbacks in salary and working hours, showed up angry and drunk on the evening of New Year's Day 1933, confronted Fay, pulled a gun, and shot him four times. Fay fell, dead.

The SIU's New York effort turned out to be supremely ironic. Irey enforced the tax laws but he never considered himself a crime-fighter, yet he and his unit were key in bringing down a host of New York City's major racketeers. Irey always went where the money trail led, and always faced huge disadvantages: his ranks were thin, his budget limited, and inevitably the SIU's interests clashed with reality. Secretary of the Treasury Morgenthau considered wiretapping "an unpleasant necessity" and "instructed Treasury agents not to supervise lines without his personal approval."[7] The SIU was not a detective agency along the lines of the Bureau of Investigation, and Irey never pretended it was. He hadn't brought his crack Chicago contingent, including Frank Wilson, to Manhattan though he did understand the value of counterintelligence. He had a superb undercover operator, Pat O'Rourke, but O'Rourke was not going to be able to penetrate the Mafia like he did Capone's circle. Nor did Irey have the intelligence apparatus to penetrate New York City's underworld, an underworld where a new and very powerful element had not only taken over, but would go on to change the face of crime in the United States.

Most important, federal law enforcement still wasn't on a firm footing. The federal constabulary was inconsistent in its strategy, lacked a counter-intelligence operation, and did not have the depth or know-how to carry out the imperatives needed. At the Justice Department, FDR's new attorney general, Homer Cummings, would devise uneven anti-racketeering legislation and would do little or nothing to cope with the growing Mafia brethren. Vice President Dawes had clearly pointed to the problem in his House speech in 1928, particularly with his specific reference to the Mafia, but his cry didn't pave the way for further inquiry. Actually, New York City's jungle of organized crime and political treachery almost made the Chicago scene look tame. For Irey, what started out with front-page fanfare and promise in April 1931, five years and six months earlier, turned out to be a half-filled glass, and probably a humbling experience. Never again would he engage in front-page imprudence against New York City's racketeers. Medalie and Dewey were gone, too, along with the momentum. The Southern District became a revolving door, an unhappy place, its effectiveness in question. The new FDR White House named Martin Conboy as Medalie's replacement. Conboy, FDR's counsel during the Beau James hearings, served from 1933 to 1935. He left, not unexpectedly, in the middle of the Schultz debacle. Conboy was the first of five lawyers who would hold the post over the next six years, a bruising turnover rate. His successor, Lamar Hardy, a former corporation counsel, ran into trouble after questionable legal dealings he made in his past came to light. The New York City Bar approved a resolution, 321-247, condemning his selection.

■

Racketeering enveloped New York City. In 1919, when Irey became the SIU chief, the underworld consisted of little more than "a ragtag collection of dope peddlers, cat burglars, and highway robbers."[8] In 1933 the historian-criminologist Harry E. Barnes told a Senate Commerce subcommittee looking at the subject of racketeering just how far crime had come: "Once in the great majority of all crimes, the thefts and pick pocketing pale into insignificance when compared to the achievements of the racketeers and gangsters."[9]

By 1930 it was hard to ignore the warnings. That June a battery of well-known names took on the subject at the three-day conference of the League for Industrial Democracy in Forest Park, Pennsylvania. Writer Paul Blanshard opened the conference by giving this definition of racketeering: "Racketeering is a scheme by which human parasites graft themselves upon and live by the industry of others, maintaining their hold by terrorism, fraud, misrepresentation and manipulation." Paul Douglas, professor of economics at the University of Chicago (and later U.S. senator from Illinois) said, "The reason the so-called decent people do not clean up the city is that the same group of politicians who protect the underworld also give favors to influential sections of the super-world, thus binding the 'respectable' people to the various machines." Writer Edward D. Sullivan called Prohibition "the chief actor in the growth of gangsterism in America" and said the "liaison" between the gangster and politician "is the greatest menace of the century."[10]

Gordon Hostetter, the executive director of the Employers Association of Chicago who lived through the Capone era, estimated that the cost of racketeering in Chicago amounted to more than $145 million a year ($1.32 billion in 1990 dollars). In 1933 Hostetter, collaborating with T. Q. Beesley, wrote, "Racketeering is beginning to emerge as the distinct contribution of the twentieth century to crime."[11] In June of that year an activist organization called the "Crusaders" filled Carnegie Hall as the "opening volley" in an "anti-racket drive." Former heavyweight boxing champion Gene Tunney spoke. The Crusaders claimed a strength of 1,250,000 young men between the ages of 21 and 45 who had come together "to clean up the aftermath of Prohibition in the form of liquor racketeers, gangsters and corrupt politicians."[12] That spring, incidentally, the foursome—Charlie Luciano, Joe Adonis, Meyer Lansky, and Jimmy Hines—enjoying a sunny day of golf on the links adjacent to the Arlington Hotel in Hot Springs, Arkansas, knew all about racketeering.

John Morton Blum noted that Secretary of the Treasury Morgenthau "commanded the most extraordinary department in the Federal government."[13] With regard to law enforcement, Morgenthau tried to keep his finger on New York City's crime and maintain an 'aggressive view outside Attorney General Cummings's questionable focus. With his characterization of Dutch Schultz as the "last of the big gangsters out," however, Morgenthau's knowledge of the underworld was limited. Many big-name racketeers, except for Waxey Gordon, were still on the street, including Schultz and the Gorilla Boys, Louis Lepke, and Jake Gurrah. The Five Mafia Families already had their claws in most of the major rackets in New York's five boroughs.

Attorney General Cummings, decidedly uneven in his law enforcement actions, did make a sterling move in the war against New York City's racketeers by bringing John Harlan Amen back to press the fight. The Justice Department's William Donovan, under President Coolidge, first sent Amen to New York City in 1927, a time when New York racketeering, then in its Golden Age, was represented by fronts such as the Building Trades Employers Association. Headed by Robert P. Brindell, the association comprised the fifteen largest construction firms. Brindell had himself elected to a life term on the Building Trades Council, known as the "Tammany Hall Annex" because many of Tammany's sachems were officials in it. "Had Benito Mussolini ever sought a model on which to build his fascist state," Leo Katcher observed, "he could not have chosen a better one than [the] Council." Brindell was a partner in an automobile agency with Arnold Rothstein, who got a kickback from life insurance sold to members of the council and its unions. Rothstein wrote $700,000 ($13.3 million in 1990 dollars) worth of insurance in one day, all on persons working for or doing business with Brindell. Contractors and builders had to supply performance bonds when a new project was begun. "These always met requirements," said Katcher, "when they were provided by Rothstein's firm."[14] Emory Buckner, as a special district attorney, handled the successful criminal prosecution of Brindell (and would later serve with distinction as the U.S. Attorney at the Southern District). The Brindell case came out of a 1921 inquiry by a joint legislative panel that was looking into how union abuses raised building costs—an Illinois state legislative committee was conducting a similar inquiry at much the same time in Chicago.

In 1927, in one of his first cases, Amen took on the ringleaders of the city's poultry racket: Joey Weiner, business agent for Local 440 of the Amalgamated Meat Cutters and Butcher Workmen of North America, and Arthur "Tootsie" Herbert. "Tootsie," who won the sobriquet for his love of good clothes and the perfumed hair oil he used to plaster his locks of curly, black hair, was secretary-treasurer of the chicken driver's union that became Local 167 of the Teamsters Union. He also was the boss of the Metropolitan Feed Company and had organized the New York Live Poultry Chamber of Commerce, a trade association "to protect" the businessman. These phony associations, one of racketeering's most enduring and polished weapons, flourished in New York City. The poultry association paid Tootsie $3,800 ($64,800 in 1990 dollars) a week. To unload a railcar of poultry was twice as expensive in New York City as it was in Philadelphia. On the side, Tootsie ran a loan shark operation that victimized members of his own union. In 1928 Amen won an antitrust conviction of Weiner, Tootsie, and Tootsie's older and more violent brother, Charles—only to receive his first dose of how the federal courts treated racketeers.

U.S. Circuit Judge John C. Knox gave Tootsie eight weeks in the federal house of detention, Charles four weeks with a suspended sentence, and Weiner a suspended sentence because he had just served three years on Welfare Island for assaulting a recalcitrant poultry dealer. The trio, incidentally, paid their counsel fees by levying an assessment of $50 ($900 in 1990 dollars) on members of their locals and by making "special collections" from poultry merchants. Tootsie, after extorting his defense fees, was still short of cash and borrowed $4,900 ($67,300 in 1990 dollars) from Arnold Rothstein.

For Amen— like Irey, the personification of the reliable, incorruptible public servant—the outlook upon his return appeared to be optimistic. The backlash against racketeering was growing; Cummings had anti-rackets legislation on the way. No longer would Amen have to rail against the "ridiculously small penalties" judges handed to racket bosses—courtly henpecks that were a primary factor in the comfortable advance of racketeering.[15]

On Monday, February 18, 1934, Cummings sent twelve measures to Congress designed to strengthen the government's arm in its battle against racketeers and criminals. It was the most sweeping law enforcement legislation ever presented to Congress and sought to extend federal control over crime in unprecedented ways. FDR's administration had tossed a red flag in the face of the long-held and dominant belief that law enforcement was local and Washington ought to keep it that way. The thrust of the new legislation dealt with turning a wide range of criminal activity into federal offenses. On the issue of racketeering, one measure made it a felony to commit an act restraining interstate or foreign commerce if such an act involved extortion, violence, coercion, or intimidation. It contained broader language than the Sherman Act, then being used against racketeers.

The crime package came twenty-three months after the kidnapping of the twenty-month-old son of Charles and Anne Lindbergh, eight months after the Union Station massacre in Kansas City, and at the point when celebrity bandits such as "Pretty Boy" Floyd, John Dillinger, and "Baby Face" Nelson had burst on the scene, becoming front-page news across the country. It contained a raft of measures specifically aimed at the celebrity bandits. It established federal penalties for robbing a bank, transporting a car across state lines, fleeing across state lines to avoid prosecution in felony cases, and assaulting or killing a federal officer. It armed federal agents and limited alibi defenses. The latter involved the right of appeal in certain types of habeas corpus cases and allowed the mate of a defendant to be a witness in criminal prosecutions. Another measure strengthened the Lindbergh kidnapping statute by stipulating that if a kidnapped person was held for more than two days, the action became a federal offense.

In a message with the legislation, Cummings sought to justify these broadened powers this way: The bills "are drawn along reasonably conservative lines and within constitutional limits." They are required because "roving criminals bent upon the commission of various types of predatory crime, constitute a growing menace to law and orderly government. . . . [They] operate in organized groups and do not confine their unlawful activities to any particular city, county or state, but, on the contrary, move rapidly across state lines from the scene of one crime of violence to another."[16]

In his mention of "organized groups," Cummings was referring to armed bands like Dillinger's gang, not the Mafia's Five Families. When he appeared before the Senate Judiciary Committee on March 18 to testify on behalf of the legislation, Cummings showed faint understanding of the criminal underworld he wanted to bring down. He told the committee that if he had to, he preferred to deal with racketeers like Al Capone rather than with Roger "Terrible" Touhy. Touhy and his five brothers were stone enemies of Capone and controlled the bootlegging operations in Des Plaines, a Chicago suburb. For years they successfully fended off Capone's attempts to take over their racket enterprises. Cummings explained that the Capone group was of a "much higher type. It is not so brutal as the Touhys and not so likely to take off a man's ear or gouge out his eye." (Homer Cummings, who died in 1956 at age eighty-six, wasn't around to see the final irony in his belief that Touhy was more "brutal" than Capone. In 1959 Capone's heirs finally caught up with Touhy outside his sister's house in Chicago and shot him dead.)

As his package of legislation moved through Congress, Cummings's rhetoric began drawing scrutiny. He declared that 200,000 armed gangsters were loose in the country, a statement that one congressman called "asinine."[17] The *New York Times* decided to review the statistics in a less profane way. If the attorney general was right, an editorial asserted, it meant there were at least 10,000 gangs operating with at least twenty members each, which "outnumber the joint strength of our army and navy." Then the editorial pointed out, "Whether the way to combat them is through the federal government or to break up the local alliances between the underworld and the politicians is a good subject for debate."[18] Cummings's remarks were not informed, and neither was a debate about "local alliances" necessary. The Treasury's SIU had been successful in bringing down the ranking power of the country's best-known local alliance—Al Capone of Chicago. Little debate was needed on the importance of attacking these local alliances—and unrelentingly.

Cummings's legislative package did not contain a single imperative to help the more difficult work of Irey's SIU in investigating financial conspirators. Cummings did give the back of his hand to the matter, though he was not going to acknowledge it. In May he called reporters to his office to announce that he was seeking appropriations to add seventy operatives to the Justice Department. Of that number, 200 would be used as additional agents for the Division of Investigation, while seventy accountants would be brought on to examine banks, where clues to law violators could be unearthed. This was not about enlarging the federal effort as much as it was about duplicating Irey's work—and recognizing its value too.

By mid-April the Senate had approved eight of the twelve crime measures. Much of the debate occurred in the House Judiciary Committee, where members were still arguing about the wisdom of enlarging federal control over crime. One measure in particular made the members hesitant. It allowed federal agents to arrest a suspect in a state other than that in which he committed the crime and was being called a "radical departure from ordinary law." The debate all but ended on the night of April 22, when Bureau of Investigation agents cornered John Dillinger and his heavily armed band in Mercer, Minnesota, northeast of St. Paul. In the deadly shootout, Dillinger got away, leaving two dead, including BI Special Agent W. Carter Baum. A witness said Baby Face Nelson shot Baum. Inside of a year two BI agents had been gunned down, the other at Kansas City's Union Station massacre.

The Mercer incident grabbed as much attention as the Kansas City massacre had ten months before, even bringing comment in the British parliament. The British, of course, had always looked down on violence in the United States. Ordinarily given to underplaying its crime reportage, the *New York Times* made the Dillinger shootout its lead story, splashing it in headlines across three columns of the front page on the morning of Tuesday, April 24 (the incident occurred too late to make the final edition of the 23rd). Directly beneath the main headline was a sidebar that read, "New Dillinger Killings Stir the President and He Asks Quick Action on Crime Bills."[19]

Two days later the House Judiciary Committee approved ten of the twelve measures Cummings sent to Congress back in February. On May 4 the bills passed the House, went to conference, where the House and Senate versions were boiled down to six measures. On May 17 FDR signed them into law. He had gotten his crime package in eighty-eight days, quicker than the 100 days it took his economic legislation. It was precedent shattering: robbing a bank in the Federal Reserve System, transporting a car across state lines in the process, and assaulting a federal officer were made a federal offense. The two-year-old Lindbergh Law was strengthened. If a person were kidnapped and held more than two days, it became a federal offense. Extortion by phone or radio also became a federal offense, and federal agents were given the right to bear arms.

Who was to be the beneficiary of this imposing array of new laws? J. Edgar Hoover's Bureau of Investigation. For Hoover, FDR's signature was the moment he had been waiting for. He would leave anonymity behind. The Bureau of Investigation, which had been operating with its baby teeth for a decade—and bearing the ignominy that came with that—was about to leapfrog to the front rank of the federal detective agencies. Running down bank robbers was a suit of clothes that fit Hoover. He epitomized the belief that the "mere criminal" deserved federal attention. Stamped all over the legislation was the belief that bank robbers and kidnappers were the biggest menace.

At a crucial crossroads, officialdom had chosen to go down the wrong road. The astute Walter Lippmann in 1931, the year Capone was sent away, wrote of "the growth of a powerful underworld" that wasn't "comprehensible in the ordinary categories of crime" and spelled out the criminal distinctions that had come into play. "The mere criminal who breaks the law for his own profit, or because he is provoked by passion, or because he is degenerate, does not raise the issues with which Americans living in places like Chicago or New York are so anxiously concerned. The issues that are most deeply perplexing and ominous are those presented by the underworld which defies the law, establishes a regime of terror and violence, and draws profits for services performed by conventionally respectable members of society."[20]

One year before, Senator Royal S. Copeland's hearings on racketeering had served a clear warning. In August 1933 his committee held a public symposium on organized crime in the auditorium of the Association of the Bar of the City of New York in Manhattan, and one of the featured speakers was George Medalie, who was still serving as the U.S. attorney. Medalie minced no words: "In almost every large city, racketeers and gangsters are part of the machinery of municipal control. Not until politics is divorced from municipal control will you get rid of the gangster and the racketeers. So long as there is politics in municipal affairs where it doesn't belong, you will have racketeers." [21]

As the new laws against bank robbers and kidnappers went on the books, irony was written all over them. Bank robberies began to drop sharply. In the six months leading up to February 1934, there were 188 bank robberies, compared to the 554 robberies of a year and a half prior to that. The American Banking Association attributed the drop to the fact that the authorities were capturing many of the robbers more swiftly than before. There was another revelation: Most bank robberies had occurred in rural areas, not in regions with great banking wealth. Of eighty-six holdups of ABA members between September 1933 and February 1934, only ten were directed against banks in cities with more than a population of 50,000. Between October 1932 and August 1933, "New York State's 1,420 banks had suffered three holdups and no burglaries." [22]

Less than sixty days after FDR signed the unprecedented package, three of the nation's most notorious fugitives met their end. In July John Dillinger, thirty-one, was shot dead outside the Biograph Theater in Chicago; in October Charles "Pretty Boy" Floyd, thirty-three, was shot dead in an Ohio cornfield; and in November George "Baby Face" Nelson, twenty-six, was shot dead in a field outside Chicago. Still young men, their notoriety was short-lived. Dillinger's active life of crime—he killed ten people—totaled exactly fourteen months. He left the Indiana State Prison at Michigan City on May 22, 1933; he was slain on July 22, 1934.

As for kidnappings, an article in the May 1934 edition of *Popular Science* reported, "Of twenty-four kidnapping cases recorded since June, 1932, only one remains unsolved." In reality, major kidnapping cases like the Lindbergh abduction were so rare that the classic training police text *Modern Criminal Investigation* didn't mention them at all, "despite eighteen detailed sections that describe crime scene techniques for capital felonies."[23] According to Claire Bond Potter, the brief epidemic of social register "snatchings" in 1932 and 1933 "created a political and cultural atmosphere conducive to the creation of an interventionist federal crime policy."[24]

In 1936, two years after that package of laws had enhanced his bureau's standing, J. Edgar Hoover announced that bank robberies were declining, that the kidnapping menace had been largely eliminated, and that the activities of his bureau had contributed to that result. As if to recognize this positive step, the bureau's name was changed on May 1 to the Federal Bureau of Investigation.

As the bureau's sails eased from its success against desperadoes such as Dillinger, the brand-new federal anti-racketeering statute still presented a golden circumstance to Hoover, who had the jurisdiction to investigate racketeering. Actually, this was where the big money was flowing and where those seventy accountants Attorney General Cummings had sought could be used. The two leading Mafia figures, Charlie Luciano and Frank Costello, were taking in more cash in a week from vice and rackets than Dillinger and the entire lot of celebrity bandits had robbed from banks in their entire lives of crime. Costello, as part of his gambling empire, owned the monopoly on slot machines in New York City; Luciano ran a vice operation in addition to muscling into other rackets, such as policy, in which bets are made on numbers to be drawn by lottery, and was a big moneymaker in Harlem. Moreover, the Mafia's Five Families provided a brand new mix to politics and crime. Costello, the Luciano family underboss and likely the wealthiest mafioso, never kept ledgers and had as much political savvy as the judges and politicians he bribed. Luciano wasn't exaggerating when he called Costello "the best fixer in the whole fuckin' country."[25]

For J. Edgar Hoover, chasing down shadowy Mafia racketeers hiding under layers of political favors was a gamy exercise he wanted no part of. Attorney General Cummings's sense of immediacy never told him otherwise. The final irony to the anti-racketeering law that FDR signed in 1934 rested with John Harlan Amen, the intrepid rackets-buster whom Cummings had brought back in 1933. While waiting for Washington to pass the anti-racketeering legislation, Amen took on the case of Joseph "Socks" Lanza. Few cases in the world of racketeering had such classic ingredients.

Back in 1922 "Socks" Lanza (he acquired the sobriquet for his ability to sock a baseball), a canny, strapping, 200-pound boy-man of 20, organized Local 594 of the United Seafood Workers' Union at the Fulton Fish Market. Located on the East River in the shadows of Wall Street skyscrapers, it was the "foremost fish outlet in the United States, handling 394,000,000 pounds yearly" and the base for markets to the Mississippi River and the Great Lakes.[26] The per capita consumption of edible fresh fish product in New York was nearly thirty-two pounds. The market was also a playground of corrupt practices, in particular, a plethora of pricing schemes that drove up the cost of fish.

In 1925 Emory Buckner, the U.S. attorney for the Southern District, went after the price-fixers but to little avail. He busted up an outfit called the Fish Purchasing Corporation, known in the press as "the live fish trust." Buckner's investigators placed more than twenty witnesses from various states before a grand jury, a sizeable feat, given that most of the aggrieved in rackets cases were too intimidated to testify. They testified to the price-fixing, and Buckner got an indictment and a guilty plea from the seventeen firms and twelve individuals in the trust. U.S. District Court Judge A. N. Hand handed them an aggregate fine of $31,000 ($558,000 in 1990 dollars) and no jail time.

At Local 594, Socks's schemes had been driving up prices for more than a decade, but he eluded prosecution. In that time, he had not cared about the Local's presidency. Socks was satisfied to be its business agent, the one who made contracts for labor with the merchants and fishing captains. No crew on any of the 6,000 seagoing boats that docked at the Fulton Fish Market, for instance, could unload the catch. Local 594's members did the unloading, and Socks charged each boat captain a fee of $19 ($180 in 1990 dollars) a load for the union's benevolent fund. Skippers who protested the charge found their catch accidentally dropped off the pier. Socks also put the clamp on the giant, open air, pushcart market at nearby Peck Slip, where fish could be purchased by small retailers in ten-, twenty-five-, and fifty-pound boxes. New York City's Department of Markets, Weights, and Measures assigned spots at Peck Slip, "but after Lanza's strong-arm boys perfected their shakedown organization, it did a small vendor little good to obtain the municipal permit to do business unless he also got Lanza's permit. The municipal fee was small; Lanza's [was] small, too, though a little higher."

Like "Tootsie" Herbert, Socks organized a phony trade association. Called the Fulton Market Watchmen and Patrol Association, it provided "security" for a fee. The bustling market attracted thousands of dealers, all of whom had to leave their vehicles while doing business with the whole-salers. The NYPD patrolled the area but, "it seemed, never were [around] when a truck, unwatched by any of Lanza's men, had its tires slashed, or its contents sprayed with some stinking chemical." If you paid the asso-ciation's fee, however, your vehicle was safe. This was a cash bonanza for Socks: "Timid dealers" were shaken down for at least $40,000 annually ($720,000 in 1990 dollars).[27]

In June 1933 John Harlan Amen produced the evidence to warrant a federal indictment of Socks and fifty-three others for fixing prices and carrying on various corrupt practices at the market. In November 1935 a jury found him guilty, and he was given a two-year sentence. Amen had worked on the case for twenty-nine months, not including his work in the pre-indictment period.

During the Lanza case, Amen, armed with the new federal anti-rackets law, had begun an inquiry into tactics used by members of Local 807 of the International Brotherhood of Teamsters to block produce trucks driven by nonunion members. For nearly a year the Justice Department had been receiving complaints from out-of-state trucking companies doing business in the city that the local was charging them a fee to enter the city. In Janu-ary 1936, ten months after Amen began his inquiry, a federal grand jury indicted five members of Local 807 on charges of levying $300,000 ($4.5 million in 1990 dollars) tribute against nonunion drivers. Amen won their conviction, and the Teamsters decided to test the anti-racketeering law.

Six years later, in 1942, the case reached the U.S. Supreme Court, and the court ruled for the Teamsters. The majority opinion, written by sixty-three-year-old Justice James· F. Byrnes, decided that provisions of the law could not be applied against the Teamsters because the measure had ex-empted labor activities from its terms. In the lone dissent, Chief Justice

Harlan Stone argued there was abundant evidence to convince the jury that the Teamsters had participated in a conspiracy. In December 1945 Representative Sam Hobbs, an Alabama Democrat, persuaded the House to revise FDR's 1934 anti-racketeering law to specifically include labor unions, and President Harry S. Truman signed the revised act into law in July 1946.

■

New York City's terrain was as unfavorable to Amen as it was to Irey. There would be no more wins for the rest of the 1930s. Taking down Al Capone had been an epic battle, welded by the combination of E. Q. Johnson and the Northern District and Irey and the SIU. Similar circumstances occurred in New York City. With the triumvirate of Medalie, Dewey, and Irey providing prestige, energy, and wisdom, the Gordon case had the same makings, and FDR, likely recognizing the district chalked up some of its greatest achievements in the Republican years of the 1920s and early 1930s, for a time kept them at the Southern District. The changing political currents brought a price. Once Dewey left, Irey wasn't far behind. Their years of hard work on the Schultz case went for naught. After the flap over Lamar Hardy's appointment, the Southern District lost its punch and didn't regain it for a decade. At a time when the federal constabulary had been strengthened as never before, its reach into New York weakened.

Racketeers had such "a tremendous hold on the legitimate business life of the community" that "you could fee it," said Sol Gelb, a trial associate of Tom Dewey's.[28] Albert Marinelli, Tammany's only Italian leader and an ally of Luciano's, won the office of county clerk of New York County in 1934. Thirty-three people Marinelli named as either county committeemen or election inspectors had police records. One had eight arrests, including charges of robbery, dope dealing, and felonious assault. Another had beaten homicide charges. Marinelli's offices at 225 Lafayette Street in the Second Assembly handled the numbers rackets for the Lower East Side and had fifty-four runners. The building also housed the offices of the Five Borough Truckmen's Association, the garment truckers' racket front formed in 1932 and headed by James Plumeri, a ranking member of the Gagliano-Lucchese Mafia family.

The 1934 election that put Marinelli in office also brought Bronx-born Fiorello "The Little Flower" La Guardia as mayor, the most positive outcome of Samuel Seabury's investigation. Squat and swarthy, La Guardia wasn't as charming and silky-smooth as Beau James, but there was no question about his integrity. Still, La Guardia faced a battle that was all uphill. Shortly after "The Little Flower" started wielding a sledgehammer to Frank Costello's slot machines, the Mafia underboss converted 125,000 of them into "candy machines" and won a court injunction against further police action. After ordering his newly appointed commissioner of accounts, Paul Blanshard, to investigate every city and county department and to report any evidence of graft, incompetence, or political favoritism, La Guardia found out the extent to which Tammany was a den of thieves. Blanshard's study discovered 834 exempt positions in county offices used to reward political henchmen at a yearly outlay of $2.3 million ($36.8 million in 1990 dollars), which the city had to pay. The incompetent Thomas Crain was gone, but his Tammany-picked successor as Manhattan district attorney, William Copeland Dodge, was an ex-magistrate, which was enough to give pause. The magistrates courts had been a spawning ground of rackets and conspiracies and the primary focus of Seabury's inquiry. Before long, Dodge's tenure as a magistrate carried over into his performance as district attorney.

In March 1935 the City Affairs Committee issued a damning declaration against Dodge:

> There is a vice and crime situation in New York City today more serious than anything the community has faced since the days of William Travers Jerome. . . . Gambling is rampant, racketeering is a wide conspiracy, taking its toll of millions from business and industry, while vice is developing like a cancer at the very vitals of the city's life. There is no use in blinking or denying the situation. . . . The attitude of the District Attorney's office, as thus far disclosed, is appalling. By what right does the District Attorney ask private citizens or civic agencies to bring him evidence? When did it cease to become the responsibility of the District Attorney to find his own evidence of crime and evil and

act upon it? . . . All too evident is it that the District Attorney has no desire or intention of doing anything that he is not forced to do. . . . Mr. Dodge can put up a brave front and make beautiful gestures and speak fine words, but he is doing nothing or worse than nothing and he knows it.[29]

With the situation boiling—just as in Chicago with Big Bill Thompson and Robert Crowe in 1929—a "runaway grand jury" in the spring of 1935 demanded that Governor Herbert Lehman appoint a special prosecutor to fight racketeering.[30] Tom Dewey's name immediately came up. It had been two years since he left the Southern District; his work had not been forgotten, but crime fighting was wrapped in political partisanship. Lehman moved to appoint the special prosecutor from a list of four of the city's leading lawyers, including George Medalie. All four rejected the post but recommended to Lehman, a Democrat, that he name Dewey, a rock-ribbed Republican. Lehman balked, declaring publicly that he didn't think Dewey was "sufficiently well known" for the job. Following an acrimonious two-hour meeting with the four lawyers at his Fifth Avenue apartment in June 1935, Lehman reversed himself and announced that Dewey was "competent" for the job (a comment Dewey later called "ungracious").[31] A photograph shows both men at Lehman's desk, sitting together and smiling. Dewey accepted the appointment, but the two detested each other.

Dewey's tactics and strategies in the two years he spent as special prosecutor will endure for the ages. In pursuing racketeers, he knew he needed the full orchestra, not just a harmonious string quartet. John Harlan Amen knew that too, but under Attorney General Cummings he was a one-man band. The lawyers Dewey recruited included little-known men such as William B. Herlands and Frank S. Hogan. There were so many Phi Beta Kappa keys dangling from the watch chains of Dewey's legal staff that one of the General Sessions judges remarked that defense lawyers thought they should be classified as "dangerous weapons."[32] For the first time Dewey brought in investigative accountants, a lesson he learned from Elmer Irey. He made A. J. "Goody" Goodrich the chief accountant, and Goodrich recruited nine other accountants, who, "when racketeers refused to talk, were able to make their books talk for them."[33]

Dewey turned out to be a brilliant conductor of an amazing philharmonic. In two years he and his staff earned seventy-two convictions out of seventy-three prosecutions. The tedious work of his investigative accountants in examining the ledgers of the Perfection Coat Front Company led to the indictment of the Gorilla Boys, Louis Lepke, and Jacob Gurrah, for extortions in the garment industry amounting to $17 million ($272 million in 1990 dollars). In dealing with the $1 million-a-week loan shark racket, Dewey had thirty of the city's leading loan sharks arrested. Instead of following tradition, he received the court's permission to file criminal charges against them instead of seeking grand jury indictments. This allowed their trials to be held in the court of special sessions instead of magistrates court. Within thirty-five days, all thirty had been tried; only one went free, on a procedural error. Dewey's investigative accountants built a larceny case against Arthur "Tootsie" Herbert for stealing $49,000 ($600,000 in 1990 dollars) in union funds. Goodrich and the accountants reconstructed Tootsie's books and found he would order special assessments on all the dues-paying members, levies that ranged up to $50 ($800 in 1990 dollars). Faced with the evidence in court, Tootsie pleaded guilty midway through his trial. The case had been previously dismissed by William Copeland Dodge without even a trial, and Dewey's assessment was biting: "Everybody in the United States and Canada seemed to know who Tootsie Herbert was and what his business was. Everybody but the District Attorney of New York County. Where were the successive District Attorneys during all these years? For more than ten years the poultry racket had ruled one of the greatest industries of the city and controlled the lives of thousands."[34] The case took Dewey three months.

Dutch Schultz was the one who got away, which helps to lay out the long, saturnine tale of officialdom's ignorance of the city's Mafia families. In October 1935, shortly after his federal indictment for tax misdemeanors, Schultz was bumped off in his Newark hangout, the Palace Chop House, along with three henchmen, including jovial Otto Berman, who was such a "wizard with figures" he acquired the sobriquet Abbadabba.[35] Otto was paid

$10,000 ($160,000 in 1990 dollars) a week to rig the pari-mutuel figures at select racetracks with last-minute bets, "thereby changing the pay-off figures if it appeared that a heavily played number seemed likely to win so that the poor people of Harlem wouldn't take too much money out of the Schultz policy banks."[36] At the murder scene, police found an adding machine Schultz had used to tally up the policy take from Harlem over the last seven weeks. The tape showed an income of $827,253.54 ($13,236,056.64 in 1990 dollars) and expenses of $313,711.99 ($5,309,386.84 in 1990 dollars).

Schultz was rubbed out because he'd become too dangerous, making threats and drawing attention. Dewey was making his life so miserable that Schultz decided to kill him. Dixie Davis said he "used to sit cursing Dewey as he read in the papers about the racket investigation."[37] Schultz had his henchmen make threatening phone calls to Dewey's wife. One caller told her to go to the morgue to identify her husband's body. Schultz had fatally miscalculated: Charlie Luciano took Schultz's threats toward Dewey as real, though Schultz's fate may have already been sealed. Schultz's territory, according to Davis, was "a sort of Balkan state surrounded by hungry axis powers."[38] Luciano had begun to move in on the Dutchman's lucrative policy operations. After Schultz won over the jury in Malone and while he was hiding out from the new indictment on tax misdemeanors, Luciano arranged with Bo Weinberg to place a couple of mafiosi inside Schultz's policy bank in Harlem. Weinberg was the Schultz sidekick who ferried George McManus from the Rothstein murder scene. When Schultz learned that Weinberg had betrayed him, he killed him in a Forty-seventh Street hotel—just weeks after he killed another henchman, Jules Martin, over the theft of $21,000 ($336,000 in 1990 dollars).

Schultz was the last obstacle in the way of Luciano and his plan for the Mafia's Five Families to run the city's underworld. Luciano's interests lay in keeping the curtain drawn on the Mafia. The Dutchman's rubout served the new underworld order: any racketeer who was going to operate outside the Mafia's killing field wasn't going to survive. Two other racketeers, Jack "Legs" Diamond and Vincent "Mad Dog" Coll, did not understand this and were also killed.

No one ever expected what happened next. At one of Dewey's early strategy sessions, Eunice Hunton Carter gave Dewey the lead that started him after Luciano, then residing in his $800-a-month ($12,800 in 1990 dollars) suite at the Waldorf Towers under the sobriquet "Charles Ross." A graduate of Smith College and the only woman and black lawyer on Dewey's staff, Eunice Carter "observed on her rounds at magistrate's court that prostitutes never seemed to go to jail if they were represented by a lawyer named Abe Karp."[39] She checked the records and found she was right. Dewey's team jumped on it; Sol Gelb took charge of the case, and Frank Hogan became "Father Hogan." As "adviser, confessor, errand runner" to the prostitutes, he interviewed them at the House of Detention and "gradually convinced them that their position was hopeless unless they talked."[40] They did. One year into his post as special prosecutor, Dewey prosecuted the most important case of his career: the Boss of Bosses, Charlie Luciano. The trail from Carter's tip led to him.

Arrested in Hot Springs on April 1, 1936, and returned to New York City, Luciano went to trial the next month on charges of compulsory prostitution. Dewey accused him of running a $12-million-a-year prostitution ring that employed 200 madams and 1,000 working girls. Covering the trial in general sessions court on Foley Square was John Gunther, who had written about Chicago's rackets a decade before and would become famous with his "Inside" books. He described the confessions the prostitutes made at Luciano's trial as "wildly, almost comically fraudulent."

But jurors were swayed more by Luciano's failure to answer the questions Dewey fired at him regarding his accumulated wealth than by the testimony of the hookers. Dewey's investigative accountants made Luciano's books "talk for them," further proof of the value of following the money trail. The trial began on May 11, 1936. Judge Philip J. McCook sent the jurors out on Saturday, June 6. They returned with a guilty verdict on all counts, a verdict too late to make the Sunday editions. At his sentencing, McCook, a hard-liner in sympathy with Dewey's war on racketeers (he would later administer the oath of office to Governor Dewey) told the thirty-eight-year-old Luciano, dressed in a bluish-gray suit, white soft shirt and black tie, that he held no hope for his rehabilitation and sent him to the Clinton State Prison at bleak Dannemora for thirty to thirty-five years. What no one outside the Five Families knew was that the Boss of Bosses of the country's top criminal elite had been sent away.

Sol Gelb described Dewey's impeccable strategy in prosecuting the underworld as, "Take out the top man in any way possible." "When we went to work on prostitutes we weren't interested in prostitutes," Gelb said Dewey told him. "You're never going to eliminate prostitution, and I'm satisfied you won't wipe out prostitution, but by investigating it, we may find the weakness in the line which will lead to the big shot."[41]

Gelb didn't have an inkling of Luciano's real status, and presumably, neither did Dewey. "The Luciano case knocked off the head man in the underworld—the head man," said Gelb. "After he was convicted the news papers began to write about his position in the underworld and frankly, for the first time I realized how big he was." No one tried to map out the city's underworld until 1935, when Dewey began "staking out the terrain," according to Richard Norton Smith. In his summation to the jury, Dewey called Luciano "the greatest gangster in America." Maybe Dewey believed this. Maybe he was just using what George Medalie taught him about the "ruby rose." Dewey knew subtleties existed, once saying of a case dealing with a criminal organization: "We felt we had lifted only a corner of a curtain, raising more questions than we had answered." After spending two years as special prosecutor, he ran for district attorney of Manhattan at thirty-five in 1937. During the campaign, he told the Citizens Committee on the Control of Crime in New York: "You may definitely assume that crime, too, is incorporated." One of his last acts as district attorney before running for governor was to initiate "an unprecedented inquiry into the affairs of the Port of New York." At the time, the waterfront was a racketeering hell, where a number of the Five Families had established a profitable foothold. Neither Dewey, nor anyone else, completed the inquiry.

Dewey had all the signposts before him, but like before, he failed to recognize them. It had started more than a decade before, with Charles Dawes's warning on the House floor in 1926. It was followed the next year by writer Frederic M. Thrasher, who in painstaking detail, spelled out the role of the "gangland" in America, including where the Mafia originated and how it operated.[42] Dewey had muzzled the top of the Jewish racketeering element: Waxey was in prison, Dutch was slain, Lepke would go to Sing Sing's electric chair, and Gurrah would die in prison. Two other important names, Bugsy Siegel and Meyer Lansky, left for sunnier climes, and he had successfully prosecuted the Boss of Bosses, Charlie Luciano. This just opened the door wider for the Five Families, and they went on their merry way in the rackets. On May 11, 1938, just before he announced his candidacy for governor, Dewey told the Bar of the City of New York and the New York County Lawyers Association: "Today there is not a racketeer of first importance left in New York."[43] That sounded a lot like Secretary Morgenthau's nescient assertion that Dutch Schultz was "the last of the big-tax racketeers."

16. IREY, HOOVER, AND ANSLINGER

Elmer Irey wanted nothing to do with J. Edgar Hoover. They rarely crossed paths in their professional lives and never developed a personal friendship. "They had nothing in common," said Hugh Irey, Elmer's son. "They did their own thing, except I think that on more than one occasion, Hoover got credit for things the Treasury Department did."[1] This occurred most prominently with the Lindbergh kidnapping.

The abduction of Charles and Anne Lindbergh's twenty-month-old son, Charles Jr., from their home in Hopewell, New Jersey, on March 1, 1932, was the most publicly compelling criminal case of the decade. The couple received 40,000 letters in the first month of the kidnapping. Irey, who called it "the crime of the century," was right in the middle of it. However, he thought about the Lindbergh kidnapping the way he thought about the Capone investigation: "A case in which we had no business."[2] His idea to place gold certificates in the ransom money broke the case. Irey was near the scene already—his special force had spent the last year at the Southern District gathering evidence on Waxey Gordon, Dutch Schultz, and other racketeers. And Irey did for Lindbergh what he did not do for Medalie and Dewey: bring in members of his crack Chicago team—Art Madden, Frank Wilson, Arthur Nichols, and Pat O'Rourke—to assist in the investigation.

A bizarre turn of events brought Irey into the case. Al Capone, sitting in a Chicago jail, told Arthur Brisbane, editorial director of the Hearst newspapers, that a member of his combine named Bob Conroy had kidnapped the child and that he could get him back in exchange for his freedom. Knowing of the Treasury's role in the Capone case, Lindbergh called Secretary of the Treasury Ogden L. Mills, who happened to be his friend, and asked for his help. Ogden told Irey to meet with Lindbergh. Wilson, Madden, and O'Rourke went along. Irey spoke bluntly to the famed aviator: "Capone doesn't know who has the child, Colonel Lindbergh. He is simply trying to get out of jail. We know he thinks or says he thinks one of his gang, Bob Conroy, did it. Conroy was at least two hundred miles away, maybe more. We intend, however, to get Conroy and talk to him. But he didn't do it."[3]

J. Edgar Hoover wanted his bureau to be a part of the investigation, "which was exactly what Lindbergh did not want," according to writer Noel Behn. Hoover and his bureau became "a major nuisance" to Col. H. Norman Schwarzkopf, the New Jersey State Police superintendent, a thirty-seven-year-old West Point graduate, and a key figure in the investigation. Hoover had his agents find out what they could, Behn wrote, "without state police approval and, often, without their knowledge."[4] The day after the child's body was found, President Hoover named the FBI director to oversee and coordinate the activities of the federal agencies involved in the kidnapping. Hoover's "first move was to kick" Irey and the Secret Service off the case. "Taken aback" by Hoover's action, Lindbergh interceded with Mills. Irey was reinstated, but Hoover remained in charge.[5] In his memoir, Irey said nothing about Hoover's machinations, only that the two-and-a-half-year manhunt for the kidnappers "was filled with frustrations, sadistic humans, suicides, murders, spiritualists, hoodlums, and a weird assortment of odd creatures who wandered in and out like clowns in a funeral procession."[6]

A Lindbergh intermediary, John F. Condon, passed the ransom to a man in St. Raymond's Cemetery in the Bronx on the evening of Saturday, April 2. The kidnappers originally demanded $70,000 ($1,050,000 in 1990 dollars). Condon had a box containing $50,000 ($750,000 in 1990 dollars) and had the other $20,000 wrapped in a package. Condon said the man settled for the box containing the $50,000. In the exchange, he was handed a note that said the boy was on the boat *Nelly* off Martha's Vineyard. This turned out to be untrue. In the afternoon of May 12, the boy's body was spotted in a thicket off a muddy road two miles east of Hopewell by a man who stopped there to relieve himself.

When the marked gold certificates began appearing in New York City banks, the tellers failed to check the two-column, fifty-seven-page list of ransom-money serial numbers. Frank Wilson had "begged, threatened and harangued bankers in an effort to get them to force clerks to keep their eyes open for the ransom notes."[7]

At a Bronx service station on September 15, 1934, a driver handed a ten-dollar gold certificate to the attendant, Ernest Lyons, to pay for the gas. "Worried about counterfeit ten-dollar bills which were then flooding New York," wrote Frank Wilson and Beth Day, "Lyons jotted down the car's license number, 4U-13-41, on the certificate."[8] When the certificate went to the bank, an alert teller saw that it was part of the cash ransom and turned the license number on it over to the authorities. The license number, the authorities quickly determined, was registered to Bruno Richard Hauptmann, an unemployed carpenter. The NYPD, without telling J. Edgar Hoover, put a surveillance team on Hauptmann briefly before arresting him.

Richard Gid Powers described what happened upon Hauptmann's arrest:

> Hoover rushed to New York so he could stand beside New York City Police Commissioner John F. O'Ryan during the announcement of the Hauptmann arrest. He was also able to pose for photographs shaking hands with Special Agent T. H. Sisk and the other two agents on the New York Lindbergh Squad headed by Inspector John Lyons of the New York Police Department.[9] The *Washington Star*'s caption with this picture declared that Hoover and his men were the "Justice Board of Strategy in Lindbergh Case." Another story credited the 'sherlocks of [the] Justice Department with trapping Hauptmann and said that Hoover had supervised the interrogation.[10]

Claire Bond Potter observed that the Justice Department committed "little of its prestige" in the Lindbergh case as "the weeks of searching turned into months." J. Edgar Hoover followed a careful strategy. "Much of the New York office was assigned to the case, but the absence of memorandums in 1932–33 documenting leads, interviews, and evidence shared with other agencies reflects both Hoover's desire to keep the case to himself and the failure of the investigation." Hoover "made sure that the shortcomings of other federal investigators were noted in this period. The Treasury agent who had been 'engaged in his case since shortly after the date of the kidnapping,' Hoover complained, had not produced a report in fourteen months."[11] This was an obvious reference to Irey.

Hoover's obsessively stealthy nature knew few boundaries, even toward his peers in law enforcement. According to FBI Special Agent John Trimble, Hoover placed Irey and one of his aides under surveillance during the Lindbergh case. The reason why is not documented. But five years after the Lindbergh case was solved, Irey was still having his phones checked for signs of FBI wiretapping, according to Malachi "Mal" Harney. Harney, an aide to both Irey and Anslinger during his forty-year tenure at Treasury, said Irey and Hoover "were bitter enemies" and cited the Lindbergh case. "Irey was a good Christian who didn't cuss," Harney revealed, "but the air would be blue when the subject of the Lindbergh kidnapping case came up."[12]

While Irey's idea of marking the bills broke the Lindbergh case, he had to issue "a stuffy ultimatum" to Lindbergh that if the cache of gold certificates wasn't marked, he would withdraw from the case.[13] At that, Lindbergh relented, later telling Irey, "If it had not been for you fellows being in the case, Hauptmann would not now be on trial and your organization deserves the full credit for his apprehension."[14] Irey never mentioned in his memoir that he received a personal letter from Lindbergh. On December 30, 1932, the aviator wrote Irey a letter in longhand, thanking him for his role in solving the case. There is nothing on the record to indicate that Hoover got a similar letter.

■

There was a compelling reason for J. Edgar Hoover's stealthy attitude. Eleven months into the Lindbergh case, FDR entered the White House. In the change of administrations, heads rolled—the accepted nature of Washington politics. Irey was deeply embroiled in the Gordon and Schultz investigations in Manhattan, and since FDR allowed Medalie and Dewey to stay, even if they were rock-ribbed Republicans, Irey's job appeared safe too. Internal Revenue Commissioner David Burnet was let go. Attorney General William Mitchell was let go. What about J. Edgar Hoover?

FDR's new attorney general, Thomas J. Walsh, the Montana senator whose committee investigated the Teapot Dome scandal, had announced his intentions to reorganize the Justice Department. Repeal was on the horizon; it had been one of FDR's major campaign pledges, and the new administration was facing an outdated law enforcement constabulary made top-heavy by the 2,800-agent Prohibition Bureau, still the biggest detective agency in the federal establishment and now a part of the Justice Department. Walsh brought on as his chief assistant, Homer S. Cummings, a sixty-three-year-old well-to-do Connecticut lawyer and Yale graduate who was the mayor of Stamford, Connecticut, at age thirty. A partner in a law firm, Cummings served as the Democratic National Chairman in the Woodrow Wilson era and was in the Roosevelt-before-Chicago clique. Still in his prime—tall, energetic, the picture of health—Cummings was the White House loyalist in the Justice Department. On March 2, 1933, two days before FDR's inauguration, the seventy-four-year-old Walsh was stricken with coronary thrombosis and died within hours.

A month later Cummings took over at Justice. It was a fateful choice: he put a highly questionable stamp on the course of federal law enforcement in the 1930s. Cummings was tested in the law, but untested in his comprehension of the criminal underworld that had taken root in the country and grown into an organized and sophisticated force in his lifetime. The underworld wore a mask, and Cummings thought he saw beneath it. He could not distinguish between organized crime elements like the American Mafia, which really controlled the underworld, and desperadoes like bank robbers, thieves, and kidnappers who liked to think they were a part of it.

With an eye on the mighty Treasury Department and its force of 5,700 T-Men, one of Cummings's first moves was to recommend a super police force to lead the new administration's fight on crime. That figure of 5,700 was deceptive. The real crime fighters at the Treasury—Irey's and Harry Anslinger's contingents and Customs investigators—represented less than a tenth of the force. The rest were Secret Service personnel, White House police, Alcohol Tax unit agents, revenue agents, and the guards at Treasury, including the Mint, the Assay Office, and the Bureau of Engraving and Printing. The Treasury's investigative work wasn't lost on Cummings. Irey's unsung unit was one of the high-water marks of the three Republican administrations of the 1920s. Cummings wasn't going to call attention to this. Taking the fight to the country's criminal-political alliances and elements of organized crime was where the broad fight against crime lay. Cummings was aware the federal constabulary had been ineffective and needed to be shored up; what he wasn't aware of was where the fight should be taken.

Believing, at least, that a new order was necessary to fight crime, he moved to combine the Bureau of Prohibition, the Bureau of Identification, and the Bureau of Investigation into a new Division of Investigation at Justice. The plan sparked a side issue: it made Hoover's perch precarious, and Hoover knew it. He appeared expendable. Though he had hewed to Harlan Stone's stern injunction nine years before to build and maintain an incorruptible agency, he had not distinguished himself in those years. For a decade, Hoover and his Bureau of Investigation were nobodies.

Hoover, however, had never stopped honing his skills in staying a jump ahead of his superiors. He began lobbying for testimonials. And he knew whom to turn to at this fateful time—his old superior at Justice—the highly regarded Harlan Stone, now in his eighth year as an associate justice of the Supreme Court. Stone reached President Roosevelt through Felix Frankfurter, a trusted adviser to FDR when he was governor of New York. On April 22, 1933, FDR told Frankfurter, "It is all right about Edgar Hoover. Homer Cummings agrees with me." Hoover had already been furnishing the White House with "the same sort of informal information" he had provided to previous Oval Offices. It was the modus operandi he would use while serving a total of nine presidents and seventeen attorneys general. As

Richard Gid Powers pointed out, what counted was that Hoover's "eager willingness to provide these services must have reassured Roosevelt that here was someone with whom he could work."[15]

On June 10, 1933, FDR signed an executive order creating the Division of Investigation, effective August 10. In late July Cummings named Hoover to head it. In giving Hoover the post, he gave Hoover his way too. Major E. V. Dalrymple, chief of the Prohibition Bureau, was dismissed; his second in command, John S. Hurley, was made Hoover's assistant. Hoover, of course, wanted nothing to do with Prohibition agents. He detested them as much as he did Anslinger's drug agents, believing they were all part of a corrupted workplace. The Prohibition Bureau was abolished, and Hoover stuck the 977 agents left in a separate Alcoholic Beverage Unit at the BI. When Prohibition was repealed in December, the 977 agents Hoover never wanted were transferred back to the Treasury.

■

While the reserved Irey never captured the public's imagination like Hoover did, one of the clearest measures of the two men can be drawn from what happened to the careers of Frank Wilson of the SIU and Melvin Purvis of the FBI, each of whom were true American heroes. Wilson and Purvis distinguished themselves by helping to solve the greatest cases in the history of their respective agencies.

Wilson, with his "genius for detail" was Irey's top agent. In uncovering the evidence that sent Al Capone away, he had given new meaning to the word "driven." A sharp-faced man with a wide, grim mouth and unyielding stare, he carried out daunting and historical tasks, not once but twice. On separate occasions four years apart, he sat and grilled two of the most conspicuous public figures of the day—Al Capone and Huey Long—about their money trail. In each case, he told Irey that they should be prosecuted.

In 1936 Secretary of the Treasury Morgenthau named Wilson to head the Secret Service. There, he built another distinctive career, running the agency in exemplary fashion during World War II, a period that demanded extra effort. He was credited with developing presidential security techniques that are now standard procedures. He retired in 1947, one year after Irey left, and went on to serve as a consultant on security for the Atomic

Energy Commission. He died at Georgetown University Hospital in Washington in 1970 at age eighty-three. The same age as Irey, he outlived him by twenty-three years.

Melvin Purvis became an instant celebrity at age thirty. In his 1936 memoir (that brought him into undying conflict with J. Edgar Hoover), Purvis described the effects of "danger": "At the start of a raid, my stomach was invariably as temperamental as an Italian prima donna. It tied itself into a double-hitch or a bow knot and then was swung around on a flying trapeze. . . . After the ill-fated siege of Little Bohemia I had nervous indigestion for a week."[16] The special agent in charge of the FBI's Chicago field office, Purvis was in the shooting match that brought down John Dillinger outside Chicago's Biograph Theater on the sultry night of July 22, 1934. Three months later he was at the scene outside East Liverpool, Ohio, when marksmen with rifles drilled Pretty Boy Floyd as he ran through a cornfield. Purvis was the last person to talk to Floyd before he died, and his celebrity became an albatross. J. Edgar Hoover had built a highly regimented agency. It spoke with one collective voice and starred only one name above the title, his. There were no featured roles either. This was likely owing to Hoover's bitter experiences in the years before taking over the highly soiled agency. It was not going to be otherwise, not even for Purvis, whose sterling traits made him an overnight star at the bureau. Early on, he impressed his superiors, rising from a trainee in late 1926 to assistant special agent in charge of the Chicago field office by 1930, at twenty-seven. The rarity of one of his special agents being at the shoot-outs of both Dillinger and Floyd was too intoxicating for Hoover, who moved quickly to suffocate Purvis's newly won celebrity. The FBI director was building his legend on "getting" Dillinger. A year after the Dillinger episode, Purvis, who had been going through a series of harassments, was forced to resign.

Hoover gave the credit for bringing down Dillinger not to Purvis but to Samuel Crowley, who was in charge of a special squad searching for the bank robber. Crowley wasn't at the Biograph that historic night. "He was waiting at the Chicago field office with an open wire to Hoover's home," wrote Ovid Demaris.[17] Four months after Dillinger died in the Biograph shootout, Crowley was killed in a gun battle with Baby Face Nelson. Whatever the dispute over the roles of Crowley or Purvis on that fatal night, it was the end of the line for Purvis. As Richard Gid Powers observed, "Whenever Purvis was considered for an important job, one of Hoover's men would be sure to intervene with a damaging report."[18] In February 1960 at his residence in Timmonsville, South Carolina, Purvis, age fifty-seven, died from a bullet fired from an automatic pistol his colleagues gave him upon his resignation from the bureau. A doctor's statement said Purvis was depressed over his ill health. In the end, "by dint of constant restatement, Hoover finally managed to turn his treatment of the Dillinger case into the definitive version, and the classic victory in the FBI's war against crime," wrote Powers.[19]

■

Irey and Hoover were contemporaries who grew up in Washington and would spend their lives there. They had been at the core of federal law enforcement since the mid-1920s, when it was still in its formative years; had pointed their branches in decidedly different directions; and because of this, aside from Hoover's attempts to grab glory from Irey's achievements, there was little conflict over turf until the 1930s. Other than Irey's oblique remark in his memoir about Hoover's bureau after Secretary Mellon told him to go after Al Capone, there is nothing on the record of what each thought of the other. Any meetings—either fleeting or otherwise—are not on the record. Policy disputes between the two were rare. When they did hit the headlines, it was Hoover who did not come out looking good.

In 1938 a number of the most important German espionage agents whom FBI agents had had under surveillance slipped through their fingers and departed on steamships back to Germany. This sparked a wave of criticism, raising doubts about the bureau's effectiveness and sparking a debate on how the bureau could improve the quality of its detective work. One way to do this was to place the bureau's special agents under the Civil Service system. On Capitol Hill, this had been a long-running argument. Hoover, however, for years had fought such a move with every bone in his body.

In 1939 FDR named a committee to inquire into the improvement of the Civil Service system and also whether it should make a recommendation subjecting the FBI to the system. Hoover, in a letter of protest to the president's committee, explained, "I am not opposed to the principle of Civil Service. . . . I am a bitter opponent of the spoils system."[20] Critics, however, maintained that the other federal detective forces operating under Civil Service had "at least as satisfactory records as the FBI, and without all the shouting."[21]

The president's committee turned to Elmer Irey to canvass the problem. He reported that, except for the FBI, all of the important federal detective agencies had been functioning for years under the Civil Service system and that the advantages of the system "are so overwhelming that the application of the Civil Service to such agencies is the one certain method of securing a completely efficient, reliable and impartial investigating body." In answer to Hoover's criticism that it was a "spoils system," Irey countered, "Every administrative agency of the Government is under pressure from spoilsmen. Without the protection of the civil-service law, it is difficult to avoid political interference or pressure in selecting and separating personnel."

Irey, of course, had seen firsthand how the political-criminal alliances had corrupted Chicago, Kansas City, New York City, and elsewhere but noted that advancements were being made. Outside the federal government, "there has been growing recognition of the need for a merit system in selecting State and local law enforcement personnel," Irey said. "The Wickersham Commission in its report No. 14 on police pointed out the devastating effect spoils practices had on the operation of police groups throughout the country. The better law enforcement organizations in States, counties and cities work under a civil-service system."[22]

Hoover remained adamant. He told the House Appropriations Committee, "I think we have the highest type of personnel to be found throughout the entire Government service." He informed the president's committee, "The Federal Bureau of Investigation has the finest force of employees in any governmental agency in the United States and I believe their accomplishments will support this statement." He further declared that if his agents were put under Civil Service, the FBI would have to comply with the statutory requirement that war veterans had a preference for appointment as federal employees and that this "would materially hinder the Bureau."[23]

What developed out of the dispute over the Civil Service system was a rare look into the relative efficiency of the other investigative agencies operating under the Civil Service system, compared with the FBI. A committee chaired by Senator Harry F. Byrd of Virginia made a study in conjunction with the Brookings Institution on which of the seven most important federal detective agencies were doing the best jobs. One criteria of efficiency—which Hoover himself used—was the percentage of convictions secured in the cases investigated by the FBI and selected for indictment and court proceedings. The theory underlying this criterion was that if agents were efficient in getting evidence, a defendant would be convicted or would plead guilty. The agency with the highest percentage would be the most competent.

The study found the FBI ranked next to the bottom of the list. A Brookings researcher applied a further test, which ascertained the relative accomplishments achieved in the criminal courts by the FBI, the Secret Service, and the Post Office's inspection division. The FBI came out third. The study also maintained that the work of the other federal detective agencies was "at least as difficult and as important as the FBI's. The committee stated that in tracking down criminals who commit depredations on the Government's business activities, in particular its revenue-gathering, currency and postal activities, the Treasury and Post Office detectives combat every type of criminal from murderers, kidnappers, burglars, and highwaymen to forgers and swindlers."[24]

The study also showed the Treasury investigative staffs had done more than the FBI both in bringing money into the U.S. Treasury and in protecting the Treasury against loss. In a two-year period, Hoover said the FBI had effected savings for the benefit of the public in the amount of $155 million ($875 million in 1990 dollars). The Special Intelligence Unit, according to the study, brought in $2 billion ($30 billion in 1990 dollars).

Irey and Hoover clashed again in February 1940, when Hoover sought legislation to permit the FBI to inspect the information obtained in the 1940 census. "This attempt by the FBI to have its detectives inspect the information secured by census takers in the census of 1940 only increased the fear that it might become a central detective force with dossiers on numberless citizens," wrote Max Lowenthal. The *New York Times* broke the story, reporting that Irey and Kildroy P. Aldrich, chief inspector of the Post Office Department's "police office" "were said to have vigorously opposed legislation of the type sought by Mr. Hoover, the inference being that they would desire for themselves the right to peruse the confidential information obtained by census enumerators. Their opposition was motivated in part by two factors—the criticism which has arisen over the intimate nature of some of the questions in the census and the strong opposition in some quarters to any moves which might implement 'snooper' activities by Federal law enforcement agencies."[25] Hoover was constantly attempting to increase his bureau's powers and occasionally would spur editorial remarks such as that of *Collier's* magazine: "The FBI is superb. But human beings are ambitious; and the FBI, unchecked and unbridled, could grow to be an American Gestapo."[26] The public opposition shown by Irey and Aldrich was not generally voiced in government agencies.

■

Irey, satisfied to leave crime fighting to Hoover, believed his own role was to recover the public's money, which led him to pioneer the fight against offshore tax havens used to hide taxable income. In 1935 the Treasury began getting reports of heavy financial activity between offshore and U.S. banks, and alerted Irey. At the time, the nation was deep into the Great Depression but not everybody was suffering. Irey found Americans had formed 585 personal holding companies in four nearby countries or provinces during 1935. In Canada, Prince Edward Island had 243 and Newfoundland had 202. In the Bahamas, there were ninety-four; in Panama, forty-six. In the years from 1880 to 1924, only ninety-three companies were formed offshore for any purpose, business or otherwise. From 1924 to 1934, however, new corporations averaged twenty a year.

Irey sent SIU Special Agent William Bremmer to Nassau in 1936. He quickly found a "thriving business" among attorneys "whose chief occupation seems to be the formation of such companies." The offices of one firm, run by an attorney named Kenneth Solomon, was "literally plastered from foundation to roof with these corporate names. The name plates are about 30 inches long and 8 inches wide, and the building is so covered with them as to constitute one of the major curiosities of Nassau."[27]

The motivating force behind this of course was to hide financial proceeds—and what was the real beginning of money laundering, a phrase not coined until four decades later. Irey didn't call it that. This is what he told a congressional committee: "Some of these countries make a sort of ambulance-chasing racket out of the possibility of attracting wealthy American taxpayers. The scheme has sufficient plausibility so that no one can be sure at this time whether it is or is not a legal method of tax avoidance under our present law. It permits the taxpayer to transfer his income to countries where tax investigation by American Treasury officials is almost impossible."[28]

The first money launderer Irey ran across was a New York banker named Philip DeRonde. Formerly the president of Hibernia Trust Co. of New York and the chairman of the board of Phoenix Securities Corporation of New York, DeRonde owed $33,000 ($528,000 in 1990 dollars) in unpaid taxes and interest to the Bureau of Internal Revenue. On January 7, 1937, DeRonde made a sworn statement to Internal Revenue that he was without substantial funds and that he was seeking to settle his liability of $33,000 by offering a compromise of $1,700 ($27,200 in 1990 dollars).

Irey said Internal Revenue learned on January 8 that DeRonde received $250,000 ($4 million in 1990 dollars) from the General Investment Co., an American corporation for which he had acted as agent in the sale of the subway in Buenos Aires, Argentina. DeRonde, according to Irey, instructed the General Investment Co. to pay the $250,000 to a Bahamas corporation named Philip DeRonde, Ltd., instead of to him. The records of the registrar in the Bahamas show that the corporation had been formed three months before the transaction. The DeRonde case was the first of what became a long-running problem for the Treasury of U.S. taxpayers exploiting offshore tax havens.

What would become a major domestic and international issue in the last third of the twentieth century was already a concern by the mid-1930s. Congress stuck a surtax on personal holding companies in the Revenue

Act of 1934 as one way to stop the flow of money into offshore havens. This was not effective. Three years later, on June 18, 1937, the Joint Committee on Tax Evasion and Avoidance, chaired by Rep. Robert L. Doughton of North Carolina, launched hearings "to put on evidence with respect to the use of foreign corporations, particularly in the Bahamas, for purposes of avoiding American taxes." The hearings were called after the Treasury "was surprised and disturbed by the failure of the receipts from the income tax on March 15 to measure up to the Budget estimates." Secretary of the Treasury Morgenthau made this point in a letter dated May 29, 1937, to President Roosevelt, which the committee put in its report. Morgenthau described in detail what was happening in offshore activity and pointed out other "flagrant" ways that were being used to hide and launder income. Irey, with the evidence gathered by William Bremmer, testified at length before the committee on the SIU's investigative effort in the Bahamas. The hearings found "serious loopholes existed," and action was taken in the Revenue Act of 1938 to crack down on the problem.[29] In the years leading up to World War II, however, money laundering and the growth of tax havens never reached a scale to bring alarm. For Irey, who always worked with limited resources, the issue was moot. For him, the money trail was a domestic concern, not an international one.

■

Irey had testified before the joint committee on the tax haven issue at the time the SIU was trying to put away an old Chicago nemesis, Johnny Torrio. After leaving Chicago, the "Syndicate Superman" eluded the law, helping Luciano become the American Mafia's Boss of Bosses and lending a hand in corrupting the bail bond industry in New York City.[30] In between, he enjoyed his illegal millions by taking around-the-world cruises, once spending thirty months in Honolulu's mild clime, and shuttling between his mother's home on Long Island and his brother-in-law's residence in St. Petersburg, Florida. Then, the unexpected happened.

In May 1935 the Treasury's Alcohol Tax Unit was tipped that Torrio had a financial interest in a New York City importing firm, Prendergast and Davies Col, Ltd., which was also a wholesale liquor dealer. Alcohol Tax agents begin to tail Torrio. They arrested him in April 1936, along with two small-fries—William Stockbower, Torrio's brother-in-law, and James La Penna—for violation of the liquor laws. However, Lamar Hardy, the U.S. attorney for the Southern District confided to Hugh McQuillen, special agent in charge of the SIU's New York office, that the case "was worthless for prosecution." And would the SIU "please take over and try to save the U.S. Attorney's office some embarrassment by making an income tax case against Torrio?"[31] Irey did, in a case that, from start to finish, took four years to resolve.

On September 3, 1937, Torrio was indicted for evading income taxes for the years 1933 and 1935, but shortly thereafter new evidence was found and superseding indictments were handed up. Torrio was charged with reporting income of $18,000 ($288,000 in 1990 dollars) in 1933, when he should have reported $145,262 ($2,123,192 in 1990 dollars). For 1934 he reported income of $19,441 ($311,036 in 1990 dollars), when his income was $74,932 ($1,198,912 in 1990 dollars). In 1935 he reported income of $43,874 ($701,984 in 1990 dollars); actually it was $96,129 ($1,538,014 in 1990 dollars). Trial began on March 29, 1939. Dixie Davis, Dutch Schultz's ex-lawyer, was a witness for the prosecution and told of Torrio's activities with Dutch. The evidence was damning, and Torrio, on April 10, changed his plea to guilty. Noting Torrio's age (fifty-seven), District Court Judge John W. Clancy imposed a sentence of thirty months on the first count of tax evasion, five years on the second, and two years on the third, then suspended the latter two terms. Stockbower got a suspended sentence of one year; La Penna, nine months.

On April 15, 1941, almost two years to the day after he was sentenced, Torrio was released from Leavenworth. In 1948 Irey wrote in his memoir, "I don't know where Johnny Torrio is today. If Johnny is retired, I knew he's retired in comfort; if he's in action, I know he's the biggest gangster in America today; if he's dead, I'll bet he died with his boots on. He was the smartest and, I dare say, the best of all the hoodlums. 'Best' referring to talent, not morals."[32] Torrio died in 1957, outliving Irey by eleven years.

■

The FBI, under Hoover, failed to adequately investigate racketeering and organized crime. Its massive information and intelligence apparatus contained nothing about criminal elites such as the Five Families. The SIU's efforts, under Irey, were scattered and piecemeal, except for his investigation of the Mafia's shakedown of Hollywood. Undoubtedly, Irey's intelligence on organized crime was limited. The most notable, actually, the only one of any substance on the public record, was a missive about Charlie Luciano that Art Madden gave him at the time of the Lindbergh kidnapping. In a letter to Irey dated March 11, 1932, Madden sought to explain the circumstances surrounding Al Capone's offer to help in the kidnapping. He was even uncertain of Luciano's name, and admitted as much in his letter to Irey. Wrote Madden,

> I am advised that there is a man in the east, presumably a New York Italian, named Charles Lucky (spelling of last name is uncertain) who has more influence among the criminal Italians than Al Capone ever had. It is said that Lucky is Capone's boss and the boss of all the other Italians engaged in important violations of the law. The thought was expressed that Lucky, in view of his great influence, could do more in the Lindbergh kidnapping case, if anything could be done at all, than Capone could. I do not recall that I ever heard of Lucky, but I presume that he is as influential as he is reported to be. If this particular kidnapping is an underworld crime, perhaps means could be devised to communicate with Lucky and to get his cooperation if that has not already been done.[33]

Madden had good sources in Chicago, and that gold nugget probably came out of the Congress Hotel meeting, involving Capone and Maranzano. But like other gold nuggets dropped into the lap of lawmen about organized crime elements, no one bought it. Irey did not seize on it nor did he pass it on to Tom Dewey during their time together at the Southern District. Dewey—for all of his great success in bringing down racketeers in New York City's five boroughs—along with his talented staff, never uncovered intelligence centering on the Five Families.

Organized crime elements, whatever they were called—the "Outfit" in Chicago, the Five Mafia Families in New York, the Mayfield Road Gang in Cleveland—had become powerful operations as early as 1931. The SIU had brought down the top array of Al Capone's machine, along with an important array of other criminal-political alliances. But other elements continued to flourish. Cleveland's Mayfield Road Gang, a low-profile syndicate of Jewish racketeers, was every bit as successful as New York's Five Families, and like the Five Families, the gang used the friendship and wise advice of Meyer Lansky. The pioneering Mafia historian, Hank Messick, called the Mayfield Road Gang the "Silent Syndicate." It was made up of Morris Kleinman, Morris B. "Moe" Dalitz, Louis Rothkopf, and Samuel A. "Sam" Tucker. They conducted gambling enterprises in places like Newport, Kentucky, and went on to highly successful ventures with Lansky and Siegel in Las Vegas.

In 1931 Irey launched an inquiry of the thirty-seven-year-old Kleinman, whose rum-running in the Lake Erie region extended from Detroit to Buffalo. Kleinman never achieved the status of a Luciano, but his underworld earnings over a lifetime likely matched those of New York's Boss of Bosses. The inquiry—revenue agent Alvin Giesey was instrumental in developing the evidence—found Kleinman failed to file tax returns for the years 1929 and 1930, while depositing $1.6 million ($12 million in 1990 dollars) in eight separate bank accounts. At one point during the inquiry, Kleinman's attorney, Martin McCormack, a former U.S. attorney, threw a political punch at Irey. At a conference in Washington on December 19, 1932, McCormack told Irey that the Hoover administration had made a "promise" to Maurice Maschke, the "Republican boss of Cleveland," that there would be no prosecution "of any kind" against Kleinman. Irey ignored him. In November 1933 Kleinman was convicted of income tax evasion and sentenced to four years in prison.

Kleinman served thirty-three months before being paroled on September 1, 1936, and rejoined the Mayfield Road Gang. "Equal partners in every undertaking," Kleinman, Dalitz, Tucker, and Rothkopf became as important an organized crime element as existed in the country.[34] Through the next several decades they operated gambling joints and conducted racketeering ventures in Ohio and Kentucky, where their wealth and political influence permitted them to operate virtually unhindered. It also helped that they formed a working alliance with Mafia elements of the region. Another reason for their success was that they turned ex-enemies into friendly forces. They were "so impressed" with Alvin Giesey, the revenue agent who helped Irey's SIU gather the evidence to put away Kleinman, that they hired him after he left the Bureau of Internal Revenue in 1934.[35] Giesey would become an integral part of the Mayfield Road operation and would later give Kleinman the sobriquet "Al Capone of Cleveland."[36]

■

There was a shared antipathy between Irey and Hoover and between Harry Anslinger and Hoover, but only tiny pieces of their disputes got into the public record. Irey kept such a satisfactory distance from Hoover that there is little on the record of what Hoover thought of him. Not so for Anslinger. Hoover "didn't like him," according to William Hundley, who once served as head of the Organized Crime Section at the Justice Department.[37] And just as he did with many public figures, Hoover maintained a confidential file on Anslinger.

Anslinger's inner thoughts about Hoover are virtually nonexistent. One of the few times he did mention Hoover is revealing. In summer 1939, when Louis "Lepke" Buchalter was the target of a nationwide manhunt, Tom Dewey, then New York County district attorney, called Anslinger, Hoover, and New York City Police Commissioner Lewis Valentine to an "unprecedented secret meeting" in Manhattan over the "killing off of witnesses" in the Lepke case.[38] Lepke was the last big name left from the great racketeering era. How he measured up against Mafia chieftains such as Charlie Luciano and Frank Costello can be measured in what J. Edgar Hoover thought of him: Louis Lepke is "the most dangerous criminal in the United States."[39]

During the meeting, according to Anslinger, Hoover brought up "the question of operational procedure." This was code for, Who runs the show?—a subject uppermost to Hoover. The FBI director wanted to run things his way, with his star on the door. Dewey was already aware of Hoover's proclivities, and so was Valentine. Hoover had incurred Valentine's wrath in December 1936 for launching a "spectacular" raid on a

Manhattan apartment where bank robber–kidnapper Harry Brunette was holed up. He did so without Valentine's "consent" and "contrary to the plans carefully considered and agreed upon by the New York Police, the New Jersey State Troopers and members of the Federal Bureau of Investigation." After a siege with machine guns and gas bombs that set fire to the building, which housed twenty families, Burnett was captured. Valentine said, "I have made it a rigid policy to prohibit melodramatic raids on the hiding places of criminals." One newspaper report called Hoover "a hunter of headlines as well as of fugitive criminals."[40]

History has already recorded that from the 1920s into the late 1950s, Hoover did not focus on crime's leading element, racketeers. Former Attorney General Ramsey Clark presented one of the stoutest explanations for Hoover's attitude:

> You have to reckon the very strong human qualities of J. Edgar Hoover. He was a unique man, not at all evil by any means. He really believed deeply in integrity, as he defined it, as he saw it. He took real pride in the fact that no FBI agent was ever convicted of any corruption. It was an important gospel to him. Organized crime depends on corruption, and he knew that. You get into organized crime and it's messy as hell and you get men knocked-off and you get men bought-off and you watch the Anslingers and Hogans [Frank Hogan was the New York district attorney] and all the others struggle in the muck and mire for a full career and with no discernible impact. It's dirty, and sometimes the dirt rubs off, and he wanted clean work, easy work. He wanted to be a winner.[41]

Nonetheless, as the major federal crime fighter, Hoover failed the test in what is a critical area of law enforcement—knowing who your enemies are. Furthermore, Hoover had ignored what went on before, all the way back to Vice President Dawes's definitive speech on the House floor in 1926 that cited the Mafia. The turning point for Hoover and his bureau in recognizing the existence of the Mafia did not come until November 14, 1957, following the accidental discovery of a gathering of high-level Mafia figures at the spacious home of Joseph Barbara in Apalachin, New York. (The next morning, the *New York Times* put the story at the bottom of its front page.)

The Apalachin meeting "hit the FBI like a bomb," said William Sullivan, chief of the bureau's Research and Analysis section, which investigated "communism, espionage and the Klan."[42] Sullivan had nothing to do with criminal investigation, so he "was surprised" when Hoover called him to his office immediately after Apalachin to discuss the Mafia and was "even more surprised when he accepted my offer to do some research on organized crime for him. But he was like a drowning man, reaching for any help he could get to prevent future embarrassment, and he gave me the assignment."[43]

Sullivan had a group of "talented, dedicated men" working for him. He took the "best of them off their other cases and put them to work on a report about the Mafia." One agent "read over two hundred books on the Mafia and checked through *The New York Times* coverage of organized crime for the last hundred years." A two-volume study was put together "that proved the Mafia existed and had been operating in this country for many decades."

Sullivan was "proud" of the report he'd put together and wanted others to see it, so he sent a copy to Anslinger and Attorney General William P. Rogers. Hoover found out and, "like a shot," called Sullivan to his office and snapped, "I see no need of giving Anslinger or the attorney general copies of our study."

Sullivan replied that the copies had already been sent out that morning.

"'Retrieve them at once,' he shouted at me." Sullivan "sent some men over and they sneaked the copies out and brought them back to me. After all the study did prove that the FBI had been wrong."

On November 27, thirteen days after Apalachin, Hoover sent out a "tough, no-holds-barred edict in a letter to all field offices entitled 'The Top Hoodlum Program: Anti-Racketeering.'" Until then, according to William Roemer, "he had not found a statute on the federal books on which to peg an intelligence gathering mission against the mob."[44] The letter cited the 1946 Hobbs Anti-Racketeering Act as the statute to use. The Hobbs Act was passed as an amendment to the Anti-Racketeering Act of 1934 and was aimed at labor racketeers. The legislation was an answer to a U.S. Supreme Court decision that ruled for the Teamsters. The case involved a New York City local accused of using threats to obtain payments from out-of-town trucking companies in return for permission for their trucks to enter Manhattan. The original case, incidentally, was handled by John Harlan Amen, the great and unsung rackets prosecutor of the 1930s.

Until Anslinger, no one in the federal detective agencies tried to put together a comprehensive body of information about the Mafia; there was a limited effort along the way by such elements as the Chicago Crime Commission. After the SIU had gathered the evidence to put away Al Capone in 1931, the commission in 1932 named Murray "The Camel" Humphreys as public enemy number one. The SIU seized the moment. Nels Tessem tracked down Humphreys's "bank accounts in phony names" and found he had defrauded the government of $26,108.24 ($443,839.08 in 1990 dollars) in 1930, 1931, and 1932.[45] The Camel was indicted in June 1933 and fled to Mexico, returning after sixteen months. At trial he received an eighteen-month prison term and was fined $5,000 ($80,000 in 1990 dollars).

Anslinger spent years learning about the Mafia before it began to make sense. Growing up in Altoona, Pennsylvania, he experienced his "first brush" with Mafia-type activity while he was "a supervisor of landscape construction gangs employed in connection with the railroad." The work gangs "were made up almost entirely of Sicilian Italians, most of them recent immigrants." Anslinger recounted how he watched them paying tribute out of their "small earnings" to a "Black Hand" member called "Big-Mouth Sam," a squat, ox-shouldered, black-haired man. "Whoever balked was beaten, stabbed or shot," he said.[46]

The first time Anslinger heard a mafioso use the word "Mafia" came in January 1943 in a Kansas City drug case his agents were investigating. The bureau had placed a tap in the hotel suite of two drug traffickers, Joseph Antinori of Tampa and Tony Lopiparo of St. Louis. They were in Kansas City to confer after learning that Anslinger was on the trail of the heroin ring they were operating in the Midwest. At one point, Lopiparo asked

Antinori about conditions in his hometown. Antinori replied, "Hell, the Dagoes couldn't do any good gambling in Tampa. The city charges, the sheriff charges, and the mayor charges. They just won't let you make any money. They used to be pretty strong out here in Kansas City, but they sort of lost out. They even asked me about the Mafia"—a loud laugh—"as if I would say anything about that."[47]

About this time Anslinger and the Federal Bureau of Narcotics (FBN) began to "recognize the Mafia as something more than just another criminal gang."[48] Still, that was a lone task against great odds. Stephen Fox described what officialdom thought about the existence of a Mafia: "The concept was so preposterous, so neatly conspiratorial, that for years most other law enforcement agencies dismissed the Mafia as a myth: a peculiar fantasy maintained at the Bureau of Narcotics, perhaps under the influence of its own contraband."[49]

After the Kansas City episode, Anslinger sent a memorandum to authorities to alert them about the criminal elite. A copy of the memo wound up in the files of William B. Herlands, one of Dewey's four chief assistants when he was New York City's special prosecutor. The memo said in part, "For many years there has been in existence in this country a criminal organization, well-defined at some times and places, and at other periods rather loosely set up. This is composed of persons of Sicilian birth or extraction, often related by blood and marriage, who are engaged in the types of criminal specialties in which a code of terror and reprisal is valuable. These people are sometimes referred to as the MAFIA."[50] Since Herlands had helped Dewey carry out the nation's first broad attack on racketeers—albeit in New York City—Herlands was among the few who didn't have to be persuaded about the Mafia's influence. There is nothing on the record of what Herlands did with Anslinger's information. It is clear it wasn't used to any extent by his boss.

By then, Anslinger had the FBN compiling a file on the Mafia. It was a "Who's Who" of the "top gangsters in the United States, recording their aliases, family connections, and their criminal specialities."[51] Anslinger called it "a rewarding but frustrating job, somewhat like trying to trace the underground roots of a massive tree. We identified 1,800 of these hoodlums, all associated in a great homogeneous mass of crime. We eliminated the small-time, obscure racketeers and came up with a list of 800 big names in national (and international) crime. We arranged the names by states in a black book we called Mafia."[52] It put Anslinger's bureau a step ahead of the period. It wasn't until the John McClellan–led U.S. Senate hearings in 1962, with testimony from Joseph Valachi, that the specific structure of the Five Families became known, thirty-one years after the Five Families were organized.

17. THE "AL CAPONE" OF ST. PAUL

On Thursday evening, September 24, 1931, four men kidnapped Leon J. Gleckman from his home in St. Paul, Minnesota, secreted him, and demanded a ransom of $200,000 ($3.4 million in 1990 dollars). Eight days later, on Friday, October 2, Gleckman, ostensibly a well-to-do businessman, suddenly reappeared—in good health.

His return was treated prominently in the press. In its Saturday editions, the *St. Paul Pioneer Press* ran a picture of a smiling Gleckman, eyes aglitter, sitting with his family in their home, over this caption: "When Leon Gleckman, reported to have been kidnapped by gangsters and held for ransom, returned Friday to his home at 2185 Sargent Avenue, St. Paul, he received a warm and heartfelt greeting from his family, Mrs. Gleckman and the two children, Loraine and Helen Mae."[1] The picture showed the well-fed four in their Sunday best crowded together lovingly on a settee in the corner of their living room next to a brick fireplace. The two daughters, both under age ten, were dressed in white frocks, white socks, and black patent dress shoes with straps. Loraine, the older daughter, spliced between her parents with her arms thrown around both, grinned with joy. She and her father, both staring directly at the camera, shared a remarkable resemblance. Lighter-haired Helen Mae, looking bashful and not at the camera, sat to the left of her father, who was wearing a dark suit and dark tie. The round-faced Mrs. Gleckman, with jet-black hair and careful eyes and dressed in black with a white blouse, forced a bare smile at the camera. Had not the caption revealed the circumstance, it could have been a typical, posed photograph planned for the mantle, rather than the happy end of a nail-biting occasion.

The kidnapping of Gleckman was noteworthy outside St. Paul—to Elmer Irey in Washington. He assigned veteran special agents James N. Sullivan and Pat O'Rourke to look into the incident. Gleckman was no ordinary businessman, his kidnapping was no ordinary case, and St. Paul was no ordinary city. Like Kansas City, Toledo, Cicero, Joplin, Hot Springs, Reno, and Atlantic City, St. Paul was a safe haven for criminals. Alvin Karpis wrote, "Criminals used to talk about 'safe cities.' They were places where the fix was in from top to bottom, and guys like me could relax. The chances were slim that in those cities we'd ever get arrested."[2]

As St. Paul historian Paul Maccabee, who expertly documented Prohibition's corrupt rattle in the city's history, asserted, "When bank robbers and kidnappers arrived at the depot in downtown St. Paul, they had to identify themselves to police. You know, 'Hi, I'm a bank robber. I'm in from Chicago, how are you doing, Officer?' Usually they would pay a little tribute, so often robbers would arrive in St. Paul with stolen jewelry. Which they would hand over as a little gift to the local constabulary. They'd have to identify where they were staying, where they lived while in St. Paul."[3]

The city, lying on the Mississippi River, and adjoining Minneapolis, was safe because of "the O'Connor system."[4] O'Connor was Chief of Police John J. "the Big Fellow" O'Connor, who arrived in St. Paul from Louisville in 1857 and took over the post in 1900. He allowed criminals to stay in St. Paul—with immunity—provided they committed no crimes. His critics accused him of making the city a "refuge for crooks," but the Big Fellow responded by "insisting that St. Paul was better off if his officers forced criminals to police themselves: 'When a man knows that I know who and where he is, and that I can put my finger on him if I want him, he has every reason to behave himself.'"[5] His brother, Richard T. "the Cardinal" O'Connor, the Democratic Party boss and a St. Paul alderman, felt the same way. The Big Fellow retired in 1920 at sixty-five. He had laid such a soiled foundation that it was still difficult to distinguish between the lawful authorities and criminals. The new chief, Frank Sommers, carried on his legacy.

Leon Gleckman had first drawn Irey's attention in the early 1920s, a time when the SIU was primarily occupied with trying to police the highly corrupt Prohibition Bureau and its agents, not tax evaders. In 1922 Gleckman, age twenty-eight, was one of the owners of the Minnesota Blueing Company, located on University Avenue in Minneapolis. That August, Prohibition Bureau agents raided the company's two-story office and warehouse and found "thirteen large stills in operation." Gleckman and six others were arrested on charges of liquor conspiracy. Then, what appeared to be a normal case—involving the apprehension of a group of bootleggers—grew into "one of the most involved and dramatic in the history of the state."

On November 10 Gleckman, accompanied by his lawyer, Abraham J. "Abe" Hertz, went into federal court in Minneapolis and pleaded guilty, as did two others in the group of seven—Mose Barnett and Sol Rosenhouse. Charges against the other four had been dismissed. After Gleckman and the other two were sentenced to an eighteen-month term in Leavenworth—for an incident in which Gleckman obviously felt the four who went free were just as culpable—the real drama began. It didn't end until five years later. All during that time, Gleckman remained free on bail while his case was on appeal.

Shortly after his case went to appeal, Gleckman fired Hertz, accusing him "of improper conduct," contending that Hertz "failed to explain fully the charge against him" and that he had "pleaded guilty without realizing the seriousness of the charge." Hertz faced troubles of his own. In later proceedings involving his disbarment, he was charged with soliciting $5,000 ($95,000 in 1990 dollars) from Gleckman "on the pretext that he could 'fix' the United States circuit court of appeals" and obtain a new trial, a charge Hertz denied. While the case was on appeal, Gleckman hired Thomas V. Sullivan as his lawyer. At that point, Hertz charged his "professional standing had been injured by Sullivan's representation of the case," and that the U.S. attorney's office "was in collusion" with Gleckman.[6]

William Anderson, chief assistant U.S. attorney for the U.S. District of Minnesota in Minneapolis, was prosecuting the case. During the appeal process, Anderson filed "a confession of error on the ground that if Gleckman had pleaded not guilty the Government would not have had evidence enough to convict him."[7] An FBI report said Hertz claimed that Gleckman discussed a bribe with the U.S. attorney's office before the conviction and afterward paid Anderson to file the false confession of error in the appeals proceeding.

Amid the charges of bribery and collusion and the maze of denials and questions, who was to be believed? The federal appeals court had the Justice Department launch an investigation to sort it all out. Did Hertz solicit a bribe? Did Gleckman know about it? If so, was he behind it? Who had the most to lose? If Hertz didn't, who told Gleckman that he didn't have to plead guilty? Was someone in the U.S. attorney's office in collusion with Gleckman? What prompted Anderson to file a confession of error? How many parties did the sum of $30,000 ($570,000 in 1990 dollars) go to? This was the sum Gleckman claimed he paid in bribes to stay out of jail.

A support system unmatched by other cities marked St. Paul's courts. Aside from lawyers, those for hire included Eddie Green, an expert at identifying a vulnerable bank swollen with deposits; the robbers Frank Nash and Harvey Bailey, who provided "expertise in escape maps, jailbreaks, and the timing of bank jobs"; and a physician, Clayton E. May, who specialized in gunshot wounds, among many ill-begotten occurrences; and a "rotating supply of gunmen."[8]

The Justice Department took nearly four years to penetrate the web of duplicity the Gleckman case represented. What resulted? Disbarment proceedings were launched against Abe Hertz. He also faced jail. During the disbarment proceedings before a panel of three federal judges, Hertz denied that he had solicited a bribe. He further denied that "he knew of certain affidavits filed by Gleckman." Whereupon, the U.S. attorney's office had him indicted, charging his denials constituted perjury. Meanwhile, Paul Froelich, a St. Paul "business counselor," filed disbarment proceedings against William Anderson, charging the "misfiling or loss of certain

papers" in the Gleckman case and holding him responsible for the statement admitting the "confession of error."

By now it was 1926. Mose Barnett and Sol Rosenhouse, the two bootleggers who had pleaded guilty to liquor conspiracy along with Gleckman
back in 1922, had finished serving their prison terms. As for Gleckman,
on Christmas Eve 1926—a Friday—he was handed a holiday package: the
U.S. Circuit Court of Appeals in St. Louis upheld his conviction on liquor
conspiracy.

On Friday, March 11, 1927, at the St. Paul depot, U.S. marshals escort-
ed Gleckman aboard a train headed for Leavenworth. Gleckman had sur-
rendered the day before. At the depot, members of his family; his attorney,
Thomas Sullivan; and a group of friends saw him off. Late the next day
Gleckman donned Leavenworth's gray prison garb. It was the finale of a
five-year-old drama.

The previous day Justice Samuel B. Wilson of the Minnesota Supreme
Court, based on the recommendation of the State Board of Law Examin-
ers, dismissed the disbarment action made against William Anderson, the
chief assistant U.S. attorney. The board's recommendation said he "had
no responsibility in connection with the filing or misfiling of the papers
as charged, and that the filing of the confession of error was consistent
with an honest purpose on his part." However, the board termed the filing
of the confession of error "unwise."[9] Later, after Anderson left the federal
office, he was hired by Alexander "Jap" Gleckman, Leon's younger brother, and John "Philadelphia Johnny" Gordon, a business partner of Sam
Gleckman, another brother, after Jap and Gordon had been issued bench
warrants as material witnesses in Leon Gleckman's tax evasion case. Meanwhile, Abe Hertz was disbarred from practicing in federal court. A messy
question remained: Did any of this really clear the air?

■

On February 20, 1928, Leon Gleckman was paroled from Leavenworth
after serving 345 days of an eighteen-month sentence. He had been a model prisoner, becoming a trustee assigned to the greenhouse. Leavenworth's
psychologists examined in detail the characteristics and motives in Gleckman's personality. Their analysis showed his "problem solving abilities and

insight exceeded those of 92 percent of the inmates" and indicated that he had "a high degree of planfulness and efficiency." The file concluded that Gleckman was "a rather aggressive, pleasant appearing cooperative Hebrew. . . . His aggressiveness is characteristic of his general impressions derived from members of his race, but there is nothing offensive about them." Back in St. Paul, Gleckman began using these formidable assets, along with his Russian heritage, to a devastatingly successful degree in both his upperworld and his underworld activity.

Born in Minsk, Russia (now Belarus), in 1894, the third of eight children, he was brought to the United States through London, Nova Scotia, and Port Huron, Michigan, arriving in the winter of 1903. His father, Gershon Gleckman, "was a strict disciplinarian, a total abstainer and law-abiding man." His mother, Nechama, born in Austria, and the daughter of a rabbi, was "a religious, tolerant woman."[10] Possessing a shrewd intelligence, an easy confidence, and a marbled smoothness in dealing with people, Gleckman became one of St. Paul's most shadowy figures, a man of mystery in a city full of criminal secrets. Few figures of the era forged a more adroit front as a master fixer-racketeer in a mid-size American city. In 1922 he had been a member of a St. Paul bootlegging combine with profitable but limited success. In his second stage, he became a formidable insider, putting together a political-criminal alliance that earned him the title "Al Capone of St. Paul." The Mafia chronicler, Hank Messick, called him the "Al Capone of the Northwest."[11]

The inhabitants of St. Paul made his criminality work. The residents didn't mind John Dillinger and his gang watching a new talkie movie at the Grand Avenue Theater or carousing at a nightclub like the Boulevards of Paris, where many of the motorized cowboys often drank and played. "As kids, we thought gangsters were like football players—guys like Dillinger were heroes to us," said Charles Reiter, a former police officer. As a youth, Reiter worked at a sandwich shop where Homer Van Meter, Dillinger's first lieutenant, would stop by for an order. "Van Meter would want the special center cut of the ham, the best. He'd tip me a quarter, which was an hour's wage!"[12]

The city remained shameless in the handling of criminals. The set of rules established by Big Fellow O'Connor were still there. Prostitution and gambling prevailed. William H. "Reddy" Griffin, an Irishman from New York City, was responsible for collecting money from the brothels and gambling dens "and bringing the crisp green tributes to O'Connor's police station."[13] A tip-off system existed between police and criminals. At the top of the heap was Daniel "Dapper Dan" Hogan, who "for a decade ruled the underworld from the tables of his Green Lantern saloon on Wabasha Street, just three blocks from the Minnesota Capitol."[14] Retired St. Paul newspaper reporter Fred Heaberlin commented, "Today he'd probably be called a Godfather, sort of a father figure for hoods who were climbing the world of hoodlumism."[15] Hogan served as a fence for stolen property, hundreds of thousands in cash, and bonds from robberies, including the loot the notorious bank robber Harvey Bailey took in the Denver Mint robbery in 1922. There were so many bank robbers in town that the phrase "following the robbery, the bandits drove to the Twin Cities" became an "underworld cliché."[16] Over a ten-month span, Dapper Dan's combine robbed seven post offices in Wisconsin and Minnesota, netting more than $250,000 ($4.8 million in 1990 dollars). After postal inspectors grilled two girlfriends of members of the Hogan gang about the robberies, they were found shot to death.

■

Nine months after Gleckman returned from Leavenworth, St. Paul's underworld order changed suddenly, paving the way for Gleckman to step into the power vacuum. At 11:30 a.m., on a cold December 4, 1928, Dapper Dan Hogan, "heavy with a late-morning breakfast," climbed into his Paige coupe, turned on the ignition and stepped on the gas petal. The bomb placed beneath the floorboard exploded. The blast mangled Hogan's right leg, blew off the car's hood, "went through the top of the car, broke all the windows in the car, flattened the gears, blew the steering wheel completely off, tore part of the rear end of the engine off [and] broke all windows in the garage."[17] Nine hours later, Dapper Dan Hogan died.

With a major criminal force like Dapper Dan out of the way, Gleckman was able to move, and he did, smartly and quickly. Over the next year he fashioned a highly sophisticated criminal-political alliance. By January 1930 he was operating out of a suite of rooms at the Hotel St. Paul. His political enterprises included being a broker and master fixer between officialdom and the underworld, primarily handling payoffs between various interested parties—police officials, county commissioners, and city councilors. Political figures, including the city's commissioner of public utilities, Clyde R. May, charged rooms at the hotel to Gleckman. From an unlisted telephone in his suite, Gleckman made calls to "millionaire businessmen, politicians and underworld characters in Washington, New York City, Los Angeles, Havana and Montreal."[18] One call went to Max "Big Maxey" Greenberg, the Detroit bootlegger, who, with Waxey Gordon, had struck a deal with Arnold Rothstein in the 1920s to bring in Scotch whiskey from England.

Gleckman had the chief of police, Thomas Archibald "Big Tom" Brown, who had been elevated to the post in June 1930, in his pocket. Big Tom, six-foot-three, 280 pounds, and a policeman and detective on the force since 1914, had taken over from Frank Sommers. While a detective, he had been suspended for thirty days after a federal judge ordered that he be taken to Ohio to face charges that he had participated in a Cleveland liquor syndicate conspiracy involving Gleckman and two brothers, Abraham and Benjamin Gleeman. Big Tom rented a room at the hotel "to facilitate payoffs."[19]

Actually, Big Tom's villainy left few comparisons in police annals. Two incidents stand out. He was involved in the kidnapping by the Barker-Karpis gang of William Hamm Jr., president of the Hamm Brewing Company, and shared $36,000 ($576,000 in 1990 dollars) of the ransom with John "Jack" Peifer, a St. Paul racketeer, who also figured in the kidnapping of Leon Gleckman. Big Tom also kept the Barker-Karpis gang informed of Bureau of Investigation activities after the gang kidnapped Edward G. Bremer, the head of a St. Paul bank and son of Adolf Bremer, president of the Jacob Schmidt Brewing Company.

Gleckman would never again be busted for making bootleg whiskey, nor would he follow the deadly likes of Dapper Dan Hogan. In his life after prison, unlike Capone and more like a Mafia don, he cloaked his racketeering in secrecy. In the Capone pattern, he used the Hotel St. Paul as his headquarters, lending it the guise of openness and formality. He was never rated among the era's ranking criminal and political cutthroats, nor did he become a national figure to the extent of his namesake. He had neither Capone's murderous attitude nor his staggering wealth. His liquor syndicate included the popular Brown Derby nightclub. Big Tom wasn't going to stand for competition against Gleckman. If "any place opened, a gang of Jews who were interested in the Brown Derby would immediately go up and shoot up the competitor's place."[20] Gleckman also was one of the proprietors of the Republic Finance Company, which dealt in automobile finance. Prohibition agents placed a wiretap on Republic's phone, but telephone company representatives quickly located it; federal agents complained but could do nothing. Max Ehrlich, Gleckman's partner at Republic, said Gleckman "kept a jar on the desk where people would drop parking tickets. At the end of the week, a big Irish cop would drop by, take a fistful of cigars and bring the tickets to City Hall—and that's the last you'd hear of them. . . . Leon Gleckman was the Mayor of St. Paul, at least indirectly."[21]

■

At the time of his kidnapping, Gleckman was a power in St. Paul's underworld. After his release, he took care of the kidnappers "in his own way"—which didn't take long.[22] One of the four kidnappers, a hotel proprietor named Frank LaPre, was found dead of multiple gunshot wounds to his face on October 3, one day after Gleckman was released. Almost immediately, the other three were apprehended and soon convicted. According to a St. Paul police officer, LaPre was slain after the cops beat the names of the kidnappers out of him. An FBI informant said LaPre "was killed by [Chief of Police] Brown and others and planted in an automobile to make it look like the kidnapping gang had killed LaPre because he was thought to have double crossed them."[23] The ransom money was found in LaPre's safe. The ransom price initially was $200,000 ($3.4 million in 1990 dollars), dropped to $75,000 ($1,265,000 in 1990 dollars), and finally landed at $5,000 ($85,000 in 1990 dollars), in addition to the $1,450 ($24,650 in 1990 dollars) Gleckman was carrying. The ransom money was placed in Big Tom's campaign fund to finance his unsuccessful run for sheriff of Ramsey County (St. Paul).

Paul Maccabee noted that the Bureau of Investigation "discovered there was far more to the Gleckman kidnapping" than was publicly known. "It involved suspicious intermingling of the underworld and the police," he wrote. Engineered by John "Jack" Peifer, a St. Paul racketeer who ran a casino called Hollyhocks and liked Japanese servants because "they were very faithful and close-mouthed about what they saw or heard." Peifer's underworld activity included laundering the ransom money paid to George "Machine-Gun Kelly" Barnes in the kidnapping of Oklahoma oilman Charles Urschel. The kidnapping of Gleckman became a tale of reprisal. Gleckman apparently hijacked a shipment of Peifer's liquor. Accompanied by strongman and post office–robber William "Dutch" Canner, Peifer met with Gleckman "and threatened to kill him if he ever interfered with Peifer's business again." Big Tom figured in the incident too. According to Albert Tallerico, one of the kidnappers, Big Tom and the county attorney both warned the kidnappers that when the grand jury investigated the abduction, "if they knew what was good for them they would not mention the name of Jack Peifer."[24]

■

By 1934 St. Paul, with its combination of bootleggers, kidnappers, bank robbers, and corrupt police officials, had become a favorite haunt of John Dillinger. Attorney General Cummings was calling it "one of the three hot spots in the United States." (Chicago and Kansas City were the other two.)[25] St. Paul never reached the scale of reprisals and murders Chicago regularly experienced from gang warfare; it didn't have a Boss Pendergast, or the organized crime designs of similar-sized Toledo, Ohio, known as "Chicago on Lake Erie," where the three Licavoli brothers—Pete, James, and Thomas (Yonnie)—dominated the underworld.[26]

The brothers, long associated with Detroit's Purple Gang, moved to Toledo in mid-1931 when things got too hot after the July 1930 murder of a crusading Detroit radio announcer, Gerard E. "Jerry" Buckley. St. Paul also never attracted Capone's hungry eye, as Detroit did, when in 1927

Yonnie Licavoli, who was with him at the Fort Shelby Hotel, warned him, "Stay the hell out of Detroit. It's my territory."[27]

Gleckman's kidnapping in September 1931 came four months after Irey undertook one of his biggest missions, the special task force in New York City, and six months before the Lindbergh kidnapping. He didn't send James Sullivan and Pat O'Rourke to St. Paul until the following February. The Department of Justice and the Bureau of Investigation already had Gleckman in their crosshairs. It was the U.S. attorney for the Minnesota District, Lewis L. Drill, who first called Gleckman the "Al Capone of St. Paul," explaining in a letter in early 1933 to Attorney General William D. Mitchell that Gleckman had friends and influences and they "were not at all confined to characters of the underworld . . . on the contrary they included bankers, lawyers, and in fact persons in practically all walks of life."[28] Mitchell was a Minnesotan, born in Winona in 1874. He got his law degree at the University of Minnesota and practiced in St. Paul around the turn of the century, the time John J. O'Connor became chief of police. Mitchell was the U.S. solicitor general before taking over Justice in March 1929. And he wasn't easy on his home state, noting, "If there are two cities in America which need cleaning up, they are St. Paul and Minneapolis."[29]

In calling in Pat O'Rourke—the sure-footed bloodhound who partied with Al Capone and his henchmen in Chicago's nightclubs and who ran down Waxey Gordon in New York's Adirondacks—Irey sealed Gleckman's fate. Frank Wilson called O'Rourke "the greatest natural undercover worker the Service has ever had." A U.S. Army pilot injured in the war, O'Rourke married the nurse who attended him in the hospital. Their daughter was killed in a truck accident at age three. After that, the couple drifted apart, and O'Rourke joined the SIU "where he seemed to lose interest in everything except undercover work." O'Rourke worked out of St. Paul. According to Wilson, O'Rourke kept a room full-time at the Hotel St. Paul, "although he hardly ever stayed there, as he was constantly on duty throughout the country."[30] With both Gleckman and Police Chief Big Tom Brown occupying rooms at the same hotel, Irey did have a tidy advantage.

The SIU's investigation of Gleckman began in the spring of 1932. Newspaper accounts of the inquiry began appearing in Twin Cities' newspapers and continued throughout the summer. They were spotty in nature. One account said Gleckman was a power behind the throne in St. Paul politics, with no references to back up this contention. In May, Frank Wilson came to St. Paul to consult with Sullivan and his team. Wilson and Sullivan were close friends, going all the way back to the early 1920s in Philadelphia, where they investigated corrupt Prohibition agents. They also worked together on the big one in Chicago.

St. Paul was going through a mayoralty campaign, and the Gleckman case became political fodder. The *Pioneer Press* on May 20 reported that Mayor-elect William Mahoney charged that Gleckman "was at the head of an organization of racketeers who were in control of the city government and particularly the police department." The story went on to say, "A Ramsey County grand jury made known its intention to go into the situation charged by Mr. Mahoney beginning with its scheduled meeting next week."[31] The press in the Twin Cities did not use their investigative capacities to determine whether Mahoney's charges contained substance. Nor, in the end, was the Ramsey County grand jury given the evidence to arrive at such a conclusion. The rush of stories about Gleckman's income tax troubles and related events eventually came to a trickle, and they stopped altogether by the late fall of 1932. All the while, Sullivan, O'Rourke, and a revenue agent in Minneapolis, Leon L. Schall, continued the painstaking task of gathering evidence, an effort that took a year and a half.

On Wednesday, November 9, 1933, U.S. Attorney Lewis Drill began presenting the evidence to a federal grand jury. Two weeks later, on November 23, an indictment, charging Gleckman with evading income taxes totaling $103,000 ($1,751,000 in 1990 dollars) for the years 1929, 1930, and 1931, was handed down. His earnings for those three years were $164,924.38 ($2,638,790.08 in 1990 dollars), $128,663 ($2,058,608 in 1990 dollars), and $15,870 ($253,920 in 1990 dollars), respectively. Gleckman said his tax reports for the three years were prepared under the direction of his new lawyer, William Anderson, the former federal prosecutor.

Gleckman went on trial in federal court in Minneapolis exactly five months later, on April 23, 1934, and the revelations never stopped. In the years 1929 through 1931, testimony showed he sent a total of $40,000

($680,000 in 1990 dollars) to Cuba through the Commercial State Bank of St. Paul and the National City Bank in New York City, but the recipient of the money was unknown. He also received a check for $15,250 ($258,950 in 1990 dollars) from an unknown party in Toronto, Canada, and made payments on notes with money never in his bank accounts, according to testimony. More than a dozen people had their rooms at the Hotel St. Paul charged to Gleckman during 1931 at a cost of $5,234.65 ($88,989.05 in 1990 dollars). They included Clyde R. May, St. Paul's commissioner of public utilities; "Philadelphia Johnny" Gordon, a gangster questioned in connection with the bombing of the Boulevards of Paris nightclub and who was a business partner of Gleckman's brother, Sam; "Dr. D. Jones," whom federal officials said was a fictitious name for a city official; three women; and an array of businessmen and bankers.

Norman J. Morrison, a special assistant U.S. attorney general, was brought in as lead prosecutor. When former federal prosecutor William Anderson took the stand, Morrison accused him of letting Gleckman's liquor conspiracy case "rot in the files."[32] Anderson, Morrison also charged, caused the disappearance of a witness about to be questioned in the case. Anderson responded that he served the witness with a subpoena in another case and informed him he didn't have to remain for questioning by SIU agents. Neither was it disclosed at trial of the evidence the missing witness was expected to give. Morrison also failed to get evidence regarding Anderson's conduct. The trial judge, M. M. Joyce, held that his conduct was outside the province for which Gleckman had hired and, therefore, Gleckman could not be bound in the case by his attorney's action.

At another point, Morrison sought to prove Gleckman's "consciousness of guilt" by citing three moves he made after the SIU's Sullivan first arrived in St. Paul in early February 1932. First, a week after Sullivan arrived, Gleckman transferred up to $30,000 ($480,000 in 1990 dollars) worth of Republic Finance Company shares to one of his daughters. Second, a short time after that, he transferred garage property at 408 University Avenue to her. Last, Morrison said, Gleckman confronted William Anderson, his lawyer, and told him the two transfers were futile because of certain federal legal provisions. Immediately thereafter the finance company bought the shares back from his daughter, Morrison said, and Gleckman endorsed the payment check in her name. Judge Joyce ruled all of this out.

One of the trial's most controversial moments came during the questioning of a key prosecution witness, David Bunin, who turned on the prosecution the moment he reached the stand. Bunin was the head of University Cleaners & Dyers and had obtained loans from Gleckman. Bunin, according to Morrison, told the grand jury no less than eight times that Gleckman had a partnership interest in the company. On the stand, however, Bunin denied Gleckman had a connection to University and said Gleckman merely had interest in the company because of loans he had made to him. At that, Morrison turned to the judge and said, "I claim surprise and ask leave to cross-examine this witness. The testimony he gives now is in conflict with previous statements he made before the grand jury and to Revenue agents."

Morrison then had to impeach his own witness. Under cross-examination, he asked Bunin, "Did you tell the grand jury Gleckman had a partnership interest?" "No, I did not," Bunin replied. "I insisted the money shown on the books was a loan."

All along, the prosecution's strategy—and the outcome too—rested on the question of Gleckman's "accumulated capital" versus his current income and whether he was hiding income.[33] Morrison made point after point that Gleckman was earning income that he did not declare, but at almost every point the defense raised effective doubts about where it was coming from. Bunin's turnaround was another dagger.

John F. Dahl, Gleckman's trial counsel, laid a bold defense by asserting that Gleckman built his trade—and accumulated his capital—as a "big-shot bootlegger" before 1927 and did not have an income after that sufficient to warrant the government's tax evasion charges. Throughout the trial he drummed home this point. "Large bank deposits and other receipts in 1929, 1930 and 1931, shown by the government in presentation of its evidence against Gleckman," Dahl said, "were merely operations in pursuance of his finance and investment business."[34]

Shortly after high noon on Thursday, May 17, Judge Joyce charged the jurors, explaining to them that to convict Gleckman they must be con-

vinced he had knowledge of a greater income than was reported and pur-
posely reported less and that they must have a moral certainty that this is
true. Joyce also reminded jurors, "The failure of the defendant to keep
books or records of his affairs is not involved in the case."[35]

After three days of deliberation, jurors could not agree. Nine voted for
acquittal, and three for conviction. Judge Joyce, convinced they couldn't
reach a verdict, dismissed them on Saturday, May 19, and ruled a mistrial.
Morrison wasted little time in going after Bunin, whose court testimony
had created significant doubt against the government's case. The following
Monday, federal agents arrested Bunin and charged him with contempt of
court as the result of his testimony. The frustrated prosecutor declared, "He
deliberately and intentionally sought to block the inquiry and attempted to
conceal knowledge of Gleckman's partnership in the University Cleaners &
Dyers and resorted to deliberate subterfuge and evasion, if not falsehood
in connection with the trial."[36] Bunin was released on $500 ($8,000 in 1990
dollars) bail. In Washington, three days later, Attorney General Cummings
announced a new trial would be sought.

■

The second trial, which began on Monday, November 12, 1934, with
Norman Morrison returning as prosecutor, was full of dramatic twists, but
this time there was a certainty about its end—right from its anti-climactic
beginning. Two weeks before the start of trial, Gleckman made an "offer of
compromise" to the Bureau of Internal Revenue to pay $5,000 ($80,000 in
1990 dollars) on $63,000 ($1,008,000 in 1990 dollars) in delinquent taxes
and $40,000 ($640,000 in 1990 dollars) in accumulated penalties. He was
turned down. After that, nothing went right for Gleckman.

The second trial involved charges that he concealed $139,234
($2,229,644 in 1990 dollars) in income in the years 1929 and 1930. Mor-
rison walked into the courtroom with much more damaging evidence than
he had at the first trial, particularly with regard to Gleckman's dealings
in Cuba. This time James Sullivan—who went to Havana—and other SIU
agents were able to cite where the money had gone, to whom, and in what
specific amounts, and they were able to prove that it was money not declared as income. The $40,000 Gleckman had sent to Cuba—which was

brought out at the first trial—was bootlegging money that had gone to a Cuban, Jose Articuna, and the Mill Creek Distillery in Havana, of which only $3,000 went through Gleckman's bank account. The rest was telegraphed through banks in Canada and New York.

The most damaging testimony for Gleckman occurred when James Sullivan testified that he and revenue agent Leon Schall, in the interim between trials, had gone to Republic Finance Company to examine the books. They took a lunch break, and when they returned, the books had disappeared. Sullivan telephoned Gleckman's attorney, William Anderson, to protest, and Anderson told him he had "sent them out of the country." At the first trial Morrison was not too caustic on Anderson. This time he ripped into him, and effectively. When Anderson was called to the stand, the two got into a heated exchange, and Anderson faltered. U.S. Circuit Court Judge Robert C. Bell had to admonish him several times to observe rules of evidence "and not attempt to give hearsay testimony." One answer Anderson gave was ordered stricken from the record, and the jury was told to disregard it.

On cross-examination, Morrison had Anderson reveal some hitherto unknown background that had taken place between him and Gleckman. Gleckman had come to Anderson's office (he was then an assistant U.S. attorney) after the 1927 Supreme Court ruling in the Manly Sullivan case, which decided that illegal income earnings were taxable. According to Anderson, Gleckman told him that "he wished to pay all taxes justly assembled against him." Anderson said he went to see A. R. Knox, the deputy collector of Internal Revenue's office in St. Paul and worked out an arrangement whereby Gleckman would pay taxes for the years 1925 to 1927 on a reported income of $15,000 ($240,000 in 1990 dollars) annually.

With this revelation, Morrison demanded to know if Anderson "was working for the government or Gleckman when the three returns were made?"

Another heated exchange broke out between the two men. Finally, Morrison repeated the question, and Anderson replied that he was working for the government. Then Morrison asked him: "There was nothing in your conversations with Mr. Knox that couldn't have been handled by Gleckman himself?" "I suppose not," replied Anderson.[37]

Morrison also elicited damaging testimony about Gleckman's financial transactions. David K. Patterson, an assistant cashier at the First National Bank of St. Paul, testified that Gleckman, identifying himself as "Abraham Wynhouse," showed up at the bank with a St. Paul real estate developer named Sam M. Fink and tried to cash a check for $15,000 ($255,000 in 1990 dollars) that was made out to Fink. He was refused.

John Nelson, an assistant cashier at another bank, Forshay State Bank, testified that a cashier's check for $15,000 made out to Fink on February 25, 1929, was broken down into three cashier's checks by the bank—one payable to Charles Haim, one to Fink, and the third to Charles Grosscorth. The Haim check was paid on March 5 and deposited in Gleckman's account. Haim and Gleckman endorsed it. The Grosscorth check was paid on March 6 and deposited to Gleckman's account. Grosscorth and Gleckman had endorsed it. The remaining check in the amount of $7,450 ($126,650 in 1990 dollars) was payable to Fink. Grosscorth was the owner of a distillery in Havana, Cuba. Haim was connected to distilleries in Philadelphia and Montreal. When Haim was called to testify, Al Capone's name was raised for the first time. The prosecutor, Morrison, tried to elicit admissions from Haim of the illicit sale of liquor to Capone. Haim denied selling liquor to Capone.

Morrison hammered a final nail into the proceedings—and likely took large satisfaction from it. At the first trial, Gleckman had been helped by David Bunin's testimony that he was not a partner in the University Cleaners & Dyers. It was an important crucible toward getting the hung jury. At the second trial, Morrison produced evidence that, indeed, Gleckman was a partner in the cleaning firm and that Gleckman and Bunin had known it all along. While he was serving his sentence for bootlegging at Leavenworth in 1927, Gleckman appeared before a parole hearing. Answering questions at the time, he said he intended upon his release to reenter his business—the University Cleaners & Dyers. The SIU's James Sullivan had found the stenographer's notes taken at the parole hearing, and Morrison introduced them as evidence at the second trail.

Seventeen days after trial began, on Thursday, November 28, 1934, jurors returned a guilty verdict. They had deliberated eight hours and fifteen minutes. Gleckman was sentenced to serve eighteen months in a federal penitentiary and fined $10,000 ($160,000 in 1990 dollars) and court costs of $1,700 ($27,200 in 1990 dollars). He filed an appeal the next day, alleging twenty-six errors of law during the trial, and remained free on bond of $20,000 ($320,000 in 1990 dollars). On November 27, 1935, the U.S. Circuit Court of Appeals in St. Louis upheld his conviction. He appealed the decision to the U.S. Supreme Court, which refused to hear it.

During his appeals, Gleckman fought a variety of legal proceedings. Internal Revenue brought a claim that he owned taxes, penalties, and interest of approximately $90,000 ($1,440,000 in 1990 dollars). Gleckman was ordered to pay $6,000 ($96,000 in 1990 dollars) in court costs for the two trials; he appealed and lost. The U.S. Immigration and Naturalization Service brought deportation proceedings, charging that he never sought naturalization after coming to the United States. The office said Gleckman's father had once applied for citizenship papers but later withdrew his application. Gleckman filed a motion to forestall deportation, but it was denied.

On the morning of March 25, 1936, Gleckman, wearing a dark double-breasted suit, white shirt, and dark tie, showed up in federal district court in Minneapolis, accompanied by two lawyers, Patrick J. Ryan and Frank W. Murphy, to plead for probation. The U.S. attorney, George F. Sullivan, was preparing to object to the move. At the last minute, however, Gleckman decided to abandon the attempt. Outside the courtroom, where he usually drew a crowd, newspaper reporters asked him to comment.

Looking serious, "but not worried," he said, "I have no complaint. I had a fair trial. This is the way it has to be. So here I am and I am not kicking about something."[38]

At 3:00 p.m., Gleckman appeared at the office of U.S. Marshal J. J. Farrell to surrender. Later, he was taken to Ramsey County Jail, where he was held until Friday, when he left for Leavenworth. In prison, he and his younger brother, Alexander, were convicted of contempt of court for fixing the jury in Gleckman's first trial for tax evasion and sentenced to six months in prison. Leon fought the conviction through the courts and lost.

■

Leon Gleckman proved his elusiveness, using his wits and his money. He got out of Leavenworth a year later. He avoided deportation. He settled with Internal Revenue for less than he owed. He did give up the idea of running for the office of mayor of St. Paul. He lived for a short time in New York City but soon returned to St. Paul, perhaps because he was due to go back to jail to serve time for bribing the jury in his first tax evasion trial. It was now 1941. He had been in trouble with the federal authorities for nineteen years, ever since his arrest for bootlegging in 1922.

The news that summer was dominated by the war raging in Europe. Nazi Germany had just invaded the USSR. The United States was still in a Depression, but Leon Gleckman was prospering. On the sunny afternoon of Sunday, July 13, he played a round of golf at the Keller Golf course in Minneapolis and spent the entire evening in the clubhouse "in the company of business friends."[39] Shortly after 1:30 a.m., on Monday morning, he left the clubhouse and was driving home when his automobile hit an abutment beneath the St. Paul Union rail station at Kellogg Boulevard and Waconta Street. Alone in the car, he was nearly decapitated by the force of the collision, and he died in the police ambulance on the way to the hospital. He was forty-eight years old. Later, it was determined that his blood alcohol level was .23—the equivalence of drinking thirteen ounces of 90-proof liquor.

The next morning Gleckman's death, not the war in Europe, dominated the news. The *Minneapolis Star Tribune*'s bold black headline said, "Leon Gleckman Dies in Crash." The drop headline said, "Victim Onetime Colorful Figure in Underworld." In a column next to the Gleckman story, the newspaper ran a story headlined, "Johnson, GOP Boss, on Trial." Johnson was Enoch L. "Nucky" Johnson, the longtime political boss of Atlantic City who had gone on trial in Camden, New Jersey, in a case very similar to Gleckman's. Nucky Johnson, like Gleckman, had been brought down by Irey and the SIU.

18. THE LORD OF ATLANTIC CITY

Sheriff Enoch L. "Nucky" Johnson, who "owned Atlantic County and Atlantic City, lock, stock and barrel" and made "a lifetime career of being a crooked politician," was Elmer Irey's last case involving a political-criminal alliance and its corruption of a city.[1]

Atlantic City, where Republicans had been the kingmakers since the city's founding in 1854, pioneered political racketeering. Political corruption was turned up a notch at the turn of the century, when 230-pound Louis "The Commodore" Kuehnle became head of the Republican Party in Atlantic County. The city, with up to 500 hotels and boarding houses, was entertaining 700,000 visitors a year. Some of the world's finest hotels stood along the boardwalk. The distinctive Steel Pier, jutting 1,000 feet into the Atlantic Ocean, had opened in 1898. The cost of land near the boardwalk ranked in the millions and inspired Charles B. Darrow's Monopoly game. The Commodore, surrounded by spalpeens, made all this work for him.

"If you want to take all the power ever exercised by Boss Tweed, the Philadelphia Gang, the Pittsburgh Ring, Boss Ruef of San Francisco, and Tammany Hall, and concentrate it in one man, you would still fall a little short of Kuehnle's clutch on Atlantic City," said the *New York Sun*.[2] There were no pretensions about his power either. In its accounts of him, the *New York Times* invariably referred to him as "Boss Kuehnle," a title the newspaper never used when addressing New York City's Tammany bosses or Kansas City's Thomas Pendergast, who liked to be called the Boss. Long before Pendergast's political cunning, the Kuehnle machine was paying off election repeaters, stealing the books of Democratic challengers, and spoiling voting day in one way or another. On January 20, 1911, Frank Smathers, a Democratic candidate for the state assembly, told a special commission of the assembly that he was drugged on Election Day. According to Smathers, a powder was dissolved in a pitcher of water set in the polling place where he was acting as challenger.

Under Governor Woodrow Wilson, the special commission had been sent to Atlantic City to investigate election fraud, where they learned just how inspired the Kuehnle machine's trickery could be. William Jones, a Democratic election officer, said a foreman of the electric light company he worked for had called him "out of bed." He went to the site but failed to locate the trouble that the foreman had said to expect. By then, he had been "carted away in an automobile twelve or more miles off in the country and had to make way his way back to the polling place, getting there almost an hour late."[3]

In his meteoric political career, Wilson's success against political corruption in Atlantic City helped put him in the White House. A failed lawyer in Atlanta, Wilson became a teacher after he closed his law office and found unrivaled success in that profession. He lectured at Johns Hopkins University, went to Princeton in 1902, and became its president at age fifty-four in 1910, the same year that James Smith Jr., the "boss" of the New Jersey Democratic Party, supported him for the gubernatorial nomination. Wilson, who once exclaimed that New York was "rotten to the core," didn't become the "dignified puppet" that sleazy Smith sought.[4] Wilson turned on him, won the governorship by a landslide on November 8, 1910, prevented Smith's election to the U.S. Senate by the legislature, and wasted no time in going after Boss Kuehnle and Nucky Johnson, who was serving as the sheriff of Atlantic County, a post his father also held. His father named him an undersheriff in 1904.

Before Elmer Irey, it had been largely left to the states to go after lawbreakers. Under New Jersey law, the sheriff picked a grand jury, and in Atlantic City, Nucky picked the grand jury. Only after Governor Wilson and

Attorney General Edmund Wilson Sr. maneuvered to have an independent grand jury picked by the judicial branch did the Kuehnle machine begin to crumble. On Thursday, September 28, 1911, indictments for election fraud and graft were handed down on Kuehnle, Sheriff Johnson, the city clerk, the county engineer, the city assessor, the five members of the Board of Freeholders (which constituted the road committee that approved contracts), and Postmaster Harry Bacharach, who also happened to be the Exalted Ruler of the Elks Lodge and who had been nominated for mayor on the GOP ticket. More than 200 indictments were eventually drawn against city and county officials.

On Thursday, January 24, 1912, Boss Kuehnle, at age fifty-five, was convicted, sentenced to a year in prison, and fined $1,000 ($22,000 in 1990 dollars) after "the most remarkable case ever tried in the old Atlantic County Court House" in Mays Landing. Attorney General Wilson came down from Trenton to prosecute the case. The verdict wasn't expected by the defense, "especially after information leaked out that the jury was almost equally divided." The county clerk was so dazed by the verdict that "he forgot to dismiss the jurors."[5] Kuehnle wasn't sent away for voting fraud. He was on the Board of Water Commissioners and awarded a contract to the United Paving Company without disclosing his status as a shareholder.

One of the Commodore's confederates, boyish Nucky Johnson, born circa 1883, was only twenty-eight when he was indicted with Kuehnle in 1911. Projecting himself as a mere innocent among the gang of political thieves, Nucky beat the indictment and took over Atlantic City. It was the year before Woodrow Wilson was elected president. Inside of twenty-four months, Wilson had built an impressive résumé: president of Princeton University, governor of New Jersey, and president of the United States.

After ridding the city of Kuehnle's criminal-political alliance, Governor Wilson instituted reforms he thought would work. He set up a five-member commission to replace the cumbersome seventeen-member city council that ran Atlantic City. One of the elected commissioners was picked by his colleagues to act as mayor, and in that capacity he would be in charge of the police department, propose ordinances, and make board appointments. According to Ovid Demaris, "The proponents of commission government believed it would end corruption and increase efficiency. It did neither. Nucky's machine was so powerful that he could name the Democrats as well as Republicans who ran for office."

In 1917 Nucky helped Walter E. Edge, a forty-four-year-old Atlantic County state senator, win the governorship and was rewarded with the post of clerk of the New Jersey Supreme Court. Edge also became Nucky's political patron. Two years later, with Nucky's help, he won the U.S. Senate seat, thus enlarging Nucky's power. The coming of Prohibition broke it wide open for Nucky. In that era "it was almost as if word of the Volstead Act" never reached Atlantic City.[6] It became "Sin City, with speakeasies and whorehouses crowding every block, and with every form of gambling invented by man."[7] Nucky spun around the ocean resort town during the 1920s in a powder-blue, chauffeur-driven limousine that cost $14,000 ($252,000 in 1990 dollars) and wore a $1,200 ($21,500 in 1990 dollars) raccoon coat. This was after sleeping all day. "Breakfast was usually served at 4 p.m." and consisted of "a dozen fried eggs, from four to six chops, a ham steak, six slices of buttered toast, and as many as eight cups of coffee. After so fortifying himself, he was prepared to transact business. When his lieutenants had finished reporting at about 8:00 p.m., it was time to get dressed and go out on the town."[8]

Nucky's campaign chest was filled with protection money from vices such as gambling and prostitution and payoffs from speakeasies. In May 1928, after a decade of togetherness, Edge and Nucky split over the nominee for U.S. senator. Edge backed ex-Governor Edward C. Stokes. Nucky backed Hamilton Fish Kean. Kean was elected. Edge was named the ambassador to Great Britain. With Kean's election, a scandal ensued over vote gathering. A U.S. Senate committee investigated Nucky for allegedly buying a Senate seat for one of his followers. But in Nucky's world of politics nothing came of it, except that he became more powerful. That same year Irey's SIU took its first crack at tracking Nucky's money trail. "We were successful in prying a few more dollars from Nucky in taxes and penalties," Irey explained, "but I always felt the only real punishment he ever incurred was getting out of bed at a normal hour to discuss the charges with the investigators."[9]

By the end of the Roaring Twenties, Nucky was the Republican czar of New Jersey. The criminal-political alliance that Woodrow Wilson thought he had ridded Atlantic City of had reappeared in a more powerful and corrupt form. The next May, Nucky strolled arm in arm down the boardwalk with Al Capone during the gangland summit. As historian Nelson Johnson noted, "He was both the most powerful Republican in New Jersey, who could influence the destinies of governors and senators, and a racketeer, respected and trusted by organized crime."[10] With the rise of organized crime in the 1920s, sparked by the organization of the Five Families in New York City, half a day's drive away, Nucky was the perfect host to the biggest and best of the racketeers. He was a partner with Charlie Luciano in smuggling scotch from offshore right up to the sandy beach and onto the boardwalk. Nucky also never failed to show the common touch that turned him into a hero to the city's working class. Nelson Johnson relates an incident about "a housewife and summertime laundress in a boarding house" coming to Nucky's grand suite at the Ritz Carlton because she "was desperate for her family." Her husband had lost his entire paycheck gambling, they were heavily in debt, and they needed groceries among other things. In his sitting room, Nucky, dressed in a fancy robe and slippers, listened and, when she finished, reached into his pocket and handed her a $100 bill ($1,800 in 1990 dollars). "He told her to come back any time she had a problem."[11]

In 1934 Irey took another crack at Nucky, again getting him to settle by paying for back taxes and penalties. By then New York's Five Families had penetrated New Jersey, a state soon to achieve second ranking to New York in the number of members and associates of organized crime. Leading the pack was Joseph Adonis, who left Brooklyn when John Harlan Amen started turning up the heat and moved across the Hudson, where he established a gambling empire. As a non-Sicilian, Adonis ranked next to Meyer Lansky in his ties with Charlie Luciano. Abner "Longy" Zwillman, known as the "Al Capone of New Jersey,"[12] controlled the numbers rackets; before that, he was responsible for nearly 40 percent of all the illegal alcohol funneled into the country between 1926 and 1933, which had been carried by a fleet of thirty-three ships. Gerardo "Jerry" Catena, who for years was "the most powerful mobster operating in New Jersey,"[13] was another leading name. A stockholder in the Bally Manufacturing Corporation, the world's largest maker of slot machines, Catena filed a license application to operate a casino in Atlantic City. He owned the Runyon Sales Company, Bally's pinball machine distributor in New Jersey. Like Las Vegas and Miami, Atlantic City was an "open city," which meant that the Mafia crime families could operate in the area as long as their efforts were coordinated. By the 1960s the New Jersey State Police said eight Mafia families were operating in New Jersey, more than any other state. They were New York's Five Families along with the Scarfo, Bufalino, and DeCavalcante families. Five-foot-five Nicodemo "Little Nicky" Scarfo lived year-round in Atlantic City; Simone "The Plumber" DeCavalcante of Newark operated a plumbing supply front in Kenilworth; and Russell A. Bufalino, formerly the underboss to Joseph Barbara, operated out of northeastern Pennsylvania. The families owned pieces of Atlantic City hotels through fronts and wielded influence in the ancillary businesses that provided services and products to casinos such as garbage hauling, trucking, laundry, junket operations, limousine service, security personnel, vending machines, linen, silverware, liquor, food, and cigarettes, in addition to construction companies and some labor and service-related unions historically associated with organized crime.

■

In 1936, at one of his Friday conferences with Henry Morgenthau, the Treasury secretary asked Irey, "What goes with that fellow, Nucky Johnson?" Irey described his attempts to get the "Lord of Atlantic City" to pay his taxes and Nucky's techniques in forestalling federal prosecution. "The Secretary was not very impressed," Irey said, and he told him "to get proof that Nucky was, or was not, a tax evader."[14]

Irey pulled William Frank from the SIU's New York City office and assigned him to the case. Frank was the special agent whose testimony at the trial of Bruno Richard Hauptmann helped clinch Hauptmann's conviction as the Lindbergh baby's kidnapper-killer. On the stand, Frank had proved that Hauptmann had in his possession $49,986 ($859,762 in 1990 dollars) more than he had made—$14 less than the $50,000 ransom that was paid. Frank asked that Special Agent Edward A. Hill of the Philadelphia office work with him. Irey agreed. On November 5, 1936, the two agents rented a furnished apartment in Atlantic City. They were soon joined by Special Agent Leon R. Marshall and went undercover.

In late January 1937 Frank came to Washington to report what they had learned about Nucky.

"Chief, Atlantic City is running as wide open as anything could possibly run. Anybody can walk into a gambling room or a brothel, and half the storekeepers in town take numbers bets. Anybody you ask will tell you how much is being paid off and that Nucky is getting it."

"All of it?"

"Every dime."

"He's not paying taxes on that kind of money, Bill."

"I know he isn't, Chief." Frank proceeded to estimate Johnson's take. "Horse-rooms pay $160 [$2,400 in 1990 dollars] a week protection; numbers banks pay $133.33 [$1,999.95 in 1990 dollars] a week. Whorehouses pay $50 [$750 in 1990 dollars] a week in winter, $100 [$1,500 in 1990 dollars] a week in summer. There are twenty-five race rooms, eight brothels and nine numbers banks. We estimate the horse-rooms gross $8,000,000 [$120 million in 1990 dollars]; the numbers banks $1,500,000 [$22.5 million in 1990 dollars]; and the prostitutes $500,000 [$7.5 million in 1990 dollars]. There are five to seven hundred employed in the race rooms, between one and three hundred in the brothels and about a thousand in the numbers racket. It's a $10,000,000 [$150 million in 1990 dollars] business paying $5,700 [$85,500 in 1990 dollars] a week for protection."

Irey was impressed by his agent's "extreme thoroughness"—so much so that he envisioned "stolen records photostatted in the dark of night, and adding machines humming throughout the day." How did Frank do it? "I asked a cop!" he told Irey.[15]

■

Nucky Johnson was going to be a problem almost like none before. To say he owned Atlantic City "lock, stock, and barrel" was an understatement. Nucky could open and shut the city as easy as a pack of matches. He had taken the power of Boss Kuehnle to another level. Bill Frank's estimates were one thing; evidence that would hold up in court was another. "The intricate business of proving what we knew began," Irey said.[16] Nucky didn't keep his money in banks. The Depression had closed down fourteen of Atlantic City's sixteen banks. Nucky stole like a cat burglar, but to keep his political-criminal alliance together he piled up goodwill, by, for example, handing out hundred-dollar bills to the needy.

Irey's team decided to look at contractors first. "Road building is always a sure source of graft, if there is any grafting being done," Irey said. The agents found only one builder of consequence: Morrell Tomlin, who happened to be the son of John Tomlin, the leader of Atlantic City's First Ward and a good friend of Nucky's. From 1928 to 1935 Morrell banked $1,654,590.27 ($17,538,604.32 in 1990 dollars) and didn't pay income taxes on it. John Tomlin had filed tax returns but rigged them so that he could pay no money in the years 1930, 1931, and 1932, even though his bank deposits totaled $561,560.94 ($8,148,414.10 in 1990 dollars). "It was obvious the elder Tomlin was getting the kickbacks from his son and passing them on to Nucky," Irey observed. "Certainly his son would have been in no position to make kickbacks unless Nucky gave him the jobs." When the SIU braced the son and father, they stonewalled—even after threats of criminal prosecution.

The agents were forced to turn to the "garbage-disposal branch of contracting," but even when an Atlantic City company admitted that it evaded taxes and conspired to defraud the government and that it had given Nucky $10,000 ($160,000 in 1990 dollars) in cash for giving the company the garbage disposal contract, they couldn't make it stick. Nucky had covered the amount in his income tax return as "Other Commissions."[17]

Next, they looked at the city's most recent major construction project: the Union Station of the Pennsylvania-Reading Seashore Lines, built at a cost of $2.4 million ($38 million in 1990 dollars) in 1936. The contractor, A. P. Miller, Inc., made a profit of $240,000 ($3.6 million in 1990 dollars). The firm's books showed two items charged to legal expenses. One for $1,150 ($17,250 in 1990 dollars) seemed a logical figure to Irey. The other, for $60,000 ($900,000 in 1990 dollars), went to Joseph A. Corio, who filed no income tax return on it. Corio was Judge Joseph A. Corio, who had been with the Atlantic County Common Pleas Court since 1929. He also was A. P. Miller's counsel. Nucky would later admit at trial that Corio arranged the construction deal between the railroad and the contractor.

When Bill Frank dropped by to chat with Judge Corio about the sum and began asking some tough questions, the judge practically threw him out of his chambers. The SIU agents spent the next two months in the basement of the bank that held the judge's account, checking each check that went through the bank's records since 1935. Judge Corio had explained to Frank that he had spent $40,000 ($640,000 in 1990 dollars) of the $60,000 ($960,000 in 1990 dollars) on "expenses" and kept the remaining $20,000 ($320,000 in 1990 dollars). The bank's records showed that Corio hadn't paid out $40,000 in expenses, as he had claimed, and had further defrauded the government of taxes of an additional $9,000 ($144,000 in 1990 dollars). When Frank confronted him with this, Corio admitted that he made an error about the $9,000 and planned to pay the penalties, but he refused to say what he did with the $40,000. On May 10, 1938, a federal grand jury indicted Corio. The same day, however, Corio suffered a nervous breakdown and spent the rest of the year hospitalized. Just before his trial was scheduled to begin on January 30, 1939, he got "a severe attack of conscience" and spilled everything.[18]

The Miller firm got the railroad station contract on the promise to pay Nucky Johnson 60 percent of the profits, according to Corio. It was also decided to beat the taxes on the profits and the payoff too. The net profit was $70,000 ($1,120,000 in 1990 dollars). Miller kept $10,000 ($160,000 in 1990 dollars) for expenses and paid $60,000 of it to Corio as a legal fee, thus saving Miller $25,000 ($400,000 in 1990 dollars) in personal and corporation taxes. Of this, Corio was to pay a tax of $13,200 ($221,200 in 1990 dollars), leaving $46,800 ($748,800 in 1990 dollars). Of the $46,800, Corio said, he kept $9,400, Miller kept $9,400 ($150,400 in 1990 dollars), and the remaining $28,000 ($448,000 in 1990 dollars) went to Nucky Johnson. Corio, however, decided to keep the $13,200 ($211,200 in 1990 dollars) and not pay any taxes.

Corio and Anthony P. Miller, the contractor, delivered the $28,000 ($448,000 in 1990 dollars) to Johnson at his home in Atlantic City on September 26, 1935. Miller handed him the money in cash. "Miller said to Johnson, 'Count it,'" Corio related.[19] "He did and then put it in the pocket of his suit."

■

On Wednesday, May 10, 1939, a federal grand jury in Newark indicted Nucky Johnson, Corio, Anthony P. Miller, Japhet Garwood, and A. P. Miller, Inc., on two counts, charging evasion and conspiracy to evade income tax payments. Miller was president, and Garwood was the secretary and assistant treasurer of the firm. The *New York Times* front-page story reported in part, "The investigators allege that evidence had been found to show that Mr. Johnson received part of the profits from the [railroad] terminal job. Asked by [a] newspaperman whether Mr. Johnson allegedly received the profits because of political influence, the investigators said they could not comment but that the 'answer' probably would be given when the trial on the indictments is held."[20]

Actually, there wasn't going to be a trial, at least not in the foreseeable future. What nobody knew, except for Irey and the federal prosecutor, U.S. Attorney John J. Quinn, was that the May 10 indictment was for show. Irey later revealed that "we had little confidence" that the evidence they had in the railroad terminal case would hold up at trial. What Irey needed was more extensive evidence that would result in Nucky Johnson's conviction. That was going to require a lot more work, and most of the past year had been spent in putting together the railroad station case. No one—except Judge Corio—had turned on Nucky, but Irey figured that with the indictment there would be more. "We had always had good luck in making underlings talk by indicting their boss to prove his vulnerability," he explained.[21] The SIU proceeded to redouble its effort.

The Justice Department, meanwhile, made a coordinated attempt to keep the heat on Johnson. In Washington, the day after the indictments, Attorney General Frank Murphy announced that the case would "proceed with all possible speed" and that he would "brook no attempts at delay."[22] At their arraignment in Newark on May 19, an "unworried" Johnson, "nattily dressed in a black suit" and wearing a gray hat, and the other three men pleaded not guilty. The judge granted each bail of $5,000 ($75,000 in

1990 dollars). Nothing else was heard about the case until September 14, when it was reported that their trial "would probably be held in Camden next month."²³ After that, quietness—at least in the press—descended on the case.

In Atlantic City, Frank and the other SIU agents began digging into the three rackets making payoffs to Nucky—the brothel houses, the horse-rooms, and the numbers operations—and over the next year and a half they sought to determine Nucky's take. The brothel madams wouldn't talk. Frank found a way to determine the extent of their trade. He checked the weekly wash, which consisted of 98 percent towels. "There are so many towels to the pound, therefore the total pounds divided by the number of towels to the pound gives a very sound figure reflecting the number of customers," Irey explained. "If you know the number of customers in each house, know what they pay, and know that the madam gets half, you also know how much the madam grossed. You know what each madam's laundry bill, medical bill, rent and protection payoff was."²⁴

Next, the agents turned to the horse-rooms. They were already presenting special problems for Nucky. Over the years the New York press occasionally intruded on Nucky's doings. On New Year's Day 1930, the Hearst-owned *New York Evening Journal* began running stories about vice and graft, which suddenly seemed to be running rampant in Atlantic City. Writer Jonathan Van Meter attributes the stories to a campaign William Randolph Hearst launched against Nucky after Atlantic City's favorite son allegedly insulted actress Marion Davies (who had a close relationship with Hearst, who was married) during a visit she made. Whatever Hearst's intentions were to expose Nucky's doings, it was ironic that an insult was the motive for publishing stories that contained more than a kernel of truth. The *Journal's* stories ordered by Hearst carried such lines as these: "Gangsters roam [Atlantic City's] streets unmolested, assaulting, ravishing and murdering at will with no fear of punishment. . . . In manpower, guile, ruthlessness, a wealthy rum-gambling underworld constitutes the largest enemy ever pitted against the United States." Such reportage was only a temporary thorn in Nucky's leathery side. In 1935, however, Nucky did run into substantial trouble from the big city press.

After the *New York Sun* ran an exposé on the forty-odd horse-rooms in Atlantic City, the heat became too much, and they closed—which was a surprise. Said Irey, "Nucky's followers couldn't quite understand why he had succumbed to the pressure so completely."[25] Anyone who thought so didn't know Nucky. He proceeded to turn them into a monopoly all his own. After the horse-rooms closed, Nucky and "a stooge" named Sam Camarota went to Chicago, where they signed and sealed a deal with James M. Ragen, the general manager of Nationwide News Service, to make Camarota the exclusive agent in Atlantic City for the service. Nationwide, owned by Moses "Moe" Annenberg, furnished horse-rooms with instantaneous results, odds, and descriptions of a race and had done business with underworld heavyweights, including Frank Nitti, Meyer Lansky, and Longy Zwillman. Now, any horse-room that chose to operate in Atlantic City would have to buy its franchise from Camarota. By summer of 1935 Camarota was ready to sell the franchises, and Nucky gave the word that the horse-rooms could open. Irey described what happened next:

> Sam informed the clamoring bookies that there were too many horse-rooms in Atlantic City and that he would sell only 25 franchises. This was quite a blow to a dozen or so earnest bookmakers who found themselves frozen out and faced with the horrors of honest work. Camarota then informed the lucky 25 that the franchise would cost $200 [$3,000 in 1990 dollars] per room per week. The boys understood this perfectly, although they knew Nationwide's coast-to-coast price was $40 [$600 in 1990 dollars] a room. The $160 [$2,400 in 1990 dollars] was protection. Each Monday Bill Frank or another agent tailed Camarota as he plodded from room to room collecting his $200 in advance. He then plodded over to Nucky Johnson's where he left 25 times 140, or $4,000 [$60,000 in 1990 dollars]. The remainder, less Camarota's commission, was sent to Nationwide.[26]

■

During the time Nucky reformed the horse-rooms to his own making, he decided it was in his interest to forestall, at least in the local press, any more efforts by crusading newspaper editors. He began buying favorable coverage. In 1936 he paid the publisher of the *Atlantic City Press*, Alvin Friedberg, $9,400 ($150,400 in 1990 dollars). In 1936 he gave Friedberg $10,400 ($166,400 in 1990 dollars). In 1935 and 1936 he paid the $40 ($640 in 1990 dollars) weekly salary of Thomas Ogilvie, publisher of the *South Jersey Independent*, which eventually totaled $2,080 ($33,046 in 1990 dollars). In 1935 and 1936 Nucky also paid Louis M. Herman, an editor at the *Atlantic City Press*, a total of $11,000 ($176,000 in 1990 dollars) for making "a political survey" for him. Herman also received between $17,000 ($272,000 in 1990 dollars) and $18,000 ($288,000 in 1990 dollars) in the same period "to be paid to workers" at the newspaper. In 1935 Johnson gave the *Press* $5,000 ($80,000 in 1990 dollars) to be used "for political purposes."[27] The SIU had run down all of these transactions, which were disclosed at Nucky's trial.

In their investigation, Bill Frank and his team grilled the bookmakers who were frozen out after Nucky took over the horse-rooms. A bookie named James R. Hill had been Nationwide's agent in Atlantic City before Nucky slammed the door in his face. Bitter at Nucky's brush-off, Hill was "bursting with information," and he and other bookies gave the SIU a reasonably close estimate of the take of the various horse-rooms. Like the madams, most of the bookies admitted to their incomes and paid additional taxes and penalties to Internal Revenue. Neither of these parties, however, was going to be that helpful. As Irey explained, "In no case did we have enough to frighten them into admitting" they were paying off Nucky. Irey also didn't want to put them on the stand; they were "underworld characters" who lied "too much."[28] Camarota's testimony was also important, but he had disappeared. Irey put Pat O'Rourke on his trail. O'Rourke, of course, had batted a home run every time he stepped to the plate. He soon ran him down in Fort Lee, New Jersey—but not until early November 1941, when he was no longer important.

The key to Nucky's downfall, it turned out, lay in the numbers houses. Going after them was a complicated and lengthy affair—and a strategy that occupied the SIU for the rest of 1940 and into 1941. The numbers racket was a simple game of chance. The day's number was a three-digit figure, and "probably no city was as addicted to numbers as Atlantic City," said Irey.[29] Out of 1,500 stores in the resort, up to 800 took bets, with a daily take of approximately $6,000 ($96,000 in 1990 dollars), mostly in small change. There were more than 800 writers and dozens of pick-up men.

The numbers bankers were the problem, according to Irey. There were thirteen principal bankers who ran the city's nine numbers banks. They kept no books, used no ordinary bank, paid the same odds, used the same payoff number, and had identical commission arrangements with writers and pick-up men. All of this indicated they were operating a syndicate, and a syndicate meant Nucky Johnson "wasn't being paid off in hard-to-trace hundreds, but was getting it in one large fat chunk each week."[30] Syndicates, of course, must file corporation taxes. Hauled before a grand jury, the thirteen bankers maintained there was no syndicate and that they were operating as independents. The case came down to whether any of them would admit otherwise and, in the process, admit to paying off Nucky. They were indicted and beginning in January 1940, twenty-one people involved in the rackets, including the thirteen bankers, went to trial on charges of tax evasion, with the hope that some of them would run for cover.

The first numbers banker put on trial, Austin Clark, was found guilty and sentenced to three years for tax evasion. Eight of the bankers made the trek to Room 222 and offered to plead guilty if the Justice Department would "give them six months each." They were turned down. Three more bankers were put on trial, were found guilty, and received various sentences, none for more than two and a half years. Meanwhile, Nucky Johnson wasn't sitting still. According to Irey, "perjury, jury fixing and intimidation" became the order of the day. The "cream of Atlantic City's musclemen" sat at the trials, "glowering at witnesses."[31] Then, a break occurred.

Isaac Nutter, a lawyer for one of the bankers, won a not-guilty verdict for his client, whereupon he stiffed Nutter for the bill. "Nutter got so mad he came in and did a little talking," Irey said. Nutter said all of the bankers who had testified under oath that they were independent operators were not and therefore had perjured themselves. "He also suspected they were guilty of income-tax violations for hiding the fact that they operated as a syndicate." Irey still needed more witnesses, and Nutter decided to help.

He went to Lewisburg Penitentiary to see Herndon Daniels, one of the bankers serving a year and a half, and told Daniels that another banker in Atlantic City was sleeping with his girlfriend. After that, said Irey, all Daniels "wanted of life were a Bible and a witness stand."[32] Seated before a grand jury, Daniels testified that, indeed, the thirteen bankers operated as a syndicate, and the syndicate was paying Nucky $1,200 ($24,000 in 1990 dollars) a week for protection.

Irey brought back two other bankers serving time in Lewisburg—Austin Clark and Benny Rubenstein—for more questioning. Irey called Rubenstein's actions "unprecedented in a criminal case. He sat in his cell, refusing to say a word against Johnson, yet liberally coaching us on what questions to ask what banker." At one point Clark showed signs of weakening, but then clammed up. As he and a U.S. marshal were waiting at the railroad station for the Lewisburg train, he turned to the marshal and said, "Get the government lawyers. I want to make a statement."[33] In it, he admitted he was a member of the syndicate, a perjurer, and that he understood—but could not prove—that Nucky was being paid off. The dominoes began falling after that. Rubenstein wouldn't talk, but he did point a few fingers—which led to a numbers banker named Ralph Weloff, who happened to be the collector for Nucky Johnson. Weloff, threatened with fifteen years for perjury, lifted the latch on the whole operation.

■

On June 10, 1941, a federal grand jury in Camden indicted Johnson on three counts of personal income tax invasion for the years 1935, 1936, and 1937, but the federal judge, Albert Maris, quashed it on the grounds that the jury, which was held over without authorization, was "legally nonexistent."[34] On June 17, another grand jury indicted Nucky on the identical counts: failing to pay taxes in 1935 on an income of $171,804 ($22,748,864 in 1990 dollars), including $48,400 ($774,400 in 1990 dollars) received from operators of the numbers racket, and $28,000 ($448,000 in 1990 dollars) on the Union Railroad Depot deal. That year he reported his income as $33,404 ($535,464 in 1990 dollars) with deductions totaling $89,778 ($1,436,448 in 1990 dollars). In 1936 the indictment charged that his income totaled $92,358 ($1,436,448 in 1990 dollars), including $62,400

($998,400 in 1990 dollars) from the numbers operators, and that he paid only $1,224 ($19,784 in 1990 dollars) on a reported income of $29,958 ($479,328 in 1990 dollars). In 1937 the indictment charged that his income was $95,140 ($1,427,100 in 1990 dollars), including $33,369 ($500,235 in 1990 dollars) from numbers operators. The indictment charged that he reported his net income as $12,849 ($182,735 in 1990 dollars) and paid a tax of $852 ($12,780 in 1990 dollars), when his net income was actually $75,249 ($1,128,535 in 1990 dollars) and the tax on it was $19,611 ($294,165 in 1990 dollars). A trial date was quickly set, Tuesday, July 16, and the jury of eight men and four women was chosen on July 13. From the start, Nucky was doomed. The damning evidence and testimony revealed beyond a shadow of a doubt that Nucky corrupted everything he touched—elected officials, businessmen, policemen, newspaper editors, all had thrown in their lot with him.

In his opening statement, Joseph W. Burns, the thirty-three-year-old special assistant to the attorney general and lead prosecutor, spoke for one hour and twenty-five minutes. Johnson, he said, had police headquarters form a "special vice squad" to "frustrate public protests against gambling." Raids were permitted and fines were imposed weekly, but numbers operators were permitted to deduct their fines from their protection payments to Johnson. Though gambling in Atlantic City was illegal, Burns said, Johnson "wished to have gambling in Atlantic City and wanted it to be the Monte Carlo of America and to operate openly." The vice squad, Burns went on, "was not to prevent gambling, but to control it." Johnson was invited three times to talk to SIU agents to "make any explanation he chose." His failure to do so, Burns said, was regarded as indicating that his evasion was not accidental, "but deliberate and therefore a criminal act."[35]

The prosecution's first major witness was Judge Joseph Corio; he was devastatingly effective. On the stand, he admitted lying to save Johnson, only to be "lost and left all alone" after the SIU began investigating his role in the railroad terminal deal. Johnson "made more" from the deal than the contractor, Corio said. He also denied that he had received promises of special consideration or immunity from prosecution. Subjected to hours of cross-examination by William G. Winne, the chief defense counsel who once served as a U.S. attorney in New Jersey, Corio calmly said time and again that he had participated personally in the payoff deal. "With just as much composure," he admitted his repeated falsifications to the SIU agents and to the federal grand jury. "I had to protect Johnson. I tried to 'cover up.' I was willing to do anything in the world to save him." When Winne asked him what he expected to get as a result of his testimony, Corio said, "My position is that I am telling the truth now."[36] In addition to describing in detail the circumstances of going to Nucky's home on the day he got the $28,000 ($448,000 in 1990 dollars) in cash from Anthony Miller, Corio revealed that Nucky's nephew, Judge W. Lindley Jeffers of the Atlantic City District Court, helped draw up the papers guaranteeing Johnson three-fifths of the net profit from the railroad terminal contract.

Just as effective the next day was fifty-year-old Ralph Weloff, the numbers operator who collected the payoffs from the banks. "Did you ever give this defendant money?" Burns asked, pointing to Johnson. "Yes," Weloff said. "In 1935 I gave him money every week. The six day banks paid $125 [$2,400 in 1990 dollars] a week and the night bank paid $75 [$1,200 in 1990 dollars] and I gave $825 [$13,200 in 1990 dollars] every week to Mr. Johnson for protection." The $825 was paid during the first half of 1935, Weloff said. From July 2, 1935, until November 1937, the eight member banks contributed $150 a week each for a total of $1,200, which Weloff said he carried to Johnson. He went into the history of the payoffs, explaining that toward the end of 1933 the numbers operators thought "it would be a good investment if each would contribute a sum to be paid regularly as a guarantee of immunity from police action and against invasion of their territory by outsiders." He said he had taken the first pool of $825 to Johnson. "I told him that (the bankers) didn't want to do it (create the fund) unless something was going to be done about it. Mr. Johnson put the money in his pocket and said: 'I understand. It will be all right.' Weloff explained that the It was 'an easy matter' to handle the police. 'Whenever too many arrests were made, they (the bankers) complained to me, and I usually went to see Ralph Gold (the detective in charge of the vice squad) and complained to him. When I complained, the police eased up, and there were hardly ever any arrests at all. He said he stopped being the payoff man in November 1937 after the bankers complained he was making too many contributions 'to charitable enterprises.'"[37]

Preceding Weloff to the stand was the "cashier" of the numbers banks, Benjamin Ravniniski. Known as Benny Ray, he testified at length about the workings of the numbers racket. The combine's income, he estimated, was $5,500 ($88,000 in 1990 dollars) a day in summer and $3,700 ($59,200 in 1990 dollars) a day in the other seasons, for a total yearly take of $1.8 million ($28 million in 1990 dollars). Ravniniski confirmed that in 1935 each bank paid $125 ($2,400 in 1990 dollars) a week to Weloff "for protection," for a total of $825 ($13,200 in 1990 dollars), and that during 1936 and 1937 the total weekly payment was $1,200 ($19,200 in 1990 dollars).

Some of the most telling testimony came from William Shepherd, a black man who had served as the gatekeeper and all-around helper for Johnson. He testified that Weloff and James F. Towhey, who was identified as the bookkeeper and "contact man" of the numbers combine, were "regular visitors" to Nucky's home and "usually stayed only long enough to leave an envelope." Once, Shepherd said, he tried to keep Weloff out. Johnson overruled him, telling the bodyguard "always" to let Weloff into the house. Johnson would immediately take the money he got from Weloff and transfer it to a tin box in his bedroom. Once Shepherd looked inside the box, and "it was full of papers and money." He said, "Johnson frequently obtained large sums of money from [it] to pay the chauffeur's wages and house expenses." In a moment of boasting innocence, Shepherd said "nearly every cop in Atlantic City" visited Johnson's house. They were the "most frequent visitors" and "appeared at the cottage every day."[38] He named some of them: Ralph Gold, head of the vice squad; James McMenamin, the chief of police; and Frank Ferretti, the inspector of detectives.

In his opening address for the defense, on the first day of the trial's second week, Winne said Johnson admitted that the numbers racket paid him a total of $159,800 ($2,556,800 in 1990 dollars) in 1935, 1936, and 1937. Explained Winne, "Mr. Johnson was head of a powerful political machine and that machine needed oil to keep it running. We're not going to be hypocrites and deny we received this money."[39]

If Winne's explanation was a speeding train about to jump the tracks, the wreck occurred the next day when Johnson took the stand. There for four hours, he was "ill at ease and hesitant" even during his direct testimony. During cross-examination, he became "increasingly confused." He admitted he had never filed any accounting of his political expenses, explaining that he noted expenses on "a memorandum pad." Then he admitted that he had not done so daily and that they merely represented his recollection. He testified he kept "no regular daybook or ledger." He paid some of the money in sums of "five dollars or so" to political subordinates who approached him "with appeals for aid." Every few months, he said, he would total up the cash payments from numbers writers and the cash he had paid out, thus striking a balance between income and expenses.

The presiding judge, Albert B. Maris, at one point, interrupted to ask Johnson to inquire why he hadn't put down the full amount paid to him by the numbers rackets on his income tax return and then to explain the deductions.

"That is where I made my mistake," Johnson replied.

At another point, Burns brought out Johnson's admission that the numbers money was intended to buy his influence on behalf of an enterprise he knew to be illegal.

Q: Weren't you paid to use your influence in behalf of the numbers bankers?

A: Certainly.

Q: What did you promise to do?

A: Nothing.

Q: Didn't you know that numbers was against the law of the State of New Jersey?

A: I suppose so—if you get caught.

Q: Is that the way you feel about law violators, that they are not violating the law unless they get caught?

A: No.

Q: Did you promise to do anything to keep them from getting caught?

A: No.

Q: Then what did [Ralph] Weloff expect for his $1,200 a week?

A: Nothing that I know of. It was for the political machine to help me carry on the organization's work and elect candidates friendly to my policies.

Winne had built much of his case on the contention that the money on which Johnson had paid no income tax was really "commissions," and they had been listed on his tax returns. The case went to the jury on Thursday, July 25, and in his closing remarks that day, Winne asked the jury to consider that "we are grown up and any sophisticated person who has gotten money from this source would give it on his income tax return as 'commission.' Even the government isn't above taking tax on anybody's money, whether it is money from bootleggers or this kind of money. I'm not going to tell you that Johnson is a lily of the field. He isn't. He is a clever politician and a forceful figure in the political life of this State."[40]

■

At 5:00 p.m., on Friday, July 25, 1941, after deliberating less than five hours, the jury—four of whom were active in south New Jersey Republican politics—returned a verdict of guilty on the two counts involving the numbers racket and the $28,000 deal and not guilty on evading $1,232 in taxes in 1935. The fifty-eight-year-old Johnson "blanched" as he heard it, and his face turned "a chalky white." He was released on $25,000 ($350,000 in 1990 dollars) bail. On August 1 Judge Maris, calling Nucky a "gross perjurer," sentenced him to ten years in prison—one year less than Al Capone received—and a fine of $20,000 ($280,000 in 1990 dollars)—$30,000 ($510,000 in 1990 dollars) less than Capone was fined.[41] The next day bail was denied, and he was taken to the Mercer County jail in Trenton. In Atlantic City, meanwhile, the county's 550 employees wondered if they were going to get paid. As the county treasurer, Johnson signed their paychecks and "officials were puzzled as to who would sign the payroll."[42]

An appeal was filed immediately and thus began that long process, during which the Internal Revenue Bureau in December filed a tax lien for $206,824 ($2,895,531 in 1990 dollars). On July 1, 1942, the U.S. Circuit Court of Appeals in Philadelphia, in a 2–1 decision, upheld his conviction.

Six days later his case was taken to the U.S. Supreme Court. On October 17, 1942, the high court agreed to review his case—at the same time, it also agreed to review the case of Boss Pendergast. On February 15, 1943, the U.S. Supreme Court upheld Nucky's conviction. On March 13 it turned down a request to review the case. On September 27 Nucky filed his first application for parole, for which he was to become eligible on November 30, but it was turned down on December 8. Nucky had spent most of World War II behind bars. On Friday, August 11, 1945, the day Japan offered to accept the Potsdam ultimatum on unconditional surrender, the federal parole board granted his parole. The following Tuesday at 5:00 p.m., Nucky walked out of the U.S. penitentiary at Lewisburg, after spending four years and thirteen days behind bars.

19. "MOE" ANNENBERG

Racing-wire and publishing tycoon Moses L. "Moe" Annenberg was earning the nation's highest income, $6 million a year ($94.2 million in 1990 dollars), when he drew Elmer Irey's attention.

In acquiring and keeping his immense wealth, Annenberg did not follow the law. Nor did he tolerate his business partners, who, when they broke with him (as most did), wanted to leave with some of his capital. Inevitably, this brought lawsuits, which brought splashy headlines and stories about the huge sums that were being fought over between Annenberg and his former associates. One of the most garish began in November 1932, after a federal grand jury indicted Annenberg, his company, and his publishing associates for sending obscene literature—one of his magazines—through the mail. The case was eventually withdrawn from the courts, but his "embarrassed" publishing associates sued him; he settled by paying "a total of $2,250,000 [$36 million in 1990 dollars]."[1]

Irey, drawn to the "gaudy" figures tossed around in the lawsuits, sent Special Agent Nels Tessem in early 1935 to question the tycoon. Tessem— an experienced investigator who had played a key investigative role in the Al Capone case—went to Annenberg's office in Chicago. There, instead of offering the SIU agent an explanation, an Annenberg aide handed him his hat and pointed to the door. The rough brush-off made him think something was peculiar, and he redoubled his effort. Still, he found out little.

Annenberg ran a financial empire concealed in a maze of ventures and companies that not even Irey's agents could penetrate.

"Moe was so deft with a dollar that neither he, his heirs and assigns, nor the United States Government even knew exactly how much he was worth," said Irey.[2] Annenberg's wealth came from a publications empire that included a monopoly on racing information—the Nationwide News Service—which he had put together with a mix of brains, brawn, and deceit. Hank Messick noted, "Organized crime owes as much to Annenberg as it does to Meyer Lansky, who put off-the-top skimming from casinos on a routine basis. Moe Annenberg was for the bookies of America what Arnold Rothstein was for rum-runners and narcotics peddlers—the man who put the racket on a businesslike basis."[3] After Annenberg died in the late evening of July 20, 1942, it was an enterprise so hungrily eyed by Mafia racketeers, the brethren killed to take it over.

Wiry, bespectacled, horse-faced, and tall, Morris Annenberg was neither nice-looking nor nice. No business executive in modern times pushed the envelope between racketeering and legitimate enterprise like he did. In forging a massive and complex business operation, he wasn't reluctant to use unsavory tactics, such as bribery, intimidation, and violence. Right up to his jailing, he was still bargaining and deceiving.

An immigrant born in East Prussia on February 11, 1878, Moe's parents brought him to the United States at age four; they settled in Chicago, where Moe's father, Tobias, worked as a peddler. Moe dropped out of school at twelve, but he had a "rapier-sharp intelligence" and was already on his way to becoming the country's highest paid entrepreneur and "one of the financial wizards of the 20th Century."[4] Said Irey, "Everything he touched turned to gold and he touched everything."[5]

Annenberg cut his business teeth in the circulation wars newspaper magnate William Randolph Hearst Sr. fostered at the turn of the century. It was an era when publishers depended on muscle and intimidation when starting a newspaper, and there was no mistaking their nature. The circulation wars that broke out came as close to drawn-out, armed conflict as anyone had seen in an American city. After whipping his competitors in San Francisco and New York, Hearst launched the *Evening American* in Chicago, where, in July 1900, seven dailies already existed. "Chicago saw a new kind of circulation war," W. A. Swanberg said, "as armed thugs roamed the streets, wrecking opposition newspaper delivery trucks, dumping papers into the river and slugging news dealers who refused to take more papers than they could sell."[6] The city saw "the bloodiest and most ruthless circulation war in the history of journalism anywhere." When a truce was declared thirteen years later, twenty-seven news dealers had been murdered.[7]

Annenberg was right in the middle of it and knew the right people to use to get the upper hand in Chicago's circulation war. One hireling was Frank McErlane, a "compulsive killer."[8] After Hearst launched his tabloid *New York Daily Mirror* in 1923, he made Annenberg the publisher. He turned to Charlie Luciano to help get the new rag on the streets of a city with more dailies than Chicago. Among Annenberg's competitors was the *New York Daily News*, which proclaimed it had the nation's largest circulation. Luciano had "goon squads spread out over the city so they could seize and hold prime corners for the Mirror."[9] Said Luciano, "I always though of Annenberg as my kind of guy."[10]

After taking over as head of circulation for the Hearst newspapers and magazines, Annenberg enjoyed a side arrangement that allowed him to engage in his own business dealings. In 1922 he purchased the *Daily Racing Form* and began buying up other publications, including its competitor, the *Morning Telegraph*. He left his job with Hearst in 1926, bought into a nationwide betting syndicate in Chicago called the General News Bureau, and developed a telephone hookup that could bring the results into bookmaking parlors, most of which were operating in violation of local laws.

Soon, his only other national rival was the Greater New York News Service, lorded over by one of Manhattan's biggest racketeers, Waxey Gordon. John Cooney tells in rich detail the battle between the two, how Annenberg undercut Gordon's operation and then through a series of craftily executed maneuvers, eventually outwitted him. In the end Annenberg gained the "deep respect of gamblers who were awed by his outsmarting the ruthless Gordon."[11] But "so driven to have everything," he began undercutting his partners (and getting into a host of lawsuits).[12] In August 1934, without his partners' knowledge, he formed an opposing betting operation, Nationwide News Service. That year General's profits hit $1.4 million ($22.4 million in 1990 dollars), while Nationwide lost $3,788 ($60,608 in 1990 dollars). A year later, so ruthless and able were Annenberg's talents, Nationwide's profits hit $1.1 million ($7.6 million in 1990 dollars), while General suffered a loss of $45,634 ($730,144 in 1990 dollars). Through Nationwide, Annenberg established a monopoly on service to all the horse-betting rooms in 223 cities in the United States and Canada, becoming the American Telephone and Telegraph Company's fifth-biggest customer, behind the three newswire outlets (which serviced the nation's newspapers) and the Radio Corporation of America (RCA).

Mafia racketeers and their associates hadn't overlooked Annenberg's hugely profitable betting syndicate. Frank Erickson, a New York gambler with close ties to Frank Costello, had proposed the idea of a national wire service during the 1929 Atlantic City gathering of the brethren. Al Capone liked Erickson's idea and, upon returning to Chicago, discussed it with Annenberg, who, according to John Cooney, "flatly rejected sharing his business."[13] Still, Curt Gentry speculated, "apparently because of an understanding with the national crime syndicate, the mob kept its hands off the wire service while Annenberg still owned it."[14] Whatever did occur, Annenberg was a tough operator who had no compunction about using the same tactics Capone employed. Annenberg's General News Bureau maintained an annual slush fund of $150,000 ($2.4 million in 1990 dollars) to buy off politicians and police in Chicago.

Annenberg knew that Chicago's new underworld rulers, all of whom had been Capone's key lieutenants, could make his life difficult. After Capone was sent to Alcatraz, Annenberg left for the milder climate of Miami. There, in 1934, he purchased a daily, the *Miami Tribune*, and made the acquaintance of Meyer Lansky, who helped him bring his Nationwide News Service into the big-time racetracks such as Hialeah.

Annenberg turned the *Tribune* into a scandal sheet that beat the pants off its two competitors, the *Miami Herald* and the *Miami News*. The *Herald*'s publisher, Frank Shutts, wouldn't allow the *Tribune* in his newsroom. Despite its strong circulation, Annenberg's rag was such a "volatile paper and offended so many important people that it never gained much advertising." It did, however, give him clout he needed. He tried to use its pages to bring gambling to Florida, and he bribed a state senator, Peter Tomasello, to sponsor legislation to legalize bookmaking and gambling. When they first met, Tomasello started to spout off about his political platform. Annenberg interrupted him. "I don't care about your platform. All I want is for you to obey orders."[15]

The gambling issue failed, and with the Miami establishment against him, Annenberg, three years after buying the *Tribune*, decided to pack it in. He sold the *Tribune* to John S. Knight, the new owner of the *Herald* (who immediately scrapped it), and moved to Philadelphia, where he had purchased the *Philadelphia Inquirer*, which was one of the nation's oldest dailies (going back to 1771) and reflected the world Annenberg now wanted to engage. Things weren't going to be easy, however. He had betrayed his partners, broken bread with the Mafia, and employed whatever means necessary to achieve his end. When he was putting the General News Bureau together, a small operator in Covington, Kentucky, complained that an Annenberg enforcer told him he would be bumped off if he didn't subscribe to General. Now, sitting in the birthplace of the Declaration of Independence as the owner of a respected newspaper, he not only didn't consider that his past might catch up with him, he misjudged that politics is often unforgiving and always a perilous, wreck-strewn two-way street.

In 1938 Governor George H. Earle, the state's first Democratic governor in forty-four years, ran for reelection. In what was a polar shift away from the Republican Party, Joseph F. Guffey was also elected the first Democratic senator since 1875. Now, four years later, Annenberg intended to right that. He turned the *Inquirer* into a trumpet for the Republican gubernatorial candidate, former Superior Court Judge Arthur H. James. Besides editorial assaults on Earle, the newspaper ran a series of clever articles titled, "The Migration of Industry," which maintained that Pennsylvania "was rapidly losing jobs and industry because of tax policies instituted by the Democrats" and suggested "that ever more harmful levies were in the offing."[16] When his opponents spoke out, Annenberg's signed editorial called them "political skunks" who were "airing their poison gas at me." In reply, the publisher of the *Philadelphia Record*, J. David Stern, in a signed editorial, asked, "Is the underworld to govern Philadelphia?"[17]

Ironically, Earle had been a disappointment as governor. He was a play-boy whose term had turned out to be "as corrupt as the Republican administration he replaced." But Annenberg had also begun using the *Inquirer* to attack FDR's New Deal. Just before Pennsylvania's gubernatorial election of 1938, the White House sent Secretary of the Interior Harold Ickes to Philadelphia to give a statewide radio address. "An eloquent orator," he delivered "a no-holds-barred attack" on Annenberg.[18] But Earle still lost. Gone were the tenuous gains Democrats had made. Gone, too, was Annenberg's tenuous position in Philadelphia. That Elmer Irey had legitimate concerns about Annenberg's financial chicanery only made it easier for others in FDR's administration.

■

Irey had been proceeding slowly, for good reason. "There were hundreds of things that indicated Moe was a tax evader and a few that proved it," he said. "We knew we were a trifle short on proof and overlong on theory." Moreover, as Tessem and other agents weeded through Annenberg's massive holdings, the inquiry became the "most complex case" the Intelligence Unit had ever faced.[19]

Irey broke down a part of Annenberg's holdings. There were twenty corporations dealing with publications; five corporations and "innumerable partnerships" dealing with his racing-wire operation; sixteen corporations involving newspaper and magazine distribution outlets; and fourteen corporations involving various businesses such as real estate, insurance, theaters, liquor stores, and laundry places. Said Irey, "All these corporations locked, interlocked, and frequently became non-existent because their books had been tossed off a bridge."[20] That was where matters stood until May 1939, when, incredibly, a common mistake ended the long game.

Nels Tessem was settling in at his desk one May morning in the tiny office on South Dearborn Street that Annenberg had provided the agents as part of an arrangement to look at his books. Irey had a twenty-four-hour shift operating in the office. Tessem looked over at one of the agents who'd been working all night. "What's wrong with this dump today?" he asked. "It seems smaller than ever."

"It's probably those boxes over there," said the agent, pointing to a pile of metal boxes in a corner. "They brought 'em in this morning."

Tessem went over and started counting. There were nineteen boxes. Each one said "Private Records."[21] He looked at the labels. They indicated the boxes had been shipped from Annenberg's palatial home on Long Island. Tessem opened one, looked at a file, stiffened slightly, turned, rushed out of the office, and headed to the federal courthouse to seek a subpoena that would enable the Treasury to seize them.

The nineteen boxes, delivered early that morning, had gone to the right floor but the wrong office. They were supposed to go to Annenberg's lawyers. They contained cancelled checks, cash books, bank statements, ledgers, and correspondence, all of which Annenberg denied had existed, along with information explaining various codes he used to hide his activities. His lawyers planned to use them as background for Annenberg's defense, but the secret was out. To Irey's disbelief, they filled in all the holes in the government's case. It was a devastating blow to Annenberg.

Shortly before Tessem's discovery, a turf war between Treasury and Justice broke out over the approach to take in prosecuting Annenberg. Henry Morgenthau had begun to take an interest in the SIU's inquiry. When the Justice Department decided to pursue a parallel case against Annenberg— just as it had done in the Pendergast case—Morgenthau's interest really perked up. The year before, Thurman Arnold, the acting attorney general, had ordered the FBI to gather evidence for an antitrust action against Annenberg. Morgenthau, calling the Treasury's inquiry into Annenberg's dealings "the biggest criminal case this Administration has ever had," countered Arnold's move by reminding him that Irey's branch had been busy for three years looking into possible tax fraud by Annenberg. Key Democrats, such as Mayor Ed Kelly of Chicago, had also been vocal in opposing Irey's inquiry (Annenberg was one of Kelly's financial contributors).[22]

Partly to send a political message, partly to establish turf, Frank Murphy, the newly appointed attorney general, went public on Friday, April 21, 1939. His remarks were so nonjudgmental that one had to read between the lines to know what was happening. He announced that Annenberg was being investigated and explained that "two lines" of inquiry were being pursued. One was the income tax case that, he said, the Treasury had "recently handed findings and recommendations over to the Department of Justice." The other, he said, was the "anti-trust matter which has been under investigation for a year or more." He went on to say the tax case "involved more than $500,000." This was not only wrong but far off the mark. When the tax case was brought against Annenberg, it was the largest tax evasion case the Justice Department had ever prosecuted.

"If present plans materialize," Murphy said, "the two Annenberg cases will be offered simultaneously to a grand jury in Chicago within two or three weeks." Six days later Annenberg, after he and his attorneys met "in a personal conference" with Murphy and James W. Morris, the assistant attorney general in charge of the tax division, offered to pay "any income tax deficiency."[23]

Murphy had been a thorn in Treasury's side in the Pendergast case. Morgenthau had kept silent in that episode (much to Irey's chagrin), but he hit the ceiling after Murphy's public sounding. He went to the Oval Office to complain about Murphy's interference—and carried the day. FDR told him to go forward on the case.

The case wasn't presented in "two or three weeks," and Tessem's discovery ended the question of which "line" to follow. Six weeks passed before the materials Tessem found could be put together and the evidence presented to a grand jury. On August 11, 1939, a special grand jury in Chicago indicted Annenberg, charging him with evading $3,258,809.97 ($47,882,149.63 in 1990 dollars) in income taxes. The interest and penalties brought the amount he owed to $5,548,384.89 ($83,225,473.35 in 1990 dollars). On August 22 the same jury indicted Annenberg, and seven employees of the Consensus Publishing Company, a unit in the Annenberg horse-race information service, on charges of conspiracy to defraud the government of $77,885.53 ($1,245,968.48 in 1990 dollars) in income taxes for the years 1933 through 1936. The next day it charged that his horse-race information services constituted "an illegal monopoly" and recommended that the business be killed by legislation in the states where it was

being operated. One week later, on August 30, the jury indicted Annenberg again, along with Charles W. Bidwill and James M. Ragen. Bidwill,
owner of the Chicago Cardinals professional football team, headed a printing concern. Ragen was general manager of the Nationwide News Service,
owned by Annenberg. The indictment, unprecedented in the history of
the federal courts, charged the trio with using the mails "in furtherance of
a lottery scheme and carrying over interstate wires the mutual prices paid
at race tracks."[24] These prices were described by the grand jury as a list of
prizes awarded by means of a lottery.

Annenberg had his lawyers plea-bargain for eight months before accepting his punishment. The courtroom in the federal building in Chicago
on Tuesday, April 24, 1940, was packed. U.S. Attorney William J. Campbell;
two of his assistants, Austin Hall and William Critty; and Elmer Irey sat at
one table. Irey had decided to bring the Treasury's presence to the proceedings. The SIU had spent five years on the case. Publicly, it appeared
to be an all–Justice Department affair. In his memoir, Irey did not describe
the Annenberg case beyond Annenberg's and the SIU's role, choosing to
completely ignore the Justice Department's contribution. Irey did note
that there were "eight months of legal pleading, bickering, ultimatum, and
compromise between Uncle Sam and Moe."[25] Clearly, he did not like the
way Justice handled the case.

At trial, Annenberg, wearing a dark suit, blue shirt, and blue tie,
stepped out of a group of thirteen defendants standing in the docket and
pleaded guilty to the count in one of the indictments charging him with
evading payment of $1,217,296 ($19,476,736 in 1990 dollars) in income
taxes for 1936. He had manipulated his income in grand fashion. Gambling debts were charged off as "political contributions." He had cashed
checks for $100,000 ($1.6 million in 1990 dollars) during 1935, pooled the
money, and included it in a "fraudulent charge" of $850,000 ($13.6 million in 1990 dollars) for the purchases of 50 percent of the General News
Bureau stock. But only $750,000 ($12 million in 1990 dollars) was paid,
and he refused to say what had happened to the other $100,000.[26] When
his daughter Harriet was married, Annenberg wrote off the wedding costs,
including paying $6,444.44 ($103,111.04 in 1990 dollars) for the hotel, as

business expenses. On July 10 James Wilkerson, the federal judge who had sentenced Al Capone nine years before, sentenced Annenberg, age sixty-two but looking eighty-two, to the federal penitentiary at Lewisburg, Pennsylvania, for three years, telling him,

> Tax evaders should understand that they may not make a compromise with the Treasury Department, and then expect to receive . . . consideration in criminal cases. The court is without authority either to compromise or to pardon. It has a larger duty to the public. The main object of criminal punishment is to prevent further crime. To grant the pleas of the defendant in this case would be to say to businessmen: "You may organize your affairs in a network of corporations and avoid the payment of your just taxes and, when called to account by the government for what you really owe, nothing worse will happen to you than to be compelled to pay what you should have paid long ago."[27]

Wilkerson fined Annenberg $8 million ($120 million in 1990 dollars), the largest single tax fraud penalty in history. Internal Revenue wanted a full settlement, covering payment of back taxes, penalties, and interest for 1932 through 1938, adding up to $9.5 million ($151 million in 1990 dollars). It was arranged that Annenberg pay $3 million initially, then $1 million over the next six years. As collateral, the government was given first and second mortgages on most of his properties, though not on the *Philadelphia Inquirer*.

U.S. Marshal William H. McDonnell and Deputy Marshal Joseph Thinnes took Annenberg from Chicago to Lewisburg late on the evening of July 22, 1940. Annenberg wanted to go on his own and meet the marshals at the prison gate, but he was turned down. One week before he went away, as part of the first installment he owed on back taxes, he mailed Internal Revenue a check for $800,000 ($12 million in 1990 dollars).

20. MAFIA SHAKEDOWN IN HOLLYWOOD

"**I** had Hollywood dancin' to my tune," rat-smart Willie Bioff confessed in 1943. "We had about 20 percent of Hollywood when we got in trouble. If we hadn't got loused up we'd of had 50 percent."[1] He got "loused up" when Elmer Irey found out what he was doing.

With his "utterly ruthless talent for extortion," William Nelson "Willie" Bioff had the movie colony in his grip. Since 1934 the stagehands union local in Hollywood had been controlled—and corrupted to its core—by Bioff, the union's Hollywood delegate and enforcer, and his longtime sidekick, George W. Browne, the president of the stagehands, known formally as the International Alliance of Theatrical Stage Employees and Moving Picture Machine Operators of the United States and Canada (IATSE). Its 125,000 members were an important element of the movie industry.

In early 1938 Joseph Schenck, the founder of 20th Century Fox, wrote a dummy check for $100,000 ($1.6 million in 1990 dollars) to Bioff. Bioff accumulated the $100,000 from his cut of various extortion schemes and wanted to hide it so he could buy a ranch. Bioff arranged with Schenck to have Schenck's nephew, Arthur Stebbins, give him a check for that amount. In return, Bioff gave Stebbins $100,000 in cash. On the books, the transaction appeared as a loan from Schenck, with Bioff giving him a note. The transaction came to light during hearings into labor conditions in the movie industry, which the California legislature conducted in 1938.

The hearings, conducted by a select labor committee, ended so abruptly it raised suspicions. As a result, the state attorney general's office convened a grand jury to take a further look. It found that Bioff had "helped terminate the hearings by paying a $5,000 [$75,000 in 1990 dollars] retainer to the law firm of Assembly Speaker William M. Jones, who controlled the labor committee budget." The Schenck-Bioff revelation forced Bioff to resign from the stagehands. However, he "kept his salary and continued to make key decisions" in the union.[2]

When Irey found out that Schenck didn't declare the $100,000 check as income, he assigned SIU Special Agents Alfred "Alf" Oftedal and Charles Emory to examine the circuitous money trail. They found the high-living Schenck had always operated in shady surroundings. In the 1920s he and his brother Nicholas ran amusements parks in Manhattan and New Jersey, "a business that required continuing relationships with the local mobs."[3] They leased the film concessions at the parks to Marcus Loew, the theater magnate. Later, the brothers went to work for Loew and, in the process, introduced Arnold Rothstein to Loew. Rothstein promptly became a major stockholder in Loew, Inc. In 1932 Schenck served on the board of the Agua Caliente Jockey Club, which oversaw operations at the Tijuana racetrack. To head the betting operations at the track, he brought in Zeke Caress. Caress worked for the notorious Guy McAfee, a leader of the Anglo crime syndicate in Los Angeles. In 1935 gamblers Al and Lou Wertheimer operated a casino in Schenck's Hollywood mansion. The place didn't "quite meet their requirements" as a gambling hall, so they knocked out a couple of walls.[4] When Schenck learned that Bioff was forced to leave the IATSE, he tried to assuage Willie's disappointment by giving him tickets for a cruise to Rio de Janeiro on the liner *Normandie*.

Schenck's background left many questions, but the case was still flimsy. The dummy check was an embarrassing scam more than it was a criminal act. The $100,000 transaction was "tinged with larceny," Irey cracked, but "as close to an honest transaction as Willie ever engaged in."[5] Alf Oftedal, however, found Schenck to be "an out and out tax cheater" who was practicing the "standard tricks of fake stock transactions and phony deductions."[6]

Since 20th Century Fox's financial operations were run out of Manhattan, the case against Schenck was brought in the Southern District of New York, where in June 1939, a federal grand jury indicted Schenck on charges of avoiding $412,000 ($6,592,000 in 1990 dollars) in taxes for the years 1935, 1936, and 1937. That was where the case was supposed to end. During their investigation, however, Oftedal and Emory began to uncover Bioff's associations and his dealings in the stagehands union. With that, things took on a criminal dimension.

■

It was 1932. Al Capone was in Alcatraz. An array of his former lieutenants, including Frank "The Enforcer" Nitti, Murray "The Camel" Humphrey, Tony "Joe Batters" Accardo, and Paul "The Waiter" Ricca (born Felice DeLucia, outside Naples), were now the powers in a reformed criminal combine that dominated Chicago's underworld. None would become as domineering a figure as Capone had, of course. All except Nitti (now back on the street after serving a stretch in Leavenworth for tax evasion) had escaped jail. The grouping, with the Sicilian-born Nitti as its titular head, was a unique mix of mafiosi and non-mafiosi. A number of its leaders were neither Sicilian nor Italian, unlike New York City's Five Mafia Families, but neither did it mean they weren't acceptable to the Sicilian brethren. All had taken away an important lesson from Capone: They weren't going to be his gaudy imitators. Stealth would be the name of the game. They ended brazen operations such as wide-open brothels but kept the strip joints. Moreover, led by Nitti, they broadened their criminal empire in a way Capone never tried. Capone clubbed and murdered his way into the local labor movement. The Nitti combine decided to club and murder its way into the national union scene. The first move they made was to take over the stagehands union—and Willie Bioff and George Browne turned out to be the perfect front men.

Bioff's life had been unsavory from the start. Born in 1900 in Odessa, Russia, he came to Chicago with his parents. At age twelve, he steered male clients to whoremaster Jack Zuta's brothels. At age twenty, he was jailed twice for pimping. After leaving jail the second time, Jerry Lahey, head of the Chicago Teamsters Union, brought him on as a $35-a-week ($665 in

1990 dollars) slugger. In the late 1920s Bioff met up with Browne, then the business agent for the 450-member Chicago Local 2 of the stagehands union in the American Federation of Labor. Browne, born in 1894 in Chicago, was six years older. He quit school at age twelve and was apprenticed to the property department of a vaudeville theater. The job put him into the stagehands union, where he stayed. In 1924 he was elected sixth vice president of the IATSE and had an office in Washington, though he kept his Local 2 post. Writer George Murray said, "Browne gave the appearance of a timid businessman but the appearance was deceptive." His past was as violent and unsavory as Bioff's.

According to Murray, Browne took over the local after beating up the previous business agent. Using a piece of pipe rolled up in a newspaper, he beat him unconscious, then "momentarily panicked" when he couldn't find water to douse him.[7] He grabbed a bottle of beer and dumped the contents in his face. Shocked by the icy brew, the man revived. Gathering the strength to stagger out of the union office, the business agent was never seen on the premises again.

On January 26, 1925, Browne was being driven in a car in suburban Melrose Park by his brother-in-law, Herbert C. Green. He told Green he had some business to take care of at a restaurant owned by Ralph Amore. They stopped at the place. Green waited in the car. Words were exchanged inside, and Green could hear gunfire. Browne was wounded in the buttocks. Amore was killed. The assailant wasn't arrested, but Browne knew him. After Browne left the hospital, the assailant was found dead. Later, Herbert Green decided to run against his brother-in-law for the post of business agent of Local 2. Browne asked him to withdraw, but Green refused. Then, Willie Bioff smashed his skull with a blackjack. Green withdrew.

■

How these two unsavory characters became thugs for a criminal combine is a squalid tale of chicanery, extortion, and greed, laced with murder. Their tale opens in Chicago in 1932, shortly after theater owners had cut the salaries of stagehands in Local 2. Browne demanded the owners reinstate the reduction and threatened to shut down a number of stage shows if they didn't. In a countermove, Barney Balaban, one of the theater owners, offered to contribute to a soup kitchen that Local 2 ran. Browne and Bioff leaped at the offer. Bioff later "testified with gusto" on what happened next:[8]

> I figured right then I might as well kill a sheep as a lamb. Barney turned out to be a lamb. When he agreed to our suggestion I knew we had him. I told him his contribution would have to be $50,000 [$605,000 in 1990 dollars] unless he wanted real trouble. By that I meant we would pull his projectionists out of the theaters. He was appalled, but we turned on the heat. He finally agreed to pay us $20,000 [$340,000 in 1990 dollars]. The restoration of the pay cut was forgotten. We were not interested in that then or at any other time. We didn't care whether wages were reduced or raised. We were interested only in getting the dough, and we didn't care how we got it.[9]

Bioff and Browne each took $8,000 ($136,000 in 1990 dollars) off the top and left $4,000 ($68,000 in 1990 dollars) for the soup kitchen. To celebrate, they threw a party at a nightclub owned by Nick Circella, a member of Nitti's combine. As Circella watched Browne and Bioff toss around cash at the party, he became curious—he already knew that Browne "owned" Local 2. Late in the evening, he and Frank Rio, an ex-Capone bodyguard and Al's cousin, sidled up to their table and began asking questions. All they got back from Browne and Bioff were blank stares. Word of the party immediately got back to Paul Ricca, who knew a ripe apple when he saw one.

Considered a "specialist in theatrical entertainment," Ricca once managed the Dante, a movie theater in Chicago's Little Italy and the World Playhouse Corporation on Michigan Avenue.[10] Circella knew the trade too. He and his brother, August, had operated burlesque houses on South State Street. Ricca already had a mean eye on the motion picture industry, then in its greatest era of expansion. The talkies had replaced silent movies. In Chicago, theaters were being opened almost every month. The next day Ricca had Frank Rio confront Browne. "Petrified," Browne quickly spilled the beans about the shakedown of Barney Balaban.[11]

A few days later Browne and Bioff were summoned to a meeting at the house of Harry Hochstein in suburban Riverside. Hochstein had been

Chicago's deputy city sealer under Daniel A. Serritella, who also became Republican committeeman in the First Ward, and as such Al Capone's "principal link to City Hall."[12] In the living room sat Frank Nitti, Paul Ricca, Louis "Little New York" Campagna, Frank Rio, and Nick Circella. Nitti and Rio did most of the talking, which dealt with Browne's chances to win the presidency of the IATSE at its convention in 1934. Earlier that year, he had run for the IATSE presidency and lost.

Observed Bioff, "They wanted to know where the weak spots were throughout the country that defeated Browne in his 1932 election, that they have connections that would make it possible for Browne to change those opposition delegations in his favor." Nitti said, according to Bioff, "We will take care of Jersey and New York; we will take care of Jersey through Longy Zwillman . . . that was his contact in Jersey. He would take care of New York through Lucky Luciano and Louie Buchalter; he would take care of Cleveland through Al Paliese; he would take care of St. Louis through a Johnnie Dougherty. That is the best I can remember. And Kansas City."

There was a second meeting of the same group at Hochstein's house, and this time Louis Lepke Buchalter attended. The gathering was designed to shore up New York support for the election of Browne. "Buchalter was ordered by Nitti to contact Luciano and deliver a message to him," Bioff recalled. "That message was Local 306 was to go for George Browne, and Buchalter answered, 'I don't have to see Lucky on that matter, I will handle this myself. I will also see Kaufman and Longy from New Jersey and see to it that Longy Zwillman delivers Kaufman.'"[13] Louis Kaufman was the business agent for Local 244 in Newark.

Over the next two years the Chicago brethren hatched the takeover of the International Alliance of Theatrical Stage Employees and Moving Picture Machine Operators of the United States and Canada. At the time, most film studios operated their own chain of theaters. By controlling the projectionists, the stagehands union held the fate of most of the country's movie houses. Like imperious Roman emperors, Nitti and Ricca knew the thugs to enlist, the bases to touch, and, using Browne and Bioff as front men, how to tap the field. And as dead-on racketeers, they were ready to threaten, beat up, or kill anyone who got in their way. They devised a nimble and successful strategy.

Watching this from the sidelines was a key figure: Thomas E. "Tommy" Maloy, the longtime business agent for AFL Local 110 of the Motion Pictures Operators Union in Chicago. According to George Murray, Frank Nitti had been working with Tommy Maloy for years. Born in 1893, the year of the World's Columbian Exposition, Maloy took over the local in 1920 and, drawing an annual salary of $25,000 ($425,000 in 1990 dollars), ran "to a great extent, the entire motion picture industry in Chicago—with brass knuckles and blackjacks, blazing pistols and blasting dynamite."[14] His chief lieutenant, Dr. Emmett C. Quinn, a dentist, carried a union card but had never operated a movie projection machine in his life. The dentist was also on the payroll of the Chicago Theater, the largest in the Loop, as a "ghost" at $130 a week ($2,210 in 1990 dollars).[15]

No projectionist got into a movie house without Tommy Maloy's say. He established the rule that two projectionists had to be in the booth. But Barney Balaban and his theater chain didn't have to follow that rule. Balaban paid Maloy $150 ($2,400 in 1990 dollars) a week for years to have only one projectionist in each booth. Maloy also ran an illegal gambling parlor in the back of the union offices in a building shared by the Teamsters and the theater janitors' union—and he had the right connections. His brother Joe worked at the city hall office that handed out licenses to prospective motion picture machine operators—those, of course, who got the nod from Tommy.

In July 1931 a grand jury indicted Tommy, his brother Joe, and four others, charging them with restraint of trade, obtaining money under false pretenses, and various other counts. That fall Assistant State's Attorney Charles E. Lounsbury asked for dismissal of the criminal indictment. Maloy had spread around cash in all the right places, including $5,000 ($80,000 in 1990 dollars) to Mayor Anton "Tony" Cermak, who ran the city in the same way Big Bill Thompson did. Capone was gone, replaced by a newly structured criminal-political alliance. Complaining of Maloy's dictatorship, eight rebel projectionists sued for redress in the state court. Maloy had them fired from their jobs—and the courts upheld his right to fire them.

As Nitti and his combine continued to set the scene for Browne's take-over of the IATSE, a hitch occurred. Dwight Green, the assistant U.S. attorney who had helped in the Capone case, was tracking Maloy's money trail. The shoe dropped on May 6, 1933, when it was publicly disclosed that Maloy was under federal tax scrutiny.

Meanwhile, the combine was spreading the word on Browne's candidacy to stagehands locals throughout the Midwest. In New York City, Lepke handled his end by telling the leadership of Local 306 (the New York projectionists) how to vote. Lepke had told Nitti, "When you're talking to me it's just like you were talking to Lucky [Luciano] himself. [He knows] Harry Sherman, president of Local 306 in New York. The election is in the bag."[16]

Before the convention, the Nitti combine also met both Maloy and Browne in Maloy's office at different times to plan strategy. At the convention, Maloy would run for first vice president of the stagehands union. In June 1934 the IATSE held its national convention in Louisville, Kentucky, and Browne assumed the presidency without a hitch. Maloy took the vice presidency. They had no opposition—Lepke's sluggers had monitored the convention vote. Said George Murray, "There appeared to be more gunmen in the auditorium than voting delegates."[17] The combine, incidentally, billed the IATSE for the traveling expenses and hotel rooms of the sluggers sent to the convention—and Browne ordered their bills to be paid. Browne began drawing a salary of $25,000 ($400,000 in 1990 dollars), in addition to keeping his pay as Local 2's business agent at $250 a week ($4,000 in 1990 dollars). He brought on Bioff as his "personal representative" at $22,000 annually ($352,000 in 1990 dollars).

The extortion scheme entered its final stage at a strategy session in early 1935 at the Capone mansion in Miami, hosted by Ralph and attended by Nitti, Ricca, Campagna, Charles "Cherry Nose" Gioe, Phil D'Andrea, Francis Maritote, Bioff and Browne, Charles Fischetti, Ralph Pierce, and John Roselli, the combine's man in the Hollywood movie colony. One important person not there: Tommy Maloy. He wanted no part of the shakedown, but he also faced other trouble. On January 25, 1935, a federal grand jury charged him with failing to report $350,000 ($5,950,000 in 1990 dollars) of his income in the years 1929 to 1932, and he had also failed to report $81,000 ($1,377,000 in 1990 dollars) in income taxes due on this unreported income. Maloy's troubles were not in the combine's interests. On February 4, two days after his arraignment, Maloy was driving with Dr. Quinn on Lake Shore Drive heading for the union office. A car drew up alongside, a sawed-off shotgun appeared out of the window, and the second blast struck Maloy in the head. To make certain, the gunman also used a .45-caliber automatic pistol to put two more slugs in Maloy. Quinn wasn't hit.

George Browne, appointed caretaker of Local 110, was a pallbearer at Maloy's funeral. As soon as the funeral was over, he went directly to Maloy's office and announced that "all special permits issued by Tommy Maloy were rescinded and that anybody who was working as a projectionist in any movie theater in the Chicago area could continue to do so. This pulled the teeth of [those rebel projectionists]."

John Roselli had flown in from Los Angeles for the funeral, where Bioff and Browne met him for the first time. Born Filippo Sacco in Naples in 1885, he took his name from Cosimo Rosselli, the fifteenth-century painter who contributed frescoes of Moses on Mt. Sinai and the Last Supper to the walls of the Sistine Chapel. He immigrated in 1911, worked a short time for Johnny Torrio, and fell victim to tuberculosis. Requiring a sunny clime, he struck out for Los Angeles in 1924 and went to work as a slugger for Anthony Cornero Stralla, a flamboyant figure who wore Stetson hats and pearl-colored gloves and who was known in the Los Angeles press as "King of the Western Rumrunners."[18]

Roselli's rise paralleled the rise of organized crime in Los Angeles. He landed in the city's East Side, an immigrant ghetto that included a tight-knit Italian community where mafiosi had just begun to achieve standing. Its most prominent figure was Jack Dragna, born Anthony Rizzotti in 1891 in Corleone, Sicily. Dragna stepped onto Ellis Island at age seven. At age twenty-four, after serving a three-year sentence in San Quentin for extortion, he learned the obvious: racketeering was safer and more profitable. In the 1920s he established the Italian Protective League, enriching its status by locating it on the eleventh floor of the Law Building in downtown Los Angeles. And, though a police report pointed out that the league was "strictly a muscle outfit, preying on various business activities," Dragna never went to jail again and became the "Al Capone of Los Angeles."[19]

The Los Angeles underworld during Prohibition consisted of an unthrottled syndicate of gamblers, rum-running bootleggers, and vice operators—mostly homegrown Anglos who enjoyed success through their alliance to city hall and police connections. In the late 1920s the Dragna-Cornero-Roselli combine moved against the entrenched Anglo syndicate that had a hold on the floating casinos operating beyond the three-mile limit off Long Beach and Santa Monica. It was Roselli who went aboard the *Monfalcone*, a gambling ship off Long Beach, to tell Tutor Sherer, a syndicate member and partner in the *Monfalcone*, that Dragna wanted all profits split 50-50. Sherer and the syndicate didn't take his visit lightly. A lengthy gang war, which involved the burning of gambling ships, ensued and eventually ended in a standoff. But the Dragna-Cornero-Roselli combine was now established. Los Angeles's underworld would never be the same.

By the time of the 1935 gathering in Miami, Roselli had made a remarkable metamorphosis, turning from a tubercular, thin-faced thug with a long arrest sheet into a genial, debonair, and well-do-do gentleman-racketeer about town. He was a regular at the Olympic Auditorium, a modern boxing arena at the center of the city's sporting life. He had bought into a Sunset Strip nightclub. He lived at a stylish bungalow at the Garden of Allah, a Byzantine estate owned by a silent film star, and boasted a sixty-foot swimming pool and exotic gardens. He was the primary business representative in Los Angeles for Moe Annenberg's Nationwide News Service. When Benny Siegel arrived in town, Roselli befriended him and provided introductions to Hollywood's inner circle. Roselli was, in effect, the LA underworld's secretary of state. And, like Arnold Rothstein, he worked both sides of the labor street. In July 1933 he helped break a strike by the stagehands union against the movie moguls. Hired by Pat Casey, who handled labor liaison for the Association of Motion Pictures Producers, he enlisted a goon squad that made certain union laborers moved "efficiently across the picket lines." His "smooth management"[20] of a situation that could have easily turned violent won him "enhanced status in the film industry."

Roselli, preparing the combine's move to take over the IATSE, gave the Miami gathering a briefing on the film colony. The two Schenck brothers, both born in Russia, were among the top moguls in the movie colony. Joseph's younger brother, Nicholas, was considered "the most powerful motion picture executive in the world." He headed Loew's, Inc., a holding company of which Metro-Goldwyn-Mayer was a subsidiary. Each film studio did not have to negotiate individually; the film industry signed industry-wide contacts with four of the AFL's major unions: the International Brotherhood of Electricians, the International Brotherhood of Carpenters, the International Brotherhood of Teamsters, and the American Federation of Musicians, through what was termed "the Basic Agreement." The IATSE wasn't a part of this arrangement because it had jurisdiction in the exhibiting end of the industry, not in the production side—in effect, it had no voice in the industry and would have to become a part of the Basic Agreement.

Nitti put his finger on the problem: "What about the studio technicians corresponding to the stagehands? If they're not in Browne's union who has got them?"

Roselli replied, "Some are organized in the carpenters' union and some in the electricians."

"Okay, that's what we need to know," said Nitti. He told Browne to write to the unions and tell them he wanted those technicians returned to the IATSE's jurisdiction. Nitti went on, You go "see Nick Schenck and demand that the IATSE sit at the bargaining table with the other unions. No reason why Browne's International should not be a party to the Basic Agreement. How does that sound?"

Everyone agreed that it sounded fine. Bioff went back to Los Angeles with Roselli and began working to take control of the IATSE locals and to explain the changes that were coming with the Basic Agreement. If anyone rebelled, Roselli would supply the muscle. But none of the locals balked. It took Bioff only two weeks to establish a firm grip. For his part, Browne met with the heads of the international unions. They didn't like the idea of the stagehands becoming a part of the Basic Agreement, but Browne told them "he had no room to maneuver." They went along but still couldn't understand Browne's "adamant attitude." Browne wasn't about to explain.

■

On April 15, 1935, Browne and Bioff showed up in Nicholas Schenck's office in Manhattan for the first time. Browne told him, "When you sign the Basic Agreement next year, you'll have to sign with the IATSE as well as the other unions." A placid Schenck asked questions and heard them out before he shook hands with them as he showed them to the door. Nothing happened until September, when Schenck learned that the IATSE was threatening a strike that would paralyze film production. Browne told one of Schenck's aides he could head off the walkout for a payment of $100,000 ($1.6 million in 1990 dollars). Schenck told his aide, "Pay the money."[21] Half of it went to Nitti.

Thus began the IATSE's shakedown of the movie colony. Exhibitors and theater owners in Chicago and New York City were already being extorted. Browne and Bioff shook down Chicago film exhibitors for $150,000 ($2.4 million in 1990 dollars), New York film exhibitors for $150,000, and Hollywood's film producers for $100,000 and shared half of their take with the Chicago combine. The big movie studios were the final obstacle, but they didn't prove to be too difficult once they were threatened with strikes.

The Chicago combine adapted a variation on Dutch Schultz's methods in New York City's restaurant trade. Schultz used confederates to control the waiters' locals and charged restaurants fees to join his "association" under the pretext of maintaining labor peace. But this time it was nationwide. Browne and Bioff began installing their confederates in the stagehand locals, who in turn began to siphon off dues and extort payments under the pretext of maintaining labor peace. Intimidation was one of the cards. In Newark, Louis Kaufman, business agent of Local 244, shook down Warner Bros. Studios, according to Irey, "by having one of his attendant goons lay a loaded pistol on the desk of the Warner representative."[22]

Among the housekeeping moves, Nitti put in his stooge to handle the IATSE's books. His name was Isadore "Izzy" Zevlin; he was to be paid $75 ($1,200 in 1990 dollars) a week. "Izzy has forgot more about accounting than those Internal Revenue guys ever knew," Nitti said. When Browne asked Nitti how Zevlin could qualify for union employment, Nitti told him to run a classified ad in the newspapers, seeking a man "with exactly Izzy Zevlin's qualifications."[23] Browne kept copies of the newspaper ads in his files; if he was ever asked how they had met, he could produce the ads.

■

When Joseph Schenck went on trial at the U.S. courthouse in Manhattan's Foley Square on March 4, 1941, it was the first of three separate trials arising from the IATSE extortion. The three proceedings would take nearly three years. In each case, the defendants were convicted. When Schenck's trial opened, little was known about the Chicago combine's machinations over the last nine years. The SIU's Alf Oftedal and Charles Emory, in their investigation up until Schenck's trial, had dug up Bioff's dealings, but what they found was just the tip of the iceberg. After Schenck's trial, the iceberg began melting, and the SIU was there, to the last drop.

At the Southern District, Mathias F. Correa had just replaced John T. Cahill as the U.S. attorney. The handsome, dark-haired, thirty-year-old Correa had been Cahill's chief assistant and was a year younger than Tom Dewey when Dewey was elevated to the office. Cahill had brought the indictment against Schenck and was leaving in mixed glory. In an unprecedented case, he had just successfully prosecuted the once-invincible Martin T. Manton, chief judge of the Second District U.S. Court of Appeals, and won a conviction on conspiracy to obstruct the administration of justice and to defraud the United States. He received a two-year sentence and a fine of $10,000 ($150,000 in 1990 dollars). Judges had gone to prison, but never one so close to the top of the federal judiciary. In the 1930s Al Capone, Charlie Luciano, and Tammany boss Jimmy Hines had gone down, but not the tenth-ranking justice in the United States. Manton, in the public esteem, was subordinate only to the nine justices of the Supreme Court. He was also known as "Preying Manton." Tom Dewey, then the chief assistant in the Southern District, believed Manton was corrupt, "but I could not prove it."[24] Manton had raised Dewey's ire by releasing Louis Lepke and Jacob Gurrah on bail back in 1935 following their indictment—after personally telling Dewey that he wouldn't. Two of Manton's actions on the bench: accepting $77,000 ($1,155,000 in 1990 dollars) from a go-between for Archie M. Andrews, whose Packard razor patent suit he helped decide in Andrews's favor; and receiving $232,900 ($3,489,000 in 1990 dollars) out of $250,000 ($4,750,000 in 1990 dollars) lent through attorney Louis S. Levy to Manton's partner by the advertising firm, Lord and Thomas, whose client (and Levy's) was American Tobacco Co., for whom Manton wrote the winning opinion in a $10 million ($60 million in 1990 dollars) stockholder suit.

Mathias Correa personally prosecuted Schenck and gave him a break. The figure in the indictment that he had evaded $412,000 ($6,189,000 in 1990 dollars) in taxes was revised to $253,692 ($3,805,380 in 1990 dollars) and kept to the years 1935 and 1936, not 1937 too. Schenck expected that he would get a year's sentence, he would ask for probation, and then everything would end. "Income tax problems are always complex and subject to dispute," said Schenck. "The charges made against me are grossly unfair. Two of the best auditing firms in New York, Boyce, Hughes, and Farrell, and Webster, Horne, and Blanchard, after a recent audit, have advised me that for the years in question I have overpaid rather than underpaid my taxes."[25] His defense counsels maintained he actually paid $165,000 ($2,475,000 in 1990 dollars) too much in taxes. Charlie Chaplin, in a dark business suit, took the stand on Schenck's behalf, saying he had known him since coming to the United States in 1914 and their relationship was "one of great friendship."[26] Composer Irving Berlin; Phil S. Gibson, the chief justice of the Supreme Court of California; Will Hays, the movie industry czar; and James Farley, the former postmaster general, also spoke for the movie mogul.

The evidence, however, was too damning. Correa produced telegrams that Schenck had won $25,000 ($400,000 in 1990 dollars) in bets on the 1936 presidential election and warned that he "wanted his winnings in cash."[27] Correa used irony effectively, noting that Schenck wasn't under "dire economic necessity" to evade the law, pointing out that in 1935–1936, he earned $930,787 ($14,892,592 in 1990 dollars). Outside the courtroom, Schenck daily remained jaunty and smiled for the RKO Pathe cameras. These were Depression times. The show of wealth, the carefree attitude, his gambling winnings, the testimony that two hoods operated a casino in his mansion (which Schenck professed to know nothing about) seemed out of place.

His brother Nicholas was in the courtroom when the jury quickly returned a guilty verdict on April 17, 1941. Six days later, using Correa's recommendation, U.S. Circuit Judge Grover M. Moscowitz sentenced Schenck to three years in prison—jarring him out of his jauntiness. At age sixty-three, he obviously dreaded trading his fedora and French cuffs for stripes. Before a month passed, he had struck a deal for leniency and began to spill what he knew about Bioff and Browne.

In early May, Correa had Boris Kostelanetz, an assistant U.S. attorney who helped prosecute the case, bring Schenck before a federal grand jury. On May 23 Bioff, Browne, and Nick Circella—who was picked to take Maloy's place at Local 110—were indicted for violation of provisions of the federal anti-racketeering law and for tax evasion. It had all started at the Browne-Bioff celebration at Circella's nightclub.

Though the SIU's role in the case ended with Schenck's conviction, Alf Oftedal continued to work on the case because J. Edgar Hoover's FBI couldn't. Before Irey's investigation of Joseph Schenck started, the actor Robert Montgomery, president of the Screen Actors Guild, had become suspicious of Bioff's activities. He got the approval of the guild's board of directors for $5,000 ($70,000 in 1990 dollars) to hire two ex-FBI agents to investigate Bioff. They came up with incriminating evidence against Bioff, but neither the Justice Department nor the FBI acted on it. Aware of the demands that World War II was placing on the FBI, Irey gave Hoover's foot-dragging the benefit of the doubt, explaining that the agency "had a lot of other problems ferreting out Jap and Nazi spies." After Schenck implicated Bioff and Browne, U.S. Attorney General Francis Biddle asked Treasury Secretary Morgenthau to keep Oftedal at the Southern District to assist in putting together the case against Bioff and Browne. Said Kostelanetz of Oftedal, "Alf is the kind of guy you want to make executor of your will after meeting him once."[28]

■

The trial of Bioff and Browne began in early October 1941, and the revelations never stopped. The two, with Nitti looking over their shoulders, had been manhandling the movie moguls for years. Nicholas Schenck spent the entire day of October 9 on the stand. He told how, after Browne and Bioff, in a show of power, carried out work stoppages in theaters in Chicago and various suburbs in December 1935, movie executives caved to their demands that the IATSE take over all of the jobs—sound technicians, lab technicians, and studio mechanics—in the production end of movie-making. The IATSE already controlled the stagehands, projectionists, ushers, porters, and hatcheck concessionaires in theaters from coast to coast. The studios also signed a closed-shop agreement with the IATSE. Then, the following April, Browne and Bioff came to his Manhattan office, Schenck testified, and said they wanted $50,000 ($800,000 in 1990 dollars) a year from each of the big film-producing companies—MGM, Warner Bros., Paramount, and 20th Century Fox—and $25,000 ($400,000 in 1990 dollars) from each of the smaller ones, including Columbia and RKO. Schenck said the studios agreed on April 21, 1936, to pay. Schenck described the moment. Two days later he and Sidney R. Kent, president of 20th Century Fox (of which Joseph Schenck was board chairman), met Browne and Bioff in a room at the Waldorf-Astoria Hotel in Manhattan.

"I got the money from David Bernstein, treasurer of Loew's. All in large bills. Fifty thousand dollars in United States currency," Schenck testified. "There were twin beds right there in the hotel room. I put my money on the right-hand-side bed. Bioff took half the money and started counting it. He put the other half on the other bed and told Browne to count it. They said it was correct, fifty thousand dollars." Then Schenck walked to a window and smoked a cigarette while Kent went through the same procedure with the $50,000 ($750,000 in 1990 dollars) he had brought.

Later, when Schenck was juggling the studio's books and started worrying that stockholders would learn where the money was going, he and Bioff arranged "a way to disguise the payments." Bioff was to receive "commissions" amounting to $50,000 ($800,000 in 1990 dollars) a year on the sale of raw film to MGM. Schenck quoted Bioff on this "subagent" arrangement: "You'll have to pay enough additional so the subagent can pay income tax on the money supposedly earned. I want my fifty thousand net."

Over at Warner Bros. Studios, which had also coughed up $50,000, Harry M. Warner ran the company with his better-known brother Jack. Harry testified that just before Christmas in 1937, Bioff pressed him for an "unscheduled $20,000" ($300,000 in 1990 dollars) in cash because "the boys in Chicago are insisting on more money." Harry also testified that the studio "kited expense accounts" to cover the cash payments made to Browne and Bioff.[29]

On Thursday, November 6, the jury of twelve men got the case at 3:47 p.m. At 5:45 the jury announced it had reached a verdict: guilty. Six days later U.S. District Judge John C. Knox sentenced Browne to eight years, sentenced Bioff to ten years, and imposed $20,000 ($300,000 in 1990 dollars) fines on each. Then, Knox tacked on another sentence of ten years, execution of which was to be suspended provided the fines were paid. Circella didn't go to trial. He had disappeared.

The indictment of Bioff, Browne, and Circella back in May had placed Nitti, Ricca, and the combine in jeopardy. Johnny Roselli, in particular, saw trouble looming. After Schenck talked, Roselli was called before a federal grand jury in Manhattan—and gave perjured testimony. He told jurors that his only business transactions with Bioff involved insurance matters. As Chicago's man in Los Angeles, no one was more deeply involved or better knew Bioff's dealings. Roselli's name hadn't been included in the indictments of Bioff, Browne, and Circella. Still he was worrying about the inevitable. The day after the indictment he went to Bioff's house to "lay out an initial defense strategy."[30] Two days after that Bioff met with attorney Sidney R. Korshak at the Ambassador Hotel in Los Angeles. Korshak talked strategy with Bioff, who paid him $15,000 ($210,000 in 1990 dollars) to finance his legal expenses. The shrewd and secretive Korshak, trusted implicitly by the Chicago brethren, would become better known in the years to come.

Since Schenck's trial, Correa and Kostelanetz had been putting the bits and pieces together on the IATSE's dealings with the film studios. Bioff and Browne had been shaking the moguls down, the two prosecutors now understood, but the two weren't the only principals in the conspiracy. Harry Warner's comment about the "boys in Chicago" confirmed that. Kostelanetz noted that Bioff showed signs of being a loose cannon. Before his trial, Bioff was extradited from California to Chicago to serve a six-month term for pandering. While in jail, he told Louis "Little New York" Campagna, formerly Capone's personal bodyguard and one of the most notorious of Chicago's enforcers, that "he was resigning." Campagna fixed a cold eye on him and said, "Whoever quits us, quits feet first." This hushed up any more thoughts from Willie about leaving.

After Bioff and Browne went to prison in April 1942, Correa assigned Kostelanetz full-time to the case. Kostelanetz carried twin six-shooters. He was also trained in accounting. Born in St. Petersburg, Russia, he arrived at Ellis Island in the spring of 1920 by way of Istanbul. At age twenty-five in 1936 he got his law degree magna cum laude at St. John's University. Kostelanetz went to Chicago to grill Isadore Zevin before a federal grand jury. Zevin was the accountant Nitti had put in Browne's office to watch over the IATSE books. In October 1942 Zevin was indicted for perjury—after his testimony and the IATSE's financial records didn't add up.

Meanwhile, Alf Oftedal had been making regular visits to Bioff and Browne at the federal penitentiary in Minnesota. He coaxed, cajoled, questioned, listened, and, in every other way possible, tried to reduce their degree of separation. Late in 1942 he notified Kostelanetz that they were ready to talk. Kostelanetz had them brought to Manhattan's House of Detention. About this time Nick Circella showed signs of talking. He had been apprehended in December 1941 and, after refusing to talk, got quick justice. He pleaded guilty to racketeering charges and was sentenced to eight years in prison. Frustrated that the Chicago brethren had ignored him and reaching the conclusion that he was going to sit in a cell for a long time, he began to waver. "He never agreed to spell everything out for us, but there was a measure of cooperation," said Kostelanetz.[31]

That was enough for Ricca. Sometime in January 1943 word of Circella's "cooperation" got back to Chicago. The brethren left a terrifying warning. Circella's longtime mistress was a thirty-four-year-old "beautiful blond card dealer" named Estelle Carey.[32] On the afternoon of February 2, 1943, firefighters found her body in her charred apartment. She had been beaten with a blunt object, slashed in the face, stabbed, and set afire. A chair was used to pin her shoulders to the floor of the dining room. Upon learning of her savage murder, Circella "bit his lips, then shook his head slowly, and said: 'I don't know nothing about nothing.'" But Bioff didn't. Angry at what happened, he told Kostelanetz, "Whataya want to know, Boris?"[33]

On March 1, 1943, a federal grand jury in Chicago began hearing testimony on the IATSE-Hollywood-Chicago conspiracy. Bioff spilled enough evidence about the Hollywood plot to fill a book the size of *Gone with the Wind*. He even told about attending a dinner back in 1933 at the Casino de Paris restaurant in Manhattan, where he met Charlie Luciano, Frank Costello, and Jack Dragna—obviously involved in coast-to-coast planning. On March 19 indictments citing violations of the anti-racketeering statute were handed down in Manhattan's Southern District against Paul Ricca, Frank Nitti, Charles "Cherry Nose" Gioe, Phil D'Andrea, Louis Campagna, Francis Maritote, Ralph Pierce, and U.S. Army Private Johnny Rosselli. Rosselli arrived from Fort McPherson in Atlanta and took up temporary residence at the Waldorf-Astoria. He had enlisted in December 1942 at thirty-seven and passed the physical. He appeared in uniform at his arraignment in Manhattan. Later that day Frank Nitti was found dead alongside railroad tracks in a Chicago suburb. He had shot himself. Before the trial began, the court dismissed the indictment against Ralph Pierce, calling it too flimsy. Pierce, arrested for the murder of Tom Maloy but never tried, would later become an underboss to a yet-unknown underworld figure, Sam Giancana.

Mathias Correa had gone into the U.S. Army. On June 16 Attorney General Francis Biddle designated Kostelanetz a special assistant attorney general to direct the prosecution of the Chicago combine. It was his thirty-second birthday. With Bioff as the prosecution's principal witness, the trial took the rest of the year. Under Kostelanetz's questioning, Bioff laid out the extortion scheme in precise fashion. Isadore Zevin had kept very sweet books. Members of the stagehands union had to pay 2 percent of their salaries from July 15, 1935, to February 29, 1936, and from February 20, 1937, to December 11, 1937. The $1.5 million ($22.5 million in 1990 dollars) raised from these surcharges was supposed to pay forty or fifty union representatives $110 ($1,650 in 1990 dollars) a week. But the representatives, after cashing checks for that sum, kept only $10 ($150 in 1990 dollars) and sent $100 ($1,500 in 1990 dollars) to Zevin, the fund's custodian in Chicago. Of the entire $1.5 million, $250,000 ($3,750,000 in 1990 dollars) failed to fall into the hands of Ricca and the combine.

Three days before Christmas in 1943, a jury of nine women and three men found Ricca, Rosselli, Gioe, D'Andrea, Campagna, Maritote, and Louis Kaufman of the Newark stagehands local guilty of extorting more than $1 million ($12 million in 1990 dollars) from the motion picture industry. On December 29 U.S. Circuit Judge John Bright sentenced each of the seven defendants to ten years in prison.

When Elmer Irey initiated the investigation of Joseph Schenck in late 1938, he had little inkling of what he had on his hands. Neither did Mathias Correa nor Boris Kostelanetz. Five years later, on the day Ricca and the others were found guilty, Kostelanetz had pegged it succinctly: the cream of Chicago's underworld had been brought down—an unmatched achievement for Irey and his SIU.

21. EPILOGUE

In 1943 Elmer Irey suffered a serious heart attack. Since September 1937, he also had been serving as the coordinator of the Treasury's enforcement agencies, with the duty of overseeing the activities of the Secret Service, Coast Guard, Customs Service, Bureau of Narcotics, and the Alcohol Tax Unit. On September 1, 1946, he retired. Two years later, on July 19, 1948, he died at his home in Shady Side, Maryland, overlooking the Chesapeake Bay. At his bedside late on that Monday afternoon were his wife and his oldest son, Hugh, a thirty-four-year-old physician who was assisting his father's doctor. Irey was only sixty years old, but a series of heart attacks along with a family history of diabetes shortened his life. He left his wife, Marguerite, to whom he had been married for thirty-six years, and two sons, both physicians, and their families.

A sterling example of the selfless government servant and an incorruptible giant among his law enforcement contemporaries, Irey received a five-inch obituary stuck on page twenty-four of the next morning's *New York Times*. The newspaper simply ran the Associated Press report of Irey's death, blithely ignoring the accomplishments of a rare individual.

Irey was taken back to Washington, where the Treasury didn't give his passing any special attention. His funeral, at the Hines Funeral Home, was attended by many of his old friends, particularly those in government. Hugh remembers the circumstances of that day: "I was confined with my family and didn't see a lot of the people who attended."[1] One of those who did not attend was J. Edgar Hoover. The family received letters of condolences from some officials at the Treasury.

When Irey retired in 1946, his health was not good. He spent much of the next two years at a stucco bungalow he bought for $4,000 ($44,000 in 1990 dollars) in Sarasota, Florida, penning his memoir with a freelance writer, William J. Slocum. His memoir dealt with the key cases he had helped solve during his twenty-seven-year career at the Treasury. He had spent the last two years of that period coordinating the work of all the law enforcement branches at the Treasury, which had more than any other agency.

His achievements in helping to bring down a wildly different but corrupt grouping of silky public figures who placed themselves above the law will never be matched. He started with a force of 100 special agents in 1919–1920 that by 1940 numbered 245. Interestingly, Irey regularly received mail from people driven to disclose on those who lied to the tax collector—to the extent that he came to believe that this "common report" was the "best tipster." This led him to believe that "people who cheat the government are not likely to stop there; they go on and cheat their partners and their helpers, and these victims being human, get square by turning them in."[2] His record was quiet testimony to the fact that he got the job done when others failed. Malachi Harney, an Irey aide who had a forty-year career at the Treasury, called him "the greatest cop of the century." By comparison, Harney described J. Edgar Hoover as "a very astute empire builder."

Irey reaffirmed many times in his criminal investigations that justice was blind, and the wealthy and powerful who violated the law should be dealt with like ordinary citizens. He lived in an era when justice was very measured. The leading figures in the criminal-political alliances of the 1920s, 1930s, and 1940s could not be brought down through ordinary criminal laws—only through tax statutes. In the case for history, it will be Irey, not J. Edgar Hoover, who will be ranked as the greatest law enforcement figure of the twentieth century. Over three decades, Irey put up with

Hoover's stealthy ways, particularly the FBI director's style of grabbing un-earned credit while seeking to avoid blame under any circumstances. In his memoir, the closest Irey came to settling some old scores with Hoover capsules one of the FBI director's characteristic failings. In a brief episode in the chapter on Al Capone, Irey reveals why the Treasury and not the FBI was picked to go after the nation's biggest racketeer. It is his only comment on the public record about Hoover, and it was still indirect.

Irey wrote that when he learned from Secretary of the Treasury Andrew Mellon's "own grim lips one morning" that he was being given the assign-ment to get Capone, he "couldn't help wondering why a Treasury Depart-ment Unit charged with fighting tax, customs, and narcotics frauds should be assigned to nab a murderer, a gambler, a whoremonger and a bootleg-ger." After Mellon told Irey that the U.S. attorney in Chicago thought his unit had done a "grand job" in gathering evidence on Al's brother, Ralph, and thought "maybe you can do it on Al," Irey said, "It all became clear. Justice was willing to prosecute (by law nobody else could) but in case of failure Treasury would have to take blame, although Justice had its own investigative agents, the famous F.B.I."

Irey's publisher, Simon & Schuster, planned to publish the book, titled *The Tax Dodgers*, at Christmas 1948. Irey and William Slocum had finished writing and editing it. Consisting of chapter-by-chapter accounts of Irey's biggest cases, it was ready to go when Irey died in mid-summer. That was when trouble began.[3]

One of the chapters dealt with Moses Annenberg. Irey's memories were still fresh about Annenberg, who had a truly Midas touch and whose racketeering ways could never quite let him become the respected news-paper publisher he wanted to be. Upon Irey's death, however, Simon & Schuster told Slocum that it wanted the chapter on Annenberg taken out of the book—or it wouldn't be published. In the chapter, Irey and Slocum detailed how Treasury agents had spent four years gathering evidence on Annenberg's criminal fraud involving his vast holdings.

Slocum went to see Hugh Irey, who was then practicing medicine in Baltimore, to tell him Simon & Schuster wouldn't publish the book unless the chapter on Annenberg was removed. "I said I will not authorize it,"

Hugh Irey recalled. "I said my father would not authorize it, so I won't. Slocum said, 'Okay, then I'll have to look around.' He finally found this small publishing outfit, Greenberg, who said they would publish it."[4]

Describing the incident for the first time publicly in April 1991, forty-three years after it happened, Hugh Irey, then seventy-seven years old, told the author that Simon & Schuster applied pressure to get the book blacklisted in stores. "Simon & Schuster went out of their way to jeopardize the distribution of the book and keep it very, very limited," Hugh said. "They wouldn't let it go into certain bookstores."

The attempt to have the Annenberg episode erased from Irey's book can be circumstantially traced to Walter Annenberg and his steely zeal to rehabilitate the family name following the imprisonment of his father, Moses. Since Simon & Schuster today maintains that it has no record of a book contract with Irey, the evidence that outside interference occurred cannot be substantiated. But once Walter's role is put in perspective, it is clear he worked diligently to make certain that recollections about his racketeering father—such as Irey described in his memoir—ought not to see the light of day.

Walter was thirty-two years old when the father he adored, and who doted on him as a child and teenager, was sent to federal prison. During the trial, Walter was always at his father's side. After Moses was sentenced, Walter became "desolate and inconsolable."[5] Weymouth Kirkland, Moses's lawyer, maintained that Moses pleaded guilty on the condition that no government charges would be lodged against Walter. Even with the guilty plea, Walter "convinced himself that his father had only been as guilty as the corner grocer who had dipped into the till to pay for what he wanted."[6] He spent the rest of his life trying to live down the shame of that turbulent time.

The anxiety-ridden son faced two overriding challenges: one, to improve on his father's business legacy; the other, to right his father's scarred image. Walter grew into a successful businessman who took the publishing entity he had inherited intact from his father, Triangle Publications, and turned it into an even more successful and bigger empire, while at the same time getting rid of any of the eighty-odd companies in the Triangle grouping that appeared at all shady. In 1944 he started *Seventeen*, a highly successful magazine for teenagers, and in 1953 he started *TV Guide*, which attained the largest circulation of any publication in the world (twenty million copies) and earned him a profit of $50 million a year.

Along the way, Walter became one of the nation's richest and most private men. He owned newspapers, magazines, and television and radio stations, which made him an influential figure in the Eastern publications and media establishment. Simon & Schuster, incidentally, was an important part of the same establishment. At every step along that way, Walter attempted to broker the past about his father, starting with the parole board that freed his father from Lewisburg twenty-three months after his imprisonment. Upon his release in June 1942, Moses was sixty-four but looked eighty-four. He left prison in a wheelchair and died five weeks later. When Moses was on his deathbed, Walter, wanting them "to share in the guilt of his father's imprisonment," wrote to each member of the parole board to remind them that he had been warning them for two years that his father was a sick man.[7] In 1946, when FBI Special Agent L. V. Boardman visited Walter as part of an investigation into the shooting of James M. Ragen, a former associate of Moses, Boardman was struck at how Walter was "still preoccupied" with the way the authorities had treated his father.[8]

As publisher of the *Philadelphia Inquirer*, Walter regularly ordered names to be deleted from the newspaper's pages. This is a standard practice of all publishers and sometimes may be for legitimate cause. In Walter's case, one name happened to be an old enemy of his father's—Albert Greenfield, a Philadelphia banker who had once likened Moses to Adolf Hitler. Under Moses, the *Inquirer* had run a series of articles examining Greenfield's Banker's Trust Company, and not favorably. A reporter had interviewed Greenfield for a feature story when Walter found out about it and killed the story.

At another point, word got back to Walter that J. Edgar Hoover thought one of Triangle's magazines was going to print a story critical of the FBI. Annenberg quickly wrote Hoover to deny it and then penned, "As a matter of fact, if it should interest you, I consider your success phenomenal and a truly brilliant performance. I might add that, as a private citizen, I gain great comfort out of the knowledge that the Federal Bureau of Investigation is headed by so able an individual as yourself." It is clear that Walter did not feel the same way about Elmer Irey.[9]

Notes

Chapter 1: Law Enforcement Problems Like None Before

1. Summary of Daniel Roper's address to the twenty-fourth annual meeting of the NAM, *New York Times*, May 21, 1919.
2. Daniel C. Roper, *Fifty Years of Public Life*, in collaboration with Frank H. Lovette (Durham, NC: Duke University Press, 1941), 180.
3. *New York Times*, March 14, 1919.
4. Donald C. Gaby describes the conversion of cost in earlier years to 1990 dollars in *South Florida History Magazine*, Summer 1989. In developing the technique, Gaby credits Kevin Phillips, *The Politics of Rich and Poor—Wealth and the American Electorate in the Reagan Aftermath* (New York: Random House, 1990), 159.
5. Laurence F. Schmeckebier and Francis X. A. Eble, *The Bureau of Internal Revenue* (New York: AMS Press), 23–24.
6. Ibid., 40–41.
7. A history of the U.S. Customs House in New York City, now the National Museum of the American Indian, is in *Historic Preservation News*, Oct.–Nov.: 1994.
8. James Blaine Walker, *The Epic of American Industry* (New York: Harper & Brothers, 1949), 417.
9. Roper, *Fifty Years of Public Life*, 177.
10. Ibid., 193.
11. Leo Katcher, *The Big Bankroll: The Life and Times of Arnold Rothstein* (New York, 1958), 288.
12. Harvey W. Wiley, "An Opium Bonfire," *Good Housekeeping*, August 1912; David F. Musto, *The American Disease: Origins of Narcotic Control* (New Haven:

Yale University Press, 1973), 279. Musto's non-anecdotal work, the definitive history on the subject, cites early drug use in the United States.

13. Musto, *The American Disease*, 48

14. Ibid., 4.

15. Ibid., 130.

16. Ibid., 124.

17. *New York Times*, April 11, 1919.

18. Ibid., May 27, 1919.

19. Musto, *The American Disease*, 140.

20. *New York Times*, April 9, 1919.

21. Ibid., April 10, 1919.

22. Musto, *The American Disease*, 132.

23. *New York Times*, April 9, 1919.

24. Ibid., April 11, 1919.

25. Roper, *Fifty Years of Public Life*, 47.

26. Ibid., 17.

27. Ibid., 19.

28. Ibid., 31.

29. Ibid., 52.

30. Ibid., 54.

31. Ibid., 55.

32. Ibid.

33. Ibid, 130.

Chapter 2: The Special Intelligence Unit

1. *New York Times*, May 21, 1919.

2. Seymour Rau conviction, *New York Times*, Feb. 6, 1919; sentencing and editorial comment, ibid., Feb. 8, 1919. Three months later, the New York Circuit Court of Appeals reversed Rau's conviction "because of errors" in his trial, ruling that he was interrogated on collateral matters, which violated his rights, ibid., May 16, 1919.

3. Roper, *Fifty Years of Public Life*, 177.

4. In 1830, an Office of Instructions and Mail Depredations was established as the investigative and inspection branch at the Post Office Department.

5. Elmer Irey, *The Tax Dodgers: The Inside Story of the T-Men's War with America's Political and Underworld Hoodlums*, as told to William J. Slocum (New York: Greenberg, 1948), x.

6. Roper, *Fifty Years of Public Life*, 119. Roper was serving in the Post Office Department when he first met Alfred Burleson, then a Texas congressman.

7. Irey, *The Tax Dodgers*, x.

Chapter 3: Elmer Lincoln Irey

1. Accounts of Elmer Irey's personal life throughout the book are based on author's interviews and correspondence with Hugh Irey, his first son, and the eldest of three sons, beginning on March 9, 1991.
2. Roper, *Fifty Years of Public Life*, 63–64.
3. William A. Kenyon, *Bill Kenyon of the Postal Inspectors and Army Postal Service* (New York: Exposition Press, 1960), 12.
4. Joe Jackson, *Leavenworth Train: A Fugitive's Search for Justice in the Vanishing West* (New York: Carroll & Graf, 2001), 81.
5. Ibid., 82.
6. Ibid., 94.
7. Ibid., 76.
8. Ibid., 146.
9. Ibid., 146.
10. J. Anthony Lukas, *Big Trouble: A Murder in a Small Western Town Sets Off a Struggle for the Soul of America* (New York: Simon & Schuster, 1998), 199.
11. Ibid., 145.
12. Irey, *The Tax Dodgers*, xv.
13. Alan Hynd, *The Giant Killers* (Robert McBride & Co., New York, 1945), 26.
14. William G. Mann, "Personalities in Law Enforcement," *True Detective*, April 1939, 65, 121–122.
15. Marquis W. Childs, "The Nemesis Nobody Knows," *Saturday Evening Post*, September 16, 1939, 23, 65–73.
16. Harry J. Anslinger with J. Dennis Gregory, *The Protectors: Narcotics Agents, Citizens and Officials Against Organized Crime in America* (New York: Farrar, Straus and Company, 1964), 44.
17. Hugh Irey, interview by author.

Chapter 4: Corruption on a Staggering Scale

1. Schmeckebier and Eble, *The Bureau*, 29.
2. Ibid., 30.
3. Ibid., 31.
4. Charles Merz, *The Dry Decade* (Seattle: University of Washington Press, 1969), 111.
5. Irey, *The Tax Dodgers*, 5.
6. Merz, *The Dry Decade*, 7.
7. For Frank Wilson's role in the McConnell case, see Frank J. Wilson and Beth Day, *Special Agent: A Quarter Century with the Treasury Department and the Secret Service* (New York: Holt, Rinehart & Winston, 1963), 21.

8. Ibid., 4.

9. John Kobler, *Ardent Spirits: The Rise and Fall of Prohibition* (New York: G. P. Putnam's Sons, 1963), 272.

10. Merz, *The Dry Decade*, 56.

11. Hank Messick, *The Silent Syndicate* (New York: Macmillan, 1968), 6–7.

12. Samuel Hopkins Adams, *Incredible Era: The Life and Times of Warren Gamaliel Harding* (Boston: Houghton Mifflin Company, 1939), 235.

13. Wilson and Day, *Special Agent*, 21.

14. John Milton Cooper Jr., *Pivotal Decades: The United States 1900–1920* (New York: W. W. Norton, 1990), 196.

15. Irey, *The Tax Dodgers*, 3.

16. For Wilson letter to Roper, see Roper, *Fifty Years of Public Life*, 193–194; *New York Times*, March 7, 1920.

Chapter 5: Splendid Climate for Organized Crime

1. Matthew DeMichele and Gary Potter, "Sin City Revisited: A Case Study of the Official Sanctioning of Organized Crime in an 'Open City'" (Justice and Police Studies, Eastern Kentucky University; not dated and can be found at http://www.rootsweb.ancestry.com/~kycampbe/newportgambling.htm. Their paper later became a book: Potter, Thomas Barker, and Jenna Meglen, *Wicked Newport: Kentucky's Sin City* (Charleston, SC: History Press, 2008).

2. *New York Times*, March 11, 1919.

3. *U.S. v. Sullivan*, 274 U.S. 259.

4. Burton K. Wheeler with Paul F. Healy, *Yankee From the West* (Doubleday & Co., New York, 1962), 217.

5. Curt Gentry, *J. Edgar Hoover: The Man and the Secrets* (W. W. Norton and Company, New York), 122.

6. Gentry, *J. Edgar Hoover*, 141.

7. Raymond Moley, *Politics and Criminal Prosecution* (New York: Minton, Balch & Co., 1929), 92.

8. Ibid., 93.

9. Irey, *The Tax Dodgers*, 154.

10. Salvatore R. Martoche, "Lest We Forget: William J. Donovan," *Western New York Heritage*, 6, no. 1 (Winter 2003), 21.

11. Burdette C. Lewis, "How Racketeering Began: An Unforeseen Result of Our Anti-Trust Laws," *Review of Reviews*, 86, no. 1 (July 1932): 41–42, 54.

12. Anthony Clive Brown, *The Last Hero: Wild Bill Donovan* (New York: Times Books, 1962), 93.

13. Ralph de Toledano, *J. Edgar Hoover: The Man in His Time* (New York: Arlington House, 1973), 80.
14. Max Lowenthal, *The Federal Bureau of Investigation* (New York: William Sloane Associates, 1950), 3.
15. Ibid., 4.
16. *New York Times* editorial, Oct. 13, 1926.
17. *New York Times*, Feb. 25, 1926.
18. "Hell 'n' Maria" is part of the popular legend about Vice President Charles Dawes. See Charles G. Dawes, *Notes as Vice President, 1928–1929* (Boston: Little, Brown, 1937); Bascom N. Timmons, *Portrait of an American: Charles G. Dawes* (New York: Henry Holt, 1953); Don K. Price, "General Dawes and Executive Staff Work," *Public Administration Review*, 11, no. 3 (Summer 1951), 167–172.
19. Dawes's comments at the War Risk Board, Timmons, *Portrait of an American*, 199–200.
20. Dennis E. Hoffman, *Scarface Al and the Crime Crusaders: Chicago's Private War Against Capone* (Carbondale: Southern Illinois University Press, 1993), 19.
21. For the early days of the Chicago Crime Commission and its director, Henry Chamberlin, see John Kobler, *Capone: The Life and World of Al Capone* (New York: G. P. Putnam's Sons, 1971); J. George Murray, *The Legacy of Al Capone: Portraits and Annals of Chicago's Public Enemies* (New York: G. P. Putnam's Sons, 1975; Robert J. Schoenberg, *Mr. Capone: The Real—and Complete—Story of Al Capone* (New York: William Morrow & Co., 1992); Laurence Bergreen, *Capone: The Man and the Era* (New York, Touchstone, 1994).
22. Kobler, *Capone*, 61.
23. Ibid., 60.
24. Ibid., 197.
25. Fletcher, Dobyns. *The Underworld of American Politics*. (New York: Fletcher Dobyns, Publisher, 1932), 33.
26. Pasley, Fred D. *Al Capone: The Biography of a Self-Made Man*. (New York: Ives Washburn, Publisher, 1930), 216.
27. Kobler, *Capone*, 60.
28. Ibid., 39.
29. Moley, *Politics and Criminal Prosecution*, 85.
30. Gordon L. Hostetter and Thomas Quinn Beesley, *It's a Racket!* (Chicago: Les Quin Books, 1929), 13.
31. Pasley, *Al Capone*, 248.
32. Kobler, *Capone*, 230–231.

33. *New York Times*, Nov. 20, 1927.
34. Edward Dean Sullivan, *Chicago Surrenders* (New York: Vanguard Press, 1930), 136.
35. Kobler, *Capone*, 96.
36. Ibid., 108.
37. Dobyns, *The Underworld of American Politics*, 53.
38. Ibid., 111.

Chapter 6. "The Master of All He Surveyed"
1. Pasley, *Al Capone*, 151.
2. Ibid., 134.
3. Kobler, *Capone*, 118.
4. Ibid., 178.
5. Ibid., 177.
6. John H. Lyle, *The Dry and Lawless Years* (Upper Saddle River, NJ: Prentice-Hall, Inc., 1960), 81.
7. Kobler, *Capone*, 182.
8. Ibid., 175.
9. Ibid., 176.
10. Ibid., 176.
11. Ibid., 183.
12. Sullivan, *Chicago Surrenders*, 161.
13. Pasley, *Al Capone*, 162.
14. Ibid., 201.
15. *Chicago Tribune*, Nov. 18, 1927.
16. Lyle, *The Dry and Lawless Years*, 123.
17. Irey, *The Tax Dodgers*, 154.
18. Pasley, *Al Capone*, 177.
19. Frederic Sondern Jr., *The Brotherhood of Evil: The Mafia* (New York: Farrar, Straus, Cudahy, 1959), 72.
20. Frank Spiering, *The Man Who Got Capone* (New York: Bobbs-Merrill, 1976), 35.
21. Kobler, *Capone*, 306.
22. Spiering, *The Man Who Got Capone*, 35.
23. Kobler, *Capone*, 64.
24. Sullivan, *Chicago Surrenders*, 133.

Chapter 7: Getting Capone
1. Irey, *The Tax Dodgers*, 31.
2. Spiering, *The Man Who Got Capone*, 66.
3. Pasley, *Al Capone*, 153.

4. *75 Years of IRS Criminal Investigation History, 1910–1994,* 78. Department of the Treasury, Internal Revenue Service. Document 7233 (Rev. 96) Catalog Number 64601H. This 200-page document was published when Donald K. Vogel was serving as assistant commissioner for Criminal Investigation and was marked "Official Use Only." It is only the second document put out by the intelligence branch in its history. The first report, written under Elmer Irey's direction, covered the period from July 1, 1919 to June 30, 1936. The 124-page Irey report is a heavily-redacted document that is not numbered in regular order, leaving uncertainty as to how long it really is. Many key names are blacked out in the report; nonetheless, it is an invaluable historical work.

5. *New York Times,* Feb. 1, 1920.

6. Schoenberg, *Mr. Capone,* 124.

7. Kobler, *Capone,* 296.

8. Sullivan, *Chicago Surrenders,* 68–69.

9. *U.S. v. Sullivan, 274 U.S. 259.*

10. *U.S. v. Sullivan, 274 U.S. 259; New York Times,* May 17, 1927; *Charleston Evening Post,* May 16, 1927. The *Post,* Manly Sullivan's hometown newspaper, put the historic ruling on page 1. The *Times* put it on page 31.

11. Pasley, *Al Capone,* 87.

12. Irey, *The Tax Dodgers,* 28.

13. Pasley, *Al Capone,* 138.

14. Irey, *The Tax Dodgers,* 28.

15. Ibid., 30.

16. Ibid.

17. Bergreen, Laurence. *Capone: The Man and the Era.* (New York: Touchstone, 1994), 274.

18. Dawes, *Notes as Vice President,* 77–78.

19. Kobler, *Capone,* 227.

20. Ibid.

21. *Chicago Daily News,* March 25, 1926.

22. Pasley, *Al Capone,* 202–203

23. Irey, *The Tax Dodgers,* 20.

24. Robert J. Casey and W. A. S. Douglas, *The Midwesterner: The Story of Dwight H. Green* (Chicago: Wilcox & Follett Co., 1948), 116.

25. Ibid, 118–119.

Chapter 8: "We'll Get Right on It"

1. Irey, *The Tax Dodgers,* 27.

2. Ibid., 26.

3. Ibid., 25.

4. Ibid, 26.

5. Dobyns, *The Underworld of American Politics*, 107.

6. *Chicago Tribune*, Oct. 10, 1931.

7. Irey, *The Tax Dodgers*, 36.

8. "Undercover Man: He Trapped Capone" by Frank J. Wilson as told to Howard Whitman, *Collier's*, April 26, 1947.

9. Wilson and Day, *Special Agent*, 29.

10. Irey, *The Tax Dodgers*, 27.

11. Ibid., 36.

12. Ibid.

13. Wilson and Day, *Special Agent*, 30.

14. Irey, *The Tax Dodgers*, 36.

15. Spiering, *The Man Who Got Capone*, 47.

16. Irey, *The Tax Dodgers*, 54.

17. Wilson and Day, *Special Agent*, 23.

18. Wilson, *Collier's*, April 26, 1947.

19. Spiering, *The Man Who Got Capone*, 105.

20. Wilson and Day, *Special Agent*, 31.

21. Ibid., 35.

22. Irey, *The Tax Dodgers*, 33.

23. Ibid., 38.

24. Casey and Douglas, *The Midwesterner*, 136.

25. Ibid., 133.

26. Spiering, *The Man Who Got Capone*, 71.

Chapter 9: A Three-Year Struggle

1. Wilson, *Collier's*, April 26, 1947.

2. Irey, *The Tax Dodgers*, 45.

3. Schoenberg, *Mr. Capone*, 245.

4. Wilson and Day, *Special Agent*, 47.

5. Irey, *The Tax Dodgers*, 20.

6. *New York Times*, June 18, 1931.

7. Spiering, *The Man Who Got Capone*, 39.

8. Anthony Scaduto, "The Eliot Ness Myth," *Climax*, n.d., National Archives, Washington, D.C.

9. Hank Messick, *The Silent Syndicate*, 158.

10. Ibid., 109.

11. Irey, *The Tax Dodgers*, 60–61.
12. Wilson, "Undercover Man."
13. Ibid.
14. Ibid.
15. Irey, *The Tax Dodgers*, 57.
16. Memo dated December 18, 1930, from Burnet to Walter E. Hope, Asst. Secretary of Treasury, Herbert Hoover Library, West Branch, Iowa. Eight days after Capone was indicated for willful evasion of his income taxes, the government spurned a sum of $4 million to end the case. No details were revealed; *New York Times*, June 14, 1931.
17. Irey, *The Tax Dodgers*, 57.
18. Spiering, *The Man Who Got Capone*, 157.
19. Ibid., 165.

Chapter 10: Grim Journey to Manhattan
1. Hoover letter, dated March 16, 1931. Herbert Hoover Library, West Branch, Iowa.
2. *New York Times*, April 3, 1931.
3. Nat J. Ferber, *I Found Out: A Confidential Chronicle of the Twenties* (New York: Dial Press, 1939), 112.
4. Richard Norton Smith, *Thomas E. Dewey and His Times* (New York: Simon & Schuster, 1982), 111.
5. Ibid., 115.
6. Ibid., 88.
7. *New York Times*, April 3, 1931.
8. Spiering, *The Man Who Got Capone*, 148–149.
9. *New York Times*, June 6, 1931.
10. *New York Times*, April 4, 1931
11. *New York Times*, October 24, 1920.
12. Joseph Bonnano, *A Man of Honor: The Autobiography of Joseph Bonanno* (New York: Simon & Schuster, 1983), 65.
13. Gay Talese, *Fame and Obscurity* (New York: Dell Publishing Co., 1961), 192.
14. Thomas E. Dewey, *Twenty Against the Underworld*, (New York: Doubleday and Col., 1974), 271.
15. Burton Turkus and Sid Feder, *Murder, Inc.: The Story of the "The Syndicate"* (New York: Farrar, Straus and Young, 1951), 390.
16. Davis, "Things I Couldn't Tell till Now," Part II, *Collier's*, July 29, 1939.
17. Katcher, *The Big Bankroll*, 247.
18. Sullivan, *Chicago Surrenders*, 165.

19. Ferber, *I Found Out*, 195.

20. Donald Henderson Clarke, *In the Reign of Rothstein* (New York: Vanguard Press, 1930), xi.

21. Milton Crane, ed., *Sins of New York* (New York: Boni & Gaer, Inc., 1947), 183.

22. Craig Thompson and Allen Raymond, *Gang Rule in New York: The Story of Lawless Era* (New York: Dial Press, 1951), 55.

23. Ferber, *I Found Out*, 215.

24. Martin Gosch and Richard Hammer, *The Last Testament of Lucky Luciano* (Boston: Little, Brown, 1975), 41.

25. Leo Katcher, *The Big Bankroll: The Life and Times of Arnold Rothstein* (New York: Harper & Brothers, 1958), 285–286.

26. Clarke, *In the Reign*, 11.

27. Katcher, *The Big Bankroll*, 238.

28. Robert Lacey, *Little Man: Meyer Lansky and the Gangster Life* (Boston: Little, Brown & Company, 1991), 50.

29. Thompson and Raymond, *Gang Rule*, 66.

30. Ibid., 59.

31. Davis, "Things I Couldn't Tell till Now," Part II, *Collier's*, July 29, 1939.

32. Katcher, *The Big Bankroll*, 346.

33. Ibid., 338.

34. Ibid., 335.

35. *New York Times*, December 18, 1928.

36. *New York Times*, December 8, 1928.

37. Ibid., November 15.

38. Ibid., November 22.

39. Ibid., November 23.

40. Katcher, *The Big Bankroll*, 338–339.

41. *New York Times*, December 6, 1928.

42. Herbert Mitgang, *Once Upon a Time in New York: Jimmy Walker, Franklin Roosevelt, and the Last Great Battle of the Jazz Age* (New York: Free Press, 2000), 20.

43. Ibid., 21.

44. Lowell M. Limpus, *Honest Cop: Lewis J. Valentine* (New York: E. P. Dutton, 1939), 132.

45. Mitgang, *Once Upon a Time*, 21.

46. Katcher, *The Big Bankroll*, 341.

47. *New York Times*, December 4, 1929.

48. *New York Times*, December 6, 1929.

49. Mitgang, *Once Upon a Time*, 21; Mark A. Stuart, *Gangster #2: Longy Zwill-*

man, the Man Who Invented Organized Crime (Secaucus, NJ: Lyle Stuart, Inc., 1985), 75.

50. Gosch and Hammer, *The Last Testament*, 95.
51. Katcher, *The Big Bankroll*, 352.
52. Ibid., 245.
53. Gosch and Hammer, *The Last Testament*, 94.
54. Sann, *Kill the Dutchman!* 74.
55. Tony Sciacca, *Luciano: The Man Who Modernized the American Mafia* (New York: Pinnacle Books, 1975), 71.
56. Thompson and Raymond, *Gang Rule*, 376.
57. Kobler, *Capone*, 258.
58. Gosch and Hammer, *The Last Testament*, 87.
59. Bergreen, *Capone*, 426.
60. Sciacca, *Luciano*, 84.

Chapter 11: Where Organized Crime Really Reigned

1. Sullivan, *Chicago Surrenders*, 167.
2. Bonnano, *A Man of Honor*, 127–128.
3. Gosch and Hammer, *The Last Testament*, 140.
4. Ibid.
5. Gosch and Hammer, *The Last Testament*, 141–142.
6. Bonnano, *A Man of Honor*, 84.
7. *New York Times*, April 16, 1931.
8. *New York Times*, Sept. 12, 1931.
9. *Literary Digest*, June 15, 1929.
10. *New York Herald-Tribune*, May 17–24, 1931.
11. Walker, *Dewey*, 48.
12. Limpus, *Honest Cop*, 27.
13. Ibid., 237.
14. *New York Times*, Jan. 11, 1930.
15. National Commission on Law Observance and Enforcement, *Prohibition Survey of Illinois*, 71st Cong., 3rd sess., 293. 1931.
16. Ibid., 713.

Chapter 12: Waxey, Instead

1. Stephen Fox, *Blood and Power: Organized Crime in Twentieth-Century America* (New York: Penguin Books, 1989), 27.
2. *New York Times*, June 18, 1931.
3. Irey, *The Tax Dodgers*, 138.

4. Ibid., 143.
5. Ibid., 142–143.
6. Ibid., 139.
7. Ibid., 135.
8. Ibid., 136.
9. Ibid., 137–138.
10. Ibid., 140.
11. Ibid., 141.
12. Ibid., 137.
13. Ibid., 135.
14. Dorothy M. Brown, *Mabel Walker Willebrandt: A Story of Power, Loyalty, and Law* (Knoxville: University of Tennessee Press, 1984), 53.
15. *New York Times*, September 27, 1930.
16. Herbert Mitgang, *The Man Who Rode the Tiger* (New York: J. P. Lippincott, 1963), 205.
17. *New York Times*, March 13, 1930.
18. *New York Times*, March 15, 1930.
19. *New York Times*, March 14, 1930.
20. Mitgang, *The Man Who Rode the Tiger*, 159.
21. Alan Block, *East Side–West Side: Organizing Crime in New York, 1930–1950.* (Cardiff: University College Cardiff, 1980), 33.
22. Ibid., 204.
23. Mitgang, *Once Upon a Time*, 102.
24. Ibid., 173.
25. Ibid., 176.
26. Ibid., 348.
27. Ibid., 222.
28. Ibid., 146.
29. Ibid., 169.
30. Ibid., 254.
31. Ibid., 258.
32. Ibid., 259.
33. Ibid., 265.
34. Thomas E. Dewey, *Twenty Against the Underworld* (New York: Doubleday, 1974), 271.
35. Gus Tyler, *Organized Crime in America* (Ann Arbor: University of Michigan Press, 1962), 77.
36. Dewey, *Twenty Against the Underworld*, 281.
37. Ibid., 279.

38. Ibid., 250.
39. Ibid., 279.
40. Irey, *The Tax Dodgers*, 145–146; *New York Times*, May 22, 1933.
41. Irey, *The Tax Dodgers*, 147.
42. Dewey, *Twenty Against the Underworld*, 312–313.
43. Ibid., 312.
44. Smith, *Thomas E. Dewey*, 115.
45. Irey, *The Tax Dodgers*, 152.

Chapter 13: Anonymous Complaints About Huey Long

1. Irey, *The Tax Dodgers*, 90.
2. Don Congdon, ed., *The Thirties: A Time to Remember* (New York: Simon & Schuster, 1962), 312.
3. Harry T. Williams, *Huey Long* (New York: Alfred A. Knopf, 1970), 470.
4. Harnett T. Kane, *Huey Long's Louisiana Hayride: The American Rehearsal for Dictatorship* (Gretna, LA: Pelican Publishing Co., 1941), 49.
5. Williams, *Huey Long*, 159.
6. John Morton Blum, *From the Morgenthau Diaries: Years of Crisis, 1928–1938* (Boston: Houghton Mifflin, 1959), 97.
7. Ibid., 296.
8. Williams, *Huey Long*, 5.
9. *Washington Post*, August 28, 1946.
10. Irey, *The Tax Dodgers*, 91.
11. Ibid., 92.
12. Ibid., 91.
13. Williams, *Huey Long*, 678.
14. Ibid., 559.
15. Wheeler, *Yankee from the West*, 288–290.
16. Ibid., 290.
17. Dewey, *Twenty Against the Underworld*, 328.
18. Gosch and Hammer, *The Last Testament*, 162.
19. Ibid., 163.
20. Thompson and Raymond, *Gang Rule*, 356.
21. Thomas Kessner, *Fiorello La Guardia and the Making of Modern New York* (New York: Penguin Books, 1989), 352.
22. Hank Messick, *Secret File* (New York: G. P. Putnam's Sons, 1969), 242.
23. Williams, *Huey Long*, 631.
24. Ibid., 634.
25. Congdon, *The Thirties*, 315.

26. Williams, *Huey Long*, 813. Harold Ickes, no slouch at hurling insults, later retorted by asserting that Long had "halitosis of the intellect."
27. Ibid., 636.
28. Ibid., 637.
29. Irey, *The Tax Dodgers*, 93–94.
30. Joseph P. Lash, *Eleanor and Franklin: The Story of Their Relationship Based on Eleanor Roosevelt's Private Papers* (New York: W. W. Norton & Co., 1971), 505.
31. Irey, *The Tax Dodgers*, 96.
32. Ibid., 97.
33. Williams, *Huey Long*, 821–822.
34. Blackie Audett, *Rap Sheet: My Life Story* (New York: William Sloane Associates, 1954), 125.
35. *New York Times*, May 17, 1935.
36. Wilson and Day, *Special Agent*, 79.
37. Ibid., 83.
38. Ibid., 85–89.
39. Irey, *The Tax Dodgers*, 99.
40. Ibid., 100.
41. Williams, *Huey Long*, 873.
42. Ibid., 875.
43. Huge Irey, interview by author.
44. Irey, *The Tax Dodgers*, 100–101.
45. Kane, *Louisiana Hayride*, 182.
46. Irey, *The Tax Dodgers*, 101.
47. *New Orleans Times-Picayune*, May 30, 1936.
48. Irey, *The Tax Dodgers*, 101.
49. Huge Irey, interview by author.
50. Irey, *The Tax Dodgers*, 102–103.
51. Ibid., 103.
52. Ibid., 117.

Chapter 14: Boss Pendergast
1. Lawrence H. Larsen and Nancy J. Hulston, *Pendergast!* (Columbia: University of Missouri, 1997), 147.
2. Maurice M. Milligan, *Missouri Waltz: The Inside Story of the Pendergast Machine by the Man Who Smashed It* (New York: Charles Scribner's Sons, 1948), 78–80.
3. Michael Wallis, *Pretty Boy: The Life and Times of Charles Arthur Floyd* (New York: St. Martin's Press, 1992), 170–171.
4. Irey, *The Tax Dodgers*, 244.

5. Lear B. Reed, *Human Wolves: Seventeen Years of War on Crime* (Kansas City, MO: Brown-White-Lowell Press, 1941), 190.
6. Turkus and Feder, *Murder, Inc.*, 368.
7. Ibid., 368.
8. Alan Hynd, *The Giant Killers* (New York: Robert M. McBride & Co., 1945), 200.
9. David McCullough, *Truman* (New York: Simon & Schuster, 1992), 200.
10. Reed, *Human Wolves*, 209.
11. Milligan, *Missouri Waltz*, 103. Pendergast disclosed this in a "My Dear Jim" letter he wrote to Postmaster General James J. Farley, dated May 12, 1933.
12. Carl Sifakis, *The Mafia Encyclopedia, First edition*, 120.
13. Milligan, *Missouri Waltz*, 4.
14. Ibid., 5.
15. Audett, *Rap Sheet*, 120.
16. Milligan, *Missouri Waltz*, 144–145.
17. Audett, *Rap Sheet*, 143.
18. Larsen and Hulston, *Pendergast!* 85.
19. Milligan, *Missouri Waltz*, 97.
20. Irey, *The Tax Dodgers*, 228.
21. Ibid., 232–233.
22. Larsen and Hulston, *Pendergast!* 131.
23. Irey, *The Tax Dodgers*, 234.
24. Ibid., 235.
25. Ibid., 239.
26. Ibid., 240.
27. Ibid., 225.
28. Ibid., 226.
29. Ibid., 241–242.
30. Milligan, *Missouri Waltz*, 199.
31. Ibid., 202–203.
32. Irey, *The Tax Dodgers*, 241.

Chapter 15: Finale in New York City

1. Sann, Paul. *Kill the Dutchman! The Story of Dutch Schultz.* (New Rochelle, NY: Arlington House, 1971), 220.
2. Ibid, 220. The entire conversation between Morgenthau and La Guardia is contained in *Kill the Dutchman!*
3. Davis, "Things I Couldn't Tell till Now," *Collier's*, July 22, 1939, Part I.
4. Sann, *Kill the Dutchman!* 228.
5. Ibid.

6. *New York Times*, August 2, 1935. The *Times* sent its ace reporter, Meyer Berger, to cover the trial.
7. Blum, *Morgenthau Diaries*, 95.
8. Smith, *Thomas E. Dewey*, 109.
9. Tyler, *Organized Crime*, 179–180.
10. *New York Times*, June 27, 1930.
11. Tyler, *Organized Crime*, 49.
12. "The Great Nation-wide Campaign Against the Racketeers." *Literary Digest*, July 1, 1933.
13. Blum, *Morgenthau Diaries*, 78.
14. Katcher, *The Big Bankroll*, 272.
15. John Harlan Amen, "The Efficacy of the Antitrust Laws," *The Bar* 7, no. 2 (May 1941).
16. *New York Times*, February 19, 1934.
17. *New York Times*, May 6, 1934.
18. *New York Times*, May 8, 1934.
19. *New York Times*, April 24, 1934.
20. Walter Lippmann, "The Underworld: Our Secret Servant," *Forum*, January 7, 1931, 1–4.
21. *New York Times*, August 16, 1933.
22. "The Marines Are Coming," *Fortune*, August 24, 1934.
23. Claire Bond Potter, *War on Crime: Bandits, G-Men, and the Politics of Mass Culture* (New Brunswick, NJ: Rutgers University Press, 1988), 131.
24. Ibid., 107.
25. Gosch and Hammer, *The Last Testament*, 79.
26. *New York Times*, March 16, 1926.
27. Thompson and Raymond, *Gang Rule*, 265, 266.
28. Dewey, *Twenty Against the Underworld*, 5.
29. *New York Times*, March 16, 1935.
30. Dewey, *Twenty Against the Underworld*, 150.
31. Ibid.
32. Ibid., 80.
33. Ibid., 169.
34. Ibid., 317.
35. Davis, *Collier's*, August 12, 1939, Part IV.
36. Stanley Walker, *Dewey*, 69.
37. Davis, "Things I Couldn't Tell till Now," *Collier's, August 5, 1939*, Part III.
38. Ibid., Part III.
39. Dewey, *Twenty Against the Underworld*, 187.

40. Ibid., 195.
41. Ibid., 7.
42. Frederic Thrasher, *The Gang: A Study of 1,313 Gangs in Chicago* (Chicago: University of Chicago Press, 1927), 8.
43. Dewey, *Twenty Against the Underworld*, 402.

Chapter 16: Irey, Hoover, and Anslinger

1. Huge Irey, interview by author.
2. Irey, *The Tax Dodgers*, 67.
3. Ibid., 68.
4. Noel Behn, *Lindbergh: The Crime* (New York: Atlantic Monthly Press, 1994), 113.
5. Ibid., 186–187.
6. Irey, *The Tax Dodgers*, 66.
7. Ibid., 81.
8. Wilson and Day, *Special Agent*, 68.
9. Richard Gid Powers, *Secrecy and Power: The Life of J. Edgar Hoover* (New York: Free Press, 1988), 194.
10. Ibid.
11. Potter, *War on Crime*, 113.
12. Ovid Demaris, *The Director: An Oral Biography of J. Edgar Hoover* (New York: Harper's Magazine Press, 1975), 61.
14. Irey, *The Tax Dodgers*, 67.
15. Ibid., 87.
16. Powers, *Secrecy and Power*, 182.
17. Melvin Purvis, *American Agent* (New York: Garden City Publishing Co., 1936), 247.
18. Demaris, *The Director*, 73.
19. Powers, *Secrecy and Power*, 226.
20. Ibid., 193.
21. Lowenthal, *The FBI*, 335.
22. Ibid., 336.
23. Ibid., 341–342.
24. Ibid., 343.
25. Ibid., 345.
26. Ibid., 322–323.
27. Ibid., 328.
28. Joint Committee on Tax Evasion and Avoidance, *Hearings on Tax Evasion and Avoidance*, 75th Congress, lst Session. House Document No. 337. Irey testified on June 18, 1937. For full testimony, see 37–71.

29. Ibid., 37–38.

30. Ibid., 1, 23.

31. Messick, *Silent Syndicate*, 90.

32. Ibid., 93.

33. Irey, *The Tax Dodgers*, 165.

34. Messick, *Secret File*, 75–76.

35. Ibid., 46.

36. Ibid., 79.

37. Ibid., 43.

38. Demaris, *The Director*, 142.

39. Harry Anslinger and Will Oursler, *The Murderers: The Story of the Narcotic Gangs* (New York: Farrar, Straus and Cudahy, 1961), 49–50.

40. Turkus and Feder, *Murder, Inc.*, 331.

41. *New York Times*, December 17, 1936.

42. Curt Gentry, *J. Edgar Hoover*, 328.

43. William Sullivan with Bill Brown, *The Bureau: My Thirty Years in Hoover's FBI*, (New York: W. W. Norton, 1979), 115.

44. Ibid., 120–121.

45. William F. Roemer Jr., *Man Against the Mob* (New York: Ivy Books, 1991), 22.

46. Irey, *The Tax Dodgers*, 179.

47. Anslinger and Oursler, *The Murderers*, 9–10.

48. Fox, *Blood and Power*, 145.

49. Ibid., 144.

50. Ibid., 146.

51. Harry J. Anslinger with J. Dennis Gregory, *The Protectors: Narcotics Agents, Citizens and Officials Against Organized Crime in America* (New York: Farrar, Straus and Company, 1964), 214.

52. Ibid.

53. Ibid.

Chapter 17: The "Al Capone" of St. Paul

1. *St. Paul Pioneer Press*, Oct. 3, 1931.

2. Paul Maccabee, *John Dillinger Slept Here: A Crooks' Tour of Crime and Corruption in St. Paul, 1920–1936* (St. Paul: Minnesota Historical Society Press, 1995), 44.

3. Paul Maccabee, interview on South Dakota Public Broadcasting, March 18, 2003.

4. Maccabee, *Dillinger*, 4.

5. Ibid., 10.

6. *St. Paul Pioneer Press*, December 25, 1926.

7. *St. Paul Pioneer Press*, March 11, 1927.
8. Maccabee, *Dillinger*, 62.
9. *St. Paul Pioneer Press*, March 11, 1927.
10. Maccabee, *Dillinger*, 35.
11. Messick, *Secret File*, 56.
12. Maccabee, *Dillinger*, 215.
13. Ibid., 9.
14. Ibid., 2.
15. Ibid., 3.
16. Ibid., 94.
17. Ibid., 2.
18. *St. Paul Pioneer Press*, May 3, 1934. The *Pioneer Press* story called Greenberg "the reputed successor to Rothstein," which he was not.
19. Maccabee, *Dillinger*, 36.
20. Ibid., 63.
21. Ibid., 42.
22. Ibid., 39.
23. Ibid., 40.
24. Ibid., 39–40.
25. Ibid.
26. Harry R. Illman, *Unholy Toledo: The True Story of Detroit's Purple-Licavoli Gangs' Take-over of an Ohio City* (San Francisco: Polemic Press Publications, 1985), 96.
27. Ibid., 7.
28. Maccabee, *Dillinger*, 35.
29. Ibid.
30. Spiering, *The Man Who Got Capone*, 85.
31. *St. Paul Pioneer Press*, April 28, 1934.
32. *St. Paul Pioneer Press*, May 15, 1934.
33. *St. Paul Pioneer Press*, May 31, 1934.
34. *St. Paul Pioneer Press*, May 9, 1934.
35. *St. Paul Pioneer Press*, May 18, 1934.
36. *St. Paul Pioneer Press*, May 22, 1934.
37. *St. Paul Pioneer Press*, November 15, 1934.
38. Ibid., March 6, 1936.
39. *Minneapolis Star Journal*, July 14, 1941.

Chapter 18: The Lord of Atlantic City

1. Irey, *The Tax Dodgers*, 245.

2. Nick Tosches, *Dino: Living High in the Dirty Business of Dreams* (New York: Random House, 1992), 133.

3. *New York Times*, January 21, 1911.

4. Martin Paulsson, *The Social Anxieties of Progressive Reform: Atlantic City, 1854– 1920* (New York: New York University Press, 1994), 2.

5. *New York Times*, December 23, 1911.

6. Nelson Johnson, *Boardwalk Empire: The Birth, High Times, and Corruption of Atlantic City* (Medford, NJ: Plexus Publishing, Inc., 2002), xii.

7. Demaris, *Boardwalk Jungle*, 25–26.

8. Messick, *Secret File*, 141.

9. Irey, *The Tax Dodgers*, 246.

10. Johnson, *Boardwalk Empire*, xiv.

11. Ibid., xi.

12. Demaris, *Boardwalk Jungle*, 27.

13. Ibid., 80.

14. Irey, *The Tax Dodgers*, 247.

15. Ibid., 248.

16. Ibid.

17. Irey, *The Tax Dodgers*, 249.

18. Ibid., 252.

19. *New York Times*, July 17, 1941.

20. *New York Times*, May 11, 1939.

21. Irey, *The Tax Dodgers*, 252.

22. *New York Times*, May 12, 1939.

23. *New York Times*, May 20, 1939.

24. Irey, *The Tax Dodgers*, 254.

25. Ibid., 255.

26. Ibid.

27. *New York Times*, January 23, 1941.

28. Irey, *The Tax Dodgers*, 255–256.

29. Ibid., 258.

30. Ibid., 258–259.

31. Ibid., 260.

32. Ibid., 261–262.

33. Ibid., 264.

34. *New York Times*, June 18, 1941.

35. *New York Times*, July 16, 1941.

36. *New York Times*, July 17, 1941.

37. *New York Times*, July 18, 1941.

38. *New York Times,* July 20, 1941.
39. *New York Times,* July 22, 1941.
40. *New York Times,* July 24–25, 1941.
41. *New York Times,* July 26, 1941.
42. *New York Times,* July 27, 1941.

Chapter 19: "Moe" Annenberg
1. Messick, *Secret File,* 156.
2. Irey, *The Tax Dodgers,* 215.
3. Messick, *Secret File,* 153.
4. John Cooney, *The Annenbergs* (New York: Simon & Schuster, 1982), 32.
5. Irey, *The Tax Dodgers,* 215.
6. W. A. Swanberg, *Citizen Hearst: A Biography of William Randolph Hearst* (New York: Bantam Books, 1971), 322.
7. Gaeton Fonzi, *Annenberg: A Biography in Power* (New York: Weybright and Talley, 1970), 60.
8. Kobler, *Capone,* 96.
9. Cooney, *The Annenbergs,* 52.
10. Gosch and Hammer, *The Last Testament,* 123.
11. Cooney, *The Annenbergs,* 76.
12. Ibid., 78.
13. Ibid., 70.
14. Gentry, *Hoover,* 330.
15. Cooney, *The Annenbergs,* 89–90.
16. Ibid., 124.
17. Ibid., 126.
18. Ibid., 128–129.
19. Irey, *The Tax Dodgers,* 221.
20. Ibid., 216.
21. Ibid., 222.
22. Cooney, *The Annenbergs,* 134.
23. *New York Times,* April 22, 1939.
24. *New York Times,* August 24, 1939.
25. Irey, *The Tax Dodgers,* 223.
26. Cooney, *The Annenbergs,* 150–151.
27. *New York Times,* July 2, 1940.

Chapter 20: Mafia Shakedown in Hollywood
1. Irey, *The Tax Dodgers,* 271.

2. Charles Rappleye and Ed Becker, *All-American Mafioso: The Johnny Roselli Story* (New York: Bantam Doubleday Dell Publishing Group, Inc., 1991), 93.

3. Ibid., 61.

4. *New York Times*, March 14, 1941.

5. Irey, *The Tax Dodgers*, 285.

6. Ibid., 284.

7. Murray, *Legacy of Capone*, 262.

8. Nicholas Gage, ed., *Mafia USA* (Chicago: Playboy Press, 1972), 352.

9. Ibid., 346.

10. Murray, *Legacy of Capone*, 259.

11. Irey, *The Tax Dodgers*, 276.

12. Bergreen, *Capone*, 273.

13. William Bioff testimony, 136, 139, 403, 805, U.S. Circuit Court of Appeals, Second Circuit, C.R. 114–101, 1941.

14. Murray, *Legacy of Capone*, 230.

15. Ibid., 235.

16. Ibid., 261.

17. Ibid., 263.

18. Rappleye and Becker, *All-American Mafioso*, 39.

19. Ibid., 46.

20. Ibid., 65.

21. Murray, *Legacy of Capone*, 273, 274, 275, 276.

22. Irey, *The Tax Dodgers*, 280.

23. Murray, *Legacy of Capone*, 276.

24. Dewey, *Twenty Against the Underworld*, 453–454.

25. *New York Times*, June 4, 1940.

26. *New York Times*, April 1, 1941.

27. *New York Times*, March 6, 1941.

28. Irey, *The Tax Dodgers*, 286.

29. *New York Times*, October 10, 1941.

30. Murray, *Legacy of Capone*, 266.

31. Rappleye and Becker, *All-American Mafioso*, 32.

32. Ibid., 107.

33. Irey, *The Tax Dodgers*, 287.

Chapter 21: Epilogue

1. Hugh Irey, interview by author.

2. *New York Times*, July 14, 1940.

3. Hugh Irey, interview by author.
4. Ibid.
5. Cooney, *The Annenbergs*, 23.
6. Ibid., 152.
7. Ibid., 166.
8. Ibid., 96.
9. Ibid., 180–181.

Selected Bibliography

Adams, Henry. *The Education of Henry Adams: An Autobiography*. Boston: Houghton Mifflin Company, 1918.

Adams, Samuel Hopkins. *Incredible Era: The Life and Times of Warren Gamaliel Harding*. Boston: Houghton Mifflin Company, 1939.

Anbinder, Tyler. *Five Points*. New York: Free Press, 2001.

Anslinger, Harry, and Will Oursler. *The Murderers: The Story of the Narcotic Gangs*. New York: Farrar, Straus and Cudahy, 1961.

Asbury, Herbert. *The Gangs of Chicago: An Informed History of the Chicago Underworld*. New York: Alfred A. Knopf, 1940.

Audett, Blackie. *Rap Sheet: My Life Story*. New York: William Sloane Associates, 1954.

Barker, Thomas G., Garry Potter, and Jenna Meglen. *Wicked Newport: Kentucky's Sin City*. Charleston, SC: History Press, 2008.

Barzini, Luigi. *From Caesar to the Mafia: Persons, Places and Problems in Italian Life*. New York: Bantam Books, 1971.

Behn, Noel. *Lindbergh: The Crime*. New York: Atlantic Monthly Press, 1994.

Bennett, James O'Donnell. *Chicago Gangland: The True Story of Chicago Crime*. Chicago: The Tribune Co., 1929.

Berg, A. Scott. *Lindbergh*. New York: G. P. Putnam's Sons, 1998.

Bergreen, Laurence. *Capone: The Man and the Era*. New York: Touchstone, 1994.

Block, Alan. *East Side–West Side: Organizing Crime in New York, 1930–1950*. Cardiff: University College Cardiff, 1980.

Blum, John Morton. *From the Morgenthau Diaries: Years of Crisis, 1928–1938*. Boston: Houghton Mifflin, 1959.

Bonanno, Joseph. *A Man of Honor: The Autobiography of Joseph Bonanno.* New York: Simon & Schuster, 1983.

Borkin, Joseph. *The Corrupt Judge: An Inquiry into Bribery and other High Crimes and Misdemeanors in the Federal Courts.* New York: Clarkson N. Potter, Inc., 1962.

Brown, Anthony Clive. *The Last Hero: Wild Bill Donovan.* New York: Times Books, 1982.

Brown, Dorothy M. *Mabel Walker Willebrandt: A Study of Power, Loyalty, and Law.* Knoxville: University of Tennessee Press, 1984.

Browning, Frank, and John Gerassi. *The American Way of Crime: From Salem to Watergate, a Stunning New Perspective on American History.* New York: G. P. Putnam's Sons, 1980.

Brownlee, W. Elliot. *Federal Taxation in America: A Short History.* New York: Woodrow Wilson Center Press and Cambridge University Press, 1996.

Burnham, David. *A Law Unto Itself: Power, Politics and the IRS.* New York: Random House, 1989.

Cannadine, David. *Mellon: An American Life.* New York: Knopf, 2006.

Caro, Robert A. *The Power Broker: Robert Moses and the Fall of New York.* New York: Vintage Books, 1975.

Casey, Robert J., and W. A. S. Douglas. *The Midwesterner: The Story of Dwight H. Green.* Chicago: Wilcox & Follett Co., 1948.

Cigliano, Jan, and Sarah Bradford Landau, eds. *The Grand American Avenue 1850–1920.* San Francisco: Pomegranate Art Books, 1994.

Clarke, Donald Henderson. *In the Reign of Rothstein.* New York: Vanguard Press, 1930.

Congdon, Don, ed. *The Thirties: A Time to Remember.* New York: Simon & Schuster, 1962.

Cooney, John. *The Annenbergs.* New York: Simon & Schuster, 1982.

Cooper, John Milton Jr. *Pivotal Decades: The United States 1900–1920.* New York: W. W. Norton, 1990.

Crane, Milton, ed. *Sins of New York.* New York: Boni & Gaer, Inc., 1947.

Cressey, Donald R. *Theft of the Nation: The Structure and Operations of Organized Crime in America.* New York: Harper & Row, 1969.

Daugherty, Harry M. *The Inside Story of the Harding Tragedy.* In collaboration with Thomas Dixon. New York: Churchill Company, 1932.

Davis, Kenneth S. *FDR: The New Deal Years, 1933–1937.* New York: Random House, 1986.

Dawes, Charles G. *Notes as Vice President, 1928–1929.* Boston: Little, Brown, 1937.

Demaris, Ovid. *The Boardwalk Jungle.* New York: Bantam Books, 1986.

————. *Captive City: Chicago in Chains.* New York: Lyle Stuart, Inc., 1969.

————. *The Director: An Oral Biography of J. Edgar Hoover.* New York: Harper's Magazine Press, 1975.

————. *Dirty Business: The Corporate-Political-Money-Power Game.* New York: Harper's Magazine Press, 1974.

de Toledano, Ralph. *J. Edgar Hoover: The Man in His Time.* New York: Arlington House, 1973.

Dewey, Thomas E. *Twenty Against the Underworld.* New York: Doubleday, 1974.

Dobyns, Fletcher. *The Underworld of American Politics.* New York: Fletcher Dobyns, Publisher, 1932.

Dorsett, Lyle W. *The Pendergast Machine.* New York: Oxford University Press, 1968.

Eisenberg, Dennis, Uri Dan, and Eli Landau. *Meyer Lansky: Mogul of the Mob.* New York & London: Paddington Press Ltd., 1979.

Ferber, Nat J. *I Found Out: A Confidential Chronicle of the Twenties.* New York: Dial Press, 1939.

Finney, Guy W. *Angel City in Turmoil: A Story of the Minute Men of Los Angeles in Their War on Civic Corruption, Graft, and Privilege.* Los Angeles: Amer Press, 1945.

Floherty, John J. *Men Against Crime.* New York: J. B. Lippincott Co., 1946.

Fonzi, Gaeton. *Annenberg: A Biography of Power.* New York: Weybright and Talley, 1970.

Fox, Stephen. *Blood and Power: Organized Crime in Twentieth-Century America.* New York: Penguin Books, 1989.

Gage, Nicholas, ed. *Mafia USA.* Chicago: Playboy Press, 1972.

Gentry, Curt. *J. Edgar Hoover: The Man and the Secrets.* New York: W. W. Norton & Co., 1991.

Gosch, Martin, and Richard Hammer. *The Last Testament of Lucky Luciano.* Boston: Little, Brown, 1975.

Gunther, John. *Inside U.S.A.* New York: Harper & Brothers, 1947.

Hoffman, Dennis E. *Scarface Al and the Crime Crusaders: Chicago's Private War Against Capone.* Carbondale: Southern Illinois University Press, 1993.

Hostetter, Gordon L., and Thomas Quinn Beesley. *It's A Racket!* Chicago: Les Quin Books, 1929.

Hughes, Rupert. *The Story of Thomas E. Dewey: Attorney for the People.* New York: Grosset & Dunlap, 1944.

Hynd, Alan. *The Giant Killers.* New York: Robert M. McBride & Co., 1945.

Illman, Harry R. *Unholy Toledo: The True Story of Detroit's Purple-Licavoli Gangs' Take-over of an Ohio City.* San Francisco: Polemic Press Publications, 1986.

Irey, Elmer L. *The Tax Dodgers: The Inside Story of the T-Men's War with American's Political and Underworld Hoodlums as told to William J. Slocum.* New York: Greenberg, 1948.

Jackson, Joe. *Leavenworth Train: A Fugitive's Search for Justice in the Vanishing West.* New York: Carroll & Graf, 2001.

Jennings, Dean. *We Only Kill Each Other: The True Story of the Life and Bad Times of Bugsy Siegel.* New York: Pocket Books, 1992.

Johnson, Nelson. *Boardwalk Empire: The Birth, High Times, and Corruption of Atlantic City.* Medford, NJ: Plexus Publishing, Inc., 2002.

Kane, Harnett T. *Huey Long's Louisiana Hayride: The American Rehearsal for Dictatorship.* Gretna, LA: Pelican Publishing Co., 1941.

Katcher, Leo. *The Big Bankroll: The Life and Times of Arnold Rothstein.* New York: Harper & Brothers, 1958.

Katkov, Norman. *The Fabulous Fanny: The Story of Fanny Brice.* New York: Alfred A. Knopf, 1953.

Kavieff, Paul R. *The Purple Gang: Organized Crime in Detroit 1910–1945.* Fort Lee, NJ: Barricade Books, 2000.

Kenyon, William A. *Bill Kenyon of the Postal Inspectors and Army Postal Service.* New York: Exposition Press, 1960.

Kessner, Thomas. *Fiorello La Guardia and the Making of Modern New York.* New York: Penguin Books, 1991.

Kobler, John. *Ardent Spirits: the Rise and Fall of Prohibition.* New York: G. P. Putnam's Sons, 1973.

———. *Capone: The Life and World of Al Capone.* New York: G. P. Putnam's Sons, 1971.

Kostelanetz, Boris, and Louis Bender. *Criminal Aspects of Tax Fraud Cases.* Philadelphia: American Law Institute, 1968.

Lacey, Robert. *Little Man: Meyer Lansky and the Gangster Life.* Boston: Little, Brown & Company, 1991.

Lardner, James, and Thomas Reppetto. *NYPD: A City and Its Police.* New York: Henry Holt, 2000.

Larsen, Lawrence H., and Nancy J. Hulston. *Pendergast!* Columbia: University of Missouri, 1997.

Lash, Joseph P. *Eleanor and Franklin: The Story of Their Relationship Based on Eleanor Roosevelt's Private Papers.* New York: W. W. Norton & Co., 1971.

Limpus, Lowell, M. *Honest Cop: Lewis J. Valentine.* New York: E. P. Dutton, 1939.

Liston, Robert A. *Great Detectives: Famous Real-Life Sleuths and Their Most Baffling Cases.* New York: Platt & Munk, 1966.

Lowenthal, Max. *The Federal Bureau of Investigation*. New York: William Sloane Associates, 1950.

Lukas, J. Anthony. *Big Trouble: A Murder in a Small Western Town Sets Off a Struggle for the Soul of America*. New York: Simon & Schuster, 1998.

Lyle, John H. *The Dry and Lawless Years: The Crusade against Public Enemies and Corrupt Officials in Chicago*. Upper Saddle River, NJ: Prentice-Hall, Inc., 1960.

Lynch, Denis T. *Criminals and Politicians*. New York: Macmillan Co., 1932.

Maccabee, Paul. *John Dillinger Slept Here: A Crooks' Tour of Crime and Corruption in St. Paul, 1920–1936*. St. Paul: Minnesota Historical Society Press, 1995.

Mason, Alpheus Thomas. *Harland Fiske Stone: Pillar of the Law*. New York: Viking Press, 1956.

Mayer, Martin. *Emory Buckner: A Biography*. New York: Harper & Row, 1968.

McConaughy, John. *From Cain to Capone: Racketeering Down the Ages*. New York: Brentano's, Inc., 1931.

McCullough, David. *Truman*. New York: Simon & Schuster, 1992.

McWilliams, John C. *The Protectors: Harry J. Anslinger and the Federal Bureau of Narcotics, 1930–1962*. Newark: University of Delaware Press, 1990.

Merriam, Charles E. *Chicago: A More Intimate View of Urban Politics*. New York: Macmillan Co., 1929.

Merz, Charles. *The Dry Decade*. Seattle: University of Washington Press, 1969.

Messick, Hank. *Lansky*. New York: Berkeley Medallion Edition, 1971.

———. *Secret File*. New York: G. P. Putnam's Sons, 1969.

———. *The Silent Syndicate*. New York: Macmillan, 1968.

Milligan, Maurice M. *Missouri Waltz: The Inside Story of the Pendergast Machine by the Man Who Smashed It*. New York: Charles Scribner's Sons, 1948.

Millspaugh, Arthur C. *Crime Control by the National Government*. Washington: Brookings Institution, 1937.

Mitgang, Herbert. *The Man Who Rode the Tiger*. New York: J. P. Lippincott, 1963.

———. *Once Upon a Time in New York: Jimmy Walker, Franklin Roosevelt, and the Last Great Battle of the Jazz Age*. New York: Free Press, 2000.

Mockridge, Norton, and Robert H. Prall. *The Big Fix*. New York: Henry Holt and Co., 1954.

Moley, Raymond. *Politics and Criminal Prosecution*. New York: Minton, Balch & Co., 1929.

Morgan, John. *Prince of Crime*. New York: Stein and Day, 1985.

Murray, J. George. *The Legacy of Al Capone: Portraits and Annals of Chicago's Public Enemies*. New York: G. P. Putnam's Sons, 1975.

Murray, Robert K. *Red Scare: A Study in National Hysteria, 1919–1920*. New York: McGraw-Hill Book Co., 1955.

Musto, David F. *The American Disease: Origins of Narcotic Control.* New Haven: Yale University Press, 1973.

Nelli, Humberto S. *The Business of Crime: Italians and Syndicate Crime in the United States.* New York: Oxford University Press, 1976.

Noggle, Burl. *Teapot Dome: Oil and Politics in the 1920's.* New York: W. W. Norton and Co. Inc., l965.

O'Brien, Darcy. *Murder in Little Egypt.* New York: New American Library, 1989.

Pasley, Fred D. *Al Capone: The Biography of a Self-Made Man.* New York: Ives Washburn, Publisher, 1930.

Paulsson, Martin. *The Social Anxieties of Progressive Reform: Atlantic City, 1854– 1920.* New York: New York University Press, 1994.

Potter, Claire Bond. *War on Crime: Bandits, G-Men, and the Politics of Mass Culture.* New Brunswick, NJ: Rutgers University Press, 1988.

Powers, Richard Gid. *Secrecy and Power: The Life of J. Edgar Hoover.* New York: Free Press, 1988.

Purvis, Melvin. *American Agent.* New York: Garden City Publishing Co., 1936.

Rappleye, Charles, and Ed Becker, *All-American Mafioso: The Johnny Roselli Story.* New York: Bantam Doubleday Dell Publishing Group, Inc., 1991.

Reed, Lear B. *Human Wolves: Seventeen Years of War on Crime.* Kansas City, MO: Brown-White-Lowell Press, 1941.

Reid, Ed. *The Grim Reapers: The Anatomy of Organized Crime in America.* Chicago: Henry Regnery Co., 1969.

Reynolds, Quentin, *Courtroom: The Story of Samuel S. Leibowitz.* New York: Garden City Books, 1950.

Riordon, William L. *Plunkitt of Tammany Hall.* Boston: Bedford/St. Martin's, 1994.

Roemer, William F., Jr. *Accardo: The Genuine Godfather.* New York: Ivy Books, 1995.

———. *Man Against the Mob.* New York: Ivy Books, 1991.

Roper, Daniel C. *Fifty Years of Public Life.* In collaboration with Frank H. Lovette. Durham, NC: Duke University Press, 1941.

Russo, Gus. *The Outfit: The Role of Chicago's Underworld in the Shaping of Modern America.* New York & London: Bloomsbury, 2001.

Sann, Paul. *Kill the Dutchman! The Story of Dutch Schultz.* New Rochelle, NY: Arlington House, 1971.

Schoenberg, Robert J. *Mr. Capone: The Real—and Complete—Story of Al Capone.* New York: William. Morrow & Co., 1992.

Sciacca, Tony. *Luciano: The Man Who Modernized the American Mafia.* New York: Pinnacle Books, 1975.

Schmeckebier, Laurence F., and Francis X. A. Eble. *The Bureau of Internal Revenue.* New York: AMS Press, 1974.

Sifakis, Carl. *The Mafia Encyclopedia, First Edition.* New York: Facts on File, 1987.

———. *The Mafia Encyclopedia, Second Edition.* New York: Checkmark Books, 1999.

Smith, Richard Norton. *Thomas E. Dewey and His Times.* New York: Simon & Schuster, 1982.

Sondern, Frederic Jr. *Brotherhood of Evil: The Mafia.* New York: Farrar, Straus, Cudahy, 1959.

Spiering, Frank. *The Man Who Got Capone.* New York: Bobbs-Merrill, 1976.

Steffens, Lincoln. *The Autobiography of Lincoln Steffens.* New York: Harcourt, Brace, 1931.

Stoddard, William Leavitt. *Financial Racketeering and How to Stop It.* New York: Harper & Brothers, 1931.

Stuart, Mark A.. *Gangster #2: Longy Zwillman, the Man Who Invented Organized Crime.* Secaucus, NJ: Lyle Stuart, Inc., 1985.

Sullivan, Edward Dean. *Chicago Surrenders.* New York: Vanguard Press, 1930.

———. *This Labor Union Racket.* New York: Hillman-Curl, Inc., 1936.

Sullivan, Mark. *Our Times: America Finding Herself.* New York: Charles Scribner's Sons, 1927.

Sullivan, William. *The Bureau: My Thirty Years in Hoover's FBI.* With Bill Brown. New York: W. W. Norton, 1979.

Summers, Anthony. *Official and Confidential: The Secret Life of J. Edgar Hoover.* New York: G. P. Putnam's Sons, 1993.

Surface, William. *Inside Internal Revenue.* New York: Coward-McCann, Inc., 1967.

Swanberg, W. A. *Citizen Hearst: A Biography of William Randolph Hearst.* New York: Bantam Books, 1971.

Swisher, Carl Brent, ed. *Selected Papers of Homer Cummings: Attorney General of the United States, 1933–1939.* New York: Charles Scribner's Sons, 1939.

Talese, Gay. *Fame and Obscurity.* New York: Dell Publishing Co., 1961.

Thompson, Craig, and Allen Raymond. *Gang Rule in New York: The Story of a Lawless Era.* New York: Dial Press, 1951.

Thrasher, Frederic. *The Gang: A Study of 1,313 Gangs in Chicago.* Chicago: University of Chicago Press, 1927.

Timmons, Bascom N. *Portrait of an American: Charles G. Dawes.* New York: H. Holt, 1953.

Tosches, Nick. *Dino: Living High in the Dirty Business of Dreams.* New York: Random House, 1992.

Touhy, Roger. *The Stolen Years.* With Ray Brennan. Cleveland: Pennington Press, 1959.

Turkus, Burton, and Sid Feder, *Murder, Inc.: The Story of "the Syndicate."* New York: Farrar, Straus and Young, 1951.

Tyler, Gus. *Organized Crime in America.* Ann Arbor: University of Michigan Press, 1962.

Van Devander, Charles. *The Big Bosses.* New York: Howell, Soskin, Publishers, 1944.

Van Meter, Jonathan. *The Last Good Time: Skinny D'Amato, the Notorious 500 Club, and the Rise and Fall of Atlantic City.* New York: Crown Publishers, 2003.

Walker, James Blaine. *The Epic of American Industry.* New York: Harper & Brothers, 1949.

Walker, Stanley. *Dewey: An American of This Century.* New York: Whittlesey House, 1944.

Wallis, Michael. *Pretty Boy: The Life and Times of Charles Arthur Floyd.* New York: St. Martin's Press, 1992.

Wheeler, Burton K. *Yankee from the West: The Candid, Turbulent Life Story of the Yankee-Born U.S. Senator from Montana.* With Paul F. Healy. New York: Doubleday, 1962.

Williams, T. Harry. *Huey Long.* New York: Alfred A. Knopf, 1970.

Wilson, Frank J., and Beth Day. *Special Agent: A Quarter Century with the Treasury Department and the Secret Service.* New York: Holt, Rinehart & Winston, 1963.

Wolf, George. *Frank Costello: Prime Minister of the Underworld.* With Joseph DiMona. New York: William Morrow and Company, 1974.

Articles and Sources

Amen, John Harlan. "The Efficacy of the Antitrust Laws." *The Bar* 7, no. 2 (May 1941): 3–8.

Asbury, Herbert. "America's Number One Mystery Man." *Collier's,* two-part series, April 12 & 19, 1947.

Calder, James D. "Al Capone and the Internal Revenue Service: State-sanctioned Criminology of Organized Crime." *Crime, Law and Social Change* 17: 1–23, 1992.

Childs, Marquis. "Elmer L. Irey." *Washington Post,* August 28, 1946.

———. "The Nemesis Nobody Knows, The Story of Master Detective Irey," *The Saturday Evening Post,* September 11, 1939, 23, 65–73.

Davis, J. Richard "Dixie." "Things I Couldn't Tell till Now." *Collier's,* five-part series, July 22, 1939–August 19, 1939.

DeMichele, Matthew, and Gary Potter. "Sin City Revisited: A Case Study of the Official Sanctioning of Organized Crime in an 'Open City.'" Justice and

Police Studies, Eastern Kentucky University. http://www.rootswebancestry
.com/kycampbe/newportgambling.htm.

Department of Justice. *Bicentennial Celebration of the United States Attorneys: 1789–
1989.* Published by the Executive Office for United States Attorneys, Washington, D.C., September 1989.

Department of the Treasury. *Report Outlining the Organization, Functions, and
Activities of the Intelligence Unit Covering the Period from the Date of its Establishment, July 1, 1919.* Foreword by Elmer Irey, 1936. Washington, D.C.

Department of the Treasury. *75 Years of IRS Criminal Investigation History: 1919–
1994.* Introduction by Donald K. Vogel. Document 7233 (Rev. 2-96) Catalog Number 64601H., Washington, D.C.

"Elmer Irey Retires." *Life,* September 2, 1946, 45–46.

Fellman, David. "Some Consequences of Increased Federal Activity in Law Enforcement." *Journal of Criminal Law and Criminology,* May–June 1945, 16–33.

Gaby, Donald C. "What Would It Cost Today?" *South Florida History Magazine,*
Vol. I, No. 2 (Spring 1989), 38.

"The Great Nation-Wide Campaign Against the Racketeers." *Literary Digest,* July
1, 1933.

Gunther, John. "The High Cost of Hoodlums." *Harper's,* October 1929.

Hearings on Tax Evasion and Avoidance, Joint Committee on Tax Evasion,
June 17–18, 22–23, 1937. 85th Congress, lst Session. Irey testimony, 37–71.
Government Printing Office, Washington, D.C.

Levine, Emanuel H. "Why They 'Drilled' Dutch Schultz." *Nation,* November 20,
1935.

Lewis, Burdette C. "Behind the Crime Wave." Letter to the Editor, *New York
Times,* January 2, 1921.

———. "How Racketeering Began: An Unforeseen Result of Our Anti-Trust
Laws." *Review of Reviews* 86, no. 1 (July 1932): 41, 42–54.

Lippmann, Walter. "The Underworld: Our Secret Servant." *Forum,* January
1931, 1–4.

Mann, William G. "Personalities in Law Enforcement: Elmer Lincoln Irey."
True Detective, April 1939, 65, 121–122.

"The Marines Are Coming." *Fortune,* August 1934.

Martoche, Salvatore R. "Lest We Forget: William J. Donovan." *Western New York
Heritage,* 6, no. 1, (Winter 2003), 4–23.

"Nemesis of Capone, T-Man to Retire." *Washington Post,* August 16, 1946.

"Philadelphia Justice for Chicago's Al Capone." *Literary Digest,* June 15, 1929,
33–34, 39, 42.

"Racketeers." *New Republic,* January 7, 1931.

"Report Outlining the Organization, Function and Activities of the Intelligence Unit Covering the Period from the Date of its Establishment, July 1, 1919." Confidential report written by Elmer Irey, Treasury Department, 1937.

Russell, Francis. "The Four Mysteries of Warren Harding." *American Heritage*, April 1963, 4, 81–86.

Robins, L. H. "On the Trail of the Tax Dodger." *New York Times Magazine*, July 14, 1940, 87.

Scaduto, Anthony. "The Eliot Ness Myth." *Climax*, n.d., National Archives, Washington, D.C.

Schall, Thomas D. "Czars of the Income Tax," *Plain Talk*, September 1923, 267–270.

Schoeneman, George J., "History of the Internal Revenue Service." *I.R. News*, September 1929.

Seidman, Harold. "Labor Racketeering." *Nation*, August 16, 1933.

Stapleton, Richard M. "From Temple of Trade to Hall of Culture." *Historic Preservation News*, October–November 1994.

Wilson, Frank J. "Undercover Man: He Trapped Capone." As told to Howard Whitman. *Collier's*, April 26, 1947.

Index

About the Author

Robert Folsom was a newspaper reporter and editor for more than thirty years and is a freelance writer on law enforcement, intelligence, and counterintelligence subjects. For a decade he was Sunday managing editor of the *Fort Lauderdale News and Sun Sentinel*, where he established the first book page in the Sunday edition. A Floridian who served in the U.S. Air Force in the Korean War, he is a graduate of Florida State University, where he was editor of the student semiweekly, the *Florida Flambeau*, and was cited by the Woodrow Wilson International Center for Scholars for best essays among college students. In 1969 he left journalism to become a member of the planning team of Florida International University in Miami. Upon opening in 1972, FIU had the largest opening student enrollment of any institution in the history of American higher education. For a decade Folsom served as the university's director of information services and his work won national recognition from the Council for the Advancement and Support of Education. His work has appeared in the *New York Times*, the *New Republic*, and elsewhere.